Lecture Notes in Artificial Int

Subseries of Lecture Notes in Computer S
Edited by J. G. Carbonell and J. Siekmann

Lecture Notes in Computer Science
Edited by G. Goos, J. Hartmanis and J. van Leeuwen

Springer

Berlin
Heidelberg
New York
Barcelona
Hong Kong
London
Milan
Paris
Singapore
Tokyo

Ralf Küsters

Non-Standard Inferences in Description Logics

Springer

Series Editors

Jaime G. Carbonell, Carnegie Mellon University, Pittsburgh, PA, USA
Jörg Siekmann, University of Saarland, Saarbrücken, Germany

Author

Ralf Küsters
Christian-Albrechts-Universität zu Kiel
Institut für Informatik und Praktische Mathematik
24098 Kiel, Germany
E-mail: kuesters@ti.informatik.uni-kiel.de

Cataloging-in-Publication Data applied for

Die Deutsche Bibliothek - CIP-Einheitsaufnahme

Küsters, Ralf:
Non-standard inferences in description logics / Ralf Küsters. - Berlin ;
Heidelberg ; New York ; Barcelona ; Hong Kong ; London ; Milan ; Paris ;
Singapore ; Tokyo : Springer, 2001
    (Lecture notes in computer science ; Vol. 2100 : Lecture notes in
    artificial intelligence)
    ISBN 3-540-42397-4

CR Subject Classification (1998): I.2.3, I.2, F.4.1

ISBN 3-540-42397-4 Springer-Verlag Berlin Heidelberg New York

Springer-Verlag Berlin Heidelberg New York
a member of BertelsmannSpringer Science+Business Media GmbH

http://www.springer.de

© Springer-Verlag Berlin Heidelberg 2001
Printed in Germany

Typesetting: Camera-ready by author, data conversion by Christian Grosche, Hamburg
Printed on acid-free paper   SPIN: 10839477   06/3142   5 4 3 2 1 0

Preface

Description logics (DL) are a very successful family of logic-based knowledge representation (KR) formalisms, which provide means for the structured representation of knowledge and inference procedures for reasoning about the represented knowledge. This field (whose former names include: KL-ONE-based KR Languages, Term Subsumption Languages, Terminological KR Languages, Terminological Logics, Concept Languages) has undergone a remarkable evolution in the last 15 years. Whereas up until the late 1980s almost no complete inference procedures were known for non-trivial representation languages, there is now a rich palette of description formalisms with differing expressive power, and for which the formal and computational properties (like expressivity, decidability, complexity, connection to other formalisms) are well-investigated. In addition, modern DL systems are equipped with highly optimized implementations of complete inference procedures, which – despite their high worst-case complexity – perform very well in practice.

This satisfactory state of affairs is, however, reached only for the standard inference problems like the subsumption and the instance problem. In applications of DL systems it turned out that building and maintaining large DL knowledge bases can be facilitated by procedures for other, non-standard inference problems. For example, in applications of the system CLASSIC at AT&T Labs, two such new inference problems have turned up: generating new concepts from individuals and matching concept patterns against concepts. At the time when the research reported in this book started, the work concerning such non-standard inference problems was at its very beginning. There were first results on how to solve these problems, but they were restricted to just one representation language, and the inference procedures were again incomplete. Thus, the goal was to achieve for non-standard inference problems what the DL research of the last 15 years had accomplished for the standard inference problems.

This book is a significant step towards reaching this goal. It concentrates on two of the most prominent non-standard inference problems in description logics: (i) generating concepts from individuals by computing the most specific concept and the least common subsumer; and (ii) matching concept patterns against concepts. It provides complete results on these inference problems for two different representation languages: one that is very close to the language provided by the CLASSIC system and one that allows for existential quantification. For both languages, the important tool is a structural characterization of the subsumption problem, which is also interesting in its own right. Actually, this brings us back to the early days of DL research, since the incomplete subsumption procedures of those days did use a structural approach. However, the characterizations of subsumption given in this book are sound and complete. Interestingly, for solving non-standard inference problems, the structural approach turned out to be more appropriate than the modern tableau-based approach now used for solving the standard inference problems.

Summing up, this book provides an excellent formal foundation for research in non-standard inferences in description logic, and I hope that it will be followed up by future research on this exciting new topic.

April 2001   *Franz Baader*

Acknowledgements

This book is a revised version of my doctoral thesis, submitted to the RWTH Aachen. It would not have been written without the support, encouragement, and advice of a large number of people, whom I would like to thank.

I am indebted to my thesis advisor Franz Baader, who stimulated my interest in non-standard inferences in the first place and influenced this work to a great extent. I am also thankful to the other members of my committee, Matthias Jarke, Bernhard Nebel (second reviewer), and Wolfgang Thomas. Special thanks go to Alex Borgida, who gave me the chance to visit him at Rutgers University during the academic year 1998/99. He was a great host and I very much enjoyed working with him.

For financial and other support I owe thanks to the "Studienstiftung des Deutschen Volkes". For support during the first few months of my doctoral studies I am grateful to the "Graduiertenförderung des Landes Nordrhein-Westfalen".

I would like to thank my office mate and friend Ralf Molitor for proof-reading my thesis, encouragement, and numerous scientific and non-scientific discussions. Thanks also to my other colleagues and friends at the RWTH, who made Aachen a nice place to live. I am indebted to my friends in Grefrath for all the time we have spent together. Finally, I want to express my deep gratitude towards my parents, my brothers, and Chun Hee Kim.

April 2001   *Ralf Küsters*

Contents

1. Introduction

Description Logics (DLs) denote a family of knowledge representation formalisms that allow to represent the terminological knowledge of an application domain in a structured and well-defined way. On the one hand, the name Description Logics emphasizes that the basic elements of these logics are concept *descriptions*, i.e., expressions that are built from concept names (unary predicates) and role names (binary predicates) using the concept constructors provided by the DL. On the other hand, unlike some of their predecessor formalisms, DLs are equipped with a formal *logic*-based semantics, which is usually defined in a model-theoretic way; for some DLs it can also be declared by translating concept descriptions into first-order formulae.

As a first simple example of how to use DLs to represent knowledge let us describe some concepts of the family domain. If Human is a concept name and has-child a role name (concept names always start with upper case and role names with lower case letters), then the concept of parents can be described by the following concept description, using the concept constructor ⊓ (called concept conjunction) and ∃ (called existential restriction):

$$\text{Human} \sqcap \exists \text{has-child.Human}.$$

In the following, we refer to this concept description by Parent. Intuitively, Parent stands for the set of individuals that are human beings and that have (at least one) human child. Similarly, the concepts "mother" and "father" are described. To this end, the concept name Female is introduced to denote all female individuals; the set of all male individuals is then represented by the concept description ¬Female with '¬' standing for concept negation. Now the descriptions for the concepts mother and father read as follows:

$$\text{Human} \sqcap \text{Female} \sqcap \exists \text{has-child.Human},$$
$$\text{Human} \sqcap \neg\text{Female} \sqcap \exists \text{has-child.Human}.$$

These descriptions will be denoted Mother and Father, respectively. Their formal semantics can be fixed by translating them to first-order formulae. More precisely, concept names are turned into unary predicates and role names into binary predicates. A concept description is turned into a first-order formula with one free variable. For example, the first-order formula for Parent is

R.Küsters: Non-Standard Inferences in Description Logics, LNAI 2100, pp. 1–9, 2001.
© Springer-Verlag Berlin Heidelberg 2001

$$\mathsf{Human}(x) \wedge \exists y(\mathsf{has\text{-}child}(x, y) \wedge \mathsf{Human}(y)),$$

where x is a free variable. For a given interpretation, the meaning of Parent can now formally be specified as the set of all individuals (elements of the domain of the interpretation) that satisfy the corresponding first-order formula when substituted for its free variable.

In this work, we often consider DLs that allow to talk about the transitive closure of roles. Since transfinite closure cannot be expressed in first-order predicate logic, the semantics of these DLs will be defined in a model-theoretic way (see Section 2.2).

Standard Inferences

The main feature of DLs and DL-based knowledge representation systems are inference services which allow to derive implicit knowledge from the knowledge explicitly stored in the knowledge base. Typically, these services include computing subconcept/superconcept relationships between concept descriptions (so-called *subsumption relationships*) as well as checking whether a given individual belongs to a certain concept (so-called *instance relationships*).

From the concept descriptions of our family domain it follows that Parent is a superconcept of Mother and Father (written Mother $\sqsubseteq$ Parent and Father $\sqsubseteq$ Parent). That is, every interpretation of Parent is a superset of the interpretations of Mother and Father. A DL-system will automatically detect these subsumption relationships and will accordingly place these concept descriptions in a subsumption hierarchy (see Section 2.3 for an illustration).

In order to use these services in DL-systems, the underlying inferences, subsumption and instance checking, must be decidable (preferably with low complexity). Consequently, the expressive power of the DL needs to be restricted appropriately in order to meet the complexity requirements. However, if the expressive power of the DL is restricted too much, it might be too weak to express the relevant concepts of the application domain. Thus, one is faced with a trade-off between the complexity of the inference problems and the expressive power of the DL. This trade-off led to intensive research in the development of complete and practical inference algorithms dealing with more and more expressive DLs.

For inferences like subsumption and instance checking, which form the basis of every DL-system and are therefore called *standard inferences*, results for a great variety of DLs with differing expressive power are now available. Particularly, the boundary between decidability and undecidability as well as (for decidable DLs) the complexity of the inferences are well-investigated. Moreover, along the way, different kinds of inference algorithms have been devised. The research leading to these results can be divided into four (partly overlapping) phases, sketched only very briefly here (see Chapter 2 for a more detailed overview).

1. In the first phase, a great number of DL-systems [WS91, Pel91, MB87, Kob91, KBR86, MDW91, BFL83] was developed, based on so-called *structural subsumption algorithms*. These algorithms work in two steps: First, the concept descriptions are turned into certain normal forms. Second, these normal forms are compared syntactically to decide the subsumption relationship between the original concept descriptions. However, most such algorithms were incomplete, i.e., they did not detect all subsumption relationships. Yet, the developers were in general not aware of this fact since no formal proofs on soundness and completeness of the algorithms were carried out.

2. Only later, in the second phase, the formal analysis of inference problems set in [SS89, Pat89, Neb90a, Neb90b], revealing that already for quite unexpressive DLs reasoning was intractable (or even undecidable). One reaction to this dilemma was to further limit the expressive power of the DLs in order to get efficient as well as sound and complete inference algorithms — typically, such DLs do not allow for full negation (otherwise a reduction from SAT would yield NP-hardness right away). The most prominent system following this philosophy is CLASSIC, developed at the AT&T Labs [BPS94, BBM$^+$92, BMPS$^+$91], which still employs the structural subsumption approach.

3. In the third phase, *tableau-based algorithms*, specializations of the known algorithms for testing satisfiability of first-order predicate formulae, were integrated into DL-systems [BH91c, BFT95]. Unlike the structural subsumption algorithms, they allow to handle propositionally closed DLs [SS91, HNS90, HB91, BH91a, Baa91, BS96a, Sat96, DLNN91a, DHL$^+$92, DLNN91b]. Surprisingly, although these DLs are intractable (often PSPACE-complete), the tableau-algorithms for these logics had acceptable runtime behavior [BH91c, BFH$^+$94, BFT95].

4. Finally, in the fourth phase, the expressive power of the DLs handled by inference algorithms was extended even further by utilizing decision algorithms for the satisfiability of formulae in propositional dynamic logics (PDL) [Sch91, GL94a, Gia96, GL96, GL94b, Gia95]. Unfortunately, this has not led to practical implementations; partly because until very recently no (optimized) implementations for PDL existed, but mainly because the reductions to PDL (although polynomial) produced huge PDL-formulae. Therefore, currently researchers develop practical tableau-based algorithms for these very expressive DLs [HST99, HS99]; the first empirical results are very encouraging [Hor98a, HP98], even though now the inference problems tackled are EXPTIME-complete.

Non-Standard Inferences

Although standard inferences help structuring a knowledge base, e.g., by automatically building a concept hierarchy, they are, for example, not sufficient when it comes to (automatically) generating new concept descriptions from given ones. They also fail if concepts are specified using different vocabularies (i.e., sets of concept names and role names) or if they are described on different levels of abstraction. Altogether, it has turned out that, for building and maintaining large DL knowledge bases, besides the standard inferences, additional, so-called *non-standard inferences*, are required [MPS98].

First ad hoc implementations of such inferences have been integrated into the CLASSIC DL-system [McG96, CH94b]. The inferences involved are the *least common subsumer* (lcs), the *most specific concept* (msc), and *matching of concept descriptions*. In what follows, these inferences are briefly described and motivated (see Chapter 3 for more details).

Least Common Subsumer and Most Specific Concept. These inferences allow to abstract from given collections of concept descriptions and individuals, respectively, by extracting the commonalities of these objects. More precisely, the lcs denotes the least concept description (w.r.t. subsumption) within the given DL that subsumes all the descriptions of the collection. A concept description is the msc of a given collection of individuals if it has all individuals of the collection as instances and is the least concept description with this property.

For example, in our family domain it is easy to see that the lcs of the concept descriptions Mother and Father is Parent. Thus, in a knowledge base that only contains the concept descriptions Mother and Father the description Parent can automatically be generated using the lcs operation (provided that this operation is computable), a task not possible with only standard inferences.

This simple example might already illustrate that the lcs operation can be used to support the bottom-up construction of knowledge bases [BN98]. Namely, starting from typical examples, given by the knowledge engineer as concept descriptions, the lcs is employed to prompt new concept descriptions to the user, which generalize the examples and thereby help to refine the structure of the knowledge base. In case the examples are given as individuals, the msc operation is used in a preprocessing step to generate appropriate concept descriptions of the individuals. Inference services computing the lcs and the msc are also useful in a number of other applications, for instance, similarity-based information retrieval [MHN98, MMK99] and inductive learning [FP96, CH94b, CH94a, CBH92]. The latter application was in fact the main motivation for a group of researchers at the AT&T Labs to introduce the lcs as a new inference problem in DLs [CBH92, CH94a, FP96]. The lcs served as key operation in learning algorithms for sublanguages of CLASSIC in the PAC learning model proposed by Valiant [Val84]. The applications of lcs and msc are further described in Section 3.1.2.

Most of the initial theoretical results on the lcs are also due to the group at AT&T, which developed lcs algorithms for different sublanguages of CLASSIC [CH94b, CH94a, CBH92]. The underlying approaches of these algorithms are suitable for the considered languages. In detail, however, the algorithms suffer from several shortcomings, which make them incorrect for the DLs they are supposed to handle. As for the msc, besides heuristic algorithms for computing approximations of the msc [CH94b], as yet, no algorithms computing the msc have been proposed.

Matching of Concept Descriptions. Matching is a novel inference service that allows to replace certain concept names by concept descriptions before testing for equivalence or subsumption. Formally, given a *concept pattern D*, i.e., a concept description with *concept variables*, and a concept description C (without variables), a matching problem asks for a substitution σ (of variables by concept descriptions) such that the instance $\sigma(D)$ of D subsumes (or is equivalent to) C.

As a simple example, take the concept pattern P:

$$X \sqcap \exists\mathsf{has\text{-}child}.X$$

where X is a concept variable. Intuitively, this concept pattern speaks about people who share the same (unspecified) property X with one of their children. When X is substituted by Human, then P is equivalent to Parent. However, there is no substitution for X making P equivalent to Mother or Father, since the individuals of these concepts are required to be female or male, respectively, whereas the children of a mother, say, are not required to be female. Conversely, P matches against Human $\sqcap$ Female $\sqcap$ $\exists\mathsf{has\text{-}child}.$(Human $\sqcap$ Female) when substituting X with (Human $\sqcap$ Female).

The example illustrates that using concept patterns, matching can be employed to search the knowledge base for concepts having a certain not completely specified form. This distinguishes matching from the usual subsumption or equivalence tests where the concept descriptions to search for need to be specified completely. However, in large knowledge bases with thousands of names or knowledge bases maintained by several knowledge engineers exact descriptions are often hard to come up with (see Section 3.2).

The original motivation for introducing matching [BM96] was that concept descriptions occurring in industrial applications of the CLASSIC DL-system [MRI95, MIP+98, MW98a, MW98b, WWV+93] may become too large and complex to present them to the user as a whole — such descriptions may take 10 to 50 pages, and in some applications even five times as much [MB95, McG96]. It quickly becomes clear that such descriptions need to be pruned if users are to be able to inspect them and not be overwhelmed with irrelevant details. To this end, matching has been used to specify in a declarative manner the relevant parts of descriptions that are to be displayed to the user [McG96, MB95].

The first matching algorithm was proposed by Borgida and McGuinness for a sublanguage of CLASSIC [BM96]. However, their algorithm cannot handle arbitrary concept patterns and even for admissible patterns the algorithm does not always find a matcher even if one exists. The first complete matching algorithm was proposed by Baader and Narendran for the small sublanguage

$\mathcal{FL}_0$ of CLASSIC, which allows for concept conjunction and value restrictions [BN98]. Later, this algorithm was extended to the language $\mathcal{FL}_\neg$, which in addition allows for primitive negation [BBM98].

Summing up, the state of affairs on non-standard inferences presented so far corresponds to the one for standard inferences at the end of the first phase. That is, although first ad hoc implementations exist, the new inference problems are hardly understood from the computational point of view. For non-standard inferences, this first phase has mainly been determined by research carried out at the AT&T Labs, and it was motivated by applications of the CLASSIC DL-system.

Contribution of this Book

The main goal of this work is to take non-standard inferences to a level that corresponds to (and partly exceeds) the one at the end of the second phase for standard inferences. That is, we aim at proving formal properties of non-standard inferences (like the existence and the size of the lcs) as well as providing correct algorithms for solving these inferences together with an analysis of their complexity. As in the first phase, the focus of our investigations is on the three inferences lcs, msc, and matching.

Least Common Subsumer and Most Specific Concept. Starting from the known results in the first phase (which were exclusively concerned with sublanguages of CLASSIC), an in-depth analysis of the lcs for the language $\mathcal{ALNS}$ is presented, which contains almost all CLASSIC constructors, namely, concept conjunction, value restrictions, primitive negation, number restrictions, and same-as equalities. The analysis will overcome some shortcomings of previous results concerning the existence and the size of the lcs. Surprisingly, it turns out that these properties heavily relay on the different semantics proposed for CLASSIC concept descriptions in the literature. Finally, correct algorithms for computing the lcs in $\mathcal{ALNS}$ are provided as well as an analysis of their complexity.

The msc will not be studied for $\mathcal{ALNS}$, because its existence cannot be guaranteed in general. To overcome this problem one would have to extend the language by allowing for so-called cyclic concept descriptions, i.e., concepts that are defined in terms of cyclic terminologies interpreted with the greatest fixed-point semantics. However, for this extension of the language subsumption is undecidable (as shown by Nebel [Neb90b]). Therefore, our investigations on the msc focus on cyclic $\mathcal{ALN}$-concept descriptions (called $\mathcal{ALN}^*$-concept descriptions); $\mathcal{ALN}$ denotes a sublanguage of $\mathcal{ALNS}$ which does not allow for same-as equalities (the source of the undecidability of subsumption in the case of cyclic concept descriptions.). While up to now the msc has only been approximated, here an algorithm is presented that computes the msc exactly. Once cyclic concept descriptions are allowed, one must be able to further process these descriptions. Therefore, the lcs in $\mathcal{ALN}^*$ is explored as well.

Motivated by applications in chemical process engineering [BS96b, Sat98], the language $\mathcal{ALE}$ is studied too since it allows for existential restriction, a constructor indispensable in this domain.

Matching of Concept Descriptions. The known results on matching are extended in two directions. The first extension is concerned with identifying "interesting" sets of matchers and the second with the development of matching algorithms for more expressive DLs. Let us take a closer look at these extensions.

Matching problems may have different (often infinitely many) solutions. Not all of them can be presented to the user and not all of them are of interest to the user. Therefore, general (application independent) properties of "interesting" solutions are exhibited, formalized in terms of precedence orderings on matchers. So far, such properties have not been described in the literature. Instead, matching algorithms only computed so-called least matchers, which, however, need not exist in any DL, and are not always the most interesting matchers either.

The second extension consists in generalizing the known matching algorithms to much more expressive DLs. That is, just as for the lcs, matching problems are examined in $\mathcal{ALNS}$, $\mathcal{ALN}^*$, and $\mathcal{ALE}$. For all three DLs (as well as some sublanguages thereof), the complexity of deciding the solvability of matching problems is analyzed. We also see matching algorithms that actually compute "interesting" solutions. Remarkably, it turns out that in all these algorithms the lcs computation is needed as a subprocedure, demonstrating that these two inferences, although at first introduced independently, are actually closely related.

To sum up, this book provides an in-depth analysis as well as provably sound and complete algorithms for the three non-standard inferences lcs, msc, and matching for the DLs $\mathcal{ALNS}$, $\mathcal{ALN}^*$, and $\mathcal{ALE}$ as well as some of their sublanguages. The investigations on $\mathcal{ALNS}$ approximately correspond to what was known for standard inferences at the end of the second phase. The results for $\mathcal{ALN}^*$ and $\mathcal{ALE}$ partly take the research on non-standard inferences to the third phase, though we are far from having reached the end of this phase. Nevertheless, the hope is that the techniques developed here can be generalized and combined to be applicable to more expressive languages (corresponding to those investigated in the third phase of standard inferences) or to non-standard inferences other than lcs, msc, and matching. In fact, some of the techniques have already proved useful for rewriting of $\mathcal{ALN}$- and $\mathcal{ALE}$-concept descriptions, a novel inference problem introduced and studied in [BKM00] (see also Section 3.4).

Structure of this Book

Excluding the introduction and the conclusion (Chapter 7), this book is split into three parts. The first part (Chapter 2) gives an introduction to DLs, focusing on standard inferences. In the second part (Chapter 3), non-standard inferences are defined, their applications are sketched, and previous as well as new results are summarized. This part aims at providing an overall impression of the novel inferences rather than going into technical details. In the third part (Chapter 4, 5, and 6), the new results on non-standard inferences are proved, which means that this part contains the technical contribution of this book. Every chapter in this part consists of three sections, one for each of the DLs $\mathcal{ALNS}$, $\mathcal{ALN}^*$, and $\mathcal{ALE}$. So, for those mainly interested in one of these DLs it suffices to read the corresponding sections. Conversely, those particular interested in a certain non-standard inference problem (for whatever DL) should read the corresponding chapter. In any case, however, depending on the DL of choice it will be necessary to read (one of) the sections in Chapter 4, for subsequent chapters are building on the results presented there. The outline of the individual chapters is as follows:

- Chapter 2 provides an overview of the research that has been carried out in the field of standard inferences. It starts with introducing syntax and semantics of the DLs relevant in this book. Then, standard inferences are defined and the main approaches for solving these inferences, namely structural subsumption and tableau-based algorithms, are illustrated. Both approaches are presented since structural approaches to subsumption prove very useful for non-standard inferences, while tableau-based algorithms represent the state-of-the-art technique for deciding standard inferences.
- Chapter 3 is devoted to non-standard inferences. It contains formal definitions of the three inferences lcs, msc, and matching. In particular, for matching an important issue covered in this chapter is to identify and to formally define general properties of "interesting" matchers. Besides these formal foundations, the different applications of non-standard inferences are sketched, and previous results as well as new results are summarized. All proofs are postponed to later chapters in order to abstract from the technical details and to concentrate on the results themselves. Still, Section 3.3 offers some insight into the underlying techniques used to solve non-standard inferences. Finally, for the sake of completeness, other non-standard inferences proposed in the literature, but not covered here, are listed in Section 3.4.
- Chapter 4 prepares the ground for the proofs presented in the two subsequent chapters. More precisely, it presents the characterizations of subsumption that form the basis for all results on non-standard inferences. Just like the following two chapters, it consists of three sections, dealing with the three languages $\mathcal{ALNS}$, $\mathcal{ALN}^*$, and $\mathcal{ALE}$, respectively.
- In Chapter 5 all new results on the lcs and the msc in $\mathcal{ALNS}$, $\mathcal{ALN}^*$, and $\mathcal{ALE}$ are proved.

– Chapter 6 contains the proofs for matching in these languages.
– Finally, Chapter 7 contains a brief summary of the results achieved as well as a list of open problems.

2. Description Logics

Description Logics (DLs) are used to represent and to reason about terminological knowledge. Research in the field of DLs has mainly been driven by inventing decision algorithms for so-called *standard inference problems*, such as subsumption and instance checking, in more and more expressive DLs. Along this line, the computational complexity of standard inferences has been studied thoroughly and implementations of the developed sound and complete algorithms have been integrated into DL-systems. In what follows, we briefly review this key branch of research in DLs before, in the next chapter, *non-standard inferences* are presented (see, for instance, [DLNN97, BS00] for a more detailed description of standard inferences and the underlying techniques to solve them).

The outline of this chapter is as follows. Starting with a brief history of DLs, syntax and semantics of the DLs relevant in this book are introduced. Then, standard inference problems are defined and the main techniques for deciding these inferences are sketched. In particular, so-called structural subsumption and tableau-based algorithms are illustrated by a simple example. Whereas the latter are used in up-to-date DL-systems to decide standard inference problems in very expressive DLs, structural subsumption will play the more important role in this work. At the end of this chapter we will briefly discuss those features of structural subsumption algorithms that make them particularly suitable for solving non-standard inferences.

2.1 History

DLs have their root in the two knowledge representation formalisms Frames and Semantic Networks. *Frames* were developed by Minsky [Min75] as record-like data structures for representing prototypical situations and objects. The main idea was that a frame collects in one place all the information necessary for treating a situation. *Semantic Networks* were introduced by Quillian [Qui68] as a graph-based representation formalism to capture the semantics of natural language. The nodes of Semantic Networks represent concepts and individuals, which are linked by labeled edges. One distinguishes between property edges and IS-A-edges. As an example, consider the network depicted in Figure 2.1. One possible interpretation of this network is that the

R.Küsters: Non-Standard Inferences in Description Logics, LNAI 2100, pp. 11–31, 2001.
© Springer-Verlag Berlin Heidelberg 2001

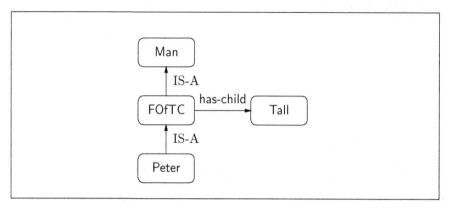

Fig. 2.1. A Semantic Network.

individual Peter is an instance of the concept FOfTC ("father of a tall child") which is a subconcept of the concept Man. All instances of FOfTC have the property that they have a tall child. Since properties of nodes are passed down along IS-A-edges, Peter inherits all properties of Man and FOfTC. In particular, Peter must have a tall child.

Since Frames and Semantic Networks are not equipped with a formal semantics, the exact meaning of a Frame and a Semantic Network is left to the intuition of the users and the programmers who implement the programs processing the frames and networks. In the above example, the network does not clarify explicitly (by syntactical means) whether all the children of instances of FOfTC are Tall or whether every father in this class has at least one tall child. In fact, the former reading would be the interpretation of choice in case FOfTC stood for "Father of tall children". Similarly, only the name of the node Peter indicates that this node is supposed to be an instance rather than a subconcept of FOfTC. In fact, different knowledge representation systems based on Semantic Networks would possibly interpret the same network in different ways.

This lack of semantics was criticized by many researchers working in the field of knowledge representation [Hay77, Hay79, Woo75, Bra77]. In response to this, Brachman [Bra77, Bra78] introduced a new graphical representation called "structured inheritance networks", which has been equipped with a formal semantics to precisely capture its meaning independently of the underlying inference machine. This representation formalism was first implemented in the system KL-ONE [BS85] and it is considered the first DL.

Specifying a formal semantics was the prerequisite for further investigations towards the expressive power of DLs as well as the computational complexity of inference problems, like computing the subconcept/superconcept hierarchy. Research carried out on this formal basis can be divided into four (partly overlapping) phases.

Phase 1: First Systems. The original system KL-ONE was followed by a great variety of successor systems, such as NIKL [KBR86], KRYPTON [BFL83], BACK [Pel91], K-REP [MDW91], LOOM [Mac91], and SB-ONE [Kob91] (where only LOOM is still "in business"). All these systems employ so-called *structural subsumption algorithms* in order to decide subsumption between concept descriptions. The basic idea of these algorithms is as follows: First, concept descriptions are turned into certain normal forms, in which implicit facts are made explicit. These normal forms can be seen as finite representations of the set of concept descriptions subsuming the original concept description. Second, subsumption between concept descriptions is tested by recursively comparing the corresponding normal forms. (See Section 2.4 for a simple example. A thorough investigation of structural subsumption algorithms for the DLs $\mathcal{ALNS}$, $\mathcal{ALN}^*$, and $\mathcal{ALE}$ is presented in Chapter 4).

The structural subsumption algorithms integrated into the first DL-systems were quite efficient, i.e., they run in polynomial time. However, for expressive DLs they were often incomplete in the sense that not all subsumption relationships are detected; even though this was not necessarily known by the designers of these systems.

Phase 2: First Complexity Results. Partially overlapping with the first phase, formal analysis of both the expressive power of DLs [Bor94] and the computational complexity of the corresponding inference problems began. It turned out that already rather unexpressive DLs have NP-hard subsumption problems [BL84, Neb90b]; thus, provided P≠NP, they do not allow for efficient (i.e., polynomial-time) subsumption algorithms. Even worse, the language underlying the first DL-system, KL-ONE, was found to have an undecidable subsumption problem [SS89].

Developers of DL-systems have reacted to this dilemma in two different ways, driven by the prevailing opinion that only polynomial-time algorithms can lead to practical implementations:

1. The inference algorithms the implementations are based on were only required to be sound, but not necessarily complete. That is, if for a subsumption test the system returns "yes", subsumption in fact holds; if, however, the system returns "no" (or "don't know"), no statement can be made. All DL-systems mentioned above follow this philosophy since they usually allow for intractable or even undecidable DLs. The major concern with these systems is that the outcome is not transparent to the users, but rather relies on their implementation.

2. DL-systems based on significantly less expressive DLs have been developed, but with sound and complete polynomial-time inference algorithms. The most prominent representative of this approach is the DL-system CLASSIC [BMPS+91, BPS94], developed at the AT&T Labs. Typical for such systems is that they cannot deal with DLs closed under negation. More precisely, although they usually allow for concept conjunction, concept disjunction is excluded. The major question here is whether such

limited DLs are sufficient in applications. Still, for the technical applications CLASSIC was designed for its expressive power turned out to be sufficient [WWV+93, MW98a, MW98b, MIP+98].

Phase 3: Tableau-Based Algorithms. In order to be able to handle DLs with full negation, Schmidt-Schauß and Smolka [SS91] developed a sound and complete tableau-based algorithm for a DL that they called $\mathcal{ALC}$ (for "attributive concept description language with complements"). Today, $\mathcal{ALC}$ is considered the standard DL. The algorithm proposed by Schmidt-Schauß and Smolka is a specialization of the tableau calculus for first-order predicate logic (FOL) — its termination can be established because in $\mathcal{ALC}$ quantifiers only occur in a restricted form; see Section 2.4 for a brief description of tableau-algorithms. At that time, however, the authors were not aware of the close connection between their rule-based algorithm working on constraint systems and tableau-procedures for FOL. More interestingly, after Schild has pointed out that $\mathcal{ALC}$ is just a syntactic variant of propositional multi-modal logic $\mathbf{K}_n$ [Sch91], the algorithm by Schmidt-Schauß and Smolka turned out to be a re-invention of the known tableau-algorithm for $\mathbf{K}_n$.

In any case, a major step towards complete subsumption algorithms for expressive DLs was made, and soon the first tableau-algorithm for $\mathcal{ALC}$ was extended to various other DLs (see, e.g., [HNS90, HB91, BH91a, Baa91]), and also to other inference problems such as instance checking (see, e.g., [Hol90]).

At the same time, the analysis of the worst-case complexity of reasoning in DLs, already started in the second phase, was continued, resulting in tight complexity bounds for various DLs (see, e.g., [DLNN91a, DHL+92, DLNN91b]). Again, one could benefit from the correspondence between $\mathcal{ALC}$ and $\mathbf{K}_n$. For instance, Ladner [Lad77] has shown that satisfiability in $\mathbf{K}_n$ is PSPACE-complete, thus also in $\mathcal{ALC}$.

These results confirmed that already quite unexpressive DLs were intractable. However, the first DL-systems employing tableau-algorithms (KRIS [BH91b] and CRACK [BFT95]) demonstrated that, in spite of the discouraging complexity results, the algorithms had quite acceptable runtime behavior in practice [BFH+94]. In highly optimized systems, such as FACT [Hor98b, HPS99], the performance was even improved significantly.

Phase 4: Algorithms and Systems for Very Expressive DLs. Building on the observation that some DLs are syntactic variants of the propositional dynamic logic (PDL), once more first noted by Schild [Sch94], De Giacomo and Lenzerini provided (often quite involved) polynomial-time reductions from subsumption in various DLs to the satisfiability of PDL-formulae [GL94a, Gia96, GL96, GL94b, Gia95]. Since satisfiability of PDL-formulae is EXPTIME-complete [FL79], the reductions yield exponential-time inference algorithms for DLs whose expressive power goes far beyond that of $\mathcal{ALC}$. From the (worst-case) complexity point of view, these algorithms are optimal, for reasoning in these logics is EXPTIME-hard as well (easily seen via reduction from satisfiability in PDL). From a practical point of view, however, two problems emerged. On the one hand, at the time the reductions were proposed, no implementations existed. Only recently efficient implementations for PDL have been developed [HP98]. On the other hand, even though the reductions to PDL are polynomial, they produce formulae that cannot be handled by current implementations. To overcome these problems, current research aims at building practical tableau-based algorithms that directly work on the expressive languages without taking the detour to PDL [HST99, HS99]. Some of these algorithms are already integrated in DL-systems, like FACT [HT00, HST00] and RACE [HM00]. Again, despite of EXPTIME-hardness of reasoning, the runtime behavior of these systems is acceptable. Thus, as far as DLs are concerned, even EXPTIME-algorithms cannot a priori be considered impractical.

On the contrary, current DL-systems incorporating such algorithms are successfully integrated in various tools. For example, the tool i•com [FN00], which provides a graphical user interface supporting the design and integration of conceptual models as enhanced Entity-Relationship diagrams [CGL+98a, CDGR99]. Internally, these diagrams are represented by an expressive DL [CLN99], and an underlying inference engine, the DL-system FACT, is used to reason about the diagrams (more precisely, their DL counterparts). That is, consistency of entities and relations can be checked and implicit IS-A links are exhibited. In case of inconsistencies or unexpected IS-A links the user can modify the conceptual model appropriately.

Besides their good properties in practice, researchers have tried to gain a theoretical understanding of why description logics and modal logics provide such a good balance between expressive power and computational complexity [Var97]. To this end, the model-theoretic properties of these logics have been studied, and one has tried to identify fragments of FOL (or extensions thereof by fixed-point constructors) with properties similar to those of description and modal logics (see [Grä99b] for an overview). Among the fragments are the two-variable fragment of FOL (with counting) [GOR97, GOR99] as well as the so-called guarded fragment of FOL and guarded fixed point logics [AvBN98, Grä99a, GW99]. As it stands, the properties of the latter kind of logic seem to come closest to the model-theoretic and algorithmic properties of description and modal logics.

2.2 Syntax and Semantics of Description Logics

DL-systems consist of two components. First, the *knowledge base* (KB), which can further be divided into the TBox and the ABox. Second, the *reasoning engine*, which implements the various inference services. We will come back to the latter component in Section 2.3 and for now concentrate on KBs. A *TBox* stores the conceptual knowledge (vocabulary) of an application domain, while an *ABox* introduces the assertional knowledge (world description). The concepts occurring in a KB are represented by concept descriptions. Syntax

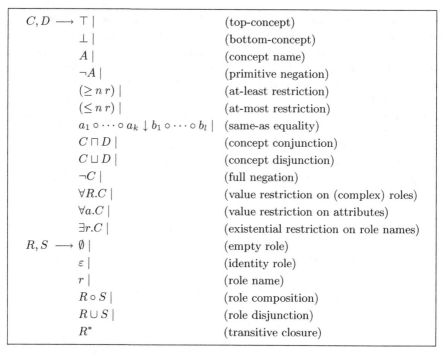

$C, D \longrightarrow$	$\top \mid$	(top-concept)
	$\bot \mid$	(bottom-concept)
	$A \mid$	(concept name)
	$\neg A \mid$	(primitive negation)
	$(\geq n\, r) \mid$	(at-least restriction)
	$(\leq n\, r) \mid$	(at-most restriction)
	$a_1 \circ \cdots \circ a_k \downarrow b_1 \circ \cdots \circ b_l \mid$	(same-as equality)
	$C \sqcap D \mid$	(concept conjunction)
	$C \sqcup D \mid$	(concept disjunction)
	$\neg C \mid$	(full negation)
	$\forall R.C \mid$	(value restriction on (complex) roles)
	$\forall a.C \mid$	(value restriction on attributes)
	$\exists r.C \mid$	(existential restriction on role names)
$R, S \longrightarrow$	$\emptyset \mid$	(empty role)
	$\varepsilon \mid$	(identity role)
	$r \mid$	(role name)
	$R \circ S \mid$	(role composition)
	$R \cup S \mid$	(role disjunction)
	$R^* $	(transitive closure)

Fig. 2.2. Syntax of Concept Descriptions.

and semantics of concept descriptions are determined by the DL underlying the system. In what follows, we introduce concept descriptions, TBoxes, and ABoxes for the DLs relevant in this work.

2.2.1 Concept Descriptions

Starting with *concept names*, *role names*, and *attribute names*, complex concept descriptions and roles are built inductively using *concept* and *role constructors*. Primarily, the various DLs differ in the number and kind of the constructors they provide.

Throughout this book let N_C, N_A, and N_R denote disjoint sets of concept names, attribute names, and role names. In the following, let $A \in N_C$ denote a concept name, $a, a_1, \ldots, a_k, b_1, \ldots, b_l \in N_A$ attribute names, $r, s \in N_R$ role names as well as n a non-negative integer, R, S (complex) roles and C, D (complex) concept descriptions.

With these notations, *concept descriptions* are formed according to the syntax rules depicted in Figure 2.2. Often we dispense with $\circ$ in the composition of roles and attributes. For example, instead of $r \circ s$ or $a_1 \circ \cdots \circ a_k$ we simply write rs and $a_1 \cdots a_k$. We also note that complex roles R can be viewed as regular expressions over N_R, which define regular languages. Therefore, instead of $\forall R.C$, we occasionally write $\forall L.C$ for some regular language L over N_R.

A concept description of the form $\forall r_1.\cdots.\forall r_k.C$ is sometimes abbreviated by $\forall r_1 \cdots r_k.C$ where the r_i's may be role names as well as attribute names. Even if $r_1 \cdots r_k$ is confused with a complex role this causes no harm, since the interpretations will coincide.

In subsequent chapters, we occasionally refer to the size $|\cdot|$ of concept descriptions. The size function $|\cdot|$ is defined inductively as follows:

- $|\top| := |\bot| := |A| := |\neg A| := 1$;
- $|(\geq n\,r)| := |(\leq n\,r)| := 2 + \lceil log(n+1) \rceil$ (binary encoding of n);
- $|a_1 \cdots a_k \downarrow b_1 \cdots b_l| := l + k$;
- $|C \sqcap D| := |C \sqcup D| := |C| + |D|$;
- $|\neg C| := |C|$;
- $|\forall r.C| := |\forall a.C| := |\exists r.C| := 1 + |C|$. (The size of value restrictions on complex roles is not needed.)

We will also refer to the depth, $depth(C)$, of concept descriptions C, which is the maximum number of nested value or existential restrictions. Again, value restrictions on complex roles are not taken into account:

- $depth(\top) := depth(\bot) := depth(A) := depth(\neg A) := 0$;
- $depth(\geq n\,r) := depth(\leq n\,r) := 0$;
- $depth(a_1 \cdots a_k \downarrow b_1 \cdots b_l) := 0$;
- $depth(C \sqcap D) := depth(C \sqcup D) := max\{depth(C), depth(D)\}$;
- $depth(\neg C) := depth(C)$;
- $depth(\forall r.C) := depth(\forall a.C) := depth(\exists r.C) := 1 + depth(C)$.

The DLs we are concerned with here only allow for subsets of the constructors listed above. Concept descriptions in a DL $\mathcal{L}$ are called $\mathcal{L}$-concept descriptions. In the following, we define the various DLs relevant in this work. They can be split into three classes, namely, sublanguages of $\mathcal{ALNS}$, $\mathcal{ALN}^*$, and $\mathcal{ALE}$.

Table 2.1 lists the constructors that are allowed in the language $\mathcal{ALNS}$ and its sublanguages. $\mathcal{ALNS}$ represents the core language of CLASSIC [BPS94].[1] Just like CLASSIC, this language excludes concept disjunction and full negation; only primitive negation is allowed, i.e., negation in front of concept names. Moreover, in value restrictions only role names instead of complex roles are permitted. Note that, in $\mathcal{FLN}$, the bottom-concept as well as primitive negation is not allowed. Nevertheless, as the semantics will reveal, these constructors can be simulated by number restrictions.

As an example of an $\mathcal{ALNS}$-concept description consider the following concept:

---

[1] Unlike CLASSIC, $\mathcal{ALNS}$ does not allow for the constructors fills, one-of, min, and max. See [BPS94] for the definition of these constructors.

Table 2.1. The Languages $\mathcal{ALNS}$ and Relevant Sublanguages.

Concept constructors	$\mathcal{LS}$	$\mathcal{FL}_0$	$\mathcal{FL}_\neg$	$\mathcal{FLN}$	$\mathcal{ALN}$	$\mathcal{ALNS}$
$\top$	x	x	x	x	x	x
$\bot$			x		x	x
$\neg A$			x		x	x
$(\geq n\, r)$				x	x	x
$(\leq n\, r)$				x	x	x
$a_1 \circ \cdots \circ a_k \downarrow b_1 \circ \cdots \circ b_l$	x					x
$(C \sqcap D)$	x	x	x	x	x	x
$\forall r.C$		x	x	x	x	x
$\forall a.C$						x

$$\text{Lemon} := \text{Car} \sqcap \forall \text{model}.\text{Model} \sqcap$$
$$\forall \text{madeBy}.\text{Manufacturer} \sqcap \forall \text{repairs}.\text{RepairReport} \sqcap$$
$$\text{madeBy} \downarrow \text{model} \circ \text{madeBy} \sqcap (\geq 10\,\text{repairs})$$

where Car, Model, Manufacturer, and RepairReport are concept names, model and madeBy are attribute names, and repairs is a role name. Intuitively, the $\mathcal{ALNS}$-concept description Lemon describes those cars that have had frequent (at least 10) repairs. The same-as equality guarantees that the manufacturer of a car and the manufacturer of the model of the car coincide.

Now, let us turn to the DL $\mathcal{ALN}^*$, which extends $\mathcal{ALN}$ by the role constructors presented above. Table 2.2 contains a list of all constructors allowed in $\mathcal{ALN}^*$-concept descriptions and defines some relevant sublanguages of $\mathcal{ALN}^*$. At this point, we should point out already that there is a 1-1 correspondence between $\mathcal{ALN}^*$-concept descriptions and cyclic TBoxes over the language $\mathcal{ALN}$. We will come back to this at the end of the following section, after having introduced TBoxes.

An example of an $\mathcal{ALN}^*$-concept description is

$$\text{Momo} := \forall \text{has-child}^*.\text{Male},$$

which intuitively describes all man with only man offspring. In particular, has-child* is interpreted as reflexive-transitive closure of the role has-child, thus representing the role "offspring".

The third class of languages we deal with are sublanguages of $\mathcal{ALC}$ that allow for existential restrictions, but exclude concept disjunction and full negation. In Table 2.3 the syntax of these sublanguages is defined.

A simple example of an $\mathcal{ALE}$-concept description is the one representing fathers with only sons:

$$\text{FatherOfSons} := \text{Man} \sqcap \exists \text{has-child}.\text{Human} \sqcap \forall \text{has-child}.\text{Man}.$$

Table 2.2. The Language $\mathcal{ALN}^*$ and Relevant Sublanguages.

Concept constructors	$\mathcal{FL}_0^*$	$\mathcal{FLN}^*$	$\mathcal{ALN}^*$
$\top$	x	x	x
$\bot$			x
$\neg A$			x
$(\geq n\, r)$		x	x
$(\leq n\, r)$		x	x
$(C \sqcap D)$	x	x	x
$\forall R.C$	x	x	x
Role constructors			
$\emptyset$	x	x	x
ε	x	x	x
r	x	x	x
$R \circ S$	x	x	x
$R \cup S$	x	x	x
R^*	x	x	x

Table 2.3. The Language $\mathcal{ALC}$ and Relevant Sublanguages.

Concept constructors	$\mathcal{EL}$	$\mathcal{FLE}$	$\mathcal{ALE}$	$\mathcal{ALC}$
$\top$	x	x	x	x
$\bot$			x	x
$\neg A$			x	x
$(C \sqcap D)$	x	x	x	x
$(C \sqcup D)$				x
$\forall r.C$		x	x	x
$\exists r.C$	x	x	x	x

We now formally fix the meaning of concept descriptions in the usual model-theoretic way, using the notion of an interpretation.

Definition 2.2.1. *An* interpretation $\mathcal{I}$ *is a tuple* $(\Delta^{\mathcal{I}}, \cdot^{\mathcal{I}})$, *which consists of a non-empty* domain $\Delta^{\mathcal{I}}$ *and an* interpretation function $\cdot^{\mathcal{I}}$ *that assigns to every concept name, A, a set* $A^{\mathcal{I}} \subseteq \Delta^{\mathcal{I}}$, *to every attribute name, a, a partial function from* $\Delta^{\mathcal{I}}$ *into* $\Delta^{\mathcal{I}}$, *and to every role name, r, a binary relation* $r^{\mathcal{I}} \subseteq \Delta^{\mathcal{I}} \times \Delta^{\mathcal{I}}$.

Occasionally, we require attributes to be interpreted as total functions. Attributes interpreted in this way are called *total attributes*; the others are called *partial*. If nothing is said, attributes are assumed to be partial.

Before we can define the interpretation of concept descriptions, we need to extend the interpretation function to complex roles:

$$\emptyset^{\mathcal{I}} := \emptyset,$$
$$\varepsilon^{\mathcal{I}} := \{(d,d) \mid d \in \Delta^{\mathcal{I}}\},$$
$$(R \cup S)^{\mathcal{I}} := R^{\mathcal{I}} \cup S^{\mathcal{I}},$$
$$(R \circ S)^{\mathcal{I}} := R^{\mathcal{I}} \circ S^{\mathcal{I}}, \text{ and}$$
$$(R^*)^{\mathcal{I}} := \bigcup_{i=0}^{\infty} (R^i)^{\mathcal{I}},$$

where $R^{\mathcal{I}} \circ S^{\mathcal{I}}$ denotes the usual composition between binary relations, i.e., $R^{\mathcal{I}} \circ S^{\mathcal{I}} := \{(d,f) \mid \text{ there exists } e \in \Delta^{\mathcal{I}} \text{ with } (d,e) \in R^{\mathcal{I}} \text{ and } (e,f) \in S\mathcal{I}\}$, and R^i denotes the composition $R \circ \cdots \circ R$ of length i; $R^0 := \varepsilon$.

We now extend interpretation functions to concept descriptions. For this purpose, some additional notation is needed. If $d \in \Delta^{\mathcal{I}}$, then for a (complex) role define $R^{\mathcal{I}}(d) := \{e \mid (d,e) \in R^{\mathcal{I}}\}$ to be the set of R-successors of d. For an attribute a, we say that $a^{\mathcal{I}}$ is defined on d, if d belongs to the domain of $a^{\mathcal{I}}$. In this case, by abuse of notation, $a^{\mathcal{I}}(d)$ either denotes the image of d or a singleton containing this image; otherwise, if $a^{\mathcal{I}}$ is not defined on d, then $a^{\mathcal{I}}(d)$ denotes the empty set. A sequence (composition) $a_1 \cdots a_k$ of attributes a_i is interpreted as partial function by $(a_1 \cdots a_k)^{\mathcal{I}}(d) := a_k^{\mathcal{I}}(\cdots a_1^{\mathcal{I}}(d) \cdots)$. The inductive extension of $\cdot^{\mathcal{I}}$ to concept descriptions is now specified as follows, where for a given concept description C, $C^{\mathcal{I}}$ will be referred to as the *extension of C* (under $\mathcal{I}$):

$$\top^{\mathcal{I}} := \Delta^{\mathcal{I}},$$
$$\bot^{\mathcal{I}} := \emptyset,$$
$$(\neg A)^{\mathcal{I}} := \Delta^{\mathcal{I}} \setminus A^{\mathcal{I}},$$
$$(\geq n\, r)^{\mathcal{I}} := \{d \mid card\{r^{\mathcal{I}}(d)\} \geq n\},$$
$$(\leq n\, r)^{\mathcal{I}} := \{d \mid card\{r^{\mathcal{I}}(d)\} \leq n\},$$
$$(a_1 \cdots a_k \downarrow b_1 \cdots b_l)^{\mathcal{I}} := \{d \mid (a_1 \cdots a_k)^{\mathcal{I}} \text{ and } (b_1 \cdots b_l)^{\mathcal{I}} \text{ are defined}$$
$$\text{on } d \text{ and } (a_1 \cdots a_k)^{\mathcal{I}}(d) = (b_1 \cdots b_l)^{\mathcal{I}}(d)\},$$
$$(C \sqcap D)^{\mathcal{I}} := C^{\mathcal{I}} \cap D^{\mathcal{I}},$$
$$(C \sqcup D)^{\mathcal{I}} := C^{\mathcal{I}} \cup D^{\mathcal{I}},$$
$$(\neg C)^{\mathcal{I}} := \Delta^{\mathcal{I}} \setminus C^{\mathcal{I}},$$
$$(\forall R.C)^{\mathcal{I}} := \{d \mid R^{\mathcal{I}}(d) \subseteq C^{\mathcal{I}}\},$$
$$(\forall a.C)^{\mathcal{I}} := \{d \mid a^{\mathcal{I}}(d) \subseteq C^{\mathcal{I}}\},$$
$$(\exists r.C)^{\mathcal{I}} := \{d \mid r^{\mathcal{I}}(d) \cap C^{\mathcal{I}} \neq \emptyset\}.$$

As mentioned above, complex roles R define regular languages L_R. The semantics of L_R can be defined by

$$L_R{}^{\mathcal{I}} := \bigcup_{w \in L_R} w^{\mathcal{I}}$$

where with $w = r_1 \cdots r_k$, $w^{\mathcal{I}}$ denotes the composition $r_1^{\mathcal{I}} \circ \cdots \circ r_k^{\mathcal{I}}$. By structural induction on R it is easy to prove that $R^{\mathcal{I}} = L_R{}^{\mathcal{I}}$. This implies, when defining $(\forall L_R.C)^{\mathcal{I}} := \{d \mid (L_R)^{\mathcal{I}}(d) \subseteq C^{\mathcal{I}}\}$, that

$$(\forall R.C)^{\mathcal{I}} = (\forall L_R.C)^{\mathcal{I}}.$$

Thus, the two different notations for value restrictions on complex roles are in fact equivalent. Finally, it is easy to verify that

$$(\forall L_R.C)^{\mathcal{I}} = \bigcap_{w \in L_R} \{d \mid w^{\mathcal{I}}(d) \subseteq C^{\mathcal{I}}\}.$$

As an aside, we note that the semantics of concept descriptions (at least for some DLs) can also be declared by turning concept descriptions into first-order formulae with one free variable [Bor94]. $\mathcal{ALC}$-concept descriptions, for instance, can even be expressed in the two-variable fragment L^2 of first-order logic — a fragment of first-order logic known to be decidable, [Mor75]. As a simple example, consider the concept $\forall r.A$, which corresponds to the following first-order formula

$$\forall y(r(x, y) \longrightarrow A(y))$$

with free variable x. In the literature, also other (decidable) fragments of first-order logic have been identified to which many DLs can be reduced (see, e.g., [GOR97, Grä99a]). Note, however, that the concept Momo introduced above cannot be expressed in first-order logic, since it is well-known that the transitive closure of binary relations is beyond the expressive power of classical first-order logic. Thus, in terms of expressive power, first-order formulae and some of the DLs considered in this work (namely the (sublanguages of) $\mathcal{ALN}^*$ in Table 2.2) are incomparable.

2.2.2 Terminologies (TBoxes)

Concept descriptions are used in a TBox to define the concepts of the application domain. In particular, TBoxes allow to introduce names for concept descriptions.

In the following, let $\mathcal{L}$ denote some DL. Then, $\mathcal{L}$-TBoxes are defined as follows.

Definition 2.2.2. An $\mathcal{L}$-concept definition *is of the form* $A \doteq C$, *where* $A \in N_C$ *is a concept name and* C *is an* $\mathcal{L}$-concept description. *An* $\mathcal{L}$-TBox $\mathcal{T}$ *consists of a finite set of* $\mathcal{L}$-concept definitions. *A concept name is called* defined *(in* $\mathcal{T}$) *if it occurs on the left-hand side of a concept definition, otherwise it is called* primitive. *We require defined names to occur exactly once on the left-hand side of concept definitions in* $\mathcal{T}$. *The concept description* C *in the definition* $A \doteq C$ *of* A *is called* defining concept *of* A *and it is referred to by* $\mathcal{T}(A)$.

Note that defined names can be used within defining concepts. However, if the language $\mathcal{L}$ does only allow for primitive negation (as opposed to full negation), then negation is only allowed in front of primitive concepts. (Otherwise, full negation could be emulated.)

In the literature, also TBoxes have been considered that allow for axioms of the form $A \sqsubseteq C$, or even general inclusion axioms, $C \sqsubseteq D$, where both C and D may be complex concept descriptions (see, e.g., [Gia95, Cal96, GL96, HST99]). Such TBoxes can, for example, be used to express schemas in data models, like Entity-Relationship diagrams [CLN99, CGL$^+$98a]. However, these kinds of TBoxes are not further investigated here; we will always stick to Definition 2.2.2.

A TBox $\mathcal{T}$ is called cyclic if there exists at least one concept name which (directly or indirectly) occurs in its own definitions. Formally, cycles are defined as follows: Let A denote a defined concept and B be a concept name. We say that A directly uses B if B occurs in $\mathcal{T}(A)$. Now, if "uses" denotes the transitive closure of "directly uses", then $\mathcal{T}$ is cyclic if there is a defined concept in $\mathcal{T}$ that uses itself. Otherwise, $\mathcal{T}$ is acyclic.

In the remainder of this subsection, the semantics of TBoxes is defined. While for acyclic TBoxes there is one canonical way of fixing the meaning, for cyclic TBoxes there are several reasonable semantics, including fixed-point semantics. Using $\mathcal{ALN}$-TBoxes, we illustrate that cyclic TBoxes together with fixed-point semantics can be used to increase the expressive power of a DL. In fact, there is a 1-1 correspondence between concept defined in a cyclic $\mathcal{ALN}$-TBox and $\mathcal{ALN}^*$-concept descriptions.

Semantics of Acyclic TBoxes. The meaning of a TBox is defined by the set of its models.

Definition 2.2.3. *An interpretation $\mathcal{I}$ is a* model *of a TBox $\mathcal{T}$ if every concept definition $A \doteq C$ in $\mathcal{T}$ is satisfied, i.e., $A^\mathcal{I} = C^\mathcal{I}$.*

A *primitive interpretation* $\mathcal{J}$ of $\mathcal{T}$ only interprets the primitive concepts, roles, and attributes (if any) of $\mathcal{T}$, i.e., the interpretation of the defined name in $\mathcal{T}$ is omitted. An *extension* $\mathcal{I}$ of $\mathcal{J}$ is an interpretation that interprets the defined concepts of $\mathcal{T}$ and that coincides with $\mathcal{J}$ on the domain as well as the interpretation of the primitive concepts, roles, and attributes.

In acyclic TBoxes, the semantics of defined names is uniquely determined given a primitive interpretation. This means that, for every primitive interpretation $\mathcal{J}$ of a TBox $\mathcal{T}$, there exists a unique extension $\mathcal{I}$ of $\mathcal{J}$ to a model of $\mathcal{T}$. To see this, we need to define unfolded TBoxes.

A TBox is *unfolded* if there exists no defining concept containing defined names. Clearly, every given acyclic TBox $\mathcal{T}$ can be turned into an equivalent unfolded TBox $\mathcal{T}'$ by exhaustively substituting defined names on the right-hand side of concept definitions by their defining concepts. Every concept definition in $\mathcal{T}'$ is of the form $A \doteq C'$ where C' does not contain defined names. This concept description is called the *unfolded defining concept* of

Man $\doteq$ Human $\sqcap$ Male

Parent $\doteq$ Human $\sqcap$ $\exists$has-child.Human

Father $\doteq$ Man $\sqcap$ Parent

Grandfather $\doteq$ Father $\sqcap$ $\exists$has-child.Parent

FatherOfSons $\doteq$ Father $\sqcap$ $\forall$has-child.Man

Fig. 2.3. An Example TBox in the Family Domain.

A. Nebel, [Neb90a], has shown that the size of $\mathcal{T}'$ may grow exponentially in the size of $\mathcal{T}$.

As an example of the unfolding process, Figure 2.3 depicts a TBox defining concepts in the family domain. In the corresponding unfolded TBox the defining concept of, say, Father is Human $\sqcap$ Male $\sqcap$ Human $\sqcap$ $\exists$has-child.Human, obtained by substituting Man and Parent with their defining concepts.

Now, given a primitive interpretation $\mathcal{J}$ of an acyclic TBox $\mathcal{T}$, every extension $\mathcal{I}$ of $\mathcal{J}$ to a model of $\mathcal{T}$ satisfies $A^{\mathcal{I}} = C'^{\mathcal{J}}$ for every defined name A in $\mathcal{T}$ and its unfolded defining concept C'. Thus, the meaning of every defined name of $\mathcal{T}$ is uniquely determined given $\mathcal{J}$ and $\mathcal{T}$.

Semantics of Cyclic TBoxes. In general, for cyclic TBoxes primitive interpretations cannot uniquely be extended to models of the TBox (see [Baa96] for an example). Nevertheless, all models of cyclic TBoxes can be described as fixed-points of the following mapping: Let $\mathcal{E}_{\mathcal{J}}$ denote the set of extensions of $\mathcal{J}$. The mapping

$$\mathcal{T}_{\mathcal{J}} : \mathcal{E}_{\mathcal{J}} \longrightarrow \mathcal{E}_{\mathcal{J}}$$

is defined by $A^{\mathcal{T}_{\mathcal{J}}(\mathcal{I})} := \mathcal{T}(A)^{\mathcal{I}}$ for every defined concept A of $\mathcal{T}$ and extension $\mathcal{I} \in \mathcal{E}_{\mathcal{J}}$. Observe that with this definition, $\mathcal{T}_{\mathcal{J}}$ is completely specified since $\mathcal{T}_{\mathcal{J}}$ must coincide with $\mathcal{J}$ on the primitive names, roles, and attributes of $\mathcal{T}$.

Lemma 2.2.1. *Let $\mathcal{T}$ be a TBox, $\mathcal{J}$ be a primitive interpretation, and $\mathcal{I}$ be some extension of $\mathcal{J}$. Then, $\mathcal{T}_{\mathcal{J}}(\mathcal{I}) = \mathcal{I}$ iff $\mathcal{I}$ is a model of $\mathcal{T}$.*

Unlike acyclic TBoxes, in general cyclic TBoxes do not allow to extend every primitive interpretation to a model of the TBox. For example, there does not exist a model of the TBox $A \doteq \neg A$ since for every interpretation $\mathcal{I}$, $A^{\mathcal{I}}$ and $(\neg A)^{\mathcal{I}}$ are disjoint. In terms of our mapping, this means that $\mathcal{T}_{\mathcal{J}}$ does not have a fixed-point.

In order to identify (cyclic) TBoxes $\mathcal{T}$ that allow to extend every primitive interpretation $\mathcal{J}$ to a model of the TBox, we need to introduce a partial ordering $\preceq$ on $\mathcal{E}_{\mathcal{J}}$: $\mathcal{I} \preceq \mathcal{I}'$ iff $A^{\mathcal{I}} \subseteq A^{\mathcal{I}'}$ for all defined concepts A in $\mathcal{T}$. Since every family of interpretations $\mathcal{I}_i \in \mathcal{E}_{\mathcal{J}}$ has a least upper bound, namely, the interpretation $\mathcal{I}_0$ with $A^{\mathcal{I}_0} = \bigcup_i A^{\mathcal{I}_i}$ for every defined concept A in $\mathcal{T}$, the tuple $(\mathcal{E}_{\mathcal{J}}, \preceq)$ establishes a complete lattice. The mapping $\mathcal{T}_{\mathcal{J}}$ is called *monotone* on this lattice if $\mathcal{T}_{\mathcal{J}}(\mathcal{I}) \preceq \mathcal{T}_{\mathcal{J}'}(\mathcal{I}')$ whenever $\mathcal{I} \preceq \mathcal{I}'$.

Tarski's Fixed-Point Theorem says that for monotone functions on a complete lattice there always exists a (least and greatest) fixed-point. In our setting this means that, if $\mathcal{T}_{\mathcal{J}}$ is monotone, then there exist least and greatest fixed-points of $\mathcal{T}_{\mathcal{J}}$. An interpretation $\mathcal{I}$ is a least (greatest) fixed-point of $\mathcal{T}_{\mathcal{J}}$ if i) $\mathcal{T}_{\mathcal{J}}(\mathcal{I}) = \mathcal{I}$ and ii) $\mathcal{T}_{\mathcal{J}}(\mathcal{I}') = \mathcal{I}'$ implies $\mathcal{I} \preceq \mathcal{I}'$ ($\mathcal{I}' \preceq \mathcal{I}$).

A simple syntactic restriction that guarantees $\mathcal{T}_{\mathcal{J}}$ to be monotone is that, if $\mathcal{T}$ does contain negation at all, then only in front of primitive concepts. Such TBoxes are called *negation free*. Except for $\mathcal{ALC}$-TBoxes, this requirement is met by all DLs introduced in Section 2.2.1.

According to Tarski's theorem, for negation free TBoxes every primitive interpretation $\mathcal{J}$ can be extended to a model of a TBox $\mathcal{T}$. Moreover, there always exists a least (greatest) model of $\mathcal{T}$, i.e., one that is the least (greatest) fixed-point of $\mathcal{T}_{J}$.

Definition 2.2.4. *Let $\mathcal{T}$ be a negation free (possibly cyclic) TBox.*

1. *The* descriptive semantics *allows for all models of $\mathcal{T}$ as admissible models (see Definition 2.2.3).*
2. *The* least fixed-point semantics *(lfp-semantics) allows only for those models of $\mathcal{T}$ that come from the least fixed-point of a mapping $\mathcal{T}_{\mathcal{J}}$ (lfp-models).*
3. *The* greatest fixed-point semantics *(gfp-semantics) allows only for those models of $\mathcal{T}$ that come from the greatest fixed-point of a mapping $\mathcal{T}_{\mathcal{J}}$ (lfp-models).*

In the literature there have been many discussions about what is the appropriate semantics of cyclic TBoxes. At the beginning, people wanted to circumvent the problem altogether by not allowing for cycles in the first place. The first thorough investigation of terminological cycles is due to Nebel [Neb87, Neb91, Neb90a], who showed that the appropriate semantics of cyclic TBoxes depends on the application under consideration. To get a better understanding of the different semantics, Baader [Baa96] provided an automata-theoretic characterization of the semantics of cyclic $\mathcal{FL}_0$-TBoxes, which later on was extended to $\mathcal{ALN}$-TBoxes [Küs98]. Finally, researchers augmented logics with fixed-point operators in order to switch between different semantics [Gia95, CGL99]. The logics proposed are syntactic variants or extensions of the modal μ-calculus, [Koz83]. However, while these logics are introduced for knowledge representation purposes, the interest in the μ-calculus stems from the verification of concurrent programs.

Cyclic $\mathcal{ALN}$-TBoxes and $\mathcal{ALN}^*$-Concept Descriptions. With the help of cyclic $\mathcal{ALN}$-TBoxes so-called cyclic $\mathcal{ALN}$-concept descriptions can be defined.

Definition 2.2.5. *A cyclic $\mathcal{ALN}$-concept description is a tuple $C = (A, \mathcal{T})$ where A denotes a defined name in the (cyclic) $\mathcal{ALN}$-TBox $\mathcal{T}$. Given a prim-*

itive interpretation $\mathcal{J}$ of $\mathcal{T}$, the semantics of C is determined by $C^{\mathcal{I}} := A^{\mathcal{I}}$ where $\mathcal{I}$ is the gfp-model of $\mathcal{T}$ w.r.t. $\mathcal{J}$.[2]

As shown in [Küs98] (see also Section 4.2), there is a 1-1 correspondence between cyclic $\mathcal{ALN}$-concept descriptions and $\mathcal{ALN}^*$-concept descriptions. More precisely, one can show that for every $\mathcal{ALN}^*$-concept description D there exists an equivalent cyclic $\mathcal{ALN}$-concept description C, i.e., for all interpretations $\mathcal{I}$, $D^{\mathcal{I}} = C^{\mathcal{I}}$. Conversely, for every cyclic $\mathcal{ALN}$-concept description C there exists an equivalent $\mathcal{ALN}^*$-concept description D.

As an example, the $\mathcal{ALN}^*$-concept description Momo can be turned into the cyclic $\mathcal{ALN}$-concept description (Momo, $\mathcal{T}$), where now Momo denotes a defined concept in the TBox $\mathcal{T}$ given by:

$$\text{Momo} \doteq \text{Male} \sqcap \forall\text{has-child.Momo}.$$

2.2.3 World Descriptions (ABoxes)

The second component of DL knowledge bases are ABoxes. Whereas TBoxes restrict the set of possible worlds, ABoxes allow to describe a specific state of the world by introducing individuals together with their properties. Throughout this book the set of individuals is denoted by N_I. This set is disjoint from the sets N_C, N_R, and N_A. If $\mathcal{L}$ denotes some DL, then $\mathcal{L}$-ABoxes are defined as follows:

Definition 2.2.6. *A concept assertion is of the form $C(a)$ where C is a concept description and $a \in N_I$ is an individual. A role assertion is of the form $r(a, b)$ where $r \in N_R$ is a role name and $a, b \in N_I$ are individuals. An ABox $\mathcal{A}$ is a finite set of assertions, i.e., concept and role assertions. If all concept descriptions occurring in $\mathcal{A}$ are $\mathcal{L}$-concept descriptions, then $\mathcal{A}$ is called $\mathcal{L}$-ABox. In case $\mathcal{A}$ is defined with respect to an TBox, then the concept descriptions in $\mathcal{A}$ may contain defined names of the TBox.*

A simple example of an ABox specified with respect to the TBox depicted in Figure 2.3 is

$$\text{Man(Peter), has-child(Peter, Paul), Man(Paul)}.$$

Intuitively, this ABox says that Peter is a man with a son, namely Paul.

In order to formally specify the semantics of ABoxes, interpretations $\mathcal{I}$ are extended to map every individual $a \in N_I$ to an element $a^{\mathcal{I}} \in \Delta^{\mathcal{I}}$. It is required that different individuals are mapped to different domain elements (*unique name assumption*).

Definition 2.2.7. *An interpretation $\mathcal{I}$ is a model of an ABox $\mathcal{A}$, if all concept assertions $C(a) \in \mathcal{A}$ and role assertions $r(a, b) \in \mathcal{A}$ in $\mathcal{A}$ are satisfied, i.e., $a^{\mathcal{I}} \in C^{\mathcal{I}}$ and $(a^{\mathcal{I}}, b^{\mathcal{I}}) \in r^{\mathcal{I}}$.*

---

[2] Since $\mathcal{I}$ is uniquely determined by $\mathcal{T}$ and $\mathcal{J}$, we will not distinguish between $\mathcal{J}$ and $\mathcal{I}$ in the sequel.

2.3 Standard Inferences

So far, we have introduced syntax and semantics of knowledge bases. The main purpose of a knowledge representation system is to reason about the (conceptual and assertional) knowledge stored in such knowledge bases. There are some reasoning services (almost) all DL-systems provide. In the following, we will introduce the underlying inference problems — here called *standard inferences*.

Reasoning about Conceptual Knowledge. We start with the definition of the basic inferences on concepts. All notions can be defined with or without an underlying TBox $\mathcal{T}$.

- A concept description C is called *satisfiable* if there exists an interpretation $\mathcal{I}$ with $C^{\mathcal{I}} \neq \emptyset$; C is called *satisfiable modulo* $\mathcal{T}$ if there exists a model $\mathcal{I}$ of $\mathcal{T}$ with $C^{\mathcal{I}} \neq \emptyset$.
- Given concept descriptions C and D, D is said to *subsume* C ($C \sqsubseteq D$ for short) if $C^{\mathcal{I}} \subseteq D^{\mathcal{I}}$ for all interpretations $\mathcal{I}$; D *subsumes* C *modulo* $\mathcal{T}$ ($C \sqsubseteq_{\mathcal{T}} D$) if the above holds for all models $\mathcal{I}$ of $\mathcal{T}$.
- The concept descriptions C and D are called *equivalent* ($C \equiv D$) if $C^{\mathcal{I}} = D^{\mathcal{I}}$ for all interpretations $\mathcal{I}$; C and D are *equivalent modulo* $\mathcal{T}$ ($C \equiv_{\mathcal{T}} D$) if this holds for all models $\mathcal{I}$ of $\mathcal{T}$.

Before we discuss simple properties of these inferences as well as their interconnection, let us first sketch how one can benefit from these inferences in DL-systems.

Checking satisfiability can be used to test whether a concept can contain individuals. If this is not the case, i.e., the concept is self-contradictory, a modeling error has occurred, and the concept must be changed.

Checking subsumption relationships between concepts is used to compute the subconcept/superconcept hierarchy of the concepts defined in a TBox. For example, given the TBox depicted in Figure 2.3, a DL-systems can automatically come up with the hierarchy shown in Figure 2.4 (provided that subsumption is decidable). Such a hierarchy can then be used to evaluate the adequacy of a TBox with respect to the application domain the TBox is supposed to describe. If concepts occur at unexpected positions in the hierarchy, then this indicates a mismatch between the intuition underlying a concept and its representation in the TBox. Hierarchies can also facilitate the reuse of concepts and their instances, for one can browse the knowledge base along the hierarchy as opposed to searching through the whole knowledge base.

Finally, testing equivalence allows to check whether a concept to be added to the knowledge base already exists.

Now, let us examine the connections between the different inference problems. The first observation is that deciding the satisfiability of a concept can be reduced to subsumption because a concept description C is unsatisfiable modulo $\mathcal{T}$ iff $C \sqsubseteq_{\mathcal{T}} \bot$. Conversely, for DLs that allow for full negation

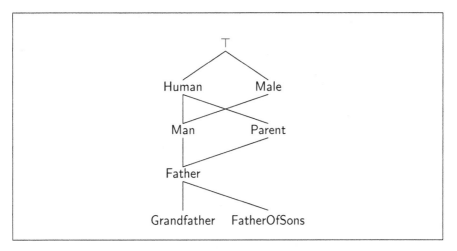

Fig. 2.4. Subsumption Hierarchy.

(like $\mathcal{ALC}$) subsumption can be reduced to unsatisfiability since $C \sqsubseteq_{\mathcal{T}} D$ iff $C \sqcap \neg D \equiv_{\mathcal{T}} \bot$. Finally, testing equivalence can be reduced to subsumption checking because $C \equiv_{\mathcal{T}} D$ iff $C \sqsubseteq_{\mathcal{T}} D$ and $D \sqsubseteq_{\mathcal{T}} C$. On the other hand, $C \sqsubseteq_{\mathcal{T}} D$ iff $C \equiv_{\mathcal{T}} C \sqcap D$.

For all inference problems introduced above, acyclic TBoxes can be eliminated. The idea is that, given an acyclic TBox $\mathcal{T}$, one computes the corresponding unfolded TBox $\mathcal{T}'$ and then substitutes all defined names occurring in the inference problem by their unfolded defining concepts. As an example consider the problem $C \sqsubseteq_{\mathcal{T}} D$. If C' and D' are obtained by replacing all defined concepts in C and D by their unfolded defining concepts, then deciding $C \sqsubseteq_{\mathcal{T}} D$ is equivalent to deciding $C' \sqsubseteq D'$. As shown by Lutz [Lut99], this approach of deciding subsumption modulo acyclic TBoxes is not always optimal from the complexity point of view.

Still, in all investigations carried out in this work, we usually do not take TBoxes into account. An exception are $\mathcal{ALN}^*$-concept descriptions since, as mentioned in the previous section, they can be defined by cyclic $\mathcal{ALN}$-TBoxes using gfp-semantics. Hence, for $\mathcal{ALN}^*$, (cyclic) TBoxes are always present implicitly.

As mentioned in Section 2.1, standard inferences have been studied exhaustively. In particular, the complexity of reasoning in $\mathcal{ALNS}$, $\mathcal{ALN}^*$, and $\mathcal{ALE}$, is well-investigated. Table 2.4 summarizes the complexity of deciding satisfiability and subsumption in these languages and some sublanguages, where PSPACE and NP mean PSPACE-complete and NP-complete, respectively; P means that the problem is in P (completeness has usually not been investigated for this complexity class). These results can be derive from the characterizations of subsumption presented in Chapter 4. They are proved

Table 2.4. Complexity Results for Standard Inferences (with empty TBox)

	$\mathcal{ALNS}$	$\mathcal{FL}_0^*$	$\mathcal{FLN}^*/\mathcal{ALN}^*$	$\mathcal{EL}$	$\mathcal{FLE}$	$\mathcal{ALE}$
Satisfiability	P	P	PSPACE	P	P	NP
Subsumption	P	PSPACE	PSPACE	P	NP	NP

in [KB99] (for $\mathcal{ALNS}$), [Küs98] (for $\mathcal{ALN}^*$ and its sublanguages), [BKM99] (for $\mathcal{EL}$), and [DHL⁺92] (for $\mathcal{FLE}$ and $\mathcal{ALE}$).

Reasoning about Assertional Knowledge. For ABoxes the standard inference problems are satisfiability and instance checking. Given a TBox $\mathcal{T}$, an ABox $\mathcal{A}$, a concept description C, and an individual a in $\mathcal{A}$, these problems are defined as follows:

- $\mathcal{A}$ is called *consistent* if there exists a model $\mathcal{I}$ of $\mathcal{A}$; $\mathcal{A}$ is *consistent modulo* $\mathcal{T}$ if there exists a model of $\mathcal{A}$ and $\mathcal{T}$.
- The individual a is said to be an *instance* of C ($a \in_{\mathcal{A}} C$) if $a^{\mathcal{I}} \in C^{\mathcal{I}}$ for all models $\mathcal{I}$ of $\mathcal{A}$; a is an *instance of* C *modulo* $\mathcal{T}$ ($a \in_{\mathcal{A},\mathcal{T}} C$) if the above holds for all models of $\mathcal{A}$ and $\mathcal{T}$.

In our family knowledge base, we can deduce that Peter is an instance of Father, i.e., Peter $\in_{\mathcal{A},\mathcal{T}}$ Father. However, Peter $\in_{\mathcal{A},\mathcal{T}}$ FatherOfSons does not hold because from the ABox we cannot conclude that Paul is the only son of Peter.

There is a close interconnection between the inference problems specified above. First, consistency of ABoxes can be reduced to instance checking since an individual is an instance of the bottom-concept iff the ABox is inconsistent. Conversely, for languages that allow for full negation, instance checking can be reduced to consistency as follows: $a \in_{\mathcal{A},\mathcal{T}} C$ iff the knowledge base consisting of $\mathcal{T}$ and $\mathcal{A} \cup \{\neg C(a)\}$ is inconsistent. As before, one can use the unfolding trick to get rid of acyclic TBoxes.

Throughout this book, we do not take TBoxes into account when reasoning about ABoxes. Only for $\mathcal{ALN}^*$-ABoxes, (cyclic) TBoxes are present implicitly.

2.4 Decision Algorithms

As mentioned in Section 2.1, basically two types of algorithms, namely, *structural subsumption* and *tableau-based* algorithms have been employed to decide standard inference problems. Nowadays, tableau-algorithms represent the state of the art technique to decide standard inferences for a great variety of very expressive DLs. Conversely, structural subsumption algorithms are only applicable to less expressive DLs, for example those that do not allow for concept disjunction and full negation. However, they prove to be very useful for solving non-standard inferences. Therefore, Chapter 4 is devoted to structural characterizations of subsumption, which form the basis for investigations on non-standard inferences in subsequent chapters.

In this section, the underlying ideas of both the structural and the tableau-based approach are illustrated by a simple example. At the end of this section, we sketch those features of structural algorithms, which, intuitively, make them more suitable for solving non-standard inferences than tableau-based algorithms. More than an intuition cannot be given at this point since the precise relationship between the two kinds of algorithms is not yet clarified.

As a running example we take the following $\mathcal{ALE}$-concept descriptions

$$C_{ex} := \exists r.P \sqcap \forall r.Q \sqcap \forall r.Q',$$
$$D_{ex} := \exists r.(P \sqcap Q) \sqcap \forall r.Q',$$

and consider the problem of deciding $C_{ex} \sqsubseteq D_{ex}$ (which obviously is a valid subsumption relationship).

Structural Subsumption Algorithms. The main idea underlying structural subsumption algorithms is as follows: First, turn the given (potential) subsumee into its normal form by making implicit knowledge explicit. Then, syntactically compare the (potential) subsumer with the normal form of the (potential) subsumee in order to decide subsumption.

To obtain the normal form, one gathers all information "at one place". In our example, one must apply the following (equivalence preserving) normalization rules to the subsumee C_{ex}:

$$\forall r.E \sqcap \forall r.F \longrightarrow \forall r.(E \sqcap F),$$
$$\exists r.E \sqcap \forall r.F \longrightarrow \exists r.(E \sqcap F) \sqcap \forall r.F.$$

We obtain the following normalized concept description:

$$C'_{ex} := \exists r.(P \sqcap Q \sqcap Q') \sqcap \forall r.(Q \sqcap Q').$$

In the second step of the subsumption algorithm, one checks whether for all names and restrictions on the top-level of the potential subsumer there exist more specific expressions on the top-level of the normal form of the subsumee. Then, recursively all restrictions are processed.

In the example, the conjuncts $\exists r.(P \sqcap Q)$ and $\forall r.Q'$ of D_{ex} are considered one at a time, and then the descriptions within these restrictions are treated recursively. Let us start with $\exists r.(P \sqcap Q)$. If at all, this restriction can only subsume the conjunct $\exists r.(P \sqcap Q \sqcap Q')$ in C'_{ex}. Recursively, checking subsumption between these expressions leads to testing $P \sqcap Q \sqcap Q' \sqsubseteq P \sqcap Q$, which returns a positive answer. Then, it remains to check subsumption between $\forall r.Q'$ in D_{ex} and $\forall r.(Q \sqcap Q')$ in C_{ex}, which is again successful since $Q \sqcap Q' \sqsubseteq Q'$. Thus, with input $C_{ex} \sqsubseteq D_{ex}$, the structural subsumption algorithm returns 'yes'.

Note that, if C_{ex} had not been normalized, e.g., the value restriction had not been propagated to the existential restriction, then for the existential restriction $\exists r.(P \sqcap Q)$ in D_{ex} there would not have been a more specific conjunct on the top-level of C_{ex}. In this case, the algorithm would come back with the wrong answer.

Tableau-Based Algorithms. These algorithms are usually employed for DLs that allow for full negation, and subsumption is reduced to deciding satisfiability of concepts: $C \sqsubseteq D$ iff $C \sqcap \neg D$ is unsatisfiable.

As for our running example, we can view C_{ex} and D_{ex} as $\mathcal{ALC}$-concept descriptions. Then, an $\mathcal{ALC}$ tableau-algorithm tries to decide satisfiability of

$$
\begin{aligned}
C_{ex} \sqcap \neg D_{ex} &= \exists r.P \sqcap \forall r.Q \sqcap \forall r.Q' \sqcap \neg(\exists r.(P \sqcap Q) \sqcap \forall r.Q') \\
&\equiv \exists r.P \sqcap \forall r.Q \sqcap \forall r.Q' \sqcap (\forall r.(\neg P \sqcup \neg Q) \sqcup \exists r.\neg Q') =: E_{ex}.
\end{aligned}
$$

The concept description E_{ex} is the *negation normal form* of $C_{ex} \sqcap \neg D_{ex}$, i.e., negation only occurs in front of concept names. This normal form is needed for technical reasons, and unlike the normal form in the structural case, its purpose is not to make implicit knowledge explicit.

The general idea of a tableau-algorithm is to build a model $\mathcal{I}$ with $E_{ex}^{\mathcal{I}} \neq \emptyset$ in order to prove satisfiability of E_{ex}. The first step is to generate an individual, say a_0, that is supposed to be an element of $E_{ex}^{\mathcal{I}}$. Then, the remaining task is to extend the model $\mathcal{I}$ in such a way that $a_0 \in E_{ex}^{\mathcal{I}}$ actually holds.

Let us illustrate this by our running example. In order to guarantee $a_0 \in E_{ex}^{\mathcal{I}}$ one needs to extend $\mathcal{I}$ in such a way that all constraints contained in E_{ex} are satisfied. The starting point is an interpretation $\mathcal{I}$ which contains a_0 in its domain and which maps all concept names and role names onto the empty set. Due to the first conjunct on the top-level of E_{ex} we deduce that there must exist an individual a_1 with $(a_0, a_1) \in r^{\mathcal{I}}$ and $a_1 \in P^{\mathcal{I}}$. Thus, the domain of $\mathcal{I}$ and the extensions of r and P are modified accordingly. Because of the two value restrictions $\forall r.Q$ and $\forall r.Q'$ in E_{ex}, additional constraints are *propagated* to a_1. Consequently, $\mathcal{I}$ is augmented to satisfy $a_1 \in P^{\mathcal{I}} \cap Q^{\mathcal{I}} \cap Q'^{\mathcal{I}}$. It remains to extend the model to ensure $a_0 \in (\forall r.(\neg P \sqcup \neg Q) \sqcup \exists r.\neg Q')^{\mathcal{I}}$. Hence, a_0 must belong to one of the two disjuncts. If a_0 belongs to the first one, then again further constraints are imposed on a_1, namely $a_1 \in (\neg P \sqcup \neg Q)^{\mathcal{I}}$. However, together with the already existing constraints on a_1 neither $a_1 \in (\neg P)^{\mathcal{I}}$ nor $a_1 \in (\neg Q)^{\mathcal{I}}$ can be satisfied. Therefore, the algorithms backtracks and checks whether $\mathcal{I}$ can be extended in such a way that $a_0 \in (\exists r.\neg Q')^{\mathcal{I}}$ holds. To satisfy this condition, an individual, a_2, is added to $\mathcal{I}$ with $(a_0, a_2) \in r^{\mathcal{I}}$ and $a_2 \in (\neg Q')^{\mathcal{I}}$. In this situation, one should not assume that $a_1 = a_2$ since otherwise one would impose additional constraints on both individuals which, however, need not hold in general. Just like for a_1, the two value restriction on a_0, namely $\forall r.Q$ and $\forall r.Q'$, are propagated to a_2, which means that a_2 must satisfy $a_2 \in (\neg Q')^{\mathcal{I}} \cap Q^{\mathcal{I}} \cap Q'^{\mathcal{I}}$. Again, these constraints are contradicting. At this point, no alternative is left to try. Since it is not possible to construct a model $\mathcal{I}$ that shows that E_{ex} (and thus, $C_{ex} \sqcap \neg D_{ex}$), is satisfiable, the tableau-algorithm returns 'yes' indicating that $C_{ex} \sqsubseteq D_{ex}$ holds.

Comparing Structural and Tableau-Based Algorithms. The main feature of structural subsumption algorithms is that concept descriptions are turned into normal forms. These normal forms can be concept descriptions, like C'_{ex} in the example, or other mathematical objects, like trees or systems of finite automata (see Chapter 4.1). Intuitively speaking, their common property is that they are finite representations of the set of all implications that can be drawn from the original concept descriptions. Therefore, the task of a structural subsumption algorithm can be described as checking whether the set of all implications of the (potential) subsumer is "contained" in the set of all implications of the (potential) subsumee.

Conversely, tableau-algorithms do not make implications explicit on the description level, but rather generate interpretations. For instance, value restrictions are only dealt with indirectly by propagating them onto the individuals generated in an interpretation. In our example, the fact $C_{ex} \sqsubseteq \forall r.(Q \sqcap Q')$ is only taken care of by propagating Q and Q' onto the r-successors a_1 and a_2 of a_0. The value restriction itself is not represented in the generated interpretation.

As we will see in the subsequent chapters, finite representations of *all* implications that can be derived from concepts form the basis of our algorithms solving non-standard inferences. The normal forms employed in structural subsumption algorithms exactly provide us with these kinds of representations. Tableau-algorithms, on the other hand, do not provide comprehensive information about one concept. Implications are not gathered and made explicit, but are only derived "on demand", e.g., by propagating value restrictions.

3. Non-Standard Inferences

As described in the previous chapter, during the last fifteen years DLs have been investigated thoroughly with respect to their expressive power and the complexity of the standard inference problems. In some applications it has turned out, however, that additional *non-standard inferences* are needed to support the construction and maintenance of large DL knowledge bases. Some systems, e.g., Classic, contain ad hoc implementations of such novel inferences, mostly without having defined them formally or having investigated their computational complexity. This situation corresponds to the early days of DLs where systems have been built without an exact understanding of the formal properties of the implemented reasoning services. In this book, we aim at taking non-standard inferences to a formal level by providing precise definitions, complete algorithms, and first complexity results.

We concentrate on the three non-standard inferences *least common subsumer* (lcs), *most specific concept* (msc), and *matching of concept descriptions*. Originally, all three inferences have been introduced and implemented at the AT&T Labs motivated by applications of the DL-system Classic.

This chapter provides a survey of these inferences, including their applications as well as previous and new complexity results. All proofs and algorithms are postponed to subsequent chapters. For the sake of completeness, novel inferences not covered in this book are briefly discussed.

The chapter is structured as follows. In the first section, we formally define lcs and msc and explain some simple properties. We also sketch the possible applications of these non-standard inferences and review previous results known from the literature. An overview of the contributions of this book to the lcs and msc computation concludes the section. All algorithms and proofs are presented in Chapter 5. Section 3.2 covers the different aspects of matching, similar to the preceding section, including the formal definition of matching problems, their applications, known results, and the new contributions. Again, the algorithms and proofs are postponed to a later chapter (Chapter 6). Nevertheless, to get an idea of the theoretical background, Section 3.3 sketches the underlying techniques used to solve non-standard inferences. Finally, the last section discusses some novel inferences proposed in the literature but not further investigated in the present book.

R.Küsters: Non-Standard Inferences in Description Logics, LNAI 2100, pp. 33–72, 2001.
© Springer-Verlag Berlin Heidelberg 2001

3.1 LCS and MSC

In this section, we provide a formal definition of lcs and msc, and state basic properties of these inferences (Section 3.1.1). Their main applications are summarized in Section 3.1.2. The last two subsections give an overview of known and new theoretical results on these inferences. All technical details are postponed to Chapter 5 in order to concentrate on the results themselves.

3.1.1 Definition of LCS and MSC

In what follows, let $\mathcal{L}$ denote some DL. In subsequent chapters, $\mathcal{L}$ will usually stand for one of the DLs $\mathcal{ALNS}$, $\mathcal{ALN}^*$, and $\mathcal{ALE}$, or a sublanguage.

Least Common Subsumer. Intuitively, the least common subsumer of a given sequence of concept descriptions is a description that represents the properties that all the elements of the sequence have in common. More formally, it is the most specific concept description that subsumes the given descriptions:

Definition 3.1.1. Let $C_1, \ldots, C_k$ be $\mathcal{L}$-concept descriptions. The $\mathcal{L}$-concept description C is a least common subsumer (lcs) of $C_1, \ldots, C_k$ if, and only if,

1. $C_i \sqsubseteq C$ for all $i = 1, \ldots, k$; and
2. C is the most specific concept with this property, i.e., for every $\mathcal{L}$-concept description E, if $C_i \sqsubseteq E$ for all $i = 1, \ldots, k$, then $C \sqsubseteq E$.

First note that there need not necessarily exist an lcs for a given sequence of concepts. We will come back to the different reasons of this phenomenon later on. However, if an lcs exists, then it is uniquely determined up to equivalence. In fact, as an easy consequence of the definition of the lcs one can show the following lemma.

Lemma 3.1.1. If C and D are least common subsumers of $C_1, \ldots, C_k$, then $C \equiv D$.

Therefore, by abuse of language and notation, we will talk about *the* least common subsumer

$$lcs(C_1, \ldots, C_k)$$

of the concept descriptions $C_1, \ldots, C_k$. In view of Lemma 3.1.1, the concept description $lcs(C_1, \ldots, C_k)$ denotes a representative of the equivalence class (induced by the equivalence relation $\equiv$) of all least common subsumers of $C_1, \ldots, C_k$. We will elaborate on this in the following by providing a more abstract view on the lcs. To this end, some more notions are introduced.

Obviously, the set of all $\mathcal{L}$-concept descriptions along with the subsumption relation $\sqsubseteq$ (Section 2.3) defines a *quasi-ordering*, i.e., a reflexive and transitive ordering. Recall that $\equiv$ is the equivalence relationship induced by $\sqsubseteq$, i.e., $C \equiv D$ iff $C \sqsubseteq D$ and $D \sqsubseteq C$. Given a (possibly infinite) set S of concept descriptions, a description $C \in S$ is *minimal* in S, if $C \equiv D$ whenever $D \in S$ and $D \sqsubseteq C$; C is a *least* element in S, if $C \sqsubseteq D$ for all $D \in S$. For concept descriptions C the corresponding equivalence class is defined by $[C] := \{D \mid C \equiv D\}$. As usual, given a quasi-ordering $\sqsubseteq$, a *partial ordering* $\preceq$ on equivalence classes induced by $\sqsubseteq$ can be defined, i.e., a reflexive, antisymmetric, and transitive relation: $[C] \preceq [D]$ iff $C \sqsubseteq D$. Note that, since $\sqsubseteq$ is a quasi-ordering, $\preceq$ is well-defined. We write $[C] \prec [D]$ in case $[C] \preceq [D]$ and $[C] \neq [D]$. With $[S] := \{[C] \mid C \in S\}$ the definition of minimal and least elements carries over to the partial ordering as follows: $[C] \in [S]$ is *minimal* in $[S]$, if $[D] = [C]$ whenever $[D] \in [S]$ and $[D] \preceq [C]$; $[C] \in [S]$ is a *least* element in $[S]$, if $[C] \preceq [D]$ for all $[D] \in [S]$. Clearly, $[S]$ can have at most one least element: if $[C]$ and $[D]$ are both least elements, then $[C] \preceq [D]$ and $[D] \preceq [C]$ implies $[C] = [D]$. Thus, least elements in $[S]$ (if any) are uniquely determined.

According to Lemma 3.1.1, if an lcs of $C_1, \ldots, C_k$ exists, then the set of all the least common subsumers of $C_1, \ldots, C_k$ forms an equivalence class. Exploiting the ordering $\preceq$ introduced above, this class is *the* least element in $[S]$ where S denotes the set of all concept descriptions subsuming $C_1, \ldots, C_k$. In view of this, $lcs(C_1, \ldots, C_k)$ denotes a representative of the least element in $[S]$. This justifies to refer to *the* lcs of $C_1, \ldots, C_k$.

Beside this interpretation of the lcs as least element in the partial ordering $([S], \preceq)$, one can also view the lcs (and more precisely its equivalence class) as supremum of elements in a lattice.

Recall that a lattice is a partial ordering $(L, \leq)$ such that for all elements $l, l' \in L$ there exists a supremum, s, and an infimum, i, of these elements, i.e., $l, l' \leq s$, and for all $h \in L$ with $l, l' \leq h$, $s \leq h$, and symmetrically, $l, l' \geq i$, and for all $h \in L$ with $l, l' \geq h$, $i \geq h$. See, for instance, [Grä73] for more on lattices.

Now, let $\mathcal{E}$ denote the set of all equivalence classes of $\mathcal{L}$-concept descriptions. Just as $([S], \preceq)$, $(\mathcal{E}, \preceq)$ defines a partial ordering. If we assume that i) $\mathcal{L}$ allows to express concept conjunction and ii) for every finite set of $\mathcal{L}$-concept descriptions the lcs exists, $(\mathcal{E}, \preceq)$ defines a lattice, because for every given finite subset $\{[C_1], \ldots, [C_k]\}$ of $\mathcal{E}$, the class $[C_1 \sqcap \cdots \sqcap C_k]$ is the infimum and $[lcs(C_1, \ldots, C_k)]$ is the supremum of the elements $[C_1], \ldots, [C_k]$.

We will now turn our attention to the existence of the lcs. If $\mathcal{L}$ allows for concept disjunction (like $\mathcal{ALC}$), then the lcs is guaranteed to exist since

$$lcs(C_1, \ldots, C_k) \equiv C_1 \sqcup \cdots \sqcup C_k.$$

In general, however, the lcs need not exist. In light of the partial ordering $([S], \preceq)$ with S defined as the set of all subsumers of $C_1, \ldots, C_k$, this means that $[S]$ need not contain a least element. (From the lattice point of view, this means that, even if $\mathcal{L}$ allows for concept conjunction, $(\mathcal{E}, \preceq)$ is only a lower semi-lattice.) Three different phenomenons may cause the absence of a least element, and thus, an lcs:

1. $[S]$ might be empty, i.e., there does not exist a common subsumer in the first place.

   This cannot happen if the language $\mathcal{L}$ allows for the top-concept (like all languages we are dealing with), since $\top$ subsumes all other concepts. In particular, it subsumes $C_1, \ldots, C_k$.

2. $[S]$ might contain different minimal elements. Since the least element (i.e., the lcs) would be placed below all these minimal elements, there cannot exist a least element.

   Again, this is impossible for all the languages we consider here since they allow for concept conjunction: If C and D subsume $C_1, \ldots, C_k$, then $C \sqcap D$ is a common subsumer as well. Thus, there cannot exist different minimal elements $[C]$ and $[D]$ in $[S]$, since the class $[C \sqcap D]$ still belongs to $[S]$ and it is strictly smaller than the two "minimal" elements.

3. $[S]$ might contain an infinite decreasing chain $[D_1] \succ [D_2] \succ \cdots$ Although, the existence of such a chain is not sufficient for the absence of a least element in $[S]$, one can easily verify that it is necessary if the previous two cases do not hold.

   In Section 5.1.2 it is shown that there exist two $\mathcal{ALNS}$-concept descriptions, for the time being call them C and D, for which the lcs does not exist in case attributes are interpreted as total functions. Since $\mathcal{ALNS}$ allows for the top-concept and concept conjunction, $[S]$ (with S the set of subsumers of C and D) is not empty and does not contain two distinct minimal elements. Thus, $[S]$ must contain an infinite decreasing chain.

The following lemma shows that, in order to prove for arbitrary DLs $\mathcal{L}$ that the lcs of finite sequences of concept descriptions always exists and that it can be computed effectively, it is sufficient to provide an algorithm computing the lcs of two concept descriptions at a time.

Lemma 3.1.2. *Let $C_1, \ldots, C_k$ be $\mathcal{L}$-concept descriptions. Then,*

$$lcs(C_1, \ldots, C_k) \equiv lcs(C_k, lcs(\cdots lcs(C_2, C_1) \cdots)).$$

However, when it comes to computational complexity one needs to distinguish between the binary lcs operation and the one that works on sequences of concept descriptions. In fact, for most languages investigated in Chapter 5 one obtains different complexity results for the binary and k-ary lcs operation.

Most Specific Concept. Intuitively, the most specific concept of individuals described in an ABox is a concept description that represents all the properties of the individuals including the concept assertions they occur in and their relationship to other individuals.

Definition 3.1.2. *Let $\mathcal{A}$ be an $\mathcal{L}$-ABox and $a_1, \ldots, a_k$ be individuals of $\mathcal{A}$. Then, C is a most specific concept (msc) of $a_1, \ldots, a_k$ if, and only if,*

1. $a_i \in_{\mathcal{A}} C$, for all $i = 1, \ldots, k$; and
2. C is the most specific concept with this property, i.e., for all $\mathcal{L}$-concept descriptions E, if $a_i \in_{\mathcal{A}} E$ for all $i = 1, \ldots, k$, then $C \sqsubseteq E$.

Similar to the lcs, a most specific concept is uniquely determined up to equivalence. More precisely, the set of most specific concepts of individuals $a_1, \ldots, a_k$ forms an equivalence class, and if S is defined to be the set of all concept descriptions that have $a_1, \ldots, a_k$ as their instance, then this class is the least element in $[S]$ (w.r.t. $\preceq$ as defined above). Analogously to the lcs, we refer to one of its representatives by

$$msc(a_1, \ldots, a_k).$$

For the same three reasons listed above, the msc need not exist. Again, only the third phenomenon can actually occur in the languages considered here. The following example presents an $\mathcal{ALE}$- and $\mathcal{ALN}$-ABox illustrating this.

Example 3.1.1. If $\mathcal{A}$ consists of the role assertion

$$r(a, a),$$

then the $\mathcal{ALE}$-concept descriptions $D_0 := \top$, $D_i := \exists r.D_{i-1}$, $i \geq 1$, have the individual a as their instance. Moreover, $[D_0] \succ [D_1] \succ \cdots$

Similarly, if we add the concept assertion

$$(\leq 1\, r)(a)$$

to $\mathcal{A}$, then the same holds for the $\mathcal{ALN}$-concept descriptions $E_0 := (\geq 1\, r) \sqcap (\leq 1\, r)$, $E_i := E_{i-1} \sqcap \forall r.E_{i-1}$.

In fact, it is easy to verify that in $\mathcal{ALE}$ and $\mathcal{ALN}$, a does not have a most specific concept. However, the $\mathcal{ALN}^*$-concept description $E := \forall r^*.((\geq 1\, r) \sqcap (\leq 1\, r))$ is the msc of a. The class $[E]$ can be seen as the limes of the chain $[E_0] \succ [E_1] \succ \cdots$

In Section 5.2.2, we will show that for $\mathcal{ALN}^*$-concept descriptions the msc of individuals represented in $\mathcal{ALN}^*$-ABoxes always exists and that it can be computed effectively. Thus, $\mathcal{ALN}^*$ is the right language extension in order to guarantee the existence of the msc.

Up to now, it is, however, not known which language extension of $\mathcal{ALE}$ should be considered in order to guarantee the existence of the msc. A possible candidate seems to be the set of *cyclic* $\mathcal{ALE}$-concept descriptions, i.e., concepts defined by means of cyclic $\mathcal{ALE}$-TBoxes equipped with gfp-semantics (cf. Section 2.2.2). In the example, the concept A defined by the TBox

$$A \doteq \exists r.A$$

yields an msc of a. Intuitively, A says that every individual in an extension of A is the starting point of an infinite r-chain.

In the remainder of this subsection, we show that there exists a close connection between the lcs and the msc. On the one hand, computing the lcs can be reduced to computing the msc. Given the ABox

$$C_1(a_1), \ldots, C_k(a_k)$$

the msc, $msc(a_1, \ldots, a_k)$, of $a_1, \ldots, a_k$ is equivalent to $lcs(C_1, \ldots, C_k)$.

On the other hand, the next lemma illustrates that for computing the msc of a sequence of individuals one only needs an lcs algorithm and an algorithm that realizes the unary msc operation.

Lemma 3.1.3. *Let $\mathcal{A}$ be an $\mathcal{L}$-ABox and $a_1, \ldots, a_n$ be individuals of $\mathcal{A}$. Then,*

$$msc(a_1, \ldots, a_k) \equiv lcs(msc(a_1), \ldots, msc(a_k)).$$

As an aside we note that, for languages $\mathcal{L}$ that allow for the one-of concept constructor $\{a_1, \ldots, a_k\}$, which given an interpretation $\mathcal{I}$ is interpreted as $\{a_1, \ldots, a_k\}^{\mathcal{I}} := \{a_1^{\mathcal{I}}, \ldots, a_1^{\mathcal{I}}\}$, the computation of the msc is trivial since

$$msc(a_1, \ldots, a_k) \equiv \{a_1, \ldots, a_k\}.$$

This phenomenon corresponds to the situation where the lcs is considered in a language that allows for concept disjunction ($lcs(C, D) \equiv C \sqcup D$).

3.1.2 Applications of LCS and MSC

The lcs and msc have been introduced and used in a number of applications. These range from solving standard inferences to supporting the bottom-up construction of knowledge bases. In what follows, we present an overview of the various applications proposed in the literature.

Solving Standard Inferences. In many cases, adding concept disjunction to a DL increases the complexity of reasoning. Since in the early days of DLs the predominating opinion was that only polynomial subsumption algorithms can be used reasonably in practice, one was interested in alternatives to concept disjunction. The idea was to replace disjunctions like $C_1 \sqcup \ldots \sqcup C_n$ by the lcs of $C_1, \ldots, C_n$. In [CBH92, BE89], this operation is called *knowledge-base vivification*. Although, in general, the lcs is not equivalent to the corresponding disjunction, it is the best approximation of the disjunctive concept within the available language. As pointed out before, in case the language allows for concept disjunction, the lcs operation corresponds to the disjunction of concepts. Nowadays, state of the art DL-systems like FACT [Hor98a] incorporate reasoning engines that are optimized in such a way that, in terms of efficiency, dealing with concept disjunction is not a problem. Thus, the lcs as "weak disjunction" operator is not an issue anymore.

Provided that the msc C_a of an individual a presented in an ABox $\mathcal{A}$ always exists and that it can be computed effectively, instance checking can be reduced to testing subsumption because of the following equivalence:

$$a \in_{\mathcal{A}} C \quad \text{iff} \quad C_a \sqsubseteq C.$$

The first algorithms proposed for instance checking tried to exploit this connection between instance checking and subsumption (see, e.g., [Neb90a, DE92, DLN90, DLNS94]). The problem of these approaches, however, is that in the languages under consideration the msc need not exist in general (cf. Example 3.1.1). Moreover, algorithms for computing the msc were not known at that time. (In fact, the algorithm presented in Section 5.2.2 is the first msc algorithm for a non-trivial language.) Therefore, msc's were only approximated by collecting all informations of an individual necessary to decide the instance relationship. This problem was called *realization*. In some cases, the approximated msc did not contain enough information, which then led to incomplete instance algorithms. Today, the reduction of instance checking to subsumption is (mostly) abandoned in favor of tableau-based algorithms, which reduce the problem of instance checking to the consistency of ABoxes (as illustrated in Section 2.4).

Summing up, the lcs and the msc no longer play an important rôle for solving standard inferences. Current tableau-techniques are much more suitable for this task, in particular in very expressive DLs.

Learning from Examples. Finding the most specific concept that generalizes a set of examples is a common operation in inductive learning, called learning from examples. The problem of learning from examples is to extrapolate a general description of a *target concept* C (or some reasonable approximation thereof) from a set of *training examples*—things that have been labeled by an oracle as positive if they are elements of C and negative otherwise. Cohen and Hirsh [CH94a] as well as Frazier and Pitt [FP96] investigated the learnability of sublanguages of CLASSIC with regard to the PAC learning model proposed by Valiant [Val84] where "PAC" stands for "Probably Approximately Correct". In these works the training examples are assumed to be concept descriptions and the lcs computation is used as a subprocedure in their learning algorithm. In [CH94b], examples are assumed to be individuals defined in an ABoxes. For the experimental results presented there, an approximation of the msc was employed to abstract from the examples in a preprocessing step. In a second step, the commonalities of these msc's were computed by the lcs operation in order to obtain hypotheses for the target concept. It should be stressed at this point that the msc was only approximated since, at this time, no algorithm computing the exact msc for (sublanguages of) CLASSIC was known and since the implementations of the lcs operation could not process exact representations of the msc either.

Similarity-Based Information Retrieval. In [MHN98, MMK99], the lcs operation is used as a subtask for similarity-based information retrieval. The goal is to provide the user of an information system with an example-based query mechanism. The knowledge of the system is represented in an ABox and queries are subsets of individuals described in the ABox. In principle, answers to such queries are computed in three steps: First, the msc's of the user-selected examples are computed. Then, a retrieval concept is derived by determining the lcs from the msc's thus obtained. Finally, all instances of the retrieval concept are computed. However, the DLs used do not guarantee the existence of an msc. Therefore, only approximations of msc's are computed.

In [MMK99], a probabilistic lcs is introduced based on P-Classic [KLP97]. The hope is that with a probabilistic version of the lcs an example-based query yields individuals that are closer related to the original examples.

Bottom-Up Construction of Knowledge Bases. Traditionally, a DL-knowledge base is built by first formalizing the relevant concepts of the domain (its terminology, stored in the TBox) by concept descriptions. In a second step, the concept descriptions are used to specify properties of objects and individuals occurring in the domain (the world description, stored in the ABox). As pointed out previously, the standard inferences provided by all DL systems support both steps by providing reasoning engines for classifying concepts and individuals as well as checking for inconsistencies: Testing for subsumption (classification of concepts) allows one to structure the terminology in the form of a subsumption hierarchy. This hierarchy provides useful information on (implicit) connections between different concepts, and can thus be used to check (at least partially) whether the formal descriptions capture the intuitive meaning of the concepts. Instance checking (classification of individuals) provides useful information on the properties of an individual, and can again be used for checking the adequacy of the knowledge base with respect to the application domain it is supposed to describe. Finally, if a knowledge base is inconsistent (i.e., self-contradictory), then it is clear that a modeling error has occurred, and the knowledge base must be changed.

This traditional "top down" approach for constructing a DL knowledge base is not always adequate, though. On the one hand, it need not be clear from the outset which are the relevant concepts in a particular application. On the other hand, even if it is clear which (intuitive) concepts should be introduced, it is in general not easy to come up with formal definitions of these concepts within the available description language. For example, in an application in chemical process engineering [BS96b, Sat98], the process engineers prefer to construct the knowledge base (which consists of descriptions of standard building blocks of process models, such as reactors) in the following "bottom up" fashion [BK98, BKM99]: first, they introduce several "typical" examples of the standard building block as individuals in the ABox, and then they generalize (the descriptions of) these individuals into a concept description that (a) has all the individuals as instances, and (b) is the most specific description satisfying property (a). Computing the lcs and the msc are inference services that exactly fit into this "bottom-up" approach of building knowledge bases. In particular, the task of computing descriptions satisfying (a) and (b) from above can be split into two subtasks: computing the msc of a single ABox individual, and computing the lcs of the concepts thus obtained. The main difference to the application scenario sketched before (information retrieval) is that here the computed concept description is presented to the knowledge engineer as a suggestion for a new concept that can be added to the TBox. Typically, it must be modified by the knowledge engineer in order to obtain a concept that corresponds to the engineer's intuition. Nevertheless, the computed concept is a good starting point for deriving the final concept that is actually added to the TBox.

The experiments carried out for the process engineering domain supports this impression [BKM00]. It turned out, however, that in order to obtain concept descriptions that can in fact be understood by the knowledge engineer, i.e., descriptions of small size, one needs to rewrite the computed concepts. We will come back to this issue in Section 3.4. It should also be mentioned that the empirical investigations used "typical" standard building blocks that were given by concept descriptions rather than individuals, since for the DL employed in the process engineering application msc algorithms are not known up to now.

3.1.3 Previous Results

All previous investigations concerning the lcs essentially deal with sublanguages of $\mathcal{ALNS}$. The lcs was originally introduced by Cohen, Borgida, and Hirsh [CBH92], who proposed algorithms for computing the lcs in the languages $\mathcal{ALN}$ and $\mathcal{LS}$. In [CH94a], the algorithm for $\mathcal{LS}$ was extended to CORECLASSIC, which additionally allows for value restrictions (see [CH94b] for experimental results). Finally, Frazier and Pitt, [FP96], claimed to have an lcs algorithm for full CLASSIC, i.e., the language $\mathcal{ALNS}$ extended by the fills and the one-of operator as defined in [BPS94].

Unfortunately, the results presented in these works suffer from several shortcomings, which make them valid only for certain fragments of the considered languages.

First, in none of these works unsatisfiable subexpressions, which can occur in $\mathcal{ALN}$ and CLASSIC, are dealt with correctly.

Second, for languages that involve same-as equalities the lcs algorithms are based on graphs which are equipped with a formal semantics. However, the semantics they propose are only well-defined for acyclic graphs. In particular, for the algorithms presented in [CH94a, FP96] this means that the proofs of correctness only hold for concept descriptions that do not induce cyclic graphs. For instance, this excludes same-as equalities like $\varepsilon \downarrow$ spouse $\circ$ spouse.

Finally, and most importantly, all aforementioned works do not state whether partial or total attributes are used, i.e., whether attributes are interpreted as partial or total functions. Looking at the respective lcs algorithms presented in the mentioned papers, it turns out that in some papers attributes are assumed to be total while they are partial in others. One of the surprising results proved in the present book is that, as far as the lcs is concerned, one

Table 3.1. Complexity Results for the Computation of the lcs. Note that for $\mathcal{LS}$ with total attributes the lcs need not exist (Theorem 5.1.3). However, the existence can be checked via a polynomial-time algorithm (Corollary 5.1.8).

	$\mathcal{ALN}$	$\mathcal{LS}$ (total attributes)	$\mathcal{ALNS}$ (partial attributes)
binary	P (Corollary 5.1.3)	EXPTIME (Corollary 5.1.9)	P (Corollary 5.1.1)
sequence	P (Corollary 5.1.3)	EXPTIME (Corollary 5.1.9)	EXPTIME (Corollary 5.1.2)

must strictly distinguish between total and partial attributes (see the next subsection for details).

As for the msc, up to now algorithms have been proposed that compute only approximations of the msc. The reason for this is that in most languages considered until now in the literature, the msc need not exist.

3.1.4 New Results

In this subsection, the results proved in this book concerning the lcs and the msc are summarized. The actual proofs can be found in Chapter 5. The languages that have been investigated are (sublanguages of) $\mathcal{ALNS}$ and $\mathcal{ALN}^*$.[1] Moreover, for the sake of completeness results on the lcs in $\mathcal{ALE}$ are presented since they are needed for matching (see [BKM98a, BKM99] for proofs).

Least Common Subsumer. In Section 5.1, previous results on the lcs in sublanguages of $\mathcal{ALNS}$ are revised and extended. In particular, the three problems mentioned above, namely, dealing with unsatisfiable subexpressions and certain same-as equalities (like $\varepsilon \downarrow$ spouse $\circ$ spouse) as well as the impact of the different semantics for attributes are settled.

More precisely, a correct lcs algorithm for $\mathcal{ALNS}$-concept descriptions with partial attributes is developed (Section 5.1.1). This algorithm can deal with descriptions that contain unsatisfiable subexpressions and arbitrary same-as equalities. The algorithm also shows that in $\mathcal{ALNS}$ the lcs always exists and that for two concepts it can be computed in polynomial-time. For sequences of concept descriptions, however, the lcs may grow exponentially in the size of the sequence and there exists an exponential-time algorithm for computing it.

Most surprising are the results on the lcs when attributes are interpreted as total functions (as partly done in previous works). In this case, as shown for the language $\mathcal{LS}$ in Section 5.1.2, the lcs need not exist. Although one can

---

[1] In [KB99], the results for $\mathcal{ALNS}$ are extended to full CLASSIC, i.e., the language that extends $\mathcal{ALNS}$ by the fills and one-of operator [BPS94].

Table 3.2. Complexity Results for lcs and msc in $\mathcal{ALN}^*$.

lcs		msc
binary	sequence	
$\leq$EXPTIME	EXPTIME	$\geq$EXPTIME $\leq$2EXPTIME
(Corollary 5.2.1)	(Corollary 5.2.2)	(Corollary 5.2.7)

decide the existence of the lcs of two $\mathcal{LS}$-concept descriptions in polynomial time, the size of such an lcs may explode when going from partial to total attributes. More precisely, while in $\mathcal{LS}$ with partial attributes the size of the lcs of two concept descriptions can polynomially be bounded, it is exponential for total attributes and there exists a (necessarily) worst-case exponential-time algorithm computing the lcs. Presumably, for extensions of $\mathcal{LS}$, like $\mathcal{ALNS}$, these results also hold. Altogether this shows that although the distinction between partial versus total attributes has not been considered so essential until now, the different semantics of attributes have significant effects on the existence and the complexity of the lcs for languages that involve the same-as constructor.

Table 3.1 summarizes the complexity results just sketched, distinguishing between the lcs taking two concept descriptions as input (binary lcs) and the one that works on sequences. In this table, "P" ("EXPTIME") means that there exists a polynomial (exponential) time algorithm for computing the lcs. More precisely, the entry "EXPTIME" says that the lcs algorithm is necessarily worst-case exponential since the size of the computed lcs may grow exponentially in the size of the input concepts.

As an aside, it was pointed out in [CBH92] (see also Section 5.1) that concept descriptions in $\mathcal{LS}$ with total attributes correspond to finitely generated right-congruences [Eil74]. Moreover, the lcs of two concept descriptions coincides with the intersection of right-congruences. Thus, our results show that the intersection of finitely generated right-congruences is not always a finitely generated right-congruence, and that there is a polynomial-time algorithm for deciding this question. In addition, if the intersection can be finitely generated, then the generating system can be computed by a (necessarily) worst-case exponential-time algorithm in the size of the generating systems of the given right-congruences.

Let us now turn to the language $\mathcal{ALN}^*$, dealt with in Section 5.2. Investigating the lcs in this language is motivated by the fact that for $\mathcal{ALN}^*$ the msc always exists. Once one allows for $\mathcal{ALN}^*$-concept descriptions, the lcs must operate on these kinds of concepts as well. It turns out (Section 5.2.1) that in $\mathcal{ALN}^*$ the lcs always exists and that it can be computed in exponential time (Section 5.2.1). The complexity of the algorithm complies with the size of the lcs of a sequence of $\mathcal{ALN}^*$-concept descriptions, which can grow exponen-

Table 3.3. Complexity Results for the Computation of the lcs in $\mathcal{ALE}$ and Its Sublanguage $\mathcal{EL}$.

	$\mathcal{EL}$	$\mathcal{ALE}$
binary	P	EXPTIME
	([BKM99], Corollary 5.3.1)	([BKM99], Theorem 5.3.1)
sequence	EXPTIME	EXPTIME
	([BKM99], Corollary 5.3.1)	([BKM99], Theorem 5.3.1)

tially in the size of the input sequence. Although the conjecture is that this holds for the lcs of two concepts as well, proving this remains an open problem. Table 3.2 shows the complexity of computing the lcs for $\mathcal{ALN}^*$-concept descriptions. The entry "$\leq$EXPTIME" for the binary lcs means that, although an exponential-time algorithm is known for computing the lcs, it is open whether this algorithm is optimal, i.e., whether there exists a PSPACE or even polynomial-time algorithm as well.

Section 5.3 summarizes the results on the lcs in $\mathcal{ALE}$ known from the literature [BKM99]. Proving these results is out of the scope of this book.[2] Nevertheless, they are needed for our investigations on matching (Section 6.3). In [BKM99] it has been shown that the lcs of two (a sequence of) $\mathcal{ALE}$-concept descriptions may grow exponential in the size of the concept descriptions and that there exists an exponential-time algorithm computing the lcs. Remarkably, even for sequences of $\mathcal{EL}$-concept descriptions this exponential blow-up cannot be avoided. For two $\mathcal{EL}$-concept descriptions there are polynomial-time computation algorithms, though. These complexity results are summarized in Table 3.3, where the entries have the same meaning as in the previous tables. Recently, a double-exponential time lcs algorithm has been proposed for a DL that extends $\mathcal{ALE}$ by number restrictions [KM01]. It is open whether there also exists an exponential-time algorithm.

Most Specific Concept. As illustrated by Example 3.1.1, the msc in $\mathcal{ALN}$, $\mathcal{ALNS}$, and $\mathcal{ALE}$ does not exist in general. Intuitively, one needs infinitely nested value and existential restrictions (the limes of the infinite decreasing chains shown in the example) to guarantee the existence of the msc. The languages that have been investigated so far, however, do not allow to express such nested restrictions. To overcome this problem, in this work $\mathcal{ALN}$ has been extended to *cyclic* $\mathcal{ALN}$-concept descriptions, i.e., those concepts defined by cyclic $\mathcal{ALN}$-TBoxes that are equipped with the gfp-semantics (Definition 2.2.5). As mentioned, these concept descriptions correspond to $\mathcal{ALN}^*$-concept descriptions.

The proofs presented in Section 5.2.2 show that cyclic $\mathcal{ALN}$-concept descriptions are in fact sufficient to guarantee the existence of the msc (Corol-

---

[2] The proofs are part of the thesis by Molitor carried out at the LuFG Theoretical Computer Science, RWTH Aachen, [Mol00] (in German).

Table 3.4. Complexity Results for Consistency and Instance Checking in $\mathcal{ALN}^*$.

consistency of of ABoxes	instance checking
PSPACE	$\geq$PSPACE $\leq$EXPTIME
(Corollary 5.2.3)	(Corollary 5.2.6)

lary 5.2.7). The msc (applied to one individual) can grow (at least) exponentially in the size of the underlying ABox and it can be computed in (at most) double-exponential time (Corollary 5.2.7). It is an open problem whether there also exists an exponential-time msc algorithm. The results on the msc are summarized in Table 3.2; the entry with preceding $\leq$ denotes a complexity upper bound, while $\geq$ indicates a complexity lower bound. As a by-product of the proofs carried out in Section 5.2.2 one obtains decision algorithms for the consistency of $\mathcal{ALN}^*$-ABoxes and the instance problem; see Table 3.4 (if neither $\leq$ nor $\geq$ is prefixed, the complexity bound is tight.)

Nebel [Neb91] has shown that the problem of testing subsumption in cyclic $\mathcal{ALNS}$-concept descriptions (defined analogously to cyclic $\mathcal{ALN}$-concept descriptions) is undecidable. This does not necessarily imply that the msc or the lcs cannot be computed effectively in this language. Nevertheless, from a practical point of view, investigating non-standard inferences for languages with undecidable standard inferences does not appear to be worth while.

As an open question remains whether for cyclic $\mathcal{ALE}$-concept descriptions the msc always exists and whether it can be computed effectively.

3.2 Matching

Rather than going into the technical aspects of matching, which are covered in Chapter 6, the present section gives an overview of the known results in the field of matching in DLs, the applications, and the new contributions of this book.

The outline of this section is as follows. First, matching problems are defined and some simple properties are stated (Section 3.2.1). Second, in Section 3.2.2, we will illustrate possible applications of matching, like pruning of concept descriptions, avoiding redundancies in knowledge bases, and integrating knowledge bases. Third, as we will see, matching problems may have (infinitely many) complex matchers as solution Thus, one is faced with the question of what are "interesting" sets of matchers to present to the user. Although the answer to this question depends on the application domain under consideration, one can identify some general properties that should be satisfied by all "reasonable" matchers. Finding such criteria is a non-trivial

problem which has not been explored sufficiently in the literature so far. In
Section 3.2.3, several criteria are discussed and formally specified by precedence orderings on matchers. Finally, known complexity results on matching
are presented (Section 3.2.4) and an overview of the results proved in this
work is provided (Section 3.2.5).

3.2.1 Definition of Matching Problems

In what follows, let $\mathcal{L}$ denote some DL. Throughout this book, $\mathcal{L}$ will usually
stand for one of the languages $\mathcal{ALNS}$, $\mathcal{ALN}^*$, and $\mathcal{ALE}$, or a sublanguage.

In order to define matching problems we need to introduce the notion of a
concept pattern and of substitutions operating on patterns. For this purpose,
we need an additional set N_X of symbols (*concept variables*) disjoint from
the set N_C of concept names, N_R of role names, and N_A of attribute names.
Informally, concept patterns are concept descriptions over the concept names
$N_C \cup N_X$. However, since $\mathcal{L}$ will be a language that does not allow for full
negation, negation is not allowed in front of variables since otherwise instances
of patterns may not belong to $\mathcal{L}$ anymore (see below for an example).

Definition 3.2.1. *If $X \in N_X$ is a concept variable, $A \in N_C$ a concept
name, $r \in N_R$ a role name, R, S complex roles, $a, a_1, \ldots, a_k, b_1, \ldots, b_l \in N_A$
attribute names, and n a non-negative integer, then concept patterns C, D
are defined according to the following syntax rules*

$$C, D \quad \longrightarrow \quad \top \mid \bot \mid X \mid A \mid \neg A \mid (\geq n\, r) \mid (\leq n\, r) \mid a_1 \cdots a_k \downarrow b_1 \cdots b_l \mid$$

$$C \sqcap D \mid \forall R.C \mid \forall a.C \mid \exists r.C$$

$$R, S \quad \longrightarrow \quad \emptyset \mid \varepsilon \mid r \mid R \circ S \mid R \cup S \mid R^*$$

*$\mathcal{L}$-concept patterns are those patterns that only contain constructors allowed
in $\mathcal{L}$.*

For example, if X, Y are concept variables, r is a role name, and A, B are
concept names, then $D_{ex} := \mathsf{A} \sqcap X \sqcap \exists \mathsf{r}.(\mathsf{B} \sqcap Y)$ is an $\mathcal{ALE}$-concept pattern,
but $\neg X$ is not.

A *substitution* σ is a mapping from N_X into the set of concept descriptions. This mapping is extended to concept patterns in the obvious way, i.e.,

- $\sigma(\top) := \top$ and $\sigma(\bot) := \bot$,
- $\sigma(A) := A$ and $\sigma(\neg A) := \neg A$,
- $\sigma(\geq n\, r) := (\geq n\, r)$ and $\sigma(\leq n\, r) := (\leq n\, r)$,
- $\sigma(a_1 \cdots a_k \downarrow b_1 \cdots b_l) := a_1 \cdots a_k \downarrow b_1 \cdots b_l$,
- $\sigma(C \sqcap D) := \sigma(C) \sqcap \sigma(D)$,
- $\sigma(\forall R.C) := \forall R.\sigma(C)$, $\sigma(\forall a.C) := \forall a.\sigma(C)$, and $\sigma(\exists r.C) := \exists r.\sigma(C)$.

A substitution σ is called $\mathcal{L}$-*substitution* if all variables are mapped onto $\mathcal{L}$-concept descriptions. It is easy to verify that applying an $\mathcal{L}$-substitution to an $\mathcal{L}$-concept pattern yields an $\mathcal{L}$-concept description. Note, however, that at this point we make use of the fact that variables must not occur in the scope of negation. To illustrate this, consider the inadmissible concept pattern $\neg X$. Applying $\sigma(X) := (A \sqcap B)$ to $\neg X$ results in the concept $\neg(A \sqcap B)$ ($\equiv \neg A \sqcup \neg B$), which does not belong to (and cannot be expressed in) the languages we are mainly concerned with here, namely, $\mathcal{ALNS}$, $\mathcal{ALN}^*$, and $\mathcal{ALE}$. As a positive example, applying the $\mathcal{ALE}$-substitution $\sigma := \{X \mapsto A \sqcap \forall r.A, Y \mapsto A\}$ to the $\mathcal{ALE}$-concept pattern D_{ex} from above yields the $\mathcal{ALE}$-description $A \sqcap A \sqcap \forall r.A \sqcap \exists r.(B \sqcap A)$.

For a language $\mathcal{L}$ like $\mathcal{ALNS}$, $\mathcal{ALN}^*$, $\mathcal{ALE}$, and more generally for any description logic in which variables in patterns may only occur in the scope of "monotonic" operators, one easily shows the following lemma.

Lemma 3.2.1. *Let D be an $\mathcal{L}$-concept pattern and let σ, τ be two $\mathcal{L}$-substitutions such that $\sigma(X) \sqsubseteq \tau(X)$ for all variables X occurring in D. Then, $\sigma(D) \sqsubseteq \tau(D)$.*

Having defined substitutions and patterns, we distinguish two different kinds of matching problems.

Definition 3.2.2. *An $\mathcal{L}$-matching problem modulo equivalence is of the form $C \equiv^? D$ where C is an $\mathcal{L}$-concept description and D is an $\mathcal{L}$-concept pattern. A problem of the form $C \sqsubseteq^? D$ is called $\mathcal{L}$-matching problem modulo subsumption. A solution or matcher of these problems is an $\mathcal{L}$-substitution σ such that $C \equiv \sigma(D)$ and $C \sqsubseteq \sigma(D)$, respectively. A matching problem is said to be solvable if it has a solution.*

We say that two matching problems are *equivalent* in case they have the same set of solutions.

The following lemma shows that every $\mathcal{L}$-matching problem modulo subsumption can easily (in linear time) be turned into an equivalent $\mathcal{L}$-matching problem modulo equivalence provided that $\mathcal{L}$ allows for concept conjunction; the proof is straightforward.

Lemma 3.2.2. *The substitution σ solves the matching problem $C \sqsubseteq^? D$ if, and only if, it solves $C \equiv^? C \sqcap D$.*

Therefore, it suffices to devise matching algorithms for matching modulo equivalence. Nevertheless, it makes sense to treat matching problems modulo subsumption separately because solving these problems directly might be less complex. In fact, this is the case for $\mathcal{EL}$-matching problems. While deciding the solvability of $\mathcal{EL}$-matching problems modulo equivalence is an NP-complete problem, it can be carried out in polynomial time in case of subsumption (see Section 6.3.1).

The latter complexity result is an immediate consequence of the following lemma, which says that deciding the solvability of matching problems modulo subsumption can be reduced to deciding subsumption, provided that variables only occur in the scope of "monotonic" operators. The lemma immediately follows from Lemma 3.2.1.

Lemma 3.2.3. *Let $C \sqsubseteq^? D$ be an $\mathcal{L}$-matching problem modulo subsumption, and let $\sigma_\top$ be the substitution that replaces each variable by $\top$. Then, $C \sqsubseteq^? D$ has a solution if, and only if, $C \sqsubseteq \sigma_\top(D)$.*

Instead of single matching problems, one can also consider a finite system

$$\{C_1 \equiv^? D_1, \ldots, C_m \equiv^? D_m\}$$

of such problems.[3] A substitution is a solution of this system if, and only if, it solves all the single matching problems $C_i \equiv^? D_i$. The following lemma, which again is easy to show, states that for every such system there exists an equivalent single matching problem provided that the language allows for concept conjunction and value restrictions. (Instead of value restrictions one can also use existential restrictions.)

Lemma 3.2.4. *Let $r_1, \ldots, r_m$ be distinct role names. Then, σ solves the system $\{C_1 \equiv^? D_1, \ldots, C_m \equiv^? D_m\}$ if, and only if, it solves the single matching problem*

$$\forall r_1.C_1 \sqcap \cdots \sqcap \forall r_m.C_m \equiv^? \forall r_1.D_1 \sqcap \cdots \sqcap \forall r_m.D_m.$$

Due to this lemma we may (without loss of generality) restrict our attention to single matching problems.

Extensions of Matching Problems. Beside matching problems modulo equivalence and subsumption, extensions of these problems have also been proposed in the literature. For the sake of completeness, these extensions are listed in the remainder of this subsection. However, here we are only concerned with algorithms for the two basic types, namely, matching modulo subsumption and equivalence.

In [BKBM99], matching problems were augmented by (a system of) side conditions in order to further restrict the set of possible matchers. *Side conditions* are of the form

$$X \sqsubseteq E \quad [X \sqsubset E \text{ strict side conditions}]$$

where X is a variable and E is a concept pattern (which may contain X). A substitution σ satisfies these conditions if $\sigma(X) \sqsubseteq \sigma(E)$ $[\sigma(X) \sqsubset \sigma(E)]$. First complexity results for solving matching problems with side conditions appear in [BKBM99, BBK01].

Baader and Narendran, [BN98], have generalized matching problems to unification problems, where variables may occur on both sides of the equations (see [BS01, BS94] for an introduction to unification theory). That is, *unification problems* are of the form

---

[3] According to Lemma 3.2.2, we (w.l.o.g.) only allow for matching problems modulo equivalence in such systems.

$$D_1 \equiv^? D_2$$

where both D_1 and D_2 are concept patterns. A substitution σ is a solution of such a problem if $\sigma(D_1) \equiv \sigma(D_2)$. Analogously, one can define *disunification problems* [Bür90, Com91], which are of the form

$$D_1 \not\equiv^? D_2.$$

A substitution σ solves such a problem if $\sigma(D_1) \not\equiv \sigma(D_2)$. Note that non-strict side conditions $X \sqsubseteq E$ can be turned into (equivalent) unification problems of the form $X \equiv^? X \sqcap E$. Thus, matching problems with non-strict side conditions can easily be turned into equivalent unification problems. Moreover, matching problems with (strict) side conditions can be expressed by systems of unification and disunification problems exploiting the fact that $X \sqsubset E$ is equivalent to the system $\{X \equiv^? X \sqcap E, X \not\equiv^? E\}$.

These observations show that matching problems (even some extensions) can be reduced to unification. In [BN98], it has been shown that for $\mathcal{FL}_0$, matching problems are significantly easier to solve than unification problems. More accurately, deciding the solvability of $\mathcal{FL}_0$-matching problems modulo equivalence is a polynomial time problem, while it is EXPTIME-complete for unification. Nevertheless, this changes when languages are considered that allow for full negation, say $\mathcal{ALC}$. In $\mathcal{ALC}$-concept patterns, one allows for negation in front of variables since instantiating these patterns by $\mathcal{ALC}$-concept descriptions still yields an $\mathcal{ALC}$-concept description. Now, every $\mathcal{ALC}$-unification problem $D_1 \equiv^? D_2$ can be turned into the equivalent $\mathcal{ALC}$-matching problem $\bot \equiv^? (\neg D_1 \sqcap D_2) \sqcup (D_1 \sqcap \neg D_2)$.

The last extension of matching we want to introduce is *matching modulo TBoxes*. Formally, given a TBox $\mathcal{T}$, a matching problem modulo $\mathcal{T}$, say $C \equiv^?_{\mathcal{T}} D$, asks for substitutions σ such that $C \equiv_{\mathcal{T}} \sigma(D)$. Since, as pointed out in Section 2.2.2, $\mathcal{ALN}^*$-concept descriptions can be seen as cyclic $\mathcal{ALN}$-concept descriptions, i.e., those defined by cyclic TBoxes, $\mathcal{ALN}^*$-matching problems are in fact instances of such matching problems.

3.2.2 Applications of Matching

Unlike subsumption and equivalence tests, matching can be used to search the knowledge base for concepts having a certain not completely specified form, which is expressed by concept patterns. This capability is very useful in a number of different applications, which are sketched in this subsection.

Pruning of Concept Descriptions. In industrial applications, objects and their descriptions may become too large and complex to view in traditional ways. Simply printing (descriptions of) objects in small applications such as configuring stereo systems [MRI95, MIP+98] can easily take 10 pages, while printing objects in industrial applications such as configuring telecommunications equipment, [WWV+93, MW98a, MW98b], might take five times as

much space. In addition, if explanation facilities [MB95, McG96] are introduced and a naïve explanation is presented of all deductions, the system can
produce five times as much output again. As argued in [McG96, BKBM99], it
quickly becomes clear that object descriptions need to be pruned if users are
to be able to inspect objects and not be overwhelmed with irrelevant details.

Initially, a purely syntactic pruning mechanism was proposed to accomplish this task [McG96]. First implementations have been used in small applications [MRI95, MIP$^+$98] to save 3–5 pages of output (sometimes reducing
the object to 25 percent of its former size). As pointed out in [BKBM99], in
larger applications [MW98a, MW98b, WWV$^+$93] it can easily save 30 pages
of output per object. In [BM96], this syntactic mechanism was given a formal
semantics in terms of matching problems modulo subsumption as introduced
in Section 3.2.1.

The idea behind using matching modulo subsumption to prune concept
descriptions is as follows. A concept pattern D is thought of as a 'format
statement', describing what information is to be displayed, if the pattern
matches successfully against a specific (complicated) concept description C.
If there is no match, nothing is displayed. For example, a matcher of the
pattern

$$D := \forall \text{research-interests}.X$$

against the description

$$C := \forall \text{pets}.\text{Cat} \sqcap \forall \text{research-interests}.\text{AI} \sqcap \forall \text{hobbies}.\text{Gardening},$$

i.e., a matcher of the problem $C \sqsubseteq^? D$, assigns AI to the variable X, and thus
finds the scientific interests (in this case, Artificial Intelligence) described in
the concept. Note, however, that mapping X to the top-concept would also
yield a matcher. Yet, displaying this concept is not of any interest to the
user. In Section 3.2.3, we introduce precedence orderings on matchers that in
fact exclude such uninteresting matchers. In [BKBM99], also side conditions
(see Section 3.2.1) have been introduced to further restrict the set of possible
matchers.

Detecting and Avoiding Redundancies. This problem comes from an
application in chemical process engineering, [BS96b, Sat98], and it has first
been pointed out in [BN98]. As already mentioned in Section 3.1.2, in this
application the DL-system is used to support the design of a large terminology of concepts describing parts of chemical plants (like reactors) as well as
processes that take place in these plants. Since several knowledge engineers
are involved in defining new concepts, and since this knowledge acquisition
process takes rather long (several years), it happens that the same (intuitive)
concept is introduced several times, often with slightly differing descriptions.
Originally, the goal was to use the standard inferences, like testing for equivalence, to support avoiding this kind of redundancy. However, testing for
equivalence of concepts is not always sufficient to find out whether, for a

given concept description, there already exists another concept in the knowledge base describing the same notion. The reason is that the same atomic concept might be assigned different names or might be described on different levels of abstraction. For example, one knowledge engineer, say Alice, might simply use the concept name Woman to describe the concept of all women, while a second knowledge engineer, say Bob,[4] might represent this notion in a somewhat more fine-grained way, e.g., by using the (complex) description Female⊓Human.[5] Although these descriptions are meant to represent the same notion, they are not equivalent, and thus are redundant when contained in one knowledge base. This redundancy even accumulates if Alice and Bob use them in complex descriptions to define new concepts. For example, Alice would define the concept of all *women having only daughters*, by the concept description

$$\text{Woman} \sqcap \forall\text{has-child.Woman,}$$

whereas Bob would describe this concept by

$$\text{Female} \sqcap \text{Human} \sqcap \forall\text{has-child.}(\text{Female} \sqcap \text{Human}),$$

which, again, is not equivalent to the one Alice defined.

Matching can help to detect and avoid these kinds of redundancies. Assume, for instance, that Bob already added his description of *women having only daughters* to the knowledge base. Now, if Alice is not sure about the description used for *women*, then instead of introducing some arbitrary concept name (like Woman) she rather represents this concept by a concept variable X leaving the exact description unspecified. Then, she matches the concept pattern

$$X \sqcap \forall\text{has-child.}X$$

against the concepts of the knowledge base. In our setting, the pattern matches against Bob's description, and the resulting matcher maps X to Female ⊓ Human. From this matcher Alice can derive that i) the concept *women having only daughters* is already defined (and thus she does not need to add this concept to the knowledge base anymore) and that ii) *women* is defined by a complex description. Of course, it is not necessarily the case that matching concepts are meant to represent the same notion. Matching can, however, suggest to the knowledge engineer possible candidate descriptions.

Integrating Knowledge Bases. The problem of integrating knowledge bases is motivated by several application scenarios. First, terminologies have been developed independently by multiple research groups in a variety of application areas, including medicine, natural language processing, and logistics. In each of these cases there have been efforts at merging these terminologies

---

[4] Although Alice and Bob are famous for talking to each other a lot, this is not what interests us here.

[5] We use an example from the family domain since examples from process engineering would require too much explanation.

[KL94, NM99, MFRW00]. Second, there are many examples of *heterogeneous information sources*, such as federated databases or semi-structured data on the internet, which keep information about aspects of some single domain of discourse, and for which one desires uniform access through a "conceptual schema", mostly for the purpose of seamless querying. Predating these, a traditional step in database design has been so-called view integration [BLN86].

One approach to integrating knowledge bases is based on finding interschema assertions that relate the expressions in the constituent terminologies [BC86, CL93, CGL+98b]. For knowledge bases with many terms this task requires computer support [GLN92, CA99, MFRW00, KL94]. Most tools rely on lexical similarities between names, but they also take into account some structural information such as the subsumption hierarchy. In [BK00b], a formal framework for merging DL TBoxes has been proposed in order to explore the limits of a purely structural approach to the problem of finding interrelationships between knowledge bases. This problem amounts to finding so-called conflict-free mappings. Algorithms computing these mappings can be reduced to matching with side conditions and unification modulo TBoxes. However, up to now only little is known of the computational properties of these problems (like decidability and complexity). Thus, for the time being one needs to resort to heuristics to compute conflict-free mappings.

3.2.3 Solutions of Matching Problems

Matching problems may have an infinite number of solutions. For example, in the problem $\forall r.\bot \sqsubseteq^? \forall r.X$ an arbitrary concept description can be substituted for X. Of course, only a finite number of matchers can be presented to the user and these matchers should be "interesting" and easy to read. Therefore, one needs to state properties in order to filter out the best matchers. These properties might vary from application to application. Still, one can identify some general criteria all displayed matchers should obey. These general properties are stated here and are formalized in terms of precedence orderings on matchers. To this end, we first concentrate on matching modulo subsumption and turn to matching modulo equivalence later on.

In a nutshell, we require solutions σ of a matching problem modulo subsumption, $C \sqsubseteq^? D$, to satisfy the following two properties:

1. The instance $\sigma(D)$ of D should be as specific as possible (subsequently called *m-property*, "m" for "most specific")
2. σ should not contain redundancies (subsequently called *r-property*, "r" for "reduced").

The m-property says that one wants to bring D as close to C as possible. Indeed, this is what the first matching algorithm proposed by Borgida and McGuinness [BM96] already tried to achieve. In addition, it is desirable to obtain matchers that are as readable as possible. This requirement is captured (at least in part) by the r-property.

The main difficulty in formalizing the r-property is to specify what is meant by matchers being free of redundancies. It will be necessary to define first the notion of reduced concept descriptions, i.e., those that are free of redundancies, before turning to reduced matchers. The notion of reduction depends on the language of choice and it is a non-trivial task to come up with an appropriate definition. In fact, up to now for the extensions $\mathcal{ALNS}$ and $\mathcal{ALN}^*$ of $\mathcal{ALN}$ it is not clear how to define reduction. We will, however, provide definitions for the languages $\mathcal{ALN}$ and $\mathcal{ALE}$. Thus, for the languages $\mathcal{ALN}$ and $\mathcal{ALE}$ a more fine-grained specification of interesting solutions can be presented than for the two extensions of $\mathcal{ALN}$.

The remainder of this section is structured as follows: First, we define reduced concept descriptions in $\mathcal{ALN}$ and $\mathcal{ALE}$. Then, along with an example, the two properties of matchers sketched above are illustrated and defined formally by two precedence orderings on matchers (one for each property). These orderings are then used to specify the set of matchers that is to be displayed to the user. While for $\mathcal{ALN}$ and $\mathcal{ALE}$ both orderings are taken into account, for the extensions of $\mathcal{ALN}$ only the one capturing the m-property is employed. Subsequently, a two step generic algorithm for computing sets of "interesting" matchers (w.r.t. to the precedence orderings) is presented. We will conclude this subsection by pointing out the difficulties that occur when trying to define reduced matchers in $\mathcal{ALNS}$ and $\mathcal{ALN}^*$.

Reduced Concept Descriptions. The notion of a subdescription will form the basis of the definition of reduced concept descriptions. Roughly speaking, the concept description $\widehat{C}$ is a subdescription of the concept description C if $\widehat{C}$ is obtained from C by removing certain parts of C or replacing certain parts of C by the bottom-concept.

Definition 3.2.3. *For an $\mathcal{ALE}$-concept description C, the $\mathcal{ALE}$-concept description $\widehat{C}$ is a* subdescription *of C ($\widehat{C} \preceq_d C$) if, and only if,*

1. *$\widehat{C} = \bot$; or*
2. *$\widehat{C}$ is obtained from C by removing the top-concept, some (negated) concept names, value restrictions, or existential restrictions on the top-level of C, and for all remaining value/existential restrictions $\forall r.E / \exists r.E$ replacing E by a subdescription of E.*

Similarly, for an $\mathcal{ALN}$-concept description C, the $\mathcal{ALN}$-concept description $\widehat{C}$ is a subdescription of C ($\widehat{C} \preceq_d C$) if, and only if,

1. *$\widehat{C} = \bot$; or*
2. *$\widehat{C}$ is obtained from C by removing the top-concept, some (negated) concept names, number restrictions, or value restrictions on the top-level of C, and for all remaining value restrictions $\forall r.E$ replacing E by a subdescription of E.*

The concept description $\widehat{C}$ is a strict subdescription *of C ($\widehat{C} \prec_d C$) if $\widehat{C} \preceq_d C$ and $\widehat{C} \neq C$.*

For sublanguages of $\mathcal{ALN}$ and $\mathcal{ALE}$, subdescriptions can be defined analogously. However, in order to guarantee that subdescriptions belong to the same language as the original concept, for languages that do not allow for the bottom-concept, like $\mathcal{EL}$ and $\mathcal{FLE}$, replacing parts of C by $\bot$ is not allowed.

If everything in C is removed, then the resulting concept description is $\top$. On the other hand, if nothing is removed or replaced by $\bot$, then the resulting concept description is, of course, C.

Note that, $\preceq_d$ is a partial ordering, i.e., a reflexive, antisymmetric, and transitive relation. In particular, for the induced equivalence relation $\equiv_d$, $C \equiv_d D$ implies $C = D$, i.e., $C \equiv_d D$ just means that C and D coincide syntactically.

As an example of a subdescription let us consider the $\mathcal{ALE}$-concept description C_{ex}:

$$\mathsf{P} \sqcap \mathsf{P} \sqcap \exists r.\mathsf{P} \sqcap \exists r.(\mathsf{P} \sqcap \mathsf{Q}) \sqcap \forall r.\mathsf{P} \sqcap \forall s.(\mathsf{P} \sqcap \neg\mathsf{P}).$$

A possible (strict) subdescription $\widehat{C}_{\mathrm{ex}}$ of C_{ex},

$$\widehat{C}_{\mathrm{ex}} = \mathsf{P} \sqcap \exists r.\mathsf{Q} \sqcap \forall r.\mathsf{P} \sqcap \forall s.\bot,$$

is obtained from C_{ex} as follows: Eliminate one P and the existential restriction $\exists r.\mathsf{P}$ on the top-level of C_{ex}; in the subexpression $\exists r.(\mathsf{P} \sqcap \mathsf{Q})$ remove P; and finally, in the value restriction for s replace $(\mathsf{P} \sqcap \neg\mathsf{P})$ by $\bot$.

Note that $\widehat{C}_{\mathrm{ex}}$ is equivalent to C_{ex}, and there does not exist any strict subdescription of $\widehat{C}_{\mathrm{ex}}$ with this property. Concept descriptions like $\widehat{C}_{\mathrm{ex}}$ are called reduced. They are free of redundancies in the sense that a) nothing can be removed from them without violating equivalence and b) every inconsistency is made explicit by the bottom-concept. The following definition provides a formal specification of reduced concept descriptions.

Definition 3.2.4. *An $\mathcal{ALE}$- or $\mathcal{ALN}$-concept description C is reduced if, and only if, there does not exist a strict subdescription of C that is equivalent to C.*

It turns out that equivalent and reduced concept descriptions almost coincide syntactically provided that they are in $\forall$-normal form. To make this more precise, we need to define $\forall$-normal forms and explicate what is meant by "almost coincide".

Definition 3.2.5. *A concept description C is in $\forall$-normal form if the $\forall$-rule:*

$$\forall r.E \sqcap \forall r.F \longrightarrow \forall r.(E \sqcap F)$$

cannot be applied to some subexpression of C.

In particular, if C is in $\forall$-normal form, this implies that, for every role name r, C can have at most one value restriction of the form $\forall r.C'$ on its top-level and, recursively, in all descriptions nested in value and existential restrictions. Clearly, every $\mathcal{ALE}$- and $\mathcal{ALN}$-concept description can easily (in linear time) be turned into an equivalent concept description in $\forall$-normal form by exhaustively applying the $\forall$-rule.

With "almost coincide" we mean that concept descriptions are equal up to a (simple) equational theory.[6] For $\mathcal{ALE}$, the appropriate equational theory is called AC where 'A' stands for associativity and 'C' for commutativity. It consists of the following identities:

$$\text{(A)} \quad E_1 \sqcap (E_2 \sqcap E_3) = (E_1 \sqcap E_2) \sqcap E_3,$$
$$\text{(C)} \quad E_1 \sqcap E_2 = E_2 \sqcap E_1.$$

Let $=_{\mathsf{AC}}$ denote the congruence relation on concept descriptions induced by AC, i.e., $E =_{\mathsf{AC}} F$ iff E can be transformed into F using identities from AC. Intuitively, this means that E and F coincide up to commutativity and associativity of concept conjunction. For $\mathcal{ALE}$, the following can now be shown: Given two equivalent and reduced $\mathcal{ALE}$-concept descriptions E and F in $\forall$-normal form, it holds that $E =_{\mathsf{AC}} F$. The proof of this statement is postponed to Section 6.3.2.

For $\mathcal{ALN}$-concept descriptions, the equational theory AC alone does not suffice to relate reduced and equivalent concept descriptions. In fact, although the two reduced concepts $\forall r.\bot$ and $(\leq 0\, r)$ are equivalent, they do not coincide modulo AC. However, as will be shown in Section 6.1.3, equivalent and reduced $\mathcal{ALN}$-concept descriptions in $\forall$-normal form coincide modulo the equational theory $\mathsf{AC}\bot$, which extends AC by the following identity:

$$\text{($\bot$)} \quad \forall r.\bot = (\leq 0\, r).$$

Finally, one can show (see Section 6.1.3 and 6.3.2) that equivalent and reduced $\mathcal{ALE}$-concept descriptions ($\mathcal{ALN}$-concept descriptions) in $\forall$-normal form are the smallest representatives (in terms of size) of their equivalence class, i.e., given a reduced $\mathcal{ALE}$-concept description ($\mathcal{ALN}$-concept description) C in $\forall$-normal form, then for all $\mathcal{ALE}$-concept descriptions ($\mathcal{ALN}$-concept descriptions) E with $E \equiv C$ it holds that $|C| \leq |E|$, where $|\cdot|$ denotes the size of a concept description (see Chapter 2 for the precise definition).

The Set of "Interesting" Matchers. In what follows, we take the $\mathcal{EL}$-concept description C_{ex}

$$\mathsf{W} \sqcap \exists \mathsf{hc}.(\mathsf{W} \sqcap \exists \mathsf{hc}.(\mathsf{W} \sqcap \mathsf{D}) \sqcap \exists \mathsf{hc}.(\mathsf{W} \sqcap \mathsf{P})) \sqcap \exists \mathsf{hc}.(\mathsf{W} \sqcap \mathsf{D} \sqcap \exists \mathsf{hc}.(\mathsf{W} \sqcap \mathsf{P}))$$

and the pattern D_{ex}

$$\mathsf{W} \sqcap \exists \mathsf{hc}.(X \sqcap \exists \mathsf{hc}.(\mathsf{W} \sqcap Y)) \sqcap \exists \mathsf{hc}.(X \sqcap Y)$$

---

[6] See, e.g., [BS01] for an introduction to equational theories.

as running example in order to illustrate and formally characterize the potentially most interesting matchers (i.e., those satisfying the m- and r-property) of $\mathcal{ALN}$- and $\mathcal{ALE}$-matching problems modulo subsumption. Matching modulo equivalence and matching in $\mathcal{ALNS}$ and $\mathcal{ALN}^*$ will be taken care of later on.

Intuitively speaking, in the running example W stands for the class "Woman", D for "Doctor", P for "Professor", and the role hc is an abbreviation for "has-child". The description C_{ex} represents the concept of all grandmothers with i) one daughter who is a mother of both a female doctor and a female professor, and ii) one daughter who is a doctor herself and a mother of a female professor. The pattern D_{ex} describes grandmothers with i) a child who has some property X and who is the parent of a daughter with property Y, and ii) a child with both property X and Y. Thus, the children of the grandmothers have property X in common and one of these children shares Y with one of her nieces.

It is easy to see that the substitution $\sigma_\top$, which maps all variables onto the top-concept, is a matcher of $C_{ex} \sqsubseteq^? D_{ex}$. However, $\sigma_\top$ is obviously not an interesting matcher. We are interested in matchers that bring us as close as possible to the description C_{ex}, i.e., those satisfying the m-property. In this sense, the matcher $\sigma_1 := \{X \mapsto W \sqcap \exists hc.W, Y \mapsto W\}$ is better than $\sigma_\top$, but still not optimal. In fact, $\sigma_2 := \{X \mapsto W \sqcap \exists hc.W \sqcap \exists hc.(W \sqcap P), Y \mapsto W \sqcap D\}$ is better than σ_1 since it satisfies $C_{ex} \equiv \sigma_2(D_{ex}) \sqsubseteq \sigma_1(D_{ex})$.

We formalize this intuition with the help of the following precedence ordering on matchers. For a given matching problem $C \sqsubseteq^? D$ and two matchers σ, τ we define

$$\sigma \sqsubseteq_i \tau \text{ iff } \sigma(D) \sqsubseteq \tau(D).$$

Here "i" stands for "instance". Observe that $\sqsubseteq_i$ is a quasi-ordering, i.e., a reflexive and transitive relation. Thus, $\sqsubseteq_i$ induces the equivalence relation $\equiv_i$ on matchers: $\sigma \equiv_i \tau$ iff $\sigma \sqsubseteq_i \tau$ and $\tau \sqsubseteq_i \sigma$, i.e., $\tau(D) \equiv \sigma(D)$. The set $[\sigma]_i := \{\tau \mid \tau \equiv_i \sigma\}$ is called *i-equivalence class* of σ. Moreover, the matcher σ is called *i-minimal* (among all matchers of $C \sqsubseteq D$) if $\tau \equiv_i \sigma$ for all matchers τ with $\tau \sqsubseteq_i \sigma$. Finally, an i-equivalence class is called *minimal i-equivalence class* if it only contains i-minimal matchers. Note that every minimal i-equivalence class corresponds to the i-equivalence class of an i-minimal matcher.

By definition, the matchers satisfying the m-property are exactly those that belong to one of the minimal i-equivalence classes. The matching problem $\exists r.A \sqcap \exists r.B \sqsubseteq^? \exists r.X$ shows that there may in fact exist different minimal i-equivalence classes: The two matchers, one of which mapping X onto A and the other mapping X onto B, are i-minimal and belong to different i-equivalence classes.

Now, among the matchers that belong to minimal i-equivalence classes it remains to identify those that satisfy the r-property. For this purpose, let us go back to our running example to illustrate what it means for a matcher to obey the r-property, i.e., to be free of redundancies. In the example, there exists only one minimal i-equivalence class and σ_2 is one of the matchers in this class. However, intuitively σ_2 does not satisfy the r-property. In fact, σ_2 contains two different kinds of redundancies. First, the concept description $\sigma_2(X)$ contains a redundant subexpression since removing $\exists hc.W$ still yields a concept description equivalent to $\sigma_2(X)$. In other words, $\sigma_2(X)$ is not reduced in the sense of Definition 3.2.4. Second, W in $\sigma_2(Y)$ is redundant in that the substitution obtained by removing W from $\sigma_2(Y)$ still yields the same instance of D_{ex}, and thus belongs to the same i-equivalence class as σ_2. In our example, the only i-minimal matcher (modulo associativity and commutativity of concept conjunction) that is free of redundancies in this sense is $\sigma_3 := \{X \mapsto W \sqcap \exists hc.(W \sqcap P), Y \mapsto D\}$, which also seems to be the most intuitive solution of the problem $C_{ex} \sqsubseteq^? D_{ex}$.

Following this example, a matcher satisfies the r-property if nothing can be removed from it without the induced instance of D being changed. To make this more precise, we need to extend the ordering $\preceq_d$ on concept descriptions to matchers:[7] For matchers σ, τ define

$$\sigma \preceq_d \tau \quad \text{iff} \quad \sigma(X) \preceq_d \tau(X) \text{ for all } X \in N_X.$$

Now, matchers that obey the r-property are exactly those that are minimal among the matchers of their i-equivalence class with respect to $\preceq_d$. These matchers are called reduced or d-minimal and are defined as follows:

Definition 3.2.6. *A matcher σ of a matching problem $C \sqsubseteq^? D$ is called reduced (or d-minimal) if, and only if, $\tau \preceq_d \sigma$ implies $\tau \equiv_d \sigma$ for all matchers τ in the i-equivalence class $[\sigma]_i$ of σ.*[8]

Note that, given a reduced matcher, every concept description $\sigma(X)$ is reduced. However, as illustrated in our running example (removal of W in $\sigma_2(Y)$), just replacing all descriptions $\sigma(X)$ by equivalent and reduced descriptions does not necessarily yield a reduced matcher.

To sum up, the matchers that satisfy both the m- and r-property are exactly the i-minimal and reduced matchers. Thus, within every minimal i-equivalence class the reduced matchers need to be extracted. However, not all of these matchers need to be displayed since some matchers might syntactically resemble each other very much. The reason for this is twofold.

First, concept descriptions and their corresponding $\forall$-normal forms do not differ significantly: A matcher is in $\forall$-*normal form* if all its images are in $\forall$-normal form. Therefore, it suffices to display only those matchers that are in $\forall$-normal form.

Second, in $\mathcal{ALE}$ matchers can be grouped into equivalence classes induced by the equivalence relation $=_{AC}$: For matchers σ and τ define $\sigma =_{AC} \tau$ iff

---

[7] Since for now we only concentrate on $\mathcal{ALE}$- and $\mathcal{ALN}$-concept descriptions, $\preceq_d$ is in fact defined.

[8] Note that, just as for concept descriptions, $\tau \equiv_d \sigma$ simply means $\tau = \sigma$, i.e., $\tau(X) = \sigma(X)$ for every variable X.

$\sigma(X) =_{AC} \tau(X)$ for all variables $X \in N_X$. Matchers in one $=_{AC}$ -equivalence class only differ modulo commutativity and associativity of concept conjunction. Therefore, it suffices to display only one representative of every equivalence class. The same argument applies to matchers in $\mathcal{ALN}$, which can be grouped into $=_{AC\perp}$ -equivalences classes.

With these two additional restrictions the set of matchers that are to be displayed, called minimal set of i-minimal and reduced matchers in the sequel, can be described as follows.

Definition 3.2.7. *Let $C \sqsubseteq^? D$ be an $\mathcal{ALE}$-matching problem (or an $\mathcal{ALN}$-matching problem). Then, $\mathcal{C}$ is called a* minimal set of i-minimal and reduced matchers *if $\mathcal{C}$ is a minimal subset (w.r.t. set inclusion) of i-minimal and reduced matchers in $\forall$-normal form that contains for every minimal i-equivalence class the set of all reduced matchers of this class in $\forall$-normal form modulo AC (AC$\perp$). That is, given some i-minimal and reduced matcher σ in $\forall$-normal form there exists a matcher $\tau \in \mathcal{C}$ with $\tau =_{AC} \sigma$ ($\tau =_{AC\perp} \sigma$).*

For matching problems modulo equivalence, say $C \equiv^? D$, all matchers are i-equivalent since the induced instance of D must be equivalent to C. Thus, for these problems there exists exactly one i-equivalence class. However, similar to matching modulo subsumption one is interested in all reduced matchers in $\forall$-normal form of this class modulo AC (AC$\perp$). We will refer to this set as *minimal set of reduced matchers*.

As pointed out at the beginning of this section, the notion of reduced matchers is not defined for $\mathcal{ALNS}$ and $\mathcal{ALN}^*$. Therefore, in these languages we can only provide a less fine-grained notion of interesting solutions, which is solely based on the ordering $\sqsubseteq_i$. That is, given a matching problem $C \sqsubseteq^? D$ we are interested in a *minimal set of i-minimal matchers*, i.e., a set that contains for every minimal i-equivalence class one representative (instead of all reduced matchers of these classes). As for matching problems modulo equivalence, this means that some arbitrary matcher is displayed since the matchers of these problems all belong to one i-equivalence class. Our computation algorithms will, however, display the matcher that maps the variables on as specific concept descriptions as possible (see below).

Summing up, for matching problems modulo subsumption in $\mathcal{ALE}$ and $\mathcal{ALN}$ the minimal set of i-minimal and reduced matchers shall be presented to the user. For matching modulo equivalence this amounts to displaying the minimal set of reduced matchers. Finally, for the two extensions $\mathcal{ALNS}$ and $\mathcal{ALN}^*$ of $\mathcal{ALN}$ all matchers in a minimal set of i-minimal matchers are to be displayed.

The Approach for Computing Sets of "Interesting" Matchers. After having defined the set of "interesting" matchers, an approach for computing these matchers is presented. Again, we first concentrate on matching problems $C \sqsubseteq^? D$ modulo subsumption in $\mathcal{ALE}$ and $\mathcal{ALN}$, before turning to the extensions of $\mathcal{ALN}$ and to matching modulo equivalence.

Computing a minimal set of i-minimal and reduced matchers for the problem $C \sqsubseteq^? D$ works in two steps. In the first step, a minimal set of i-minimal matchers is computed, i.e., a set that contains one representative for every minimal i-equivalence class. Then, for every σ in this set, one tries to extract the reduced matchers in σ's i-equivalence class $[\sigma]_i$. Obviously, $[\sigma]_i$ coincides with the set of solutions of the problem $\sigma(D) \equiv^? D$. Therefore, the second step results in computing a minimal set of reduced matchers of the problem $\sigma(D) \equiv^? D$ for every matcher σ computed in the first step, i.e., the set that contains all reduced matchers in $\forall$-normal form modulo AC (AC⊥). Altogether, our approach is a generic algorithm consisting of the following two steps:

1. Compute the minimal set of i-minimal matchers of the problem $C \sqsubseteq^? D$.
2. For every matcher σ computed in the first step, determine the minimal set of reduced matchers of the problem $\sigma(D) \equiv^? D$.

For matching problems modulo equivalence one can skip the first step since all solutions form one i-equivalence class. For matching problems in $\mathcal{ALNS}$ and $\mathcal{ALN}^*$ only minimal sets of i-minimal matchers are computed, i.e., one can dispense with the second step.

In the sequel, the two steps of the generic algorithm are further refined. This will require to introduce several new notions.

Refining the First Step. The first step is broken down into two subtasks. First, a so-called i-complete set is computed, and then, this set is minimized, i.e., a *minimal* i-complete set is derived.[9]

Definition 3.2.8. *Given a matching problem $C \sqsubseteq^? D$ (or $C \equiv^? D$), a subset $\mathcal{C}$ of solutions of this problem is called* i-(co-)complete *if, and only if, for every matcher σ there exists a matcher $\sigma' \in \mathcal{C}$ such that $\sigma' \sqsubseteq_i \sigma$ ($\sigma' \sqsupseteq_i \sigma$); $\mathcal{C}$ is called* minimal i-(co-)complete *if, and only if, $\mathcal{C}$ is i-(co-)complete and any two distinct elements in $\mathcal{C}$ are i-incomparable, i.e., for all distinct matchers $\sigma, \sigma' \in \mathcal{C}$, it holds $\sigma \not\sqsubseteq_i \sigma'$.*

The following properties of (minimal) i-complete sets are easy to verify.

Lemma 3.2.5. *Given the setting of Definition 3.2.8 the following properties hold:*[10]

1. *Every i-complete set contains (at least) one representative of every minimal i-equivalence class, i.e., every i-complete set contains a minimal set of i-minimal matchers.*
2. *Every minimal i-complete set coincides with the minimal set of i-minimal matchers.*

---

[9] We also define co-complete sets since they are needed later on.
[10] Analogous properties hold for i-co-complete sets, which contain (at least) one representative of every i-equivalence class of i-maximal matchers. Also, a minimal i-co-complete set contains exactly one representative of these classes.

It should be pointed out that minimal i-complete sets need not necessarily exist because the set of matchers might contain an infinite decreasing chain of matchers (w.r.t. $\sqsubseteq_i$), for which there does not exist a limes. However, for all languages considered in this book we will show that this cannot occur. In fact, there always exist finite i-complete sets. Given such a set, a minimal i-complete set can be computed efficiently (using an oracle for deciding subsumption) by iteratively removing those matchers of the set for which there exist more specific or equivalent matchers in the set. More precisely, one can easily show the following.

Remark 3.2.1. Every finite i-complete set can be turned into a minimal i-complete set in time polynomial in the size of the i-complete set using an oracle for deciding $\sqsubseteq_i$.[11]

In the light of Lemma 3.2.5, the task of computing minimal sets of i-minimal matchers can be split into the two following subtasks: a) Compute an i-complete set, and b) turn this set into a minimal one. Conceptually, the latter subtask is not a problem once one has given an i-complete set (Remark 3.2.1). The first subtask is solved by computing so-called s-complete sets where "s" means "substitution" and stands for the ordering $\sqsubseteq_s$ on matchers: For matchers σ, τ, define

$$\sigma \sqsubseteq_s \tau \text{ iff } \sigma(X) \sqsubseteq \tau(X) \text{ for all variables } X \in N_X.$$

Now, s-equivalence and (minimal) s-(co)-complete sets are defined w.r.t. $\sqsubseteq_s$ analogously to the corresponding notions for $\sqsubseteq_i$. The following lemma shows that, in order to compute i-complete sets, it suffices to compute s-complete sets.

Lemma 3.2.6. *Every s-complete set is also i-complete.*

Proof. Let $\mathcal{C}$ be an s-complete set and let σ be some matcher. We need to show that $\mathcal{C}$ contains a matcher τ with $\tau(D) \sqsubseteq \sigma(D)$. Since $\mathcal{C}$ is s-complete there must exist a matcher τ with $\tau \sqsubseteq_s \sigma$. But now Lemma 3.2.1 implies $\tau(D) \sqsubseteq \sigma(D)$.   □

The idea behind our algorithms computing s-complete sets is to map variables on as specific concept descriptions as possible. This is exactly what previous matching algorithms have done. To be more precise, they computed so-called least matchers: A matcher σ is called *least matcher* if $\sigma \sqsubseteq_s \tau$ for every matcher τ. Note that a singleton only containing a least matcher is s-complete. Least matchers exist for all solvable $\mathcal{FL}_{\neg}$-matching problems [BBM98]. In Chapter 6.3, it will be shown that, even for matching problems in $\mathcal{ALNS}$ and $\mathcal{ALN}^*$, solvable matching problems always have a least matcher. However, the example $\exists r.A \sqcap \exists r.B \sqsubseteq^? \exists r.X$ demonstrates that for languages with existential restrictions (like $\mathcal{EL}$ and $\mathcal{ALE}$) least matchers need not exist. Thus,

---

[11] The same holds for i-co-complete sets.

for these languages, s-complete sets, in general, can contain more than just one matcher.

Summarizing, the task of computing a minimal set of i-minimal matchers can be split into a) computing an s-complete (and thus i-complete) set, and b) turning this set into a minimal i-complete set.

Refining the Second Step. Let us turn to the task of computing a minimal set of reduced matchers (for matching problems modulo equivalence). We first note that, in $\mathcal{ALE}$ ($\mathcal{ALN}$), for reduced matchers in $\forall$-normal form the equivalence relation $=_{AC}$ ($=_{AC\perp}$) coincides with s-equivalence. Thus, one does not need to distinguish between $=_{AC}$ ($=_{AC\perp}$) and $\equiv_s$ in case matchers in $\forall$-normal form are considered. The following lemma makes this connection explicit. It is a direct consequence of the relationship between $=_{AC}$ ($=_{AC\perp}$) and $\equiv$ on concept descriptions (see Theorem 6.1.2 and Theorem 6.3.6).

Lemma 3.2.7. *Let σ and τ be reduced $\mathcal{ALE}$-matchers ($\mathcal{ALN}$-matchers) in $\forall$-normal form. Then, $\sigma \equiv_s \tau$ if, and only if, $\sigma =_{AC} \tau$ ($\sigma =_{AC\perp} \tau$).*

The task of computing a minimal set of reduced matchers for matching problems modulo equivalence is again split into two subtasks. First, a so-called d-complete set is computed and then this set is turned into a minimal d-complete set.

Definition 3.2.9. *Let $C \equiv^? D$ be an $\mathcal{ALE}$-matching problem (or an $\mathcal{ALN}$-matching problem). Then, the set $\mathcal{C}$ of matchers is called d-complete if, and only if, for every matcher τ in $\forall$-normal form there exist matchers $\sigma \in \mathcal{C}$ and σ' with $\sigma' =_{AC} \sigma$ ($\sigma' =_{AC\perp} \sigma$) and $\sigma' \preceq_d \tau$; $\mathcal{C}$ is called minimal if all matchers in $\mathcal{C}$ are incomparable w.r.t. $=_{AC}$ ($=_{AC\perp}$) and $\preceq_d$.*

Similar to the i-complete case, for the languages we are concerned with in this work, we will show that every solvable matching problem modulo equivalence has a finite d-complete set that can be turned into a minimal one. Moreover, every d-complete set contains a minimal set of reduced matchers and every minimal d-complete set corresponds to a minimal set of reduced matchers.

Together with these refinements of the generic algorithm proposed above, the task of computing a minimal set of i-minimal and reduced matchers for the problem $C \sqsubseteq^? D$ can be accomplished as follows:

1. Compute a minimal set of i-minimal matchers of the problem $C \sqsubseteq^? D$:
   a) Compute an s-complete (and thus i-complete) set.
   b) Turn this set into a minimal one.
2. For every matcher σ computed in the first step, determine the minimal set of reduced matchers of the problem $\sigma(D) \equiv^? D$:
   a) Compute a d-complete set.
   b) Turn this set into a minimal one.

In Chapter 6, it will be shown how the two main tasks, namely, computing an s-complete set for matching problems modulo subsumption and computing a d-complete set for matching problems modulo equivalence, can be solved for the DLs $\mathcal{ALN}$ and $\mathcal{ALE}$. For $\mathcal{ALNS}$ and $\mathcal{ALN}^*$, it is shown how least matchers (and thus, s-complete sets) can be computed.

The Problem for $\mathcal{ALNS}$ and $\mathcal{ALN}^*$. In the remainder of this subsection we illustrate why it is difficult in $\mathcal{ALNS}$ and $\mathcal{ALN}^*$ to come up with an appropriate definition of reduced matchers. Ad hoc extensions of definitions for sublanguages do not yield satisfactory characterizations of "interesting" matchers.

Let us take a look at a first example. The class of people having only female offsprings can be represented by the $\mathcal{ALN}^*$-concept description

$$\mathsf{FD} := \forall \mathsf{hc}^*.\mathsf{W}.$$

where, as before, hc stands for the role has-child and W for the concept of all women. Now, the $\mathcal{ALN}^*$-matching problem $\mathsf{FD} \equiv^? X \sqcap Y$ has, among others, τ_0 as solution with $\tau_0(X) := \mathsf{W}$ and $\tau_0(Y) := \forall \mathsf{hc}.\forall \mathsf{hc}^*.\mathsf{W}$. Another reasonable solution is τ_1 with $\tau_1(X) := \mathsf{W} \sqcap \forall \mathsf{hc}.\mathsf{W}$ and $\tau_1(Y) := \forall \mathsf{hc}.\forall \mathsf{hc}.\forall \mathsf{hc}^*.\mathsf{W}$. Other τ_i's can be defined analogously. Intuitively, none of these matchers contains redundancies. Thus, one could call them reduced. But, of course, one cannot present this infinite number of matchers to the user. To overcome this problem, one can either think of some finite representation of this infinite set of matchers, or one needs to impose additional constraints on the matchers to be displayed (like size boundaries). It remains open whether reasonable finite representations or new constraints exist that are independent of specific applications.

A similar phenomenon occurs for $\mathcal{ALNS}$-concept descriptions. Take for example the class of all married people who love themselves most and who are married to their best friend. This can be described as

$$\mathsf{Married} := (\mathsf{love\text{-}most} \downarrow \varepsilon) \sqcap (\mathsf{best\text{-}friend} \downarrow \mathsf{spouse}).$$

Now, consider the matching problem $\mathsf{Married} \equiv^? X \sqcap Y$. One obvious solution σ_0 of this problem is to map X on $(\mathsf{love\text{-}most} \downarrow \varepsilon)$ and Y on $(\mathsf{best\text{-}friend} \downarrow \mathsf{spouse})$. Intuitively, $\sigma_0(X)$ describes "egocentric people" and $\sigma_0(Y)$ refers to all "happily married people". A similar interpretation is possible for the matcher σ_1: $\sigma_1(X) := \sigma_0(X)$ and $\sigma_1(Y) := (\mathsf{love\text{-}most} \circ \mathsf{best\text{-}friend}) \downarrow (\mathsf{love\text{-}most} \circ \mathsf{spouse})$. Of course, at this point one can proceed and define $\sigma_i(Y)$ by

$$(\mathsf{love\text{-}most}^i \circ \mathsf{best\text{-}friend}) \downarrow (\mathsf{love\text{-}most}^i \circ \mathsf{spouse})$$

where $\mathsf{love\text{-}most}^i$ denotes the word $\mathsf{love\text{-}most} \cdots \mathsf{love\text{-}most}$ of length i. Again, all these matchers can be viewed as being free of redundancies in the sense that when removing *conjuncts* the resulting substitutions are no longer matchers. The question is whether one a) should take the concept Married as "background theory" in order to keep the matchers small, b) impose some

Table 3.5. Complexity of Deciding the Solvability of Matching Problems in (Sublanguages of) $\mathcal{ALNS}$.

	$\mathcal{FL}_0$	$\mathcal{FL}_\neg$	$\mathcal{ALN}$	$\mathcal{ALNS}$
subsumption	P	P	P	P
	[BN98]	[BBM98]	(Corollary 6.1.1)	(Corollary 6.1.1)
equivalence	P	P	P	$\geq$PSPACE $\leq$EXPTIME
	[BN98]	[BBM98]	(Corollary 6.1.3)	(Corollary 6.1.2)

additional constraints on the matchers, or c) find some finite representation of the infinite set of possible matchers.

The bottom line is that for $\mathcal{ALNS}$- and $\mathcal{ALN}^*$-matching problems it might be necessary to specify further refinements of minimal i-equivalence classes with respect to the specific application domain under consideration; at least as long as no other general criteria can be found.

3.2.4 Previous Results

Matching algorithms for $\mathcal{ALN}$ extended by existential restrictions were first introduced by Borgida and McGuinness [BM96]. The main drawback of their algorithms is that they place strong restrictions on the occurrence of variables such that certain natural concept patterns are not allowed. For example, the pattern $\forall r.(X \sqcap Y) \sqcap \forall s.X \sqcap \forall t.Y$ would not be admissible. This makes it difficult to build composite patterns from simpler, previously defined ones. In addition, due to an incomplete treatment of unsatisfiable subexpressions and existential restrictions, the proposed algorithms do not always find a matcher even if one exists.

For the language $\mathcal{FL}_0$, Baader and Narendran, [BN98], devised a (necessarily worst-case exponential time) unification algorithm. From this algorithm they derived the first complete (polynomial-time) $\mathcal{FL}_0$-matching algorithm, i.e., this algorithm always computes a matcher if one exists and it indicates if the problem does not have a solution. Moreover, their algorithm does not impose restrictions on the form of the patterns. In [BKBM99], the algorithm has been extended to deal with $\mathcal{FL}_\neg$. Beside the quite restricted DLs that can be handled, the main drawback of these algorithms is that only least matchers (see the previous subsection for the definition) are computed. As illustrated previously, these matchers are usually not the ones one is really interested in since they may contain redundancies. Thus, they might be hard to read and to comprehend. A summary of the results on matching in $\mathcal{FL}_0$ and $\mathcal{FL}_\neg$ that are due to previous work is included in the first two columns of Table 3.5 and 3.8.

Table 3.6. Complexity of Deciding the Solvability of Matching Problems in (Sublanguages of) $\mathcal{ALN}^*$.

	$\mathcal{FL}_\neg^*$	$\mathcal{ALN}^*$
subsumption	PSPACE	PSPACE
	(Corollary 6.2.1)	(Corollary 6.2.1)
equivalence	$\geq$PSPACE $\leq$EXPSPACE	$\geq$PSPACE $\leq$2EXPSPACE
	(Corollary 6.2.2)	(Corollary 6.2.2)

3.2.5 New Results

In this book, the existing work on matching is extended in two directions. On the one hand, the question of what are the most "interesting" solutions of matching problems is explored in detail (Section 3.2.3). On the other hand, sound and complete matching algorithms have been devised for solving matching problems in several extensions of $\mathcal{FL}_\neg$. To be more precise, algorithms have been designed for i) the problem of deciding the solvability of matching problems, and ii) the problem of computing (interesting) matchers. According to Section 3.2.3, the latter problem comes down to computing i-complete sets (for matching problems modulo subsumption) and d-complete sets (for matching modulo equivalence). In what follows, we summarize the obtained complexity results for all these problems (see Chapter 6 for algorithms and detailed proofs).

The Decision Problem. The decision problem has been investigated for matching modulo subsumption and modulo equivalence in (sublanguages of) $\mathcal{ALNS}$, $\mathcal{ALN}^*$, and $\mathcal{ALE}$.

According to Lemma 3.2.3, deciding the solvability of matching problems modulo subsumption is not a new inference problem since it can be reduced to deciding subsumption, and conversely, subsumption can be reduced to matching modulo subsumption. Thus, the known complexity results for subsumption immediately carry over to matching modulo subsumption (see the respective entries in the Tables 3.5, 3.6, and 3.7, where "NP" means NP-complete, and analogously, "PSPACE" means PSPACE-complete).

Matching modulo equivalence, however, may add some complexity compared to a simple equivalence test. For example, although in $\mathcal{ALNS}$ and $\mathcal{EL}$ testing for equivalence can be carried out in polynomial time, matching modulo equivalence in these languages is PSPACE-hard (denoted "$\geq$PSPACE" in Table 3.5) and NP-hard (Table 3.7), respectively. The remaining lower bounds depicted in the Tables 3.6 and 3.7 are due to hardness results on deciding equivalence.

Table 3.7. Complexity of Deciding the Solvability of Matching Problems in (Sublanguages of) $\mathcal{ALE}$

	$\mathcal{EL}$	$\mathcal{ALE}$
subsumption	P	NP
	(Corollary 6.3.3)	(Corollary 6.3.13)
equivalence	NP	NP
	(Corollary 6.3.4)	(Corollary 6.3.15)

Let us now turn to the complexity upper bounds for matching modulo equivalence (marked with a preceding $\leq$ in the Tables 3.5, 3.6, and 3.7 in case the bound is not tight).

The complexity upper bounds for (sublanguages of) $\mathcal{ALNS}$ (Table 3.5) and $\mathcal{ALN}^*$ (Table 3.6) are due to an algorithm of the following form: i) Compute a candidate matcher (which then is a least matcher) and ii) check whether this candidate solves the problem. The drawback of this approach is that, except for $\mathcal{ALN}$, least matchers may be quite large, i.e., of size exponential or even double exponential in the size of the given matching problem. Consequently, the decision algorithms resulting from this approach have a high worst-case complexity. Unfortunately, for these languages no other decision algorithms are known up to now. Thus, it remains to close the (partly huge) gaps between the lower and upper bounds.

As already pointed out in Section 3.2.3, solvable $\mathcal{ALE}$-matching problems need not have least matchers. However, one can compute i-minimal matchers instead and check whether they solve the matching problem. Again, the size of these candidates may grow exponentially (even for the small language $\mathcal{EL}$) such that the resulting decision algorithms are quite complex. Fortunately, one can show that every solvable $\mathcal{ALE}$-matching problem has a matcher of size polynomially bounded in the size of the matching problem. Thus, instead of computing a candidate matcher, an NP-algorithm can simply guess a substitution (of size polynomially bounded in the size of the matching problem) and then check whether this substitution actually solves the problem. This yields an improved decision algorithm whose complexity even matches the lower complexity bounds (see Table 3.7).

Computing i-Complete Sets. Recall that (minimal) i-complete sets contain (exactly) all i-minimal matchers up to i-equivalence. These sets are of interest only for matching modulo subsumption since all solutions of matching problems modulo equivalence are i-minimal: given the problem $C \equiv^? D$, all instances of D induced by matchers are equivalent to C. In the following, we summarize the complexity results for computing i-complete sets, their cardinality, and the size of i-minimal matchers in these sets.

We will show that for (sublanguages of) $\mathcal{ALNS}$ and $\mathcal{ALN}^*$ solvable matching problems always have a least matcher. As an easy consequence

Table 3.8. Complexity of Computing i-Complete Sets, their Cardinality, and the Size of i-Minimal Matchers in (Sublanguages of) $\mathcal{ALNS}$.

i-complete sets	$\mathcal{FL}_0$	$\mathcal{FL}_\neg$	$\mathcal{ALN}$	$\mathcal{ALNS}$
computation	P	P	P	EXPTIME
	[BN98]	[BBM98]	(Corollary 6.1.5)	(Corollary 6.1.5)
cardinality	1	1	1	1
	[BN98]	[BBM98]	(Corollary 6.1.5)	(Corollary 6.1.5)
size	P	P	P	EXPONENTIAL
	[BN98]	[BBM98]	(Corollary 6.1.5)	(Corollary 6.1.5)

Table 3.9. Complexity of Computing i-Complete Sets, their Cardinality, and the Size of i-Minimal Matchers in (Sublanguages of) $\mathcal{ALN}^*$. These results are proved in Section 6.2.2 and summarized in Corollary 6.2.5.

i-complete sets	$\mathcal{FL}_\neg^*$	$\mathcal{ALN}^*$
computation	EXPTIME	$\geq$EXPTIME $\leq$2EXPTIME
cardinality	1	1
size	EXPONENTIAL	EXPONENTIAL

Table 3.10. Complexity of Computing i-Complete Sets, their Cardinality, and the Size of i-Minimal Matchers in (Sublanguages of) $\mathcal{ALE}$.

i-complete sets	$\mathcal{EL}$	$\mathcal{ALE}$
computation	EXPTIME	EXPTIME
	(Corollary 6.3.8)	(Corollary 6.3.18)
cardinality	EXPONENTIAL	EXPONENTIAL
	(Corollary 6.3.5 and 6.3.7)	(Corollary 6.3.16 and 6.3.17)
size	EXPONENTIAL	EXPONENTIAL
	(Corollary 6.3.6 and 6.3.7)	(Corollary 6.3.16 and 6.3.17)

of Lemma 3.2.1, such a matcher forms a minimal i-complete set. Thus, in these languages the cardinality of minimal i-complete sets is at most one (see Table 3.8 and 3.9). However, for $\mathcal{ALE}$ (and sublanguages thereof with existential restrictions) the cardinality of (minimal) i-complete sets may grow exponentially in the size of the matching problem (Table 3.10).

Except for $\mathcal{ALN}$ and its sublanguages, the size of i-minimal matchers may grow exponentially in the size of the given matching problems modulo subsumption (Table 3.8, 3.9, and 3.10). Consequently, algorithms computing i-complete sets need exponential time in the worst-case. As depicted in the three tables, except for $\mathcal{ALN}^*$, all matching algorithms in fact match this lower complexity bound. For $\mathcal{ALN}^*$, it remains open whether there exists an algorithm that is more efficient than the 2EXPTIME-algorithm proposed so far in this book. This is closely related to the question of what is a tight upper bound for the size of i-minimal matchers in $\mathcal{ALN}^*$.

It should be emphasized that the algorithms for (sublanguages of) $\mathcal{ALNS}$ and $\mathcal{ALN}^*$ compute *minimal* i-complete sets since a least matcher forms such a set. The algorithms for (sublanguages of) $\mathcal{ALE}$, however, only produce (not necessarily minimal) i-complete sets. Minimizing them requires some subsumption tests. Recalling that subsumption in $\mathcal{ALE}$ is an NP-complete problem and that the size of matchers in i-complete sets may be exponential in the size of the matching problem, this guarantees the existence of an EXPSPACE-algorithm for the minimization task.

Computing d-Complete Sets. As defined in Section 3.2.3, d-complete sets contain all matchers (up to s-equivalence) that are free of redundancies. These sets are only computed for matching problems modulo equivalence — for matching modulo subsumption i-complete sets are computed in a preprocessing step. Moreover, d-minimal matchers are specified only for the languages $\mathcal{ALN}$ and $\mathcal{ALE}$. As mentioned in Section 3.2.3, for extensions of $\mathcal{ALN}$ a reasonable definition remains to be established (see Section 3.2.3 for the problems one encounters).

Since the notion of d-minimality has first been introduced here, previous research has not investigated the problem of computing d-complete sets. Only least matchers have been computed.

In Section 6.3.1 and 6.3.6, it will be shown, for the languages $\mathcal{ALN}$ and $\mathcal{ALE}$ that the size of d-minimal matchers can polynomially be bounded in the size of the matching problem (Table 3.11). Therefore, one immediately obtains EXPTIME-algorithms for computing (minimal) d-complete sets: It suffices to enumerate all matchers up to the polynomial complexity bound and to filter out those that are not d-minimal or that are s-equivalent to previously computed matchers (in order to obtain a *minimal* d-complete set). Since the cardinality of minimal d-complete sets might grow exponentially (Table 3.11), this ad hoc algorithm yields a tight upper bound. However, from a practical point of view this approach is not feasible. Therefore, optimized algorithms have been developed. In particular, for $\mathcal{ALN}$-matching problems modulo equivalence it is possible to derive all d-minimal matchers from the least matcher of the given problem. For $\mathcal{EL}$ (Section 6.3.1), s-maximal matchers are computed and then the images are reduced in order to obtain a d-complete set. The hope is that in $\mathcal{FLE}$ d-complete sets can be computed via s-maximal matchers as well. Unfortunately, in $\mathcal{ALE}$ this approach probably fails to work since matching problems may have an infinite number of s-maximal matchers. In fact, other than the ad hoc algorithm no algorithm is known for computing d-complete sets in $\mathcal{ALE}$.

Table 3.11. Complexity of Computing (Minimal) d-Complete Sets, their Cardinality, and the Size of d-Minimal Matchers.

d-complete sets	$\mathcal{ALN}$	$\mathcal{ALE}$
computation	EXPTIME (Corollary 6.1.8)	EXPTIME (Corollary 6.3.19)
cardinality	EXPONENTIAL (Corollary 6.1.8)	EXPONENTIAL (Corollary 6.3.20)
size	P (Corollary 6.1.8)	P (Corollary 6.3.20)

Note that, when dealing with matching problems modulo subsumption, say $C \sqsubseteq^? D$, then d-complete sets are computed for problems of the form $\sigma(D) \equiv^? D$, where σ is an i-minimal matcher of $C \sqsubseteq^? D$. Since in $\mathcal{ALE}$ the size of σ may be exponential in the size of the original problem, d-complete sets are computed for sizable matching problems. Thus, algorithms computing these sets need *double* exponential time in the size of the original matching problem.

3.3 The Underlying Techniques

Approaches for solving non-standard inference problems are usually based on an appropriate characterization of subsumption, which often can be used to obtain a structural subsumption algorithm. Recall from Section 2.4 that structural subsumption algorithms work as follows: First, concept descriptions are turned into a certain normal form, in which implicit facts have been made explicit. Second, the normal forms are compared. As pointed out in Section 2.1, in the early days of DLs structural subsumption algorithms provided the only means for deciding subsumption. They were usually implemented as recursive algorithms working on normalized concept descriptions or graphs [Neb90a, BPS94]. Nowadays, one can distinguish two kinds of structural approaches; depending on the language of choice. In this book, one or the other approach is used to solve non-standard inferences.

In the first approach, called *language-based* or *automata-theoretic* approach, the normal form of a concept description is given in terms of certain finite or regular sets of words over the alphabet of role names. Then, subsumption can be characterized via the inclusion of these sets. This approach has originally been introduced in [Baa96] to characterize subsumption between concepts defined in cyclic $\mathcal{FL}_0$-TBoxes both to gain a better understanding of the effects of the gfp-, lfp-, and descriptive semantics, and to derive decision algorithms for subsumption. Later the results have been extended to the more expressive language $\mathcal{ALN}$ [Küs98]. In Section 4.2, we will review the characterization of subsumption in $\mathcal{ALN}$-TBoxes for the gfp-semantics. Recall that concepts defined by these TBoxes are called cyclic $\mathcal{ALN}$-concept descriptions, which correspond to $\mathcal{ALN}^*$-concept descriptions. In subsequent chapters, the language-based approach will prove very useful to solve non-standard inferences for $\mathcal{ALN}^*$-concept descriptions. In particular, it turns out that computing the lcs of $\mathcal{ALN}^*$-concept descriptions comes down to computing the intersection of regular languages occurring in the normal forms of $\mathcal{ALN}^*$-concept descriptions. Moreover, solving matching problems can be reduced to solving language equations over regular languages.

The second approach, called *graph-based* approach, turns concept descriptions into so-called description graphs. Here, subsumption of concept descriptions is characterized via the existence of certain homomorphisms between the corresponding description graphs. This approach has first been introduced in [BKM99] for the language $\mathcal{ALE}$ in order to compute the lcs between $\mathcal{ALE}$-concept descriptions. Although Borgida and Patel-Schneider [BPS94] did not explicitly characterize subsumption of CLASSIC-concept descriptions in terms of homomorphisms between description graphs, their subsumption algorithm does in fact check for the existence of an appropriate homomorphism. In Section 4.1 and 4.3 we recall the graph-based approach for the sublanguage $\mathcal{ALNS}$ of CLASSIC, and $\mathcal{ALE}$. Based on these characterizations, the lcs can be computed as the product of description graphs. Matching problems are solved by computing homomorphisms between graphs corresponding to the concept pattern and the concept description. Interestingly, to actually compute matchers, the lcs operation is needed as a subprocedure.

Summing up, the language-based approach is particularly useful to deal with cyclic concept descriptions, whereas the graph-based approach allows to deal with a number of interesting constructors, like existential restrictions and same-as equalities. Therefore, it would be interesting to combine both approaches in order to treat, say, cyclic $\mathcal{ALE}$-concept descriptions. A possible combination might result in an automata-theoretic approach, which unlike the one employed so far, is based on tree automata working on infinite trees. Another question which remains to be investigated is whether structural and tableau-based algorithms can be combined to solve non-standard inferences in more expressive languages, like those allowing for concept disjunction. As pointed out in Section 2.4, tableau-based algorithms are used to decide subsumption in very expressive DLs, while structural approaches prove very useful for solving non-standard inferences, but are restricted to quite unexpressive languages. One idea towards combining both approaches in order to get the best out of both is to use tableau-algorithms to compute normal forms of concepts.

Altogether, the hope is that the techniques for solving non-standard inferences presented in this book and those for standard inferences known from the literature can be combined in such a way that non-standard inferences can be taken to a level that comes close to what is known for standard inferences today (see Section 2.1).

3.4 Other Non-Standard Inferences

For the sake of completeness, we conclude this chapter about non-standard inferences by providing an overview of other novel inferences that have been proposed in the literature, but are not investigated here.

Concept Rewriting. A general framework for rewriting concepts using terminologies has been proposed in [BKM00]. Assume that $\mathcal{L}_1, \mathcal{L}_2$, and $\mathcal{L}_3$ are three DLs, and let C be an $\mathcal{L}_1$-concept description and $\mathcal{T}$ an $\mathcal{L}_2$-TBox. One is interested in rewriting (i.e., transforming) C into an $\mathcal{L}_3$-concept description D such that i) C and D are in a certain relationship (e.g., equivalence, subsumption), and ii) D satisfies certain optimality criteria (e.g., being of minimal size).

This very general framework has several interesting instances. In the following, we will sketch the three most interesting ones.

The first instance is the *translation of concept descriptions* from one DL into another. Here, we assume that $\mathcal{L}_1$ and $\mathcal{L}_3$ are different description languages, and that the TBox $\mathcal{T}$ is empty. By trying to rewrite an $\mathcal{L}_1$-concept C into an *equivalent* $\mathcal{L}_3$-concept D, one can find out whether C is expressible in $\mathcal{L}_3$. In many cases, such an exact rewriting may not exist. In this case, one can try to approximate C by an $\mathcal{L}_3$-concept from above (from below), i.e., find a minimal (maximal) concept description D in $\mathcal{L}_3$ such that $C \sqsubseteq D$ ($D \sqsubseteq C$). An inference service that can compute such rewritings could, for example, support the transfer of knowledge bases between different systems. Until now there are, however, no nontrivial results for this instance of the rewriting framework.

The second instance comes from the database area, where the problem of *rewriting queries using views* is a well-known research topic [BLR97]. The aim is to optimize the runtime of queries by using cached views. In the context of the above framework, views can be regarded as TBox definitions and queries as concept descriptions. Beeri et al. [BLR97] have investigated the instance where $\mathcal{L}_1$ and $\mathcal{L}_2$ allow for a language that extends $\mathcal{ALC}$ by number restrictions and role hierarchies and where $\mathcal{L}_3$ only allows for concept conjunction and disjunction. Beeri et al. are interested in maximally contained total rewritings. That is, D should be subsumed by C, contain only concept names defined in the TBox, and be a maximal concept (w.r.t. subsumption) satisfying these properties. They show that such a rewriting is computable (whenever it exists).

The third instance of the general framework, which was first proposed in [BKM00], tries to increase the readability of large concept descriptions by using concepts defined in a TBox. The motivation comes from the experiences made with non-standard inferences (like lcs, msc, and matching) in applications. The concept descriptions produced by these services are usually unfolded (i.e., do not use defined names), and are thus often very large and hard to read and comprehend. Therefore, one is interested in automatically generating an equivalent concept description of minimal length that contains the concept names defined in the underlying terminology. Referring to the framework, one considers the case where $\mathcal{L} = \mathcal{L}_1 = \mathcal{L}_2 = \mathcal{L}_3$ and the TBox is non-empty. For a given concept description C and a TBox $\mathcal{T}$ in $\mathcal{L}$ one is interested in an $\mathcal{L}$-concept description D (containing concept names defined in $\mathcal{T}$) such that $C \equiv_{\mathcal{T}} D$ and the size of D is minimal. Rewriting in this sense has been explored for the DLs $\mathcal{ALN}$ and $\mathcal{ALE}$ [BKM00]. It has turned out that rewritings can be computed by a nondeterministic polynomial algorithm that uses an oracle for deciding subsumption. The corresponding decision problem (i.e., the question whether there exists a rewriting of size $\leq k$ for a given number k) is NP-hard for both languages.

Difference Operator. Informally speaking, the difference operator allows to remove from a given description as much as possible of the information contained in another description. A first formal definition has been given by Teege [Tee94]: The difference $D - C$ between two $\mathcal{L}$-concept descriptions C and D for some DL $\mathcal{L}$ is defined as

$$max\{E \in \mathcal{L} \mid C \sqcap E \equiv D\}$$

where max is defined with respect to subsumption and C is required to subsume D.

A possible application of this operation proposed by Teege is a tutoring system where a learner is asked by the system to explain a concept. The system compares the description given by the learner with the correct description in its knowledge base. If both descriptions are equivalent, the learner knows the concept. If the learner's description subsumes the correct description the learner does not know all aspects of the concept. Conversely, if the learner's concept is subsumed by the correct one, the learner has a too specific concept in mind. In both cases, the learner can be corrected by presenting the differences between the two concepts.

However, since the difference between two concept descriptions is presented to the user (e.g., a learner), it is questionable whether it is sufficient to specify the difference exclusively by semantic means. Such a definition does not exclude unintuitive or useless representations of differences. For example, if a language allows for full negation, then $D - C$ is always equivalent to $\neg C \sqcup D$. In the application scenario sketched above this means that the learner simply gets back his/her concept and the correct one, yet without the difference between D and C made explicit. Another problem is that the description of the difference may contain redundancies, thus making it difficult to understand the description. Summing up, even though computing the difference between to concepts is an interesting new inference task, one certainly needs to refine the definition of the difference operator proposed by Teege.

Without going too much into the details, the notion of C-reduced concept descriptions (Definition 6.3.2), introduced in this book mainly for technical reasons, seems to be a promising starting point for such a refinement: Given two $\mathcal{ALE}$-concept descriptions C and D, the C-reduced concept description $D \backslash C$ of D is a subdescription of D (Definition 3.2.3) such that i) $C \sqcap D \equiv C \sqcap (D \backslash C)$, and ii) $D \backslash C$ is minimal (w.r.t. the subdescription ordering $\preceq_d$) with this property. Although, unlike Teege's definition of $D - C$, we do not need to require $D \sqsubseteq C$, let us assume $D \sqsubseteq C$ in the following in order to compare the two notions. We first consider the case where neither C nor D contain unsatisfiable subexpressions. On the one hand, under this precondition, one can show that $D \backslash C \equiv D - C$. Thus, the notion of C-reduction fits the pattern introduced by Teege. On the other hand, unlike $D - C$, $D \backslash C$ is guaranteed to be free of redundancies, which shows that in this respect the notion of C-reduction comes closer to the intuition underlying the difference operator. If C or D contain unsatisfiable subexpressions, the relationship between the two notions is not that clear anymore. This is due to the fact that in C-reduced concepts, unsatisfiable subexpressions must be made explicit by the bottom-concept, since the bottom-concept is defined to be the least concept description w.r.t. $\preceq_d$. For example, if $C = P$ and $D \equiv \bot$, then $D \backslash C = \bot$, but $D - C \equiv \neg P$. The advantage of $D \backslash C$ is that it resembles D, and thus might be better to understand for the user. Nevertheless, $D - C$ exactly captures the *semantic* difference between C and D. We leave it as future work to combine the two notions in order to get the best out of both.

4. Characterizing Subsumption

As pointed out in Section 3.3, appropriate characterizations of subsumption form the basis for algorithms solving non-standard inferences. The core of every of these characterizations lies in normal forms which provide finite representations of all implications that can be drawn from concept descriptions. Such normal forms can be stated in terms of certain concept descriptions, graphs, or systems of regular languages. Subsumption can then be described using these objects by recursive algorithms, homomorphisms, or language inclusions. Which type of characterization is employed to solve a non-standard inference problem depends on the DL of choice and the inference problem itself. Not all normal forms and characterizations are equally suitable in every situation.

In the following three sections of this chapter, the different characterizations for the languages $\mathcal{ALNS}$, $\mathcal{ALN}^*$, and $\mathcal{ALE}$ as well as relevant sublanguages thereof are presented. For the proofs of soundness and completeness, we refer the reader to the respective literature.

4.1 Subsumption in $\mathcal{ALNS}$

In this section, we present graph-based and description-based characterizations of subsumption for $\mathcal{ALNS}$ and some of its sublanguages. For the former characterization we further distinguish between a characterization based on a recursive algorithm and one that employs homomorphisms between graphs. Depending on the problem under consideration, one characterization is more appropriate than the other one. For example, the correctness of our lcs algorithm (Section 5.1) is shown by the graph-based characterization, whereas when dealing with reduced matchers (Section 6.1) the description-based characterization is employed.

The general idea of the graph-based characterization is as follows. First, the potential subsumee is turned into a so-called description graph reflecting the syntactic structure of the descriptions. Then, this graph is normalized, which means that certain inferences are made explicit and redundancies are removed by combining nodes and edges in the graph. Finally, subsumption between the potential subsumer (represented by its concept description) and

R.Küsters: Non-Standard Inferences in Description Logics, LNAI 2100, pp. 73–105, 2001.
© Springer-Verlag Berlin Heidelberg 2001

the subsumee (represented by its normalized description graph) is characterized by a recursive algorithm following the syntactic structure of the given concept description. In the literature, this kind of algorithm has been referred to as structural subsumption algorithm [Neb90a] (as opposed to the tableau-based algorithm mentioned in Chapter 2). They are usually applied to (sub-)languages of the CLASSIC DL. A sound and complete subsumption algorithm for full CLASSIC has first been described in [BPS94], where attributes are interpreted as total functions (*total attributes*). In Section 5.1, we will review this algorithm for the sublanguage $\mathcal{LS}$ of CLASSIC in order to prove results on the lcs of $\mathcal{LS}$-concept descriptions. Following the lines of [KB99], in Section 4.1.1 we present a characterization of subsumption for $\mathcal{ALNS}$-concept descriptions from which a recursive subsumption algorithm can immediately be derived.[1] Recall that $\mathcal{ALNS}$ allows for partial attributes, i.e., attributes interpreted as partial functions, whereas CLASSIC, as defined in [BPS94], allows for total attributes. For this reason, the algorithm for CLASSIC needs to be adapted.

It turns out that subsumption can also be characterized in terms of homomorphisms between description graphs where both the subsumee and the subsumer are translated into graphs. In this sense, structural subsumption algorithms decide the existence of homomorphisms between description graphs. We will present this kind of characterization both for $\mathcal{ALNS}$ and its sublanguage $\mathcal{ALN}$.

The description-based characterization of subsumption only requires the concept descriptions to be in $\forall$-normal form. Apart from this "minor" normalization step, subsumption can directly be explained based on the concept descriptions. This kind of characterization is presented for $\mathcal{ALN}$-concept descriptions; for languages including the same-as constructor only the graph-based characterization is known.

4.1.1 A Graph-Based Characterization of Subsumption

Following [BPS94, KB99], we now recall the steps necessary to establish the graph-based characterization of subsumption. We start with the definition of description graphs.

Description Graphs. Intuitively, description graphs reflect the syntactic structure of concept descriptions. A description graph is a labeled, directed graph, with a distinguished node. Roughly speaking, the edges (*a-edges*) of the graph capture the constraints expressed by same-as equalities. The labels of nodes contain, among others, a set of so-called *r-edges*, which correspond to value restrictions and which lead to *nested description graphs* representing the concepts of the corresponding value restrictions.

Before defining description graphs formally, let us first look at an example. Using the concept names Car, Model, Manufacturer, and RepairReport, the

---

[1] The algorithm presented in [KB99] includes all CLASSIC-constructors.

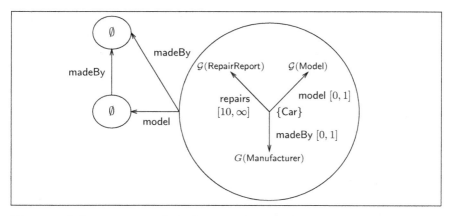

Fig. 4.1. A description graph for Lemon, where the large node is the root of the graph.

attribute names model and madeBy as well as the role name repairs, cars that have had frequent (at least 10) repairs can be represented by the following concept description:

Lemon := Car ⊓ ∀model.Model ⊓

        ∀madeBy.Manufacturer ⊓ ∀repairs.RepairReport ⊓

        madeBy ↓ model ∘ madeBy ⊓ (≥ 10 repairs)

A description graph corresponding to the concept description Lemon is depicted in Figure 4.1, where we use $\mathcal{G}$(Manufacturer), $\mathcal{G}$(Model), as well as $\mathcal{G}$(RepairReport) to denote description graphs for the concept names Manufacturer, Model, and RepairReport. These graphs merely consist of one node labeled with the corresponding concept name. In general, such graphs can be more complex since a value restriction like $\forall r.C$ leads to a (possibly complex) concept description C.

    Although number restrictions on attributes are not allowed, r-edges labeled with attributes, like model and madeBy, always have the restriction $[0, 1]$ in order to capture the semantics of attributes. Formally, description graphs, nodes, and edges are defined mutually recursively as follows:

Definition 4.1.1. *A description graph $\mathcal{G}$ is a tuple (N, E, n_0, ℓ), consisting of a finite set N of nodes; a finite set E of edges (a-edges); a distinguished node n_0 of N (root of the graph); and a labeling function ℓ from N into the set of labels. We will occasionally use the notation $\mathcal{G}.Nodes$, $\mathcal{G}.Edges$, and $\mathcal{G}.Root$ to access the components N, E and n_0 of the graph $\mathcal{G}$.*

    An a-edge is a tuple of the form (n_1, a, n_2) where n_1, n_2 are nodes and a is an attribute name.

    A label of a node is defined to be a tuple of the form (S, H), consisting of a finite set S, which may contain $\perp$ and (negated) concept names (the

atoms *of the node), and a finite set H of tuples (the* r-edges *of the node).*
We will occasionally use the notation n.Atoms and n.REdges to access the
components S and H of the node n.

An r-edge *is a tuple,* $(r, m, M, \mathcal{G}')$, *consisting of a role or attribute name*
r; *a* min, m, *which is a non-negative integer; a* max, M, *which is a non-*
negative integer or ∞; *and a (recursively nested) description graph* $\mathcal{G}'$. *The*
graph $\mathcal{G}'$ *will often be called the* restriction graph *of the node for the role r.*
We require the nodes of $\mathcal{G}'$ *to be distinct from all the nodes of* $\mathcal{G}$ *and other*
nested description graphs of $\mathcal{G}$. *If r is an attribute, then m must be 0 and*
$M \in \{0, 1\}$.

Given a description graph $\mathcal{G}$ and a node $n \in \mathcal{G}.Nodes$, we define $\mathcal{G}_n$ to
be the graph (N, E, n, ℓ); $\mathcal{G}_n$ is said to be rooted at n. A sequence $p = n_0 a_1 n_1 a_2 \cdots a_k n_k$ with $k \geq 0$ and $(n_{i-1}, a_i, n_i) \in \mathcal{G}.Edges$, $i = 1, \ldots, k$, is
called *path in* $\mathcal{G}$ *from the node* n_0 *to* n_k ($p \in \mathcal{G}$ for short); for $k = 0$ the
path p is called *empty*; $w = a_1 \cdots a_k$ is called the *label* of p (the empty path
has label ε); p is called *rooted* if n_0 is the root of $\mathcal{G}$. Occasionally, we write
$n_0 a_1 \cdots a_k n_k \in \mathcal{G}$ omitting the intermediate nodes.

Throughout this book we make the assumption that *description graphs*
are connected. A description graph is said to be *connected* if all nodes of the
graph can be reached by a rooted path and all nested graphs are connected.
The semantics of description graphs (see Definition 4.1.2) is not altered if
nodes that cannot be reached from the root are removed.

In order to merge description graphs we need the notion of "recursive set
of nodes" of a description graph $\mathcal{G}$: The *recursive set of nodes* $N_{\mathcal{G}}$ *of* $\mathcal{G}$ is the
union of the nodes of $\mathcal{G}$ and the recursive set of nodes of all nested description
graphs of $\mathcal{G}$.

Just as for concept descriptions, the semantics of description graphs is
defined by means of an interpretation $\mathcal{I}$. We introduce a function Υ which
assigns an individual of the domain of $\mathcal{I}$ to every node of the graph. This
ensures that all same-as equalities are satisfied.

Definition 4.1.2. *Let* $\mathcal{G} = (N, E, n_0, \ell)$ *be a description graph and let* $\mathcal{I}$ *be*
an interpretation. An element d of $\Delta^{\mathcal{I}}$ *is in the extension* $\mathcal{G}^{\mathcal{I}}$ *of* $\mathcal{G}$ *if, and*
only if, there is some total function Υ *from N into* $\Delta^{\mathcal{I}}$ *such that*

1. $d = \Upsilon(n_0)$;
2. *for all* $n \in N$, $\Upsilon(n) \in n^{\mathcal{I}}$; *and*
3. *for all* $(n_1, a, n_2) \in E$, $(\Upsilon(n_1), \Upsilon(n_2)) \in a^{\mathcal{I}}$.

If $\ell(n) = (S, H)$, *then an element d of* $\Delta^{\mathcal{I}}$ *is contained in the extension* $n^{\mathcal{I}}$
of n if, and only if,

1. *for all* $B \in S$, $d \in B^{\mathcal{I}}$; *and*
2. *for all* $(r, m, M, \mathcal{G}') \in H$,
   a) *there are between m and M elements d' of the domain with* $(d, d') \in r^{\mathcal{I}}$; *and*
   b) $d' \in \mathcal{G}'^{\mathcal{I}}$ *for all d' with* $(d, d') \in r^{\mathcal{I}}$.

Cohen and Hirsh [CH94a] defined the semantics of description graphs in a different way avoiding to introduce a total function Υ. However, the problem with their definition is that it is only well-defined for acyclic graphs, which, for example, excludes same-as equalities of the form $\varepsilon \downarrow \mathsf{spouse} \circ \mathsf{spouse}$.

Having defined the semantics of description graphs, subsumption and equivalence between description graphs (e.g., $\mathcal{H} \sqsubseteq \mathcal{G}$) as well as concept descriptions and description graphs (e.g., $C \sqsubseteq \mathcal{G}$) is defined in the obvious way.

Translating Concept Descriptions into Description Graphs. Following [BPS94], $\mathcal{ALNS}$-concept descriptions are turned into description graphs by a recursive process. In this process, nodes and description graphs are often merged.

Definition 4.1.3. *The* merge *of two nodes* n_1, n_2 *is a new node* $n = n_1 \oplus n_2$ *with* $n.Atoms := n_1.Atoms \cup n_2.Atoms$ *and* $n.REdges := n_1.REdges \cup n_2.REdges$.

If $\mathcal{G}_1 = (N_1, E_1, n_1, \ell_1)$ *and* $\mathcal{G}_2 = (N_2, E_2, n_2, \ell_2)$ *are two description graphs with disjoint recursive sets of nodes, then the merge of* $\mathcal{G}_1$ *and* $\mathcal{G}_2$, $\mathcal{G} := \mathcal{G}_1 \oplus \mathcal{G}_2 = (N, E, n_0, \ell)$, *is defined as follows:*

1. $n_0 := n_1 \oplus n_2$ *(where, w.l.o.g.,* n_0 *is not contained in* $N_1 \cup N_2$*);*
2. $N := (N_1 \cup N_2 \cup \{n_0\}) \setminus \{n_1, n_2\}$;
3. $E := (E_1 \cup E_2)[n_1/n_0, n_2/n_0]$, *i.e.,* E *is the union of* E_1 *and* E_2 *where every occurrence of* n_1, n_2 *is substituted by* n_0;
4. $\ell(n) := \ell_1(n)$ *for all* $n \in N_1 \setminus \{n_1\}$; $\ell(n) := \ell_2(n)$ *for all* $n \in N_2 \setminus \{n_2\}$; *and* $\ell(n_0)$ *is defined by the label obtained from merging* n_1 *and* n_2.

Now, an $\mathcal{ALNS}$-concept description C can be turned into its *corresponding description graph* $\mathcal{G}(C)$ by the following translation rules.

1. $\top$ is turned into a description graph with one node n_0 and no a-edges. Both the set of atoms and r-edges of n_0 is empty.
2. A (negated) concept name (or the bottom-concept) is turned into a description graph with one node and no a-edges. The atoms of the node contain only the (negated) concept name (or the bottom-concept) and the node has no r-edges.
3. A description of the form $(\geq k\, r)$ is turned into a description graph with one node and no a-edges. The set of atoms of the node is empty and the node has a single r-edge $(r, k, \infty, \mathcal{G}(\top))$ where $\mathcal{G}(\top)$ is specified by the first translation rule.
4. A description of the form $(\leq k\, r)$ is turned into a description graph with one node and no a-edges. The set of atoms of the node is empty and the node has a single r-edge $(r, 0, k, \mathcal{G}(\top))$.
5. A description of the form $a_1 \cdots a_k \downarrow b_1 \cdots b_l$ is turned into a graph with pairwise distinct nodes $n_1, \ldots, n_{k-1}, m_1, \ldots, m_{l-1}$, the root $m_0 := n_0$, and an additional node $n_k := m_l := n$; the set of a-edges consists of

(n_0, a_1, n_1), (n_1, a_2, n_2), ..., (n_{k-1}, a_k, n_k) and (m_0, b_1, m_1), (m_1, b_2, m_2), ..., (m_{l-1}, b_l, m_l), i.e., two disjoint paths which coincide on their starting point, n_0, and their final point, n. (Note that for $k = 0$ the first path is the empty path from n_0 to n_0 and for $l = 0$ the second path is the empty path from n_0 to n_0.) The set of atoms and r-edges of the nodes are empty.

6. A description of the form $\forall r.C$, where r is a role, is turned into a description graph with one node and no a-edges. The set of atoms of the node is empty and the node has a single r-edge $(r, 0, \infty, \mathcal{G}(C))$.

7. A description of the form $\forall a.C$, where a is an attribute, is turned into a description graph with one node and no a-edges. The set of atoms of the node is empty and the node has a single r-edge $(a, 0, 1, \mathcal{G}(C))$.[2]

8. To turn a description of the form $C \sqcap D$ into a description graph, construct $\mathcal{G}(C)$ and $\mathcal{G}(D)$ and merge them.

Figure 4.1 actually shows the description graph built in this way from the concept Lemon of our example. It can easily be verified that the translation is correct in the following sense:

Theorem 4.1.1. *A concept description C and its corresponding description graph $\mathcal{G}(C)$ are equivalent, i.e., $C^{\mathcal{I}} = \mathcal{G}(C)^{\mathcal{I}}$ for every interpretation $\mathcal{I}$.*

The main difficulty in the proof of this theorem is in showing that merging two description graphs corresponds to the conjunction of concept descriptions.

Lemma 4.1.1. *For all interpretations $\mathcal{I}$, if n_1 and n_2 are nodes, then $(n_1 \oplus n_2)^{\mathcal{I}} = n_1^{\mathcal{I}} \cap n_2^{\mathcal{I}}$; if $\mathcal{G}_1$ and $\mathcal{G}_2$ are description graphs, then $(\mathcal{G}_1 \oplus \mathcal{G}_2)^{\mathcal{I}} = \mathcal{G}_1^{\mathcal{I}} \cap \mathcal{G}_2^{\mathcal{I}}$.*

The proofs of the theorem and the lemma can be found in [BPS94, KB99].

Translating Description Graphs to Concept Descriptions. Although the characterization of subsumption does not require translating description graphs back to concept descriptions, this translation is presented here already to show that concept descriptions and description graphs are equivalent representations of $\mathcal{ALNS}$-concept descriptions. In subsequent chapters, we will then in fact need to turn graphs into concept descriptions.

A description graph $\mathcal{G}$ is turned into a concept description in a rather straightforward recursive way. The main idea of the translation stems from Cohen and Hirsh [CH94a], who employed spanning trees to translate same-as equalities. A *spanning tree* of a graph is a tree rooted at the same node as the graph and containing all nodes of the graph. In particular, it coincides with the graph except that some a-edges are removed. One possible spanning tree T for $\mathcal{G}$ in Figure 4.1 is obtained by removing the a-edge labeled madeBy whose origin is the root of $\mathcal{G}$.

---

[2] In [BPS94], the concept description $\forall a.C$ is turned into an a-edge. However, since we are dealing with partial attributes, value restrictions must be turned into r-edges in order to guarantee Υ (see Definition 4.1.2) being a total function.

Now, let $\mathcal{G}$ be a description graph and let T be a spanning tree for $\mathcal{G}$. Then, the *corresponding concept description* $C_\mathcal{G}$ is obtained as a conjunction of the following descriptions:

1. $C_\mathcal{G}$ contains (i) a same-as equality $v \downarrow v$ for every leaf n of T, where v is the label of the rooted path in T to n, and (ii) a same-as equality $v_1 a \downarrow v_2$ for each a-edge $(n_1, a, n_2) \in \mathcal{G}.Edges$ not contained in T where v_i is the label of the rooted path to n_i in T, $i = 1, 2$;
2. for every node n in T, $C_\mathcal{G}$ contains a value restriction $\forall v.C_n$, where v is the label of the rooted path to n in T, and C_n denotes the translation of the label of n, i.e., C_n is a conjunction obtained as follows:
   - every element in the atoms of n is a conjunct in C_n;
   - for every r-edge $(r, m, M, \mathcal{G}')$ of n, C_n contains (a) the number restrictions $(\geq m\ r)$ and $(\leq M\ r)$ (in case r is a role and $M \neq \infty$) and (b) the value restriction $\forall r.C_{\mathcal{G}'}$, where $C_{\mathcal{G}'}$ is the recursively defined translation of $\mathcal{G}'$.

   In case the set of atoms and r-edges of n is empty, define $C_n := \top$.

Referring to the graph $\mathcal{G} := \mathcal{G}(\mathsf{Lemon})$ in Figure 4.1, $C_\mathcal{G}$ contains the same-as equalities model ∘ madeBy $\downarrow$ model ∘ madeBy and madeBy $\downarrow$ model ∘ madeBy. Furthermore, if n_0 denotes the root of $\mathcal{G}$, $C_\mathcal{G}$ contains the value restrictions $\forall \varepsilon.C_{n_0}$, $\forall$model.$\top$, and $\forall$model madeBy.$\top$, where C_{n_0} corresponds to Lemon as defined before when removing the same-as equality. Note that, although in this case the same-as equality model ∘ madeBy $\downarrow$ model ∘ madeBy is not needed, in general one cannot dispense with these kinds of equalities, as illustrated by the following example: Without 1., (i) in the translation above, the description graph $\mathcal{G}(a \downarrow a)$ would be turned into the description $\top$, which is not equivalent to $a \downarrow a$ since the same-as equality requires instances of $a \downarrow a$ to be defined on a.

Lemma 4.1.2. *[KB99] Every description graph $\mathcal{G}$ is equivalent to its translation $C_\mathcal{G}$, i.e., for all interpretations $\mathcal{I}$: $\mathcal{G}^\mathcal{I} = C_\mathcal{G}{}^\mathcal{I}$.*

Normalizing Description Graphs. In the following, we will occasionally refer to "*marking a node incoherent*", which means that all r-edges of this node are removed and the set of atoms is set to $\{\bot\}$. "*Marking a description graph as incoherent*" means that the description graph is replaced by the graph $\mathcal{G}(\bot)$, i.e., the graph consisting only of one node with $\{\bot\}$ as its atom set and no r-edges.

One important property of normalized description graphs is that they are deterministic, i.e., for every role (attribute) every node has at most one outgoing edge (a-edge or r-edge) labeled with this role (attribute). Therefore, to turn a description graph into a normalized graph, we need to merge a-edges and r-edges as well as "lift" r-edges to a-edges.

To *merge two a-edges* (n, a, n_1) and (n, a, n_2) in a description graph $\mathcal{G}$, replace them with a single new edge (n, a, n') where n' is the result of merging n_1 and n_2. In addition, replace n_1 and n_2 by n' in all other a-edges of $\mathcal{G}$.

In order to *merge two r-edges* $(r, m_1, M_1, \mathcal{G}_1)$, $(r, m_2, M_2, \mathcal{G}_2)$ replace them by the new r-edge $(r, max(m_1, m_2), min(M_1, M_2), \mathcal{G}_1 \oplus \mathcal{G}_2)$.

To *lift up* an r-edge $(a, m, M, \mathcal{G}')$ of a node n in a concept graph $\mathcal{G}$ with an a-edge (n, a, n_1), remove it from $n.REdges$, and augment $\mathcal{G}$ by adding $\mathcal{G}'.Nodes$ to $\mathcal{G}.Nodes$, $\mathcal{G}'.Edges$ to $\mathcal{G}.Edges$, as well as adding $(n, a, \mathcal{G}'.Root)$ to $\mathcal{G}.Edges$. A *precondition* for applying this transformation is that $M = 1$, or $M = 0$ and $\mathcal{G}'$ corresponds to the graph $\mathcal{G}(\bot)$. The reason for this precondition is that if an r-edge of the form $(a, 0, 0, \mathcal{G}_a)$ is lifted without $\mathcal{G}_a$ being unsatisfiable, the fact that no a-successors are allowed is lost otherwise. Normalization rule 5 (see below) will guarantee that this precondition can always be satisfied.

A description graph $\mathcal{G}$ is transformed into *normal form* by exhaustively applying the following *normalization rules*. A graph is called *normalized* if none of these rules can be applied.

1. If some node in $\mathcal{G}$ is marked incoherent, mark the description graph as incoherent. (*Reason: Even if the node is not a root, attributes corresponding to a-edges must always have a value (since they participate in same-as equalities), and this value cannot belong to the empty set.*)
2. If some node has $\bot$, or a concept name and its negation in its atoms, mark the node incoherent. (*Reason:* $\bot \sqcap E \equiv A \sqcap \neg A \sqcap F \equiv \bot$.)
3. If some r-edge in a node has its min greater than its max, mark the node incoherent. (*Reason:* $(\geq 2\, r) \sqcap (\leq 1\, r) \equiv \bot$)
4. If some r-edge in a node has its restriction graph marked incoherent, change its max to 0. (*Reason:* $(\leq 0\, r) \equiv \forall r.\bot$.)
5. If some r-edge in a node has a max of 0, mark its restriction graph as incoherent. (*Reason: See the previous case.*)
6. If some r-edge is of the form $(r, 0, \infty, \mathcal{G}')$ where $\mathcal{G}'$ only contains one node with empty set of atoms and no r-edges, then remove this r-edge. (*Reason:* $\forall r.\top \equiv \top$.)
7. If some node has two r-edges labeled with the same role, merge the two edges, as described above. (*Reason:* $\forall r.C \sqcap \forall r.D \equiv \forall r.(C \sqcap D)$.)
8. If some description graph has two a-edges from the same node labeled with the same attribute, merge the two edges, as described above. (*Reason: See the previous case.*)
9. If some node in a graph has both an a-edge and an r-edge for the same attribute, then "lift up the r-edge" if the precondition is satisfied (see above). (*Reason: The value restrictions imposed on attributes that participate in same-as equalities must be made explicit and gathered at one place similar to the previous to cases.*)

One needs to show that applying the normalization rules to $\mathcal{G}$ does not change the semantics of $\mathcal{G}$. The main difficulty is in showing that the merging processes and the lifting preserve the semantics. The proofs of the following lemmas are routine.

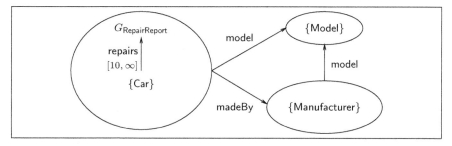

Fig. 4.2. The normal form $\mathcal{G}_{\text{Lemon}}$ of $\mathcal{G}(\text{Lemon})$, where the left-lost node is the root of $\mathcal{G}_{\text{Lemon}}$.

Lemma 4.1.3. *Let $\mathcal{G} = (N, E, n_0, \ell)$ be a description graph with two mergeable a-edges and let $\mathcal{G}' = (N', E', n', \ell')$ be the result of merging these two a-edges. Then, $\mathcal{G} \equiv \mathcal{G}'$.*

Lemma 4.1.4. *Let n be a node with two mergeable r-edges and let n' be the node with these edges merged. Then, $n^\mathcal{I} = n'^\mathcal{I}$ for every interpretation $\mathcal{I}$.*

Lemma 4.1.5. *Let $\mathcal{G} = (N, E, n_0, \ell)$ be a description graph with node n and a-edge (n, a, n''). Suppose n has an associated r-edge $(a, m, M, \mathcal{G}_a)$. Provided that the precondition for lifting r-edges is satisfied and that $\mathcal{G}' = (N', E', n', \ell')$ is the result of this transformation, then $\mathcal{G} \equiv \mathcal{G}'$.*

Having dealt with the issue of merging and lifting, it is now easy to verify that normalization does not affect the meaning of description graphs.

Theorem 4.1.2. *If $\mathcal{G}$ is a description graph and $\mathcal{G}'$ is the corresponding normalized description graph, then $\mathcal{G} \equiv \mathcal{G}'$.*

Given an $\mathcal{ALNS}$-concept description C, we refer to the *normal form of $\mathcal{G}(C)$* by $\mathcal{G}_C$. The normal form $\mathcal{G}_{\text{Lemon}}$ of the graph $\mathcal{G}(\text{Lemon})$ depicted in Figure 4.1 is given in Figure 4.2. It is obtained by lifting up the r-edge on model and madeBy, and merging the resulting a-edges with the already existing ones.

The Characterization of Subsumption. Subsumption between $\mathcal{ALNS}$-concept descriptions can now be described in terms of a recursive comparison between the potential subsumer and the normalized description graph of the subsumee along the syntactic structure of the subsumer. It turns out that it is not necessary to translate the subsumer into a normalized description graph. In [KB99], a similar characterization has been proved for arbitrary CLASSIC-concept descriptions.

Theorem 4.1.3. *Let C and D be $\mathcal{ALNS}$-concept descriptions and $\mathcal{G}_C = (N, E, n_0, \ell)$ be the normalized description graph of C. Then, $C \sqsubseteq D$ if, and only if, one of the following conditions hold:*

1. *The description graph $\mathcal{G}_C$ is marked incoherent.*
2. $D = \top$.
3. *D is a (negated) concept name or $\perp$ and it is contained in the atoms of n_0.*
4. *D is $(\geq k\, r)$ and i) some r-edge of n_0 has r as its role, and min greater than or equal to k; or ii) $k = 0$.*
5. *D is $(\leq k\, r)$ and some r-edge of n_0 has r as its role, and max less than or equal to k.*
6. *D is $a_1 \cdots a_k \downarrow b_1 \cdots b_l$, and there are two rooted paths labeled $a_1 \cdots a_k$ and $b_1 \cdots b_l$ in $\mathcal{G}_C$ ending at the same node.*
7. *D is $\forall r.C$, for a role r, and either (i) some r-edge of n_0 has r as its role and $\mathcal{G}'$ as its restriction graph with $\mathcal{G}' \sqsubseteq C$; or (ii) $\top \sqsubseteq C$ (Reason: $\forall r.\top \equiv \top$.)*
8. *D is $\forall a.C$, for an attribute a, and (i) some a-edge of $\mathcal{G}_C$ is of the form (n_0, a, n'), and $(N, E, n', \ell) \sqsubseteq C$; or (ii) some r-edge of n_0 has a as its attribute and $\mathcal{G}'$ as its restriction graph with $\mathcal{G}' \sqsubseteq C$; or (iii) $\top \sqsubseteq C$.*
9. *D is $E \sqcap F$ and both $\mathcal{G}_C \sqsubseteq E$ and $\mathcal{G}_C \sqsubseteq F$.*

The proof of Theorem 4.1.3 presented in [KB99] reveals that, for the if direction, description graphs need not be normalized.

Remark 4.1.1. Let $\mathcal{G}$ be some (not necessarily normalized description graph) and let D be an $\mathcal{ALNS}$-concept description. Then, if the conditions in Theorem 4.1.3 are satisfied, it follows that $\mathcal{G} \sqsubseteq D$.

In order to derive a recursive subsumption algorithm from Theorem 4.1.3 it is important to observe the following simple fact.

Lemma 4.1.6. *All nested description graphs of a normalized description graph are in normal form.*

Now, a recursive decision algorithm can simply check the conditions stipulated in the Theorem 4.1.3. In particular, conditions of the form $\mathcal{G}' \sqsubseteq C$ where $\mathcal{G}'$ is a nested graph of $\mathcal{G}$ can be tested recursively since $\mathcal{G}'$ is normalized and smaller than $\mathcal{G}$.

Similar to the proof in [BPS94], one can show that the normalized description graph $\mathcal{G}_C$ of C can be constructed in time polynomial in the size of C. Moreover, the conditions in Theorem 4.1.3 can be checked by a polynomial time algorithm. As a result, we obtain the following complexity result for subsumption.

Corollary 4.1.1. *For $\mathcal{ALNS}$-concept descriptions, deciding subsumption is a polynomial time problem.*

Characterizing Subsumption by Homomorphisms. Theorem 4.1.3 can also be phrased in terms of homomorphism between description graphs. We will first state this kind of characterization for the sublanguage $\mathcal{ALN}$ of $\mathcal{ALNS}$ and then generalize the characterization to the full language. We choose this stepwise presentation not only for didactic reasons, but also because the characterization for $\mathcal{ALN}$ is needed later on.

Given an $\mathcal{ALN}$-concept description C, the corresponding description graph $\mathcal{G}(C)$ consists only of one node n without any a-edges. However, the node may have a non-empty set of atoms as well as a set of r-edges. The restriction graphs of the r-edges are again graphs corresponding to $\mathcal{ALN}$-concept descriptions, i.e., they only consist of one node without a-edges. Thus, the inner structure of n can be viewed as a tree, where the root, say n', of the tree is labeled with the atoms of n. The r-edges of n correspond to outgoing edges of n' labeled with a role name as well as min, m, and max, M. They lead to the root of trees that correspond to the restriction graphs of the r-edges. In the following, these so-called $\mathcal{ALN}$-description trees are formally defined. Obviously, there is a 1-1 corresponds between $\mathcal{ALN}$-description trees and those description graphs that come from $\mathcal{ALN}$-concept descriptions.

Definition 4.1.4. An $\mathcal{ALN}$-description tree *is a tree of the form* $\mathcal{G} = (N, E, n_0, \ell)$ *where*

- *N is a finite set of* nodes *of $\mathcal{G}$;*
- *E is a finite set of* r-edges *of the form (n, r, m, M, n') with $n, n' \in N$, m a non-negative integer, and M a non-negative integer or ∞;*
- *n_0 is the* root *of $\mathcal{G}$; and*
- *ℓ is a* labeling function *mapping the nodes in N to finite sets containing $\bot$ or (negated) concept names.*

Building upon the 1-1 correspondence between $\mathcal{ALN}$-description trees and description graphs obtained from $\mathcal{ALN}$-concept descriptions, $\mathcal{ALN}$-description trees are equipped with a formal semantics analogously to description graphs. Moreover, every $\mathcal{ALN}$-concept description C can be turned into an equivalent $\mathcal{ALN}$-concept description tree, which by abuse of notation is also denoted $\mathcal{G}(C)$. (It will always be clear from the context whether $\mathcal{G}(C)$ denotes a graph or a tree.) Conversely, every $\mathcal{ALN}$-description tree $\mathcal{G}$ can be translated into an equivalent $\mathcal{ALN}$-concept description $C_\mathcal{G}$. Finally, the normalization rules carry over to $\mathcal{ALN}$-description trees in the obvious way. As before, we denote the normalized $\mathcal{ALN}$-description tree of $\mathcal{G}(C)$ by $\mathcal{G}_C$.

Homomorphisms between $\mathcal{ALN}$-description trees are defined in a straightforward manner, except for the fact that, if a node n is mapped onto an incoherent node, i.e., a node containing $\bot$, then all successors of n can also be mapped onto this node. This way of defining homomorphism takes into account that $\bot$ is subsumed by every concept description.

Definition 4.1.5. A mapping $\varphi : N_H \to N_G$ from an $\mathcal{ALN}$-description tree $\mathcal{H} = (N_H, E_H, n_H, \ell_H)$ into an $\mathcal{ALN}$-description tree $\mathcal{G} = (N_G, E_G, n_G, \ell_G)$ is called homomorphism if, and only if, the following conditions are satisfied:

1. $\varphi(n_H) = n_G$;
2. for all $n \in N_H$ either $\ell_H(n) \subseteq \ell_G(\varphi(n))$ or $\bot \in \ell_G(\varphi(n))$;

3. *for all r-edges* $(n, r, m, M, n') \in E_H$, *either i)* $\varphi(n') = \varphi(n)$ *and* $\bot \in \ell_G(\varphi(n))$ *or ii) there exists an r-edges* $(\varphi(n), r, m', M', \varphi(n')) \in E_G$ *with* $m' \geq m$ *and* $M' \leq M$.

A homomorphism φ from $\mathcal{H}$ into $\mathcal{G}$ is called *injective* if φ is an injective mapping, i.e., $\varphi(n) = \varphi(n')$ implies $n = n'$; φ is *surjective* if, for every node n in $\mathcal{G}$, there exists a node n' in $\mathcal{H}$ with $\varphi(n') = n$. Description trees $\mathcal{G}, \mathcal{H}$ are called *isomorphic* ($\mathcal{G} \cong \mathcal{H}$ for short) if there exists an isomorphism between the trees. Intuitively, this means that the trees coincide up to renaming of nodes. Formally, an isomorphism is defined as follows:

Definition 4.1.6. *A mapping* $\varphi : N_H \to N_G$ *from an* $\mathcal{ALN}$-*description tree* $\mathcal{H} = (N_H, E_H, n_H, \ell_H)$ *into an* $\mathcal{ALN}$-*description tree* $\mathcal{G} = (N_G, E_G, n_G, \ell_G)$ *is called* isomorphism *if, and only if, the following conditions are satisfied:*

1. φ *is a bijective mapping, i.e., injective and surjective.*
2. $\varphi(n_H) = n_G$.
3. *for all* $n \in N_H$, $\ell_H(n) = \ell_G(\varphi(n))$.
4. *for all r-edges* $(n, r, m, M, n') \in E_H$, $(\varphi(n), r, m, M, \varphi(n')) \in E_G$.

An equivalent way of defining an isomorphism φ from $\mathcal{H}$ onto $\mathcal{G}$ is to require a) φ to be an bijective homomorphism from $\mathcal{H}$ to $\mathcal{G}$ and b) the inverse mapping φ^{-1} to be an homomorphism from $\mathcal{G}$ into $\mathcal{H}$. (Note that φ^{-1} must be bijective if φ is.) Nevertheless, Definition 4.1.6 makes the conditions imposed on isomorphisms more explicit, which is the reason why we have chosen to specify isomorphisms in this way.

Recall that we aim at characterizing subsumption $C \sqsubseteq D$ between $\mathcal{ALN}$-concept descriptions C, D in terms of homomorphisms between $\mathcal{ALN}$-description trees of C and D. To this end, let us first take a look at the characterization provided by Theorem 4.1.3. Because of the 1-1 correspondence between $\mathcal{ALN}$-description trees and description graphs that stem from $\mathcal{ALN}$-concept descriptions, we may view $\mathcal{G}_C$ as normalized $\mathcal{ALN}$-description tree. Roughly speaking, the conditions stated in the theorem can be interpreted as recursive algorithm checking whether the tree $\mathcal{G}(D)$, which reflects the syntactic structure of D, can be embedded into $\mathcal{G}_C$. Thus, at first sight one might be tempted to think that for $\mathcal{ALN}$-concept descriptions C, D the following can be proved: $C \sqsubseteq D$ iff there exists a homomorphism from $\mathcal{G}(D)$ into $\mathcal{G}_C$. A closer look, however, reveals that there does not exist a homomorphism from $\mathcal{G}(\forall r.\top)$ or $\mathcal{G}(\geq 0\, r)$ into $\mathcal{G}_\top$, even though $\forall r.\top \equiv (\geq 0\, r) \equiv \top$. In fact, this is taken care of in the theorem (see condition 8., iii) and 4.,ii)). In case of homomorphism, this problem can be solved by $\top$-normalizing $\mathcal{G}(D)$.

An $\mathcal{ALN}$-description tree is called $\top$-*normalized* if the normalization rule 6. on page 80 cannot be applied.[3] Obviously, every $\mathcal{ALN}$-description tree can

---

[3] Of course, one needs to translate this rule to description trees meaning that the tree does not have an edge of the form $(n, r, 0, \infty, n')$, where n' is labeled with the empty set and does not have any outgoing edge.

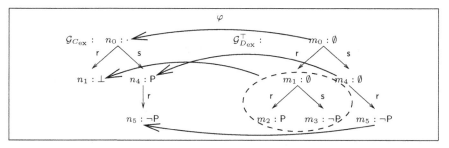

Fig. 4.3. A homomorphism from $\mathcal{G}_{D_{\mathrm{ex}}}^{\top}$ into $\mathcal{G}_{C_{\mathrm{ex}}}$, where the number restrictions $[0, \infty]$ usually attached to the edges are omitted.

be turned into $\top$-*normal form* in time linear in the size of the tree. For an $\mathcal{ALN}$-description tree $\mathcal{G}(D)$ we refer to its $\top$-normal form by $\mathcal{G}_D^{\top}$.

Now, using Theorem 4.1.3 the following characterization of subsumption can easily be proved by structural induction on D.

Corollary 4.1.2. *Let C and D be $\mathcal{ALN}$-concept descriptions. Then, $C \sqsubseteq D$ if, and only if, there exists a homomorphism from $\mathcal{G}_D^{\top}$ into $\mathcal{G}_C$.*

Since $\mathcal{G}_C$ is deterministic, i.e., for every node n and every role name r, n has at most one outgoing r-edge labeled r, there exists at most one homomorphism from $\mathcal{G}_D^{\top}$ into $\mathcal{G}_C$.

Analogously to Remark 4.1.1, we note that if there exists a homomorphism from $\mathcal{G}$ into $\mathcal{H}$, then $\mathcal{H} \sqsubseteq \mathcal{G}$. In particular, the if direction of Corollary 4.1.2 does not require the trees to be normalized.

In order to illustrate Corollary 4.1.2, consider the following $\mathcal{ALN}$-concept descriptions:

$$C_{\mathrm{ex}} := \forall r.((\geq 2\, r) \sqcap (\leq 1\, r)) \sqcap \forall s.(P \sqcap \forall r.\neg P),$$
$$D_{\mathrm{ex}} := \forall r.(\forall r.P \sqcap \forall s.\neg P) \sqcap \sqcap \forall s.\forall r.\neg P.$$

In Figure 4.3, a homomorphism from $\mathcal{G}_{D_{\mathrm{ex}}}^{\top}$ into $\mathcal{G}_{C_{\mathrm{ex}}}$ is depicted. According to Corollary 4.1.2, this implies $C_{\mathrm{ex}} \sqsubseteq D_{\mathrm{ex}}$. Observe that there does not exist a homomorphism from $\mathcal{G}(D_{\mathrm{ex}})$ into $\mathcal{G}(C_{\mathrm{ex}})$ since the unsatisfiable subexpression in C is not made explicit in $\mathcal{G}(C_{\mathrm{ex}})$. This shows that, for the only-if direction of the corollary, the description trees in fact need to be normalized.

Let us now generalize Corollary 4.1.2 to $\mathcal{ALNS}$-concept descriptions. Recall that the recursive set of nodes $N_{\mathcal{G}}$ of an $\mathcal{ALNS}$-descriptions graph $\mathcal{G}$ contains all nodes of $\mathcal{G}$ and all nodes of the nested graphs in $\mathcal{G}$. The definition of homomorphisms between trees carries over to description graphs in a rather straightforward way.

Definition 4.1.7. *Let $\mathcal{H} = (N_H, E_H, n_H, \ell_H)$, $\mathcal{G} = (N_G, E_G, n_G, \ell_G)$ be two $\mathcal{ALNS}$-description graphs. Then, a mapping $\varphi : N_H \to N_{\mathcal{G}}$ is called homomorphism from $\mathcal{H}$ into $\mathcal{G}$ if, and only if, i) the atoms of n_G contain $\bot$ and $\varphi(n) = n_G$ for every $n \in N_H$; or ii) the following conditions are satisfied:*

1. $\varphi(n_H) = n_G$;
2. for all a-edges $(n, a, n') \in E_H$, $(\varphi(n), a, \varphi(n')) \in E_G$;
3. for all $n \in N_H$: i) $n.Atoms \subseteq \varphi(n).Atoms$ and ii) for all r-edges $(r, m, M, \mathcal{H}') \in n.REdges$
   a) there exists an r-edge $(r, m', M', \mathcal{G}') \in \varphi(n).REdges$ with $m' \geq m$, $M' \leq M$, and φ restricted to $N_{\mathcal{H}'}$ is a homomorphism from $\mathcal{H}'$ into $\mathcal{G}'$; or
   b) there exists an a-edge $(\varphi(n), r, \varphi(\mathcal{H}'.Root)) \in E_G$ such that φ restricted to $N_{\mathcal{H}'}$ is a homomorphism from $\mathcal{H}'$ into the description graph $(N_G, E_G, \varphi(\mathcal{H}'.Root), \ell_G)$.

Injective and surjective homomorphisms are defined just as for $\mathcal{ALN}$. Also, isomorphisms can be defined as bijective homomorphisms such that the inverse mapping is a homomorphism as well. The following definition makes the conditions isomorphisms must obey explicit.

Definition 4.1.8. Let $\mathcal{H} = (N_H, E_H, n_H, \ell_H)$, $\mathcal{G} = (N_G, E_G, n_G, \ell_G)$ be two $\mathcal{ALNS}$-description graphs. Then, a mapping $\varphi : N_H \to N_G$ is called isomorphism from $\mathcal{H}$ into $\mathcal{G}$ if, and only if, the following conditions are satisfied:

1. Restricted on $\mathcal{H}.Nodes$, φ is a bijective mapping from $\mathcal{H}.Nodes$ onto $\mathcal{G}.Nodes$;
2. $\varphi(n_H) = n_G$;
3. for all a-edges $(n, a, n') \in E_H$, $(\varphi(n), a, \varphi(n')) \in E_G$;
4. for all $n \in \mathcal{H}.Nodes$: $n.Atoms = \varphi(n).Atoms$; and
5. for every $n \in \mathcal{H}.Nodes$, there exists a bijective mapping α from $n.REdges$ onto $\varphi(n).REdges$ such that for all r-edges $(r, m, M, \mathcal{H}') \in n.REdges$:
   a) $\alpha(r, m, M, \mathcal{H}') = (r, m, M, \mathcal{G}') \in \varphi(n).REdges$; and
   b) φ restricted on $\mathcal{H}'$ is an isomorphism from $\mathcal{H}'$ onto $\mathcal{G}'$.

From the above definition it is easy to conclude that every isomorphism φ from $\mathcal{H}$ into $\mathcal{G}$ is a bijective mapping from $N_{\mathcal{H}}$ onto $N_{\mathcal{G}}$.

As usual, $\mathcal{ALNS}$-description graphs $\mathcal{G}$, $\mathcal{H}$ are called *isomorphic* ($\mathcal{G} \cong \mathcal{H}$ for short) if there exists an isomorphism between the trees. In particular, $\mathcal{G} \cong \mathcal{H}$ means that $\mathcal{G}$ and $\mathcal{H}$ coincide up to renaming of nodes.

Similar to $\mathcal{ALN}$, an $\mathcal{ALNS}$-description graph is called $\top$-*normalized* if the normalization rule 6. on page 80 cannot be applied. Also, for an $\mathcal{ALNS}$-description graph $\mathcal{G}(D)$, we denote its $\top$-normal form by $\mathcal{G}_D^\top$. Now, using Theorem 4.1.3 one can prove the following generalization of Corollary 4.1.2.

Corollary 4.1.3. Let C and D be $\mathcal{ALNS}$-concept description. Then, $C \sqsubseteq D$ if, and only if, there exists a homomorphism from $\mathcal{G}_D^\top$ into $\mathcal{G}_C$.

Again, the if direction of this statement does not require normalized graphs, and thus the existence of a homomorphism from $\mathcal{G}$ into $\mathcal{H}$ implies $\mathcal{H} \sqsubseteq \mathcal{G}$. Also, the proof of Corollary 4.1.3 does not make use of the fact that the graphs are derived from concept descriptions. The corollary can analogously be stated in terms of description graphs only:

Remark 4.1.2. Let $\mathcal{H}$ be a $\top$-normalized $\mathcal{ALNS}$-description graph and $\mathcal{G}$ be a normalized $\mathcal{ALNS}$-description graph. Then, $\mathcal{G} \sqsubseteq \mathcal{H}$ if, and only if, there exists a homomorphism from $\mathcal{H}$ into $\mathcal{G}$.

Building upon this remark, we now show that equivalent and normalized description graphs are isomorphic, i.e., normalized graphs are unique representatives of their equivalence class. This property of normalized graphs will prove useful in Section 6.1.1, where it is employed to establish a hardness result for matching in $\mathcal{ALNS}$.

Lemma 4.1.7. *Let $\mathcal{G}$ and $\mathcal{H}$ be normalized $\mathcal{ALNS}$-description graph. Then, $\mathcal{G} \equiv \mathcal{H}$ implies $\mathcal{G} \cong \mathcal{H}$.*

Proof. If $\mathcal{G} \equiv \mathcal{H} \equiv \bot$, we know $\mathcal{G} \cong \mathcal{H} \cong \mathcal{G}(\bot)$. Now assume that $\mathcal{G}$ and $\mathcal{H}$ are not unsatisfiable.

Since every normalized description graph is $\top$-normalized, Remark 4.1.2 together with $\mathcal{G} \equiv \mathcal{H}$ implies that there exists a homomorphism φ from $\mathcal{G}$ into $\mathcal{H}$ and a homomorphism ψ from $\mathcal{H}$ into $\mathcal{G}$.

Let $n \in \mathcal{G}.Nodes$, i.e., n is a node on the top-level of $\mathcal{G}$ rather than one in some nested graph of $\mathcal{G}$. We show that $\psi(\varphi(n)) = n$. Since $\mathcal{G}$ is connected, there exists a rooted path in $\mathcal{G}$ to n labeled w for some $w \in N_A^*$. By the definition of homomorphisms, there also exists a rooted path in $\mathcal{H}$ to $\varphi(n) \in \mathcal{H}.Nodes$ labeled w. Because $\mathcal{G}$ is normalized, every node in $\mathcal{G}$ has at most one outgoing a-edge for a given attribute. Thus, ψ must map $\varphi(n)$ onto n. Analogously, for every $n \in \mathcal{H}.Nodes$ it follows $\varphi(\psi(n)) = n$. Hence, when considering the restriction of φ (ψ) to $\mathcal{G}.Nodes$ ($\mathcal{H}.Nodes$), then φ (ψ) is a bijective mapping from $\mathcal{G}.Nodes$ onto $\mathcal{H}.Nodes$ (or vice versa). Thus, the first condition in Definition 4.1.8 is satisfied for φ (ψ). The following two conditions are satisfied since φ (ψ) is a homomorphism.

Using $\psi(\varphi(n)) = n$ and the fact the φ and ψ are homomorphisms, it follows that the atoms of n and $\varphi(n)$ coincide for every $n \in \mathcal{G}.Nodes$.

In order to show that $\mathcal{G}$ and $\mathcal{H}$ are isomorphic, it remains to show condition 5. of Definition 4.1.8. Let $(r, m, M, \mathcal{G}')$ be an r-edge of n. Assume that $\varphi(\mathcal{G}'.Root) \in \mathcal{H}.Nodes$. This means that r is an attribute and $(n, r, \psi(\varphi(\mathcal{G}'.Root))) \in \mathcal{G}.Edges$. But then, n has an outgoing r-edge and an a-edge both labeled with r, which contradicts the fact that $\mathcal{G}$ is normalized. Consequently, $\varphi(n)$ must contain an r-edge $(r, m', M', \mathcal{H}')$ such that φ is a homomorphism from $\mathcal{G}'$ into $\mathcal{H}'$. For the same reason, ψ is a homomorphism from $\mathcal{H}'$ into $\mathcal{G}'$. Thus, $\mathcal{G}' \equiv \mathcal{H}'$, and by induction we deduce that φ (ψ) restricted to $\mathcal{G}'$ ($\mathcal{H}'$) is a isomorphism from $\mathcal{G}'$ onto $\mathcal{H}'$ (or vice versa). Finally, the fact that φ is a homomorphism from $\mathcal{G}$ into $\mathcal{H}$ ensures $m \leq m'$ and $M \geq M'$. Conversely, since ψ is a homomorphism from $\mathcal{H}$ into $\mathcal{G}$ we can conclude $m' \leq m$ and $M' \geq M$. This shows that for every $n.Nodes$ there exists a mapping α from $n.REdges$ into $\varphi(n).REdges$ such that the conditions a) and b) in Definition 4.1.8 are satisfied. However, it remains to show that α is bijective. Because $\mathcal{G}$ is normalized it follows that $n.REdges$ has at most one outgoing r-edge for every role. For the same reason $\varphi(n).REdges$ contains at most one r-edge for every role. Therefore, α must be injective, i.e., for every r-edge in $n.REdges$ there exists a unique corresponding r-edge in $\varphi(n).REdges$. By symmetry, for every r-edge in $\varphi(n)$ there exists a corresponding r-edge in n. Thus, there exist an injective mapping β from $\varphi(n).REdges$ into $n.REdges$. Clearly, $\alpha = \beta^{-1}$ since the mappings are uniquely determined by the role names r-edges are labeled with. In particular, α is a bijection.

This shows that $\mathcal{G}$ and $\mathcal{H}$ are isomorphic.   □

As a direct consequence of this lemma, we can deduce the following corollary.

Corollary 4.1.4. *Let C and D be $\mathcal{ALNS}$-concept descriptions. Then, $C \equiv D$ implies $\mathcal{G}_C \cong \mathcal{G}_D$.*

4.1.2 A Description-Based Characterization of Subsumption

For $\mathcal{ALN}$-concept descriptions it is possible to characterize subsumption just based on the descriptions themselves without resorting to description trees. Such a characterization only requires the concept descriptions to be in $\forall$-normal form (see Definition 3.2.5).

In order to state the description-based characterization we need to introduce some notation. For a concept description C, $\forall r.E \in C$ means that $\forall r.E$ occurs on the top-level of C; $\bot, (\leq k\,r), (\geq k\,r), A \in C$ is interpreted analogously. Now, let us assume that C is in $\forall$-normal form. Then, by definition, for a role r, C contains at most one value restriction $\forall r.E$ on its top-level. We refer to E by $C.r$. More precisely, $C.r$ is defined as follows:

$$C.r := \begin{cases} \bot, & (\leq 0\,r) \in C; \\ E, & \text{if } \forall r.E \in C \text{ and } (\leq 0\,r) \notin C; \\ \top, & \text{otherwise.} \end{cases}$$

The reason $C.r$ is defined to be $\bot$ in case $(\leq 0r) \in C$ is that $(\leq 0r) \equiv \forall r.\bot$. The set $prim(C)$ contains the bottom-concept (if any) and all (negated) concept names on the top-level of C. Finally, we define $min_r(C)$ and $max_r(C)$ as follows: $min_r(C) := max\{k \mid (\geq k\,r) \in C\}$ where $min_r(C) := 0$ if C does not have an at-least restriction on its top-level;

$$max_r(C) := \begin{cases} 0, & \text{if } C \sqsubseteq \forall r.\bot; \\ \infty, & \text{if } (\leq k\,r) \notin C \text{ for all } k \text{ and } C \not\sqsubseteq \forall r.\bot; \\ min\{k \mid (\leq k\,r) \in C\}, & \text{otherwise.} \end{cases}$$

Note that $prim(\top) = \emptyset$, $\top.r = \top$, $min_r(\top) = 0$, and $max_r(\top) = \infty$. As a simple consequence of Corollary 4.1.2, the description-based characterization of subsumption can now be stated as follows.

Theorem 4.1.4. *Let C, D be two $\mathcal{ALN}$-concept descriptions in $\forall$-normal form. Then, $C \sqsubseteq D$ if, and only if, i) $C \equiv \bot$, or ii) the following conditions are satisfied:*

1. $prim(D) \subseteq prim(C)$; *and*
2. *for every* $r \in N_R$: $min_r(D) \leq min_r(C)$, $max_r(D) \geq max_r(C)$, *and* $C.r \sqsubseteq D.r$.

In this characterization, we can dispense with explicitly normalizing the potential subsumee, because i) unsatisfiability is tested explicitly and ii) $min_r(C)$ and $max_r(C)$ deal with the subsumption relationships between number restrictions. Note that in order to derive a structural subsumption algorithm from this theorem, one needs a subprocedure checking unsatisfiability. The theorem itself leaves open how such a procedure might look like. Nevertheless, due to Corollary 4.1.1 we know that this task can be carried out in polynomial time.

4.2 Subsumption in $\mathcal{ALN}^*$

In order to provide a characterization of subsumption for $\mathcal{ALN}^*$-concept descriptions, we first present the already mentioned correspondence between $\mathcal{ALN}^*$-concept descriptions and cyclic $\mathcal{ALN}$-concept descriptions. We then exploit the automata-theoretic characterization of subsumption for cyclic $\mathcal{ALN}$-concept descriptions proposed in [Küs98] to obtain an analogous characterization for $\mathcal{ALN}^*$. The first automata-theoretic characterizations have been proved by Baader [Baa96] for the small language $\mathcal{FL}_0$, both to gain a better understanding of the effects of the gfp-, lfp-, and descriptive semantics and to derive decision algorithms for subsumption. In [Küs98], these characterizations have been extended to the more expressive language $\mathcal{ALN}$. The characterization of subsumption in $\mathcal{ALN}^*$ will directly build on these results. As a by-product, we obtain an automata-theoretic characterization of subsumption for (acyclic) $\mathcal{ALN}$-concept descriptions. As shown in [BKM98b], there is a close relation between this automata-theoretic characterization and the graph-based one presented in Section 4.1. We will come back to this point at the end of the section.

The Correspondence Between $\mathcal{ALN}^*$- and Cyclic $\mathcal{ALN}$-Concept Descriptions. Recall that cyclic $\mathcal{ALN}$-concept descriptions are defined as tuples of the form $(A, \mathcal{T})$ where A is a defined concept name in the (possibly cyclic) $\mathcal{ALN}$-TBox $\mathcal{T}$. To state the correspondence between the two DLs, we need to turn TBoxes into semi-automata. These automata are then used to define regular languages. Finally, employing a characterization of the gfp-semantics of cyclic $\mathcal{ALN}$-TBoxes [Küs98], it turns out that these regular languages conform to those occurring in $\mathcal{ALN}^*$-concept descriptions.

As usual, if Σ is a (finite) alphabet, then Σ^* denotes the set of all finite words $w = a_1 \cdots a_n$ over Σ, where n is the length of w and $a_i \in \Sigma$ for all

$i = 1, \ldots, n$. The word of length zero is the empty word which we denote by ε.

Definition 4.2.1. *A semi-automaton $\mathcal{S}$ is a triple (Σ, Q, Δ), where Σ is a finite alphabet, Q is a finite set of states, and $\Delta \subseteq Q \times \Sigma^* \times Q$ is a finite set of word-transitions.*

Note that in a semi-automaton, word-transitions with words of length at least two can easily be eliminated by replacing each of these transitions by a sequence of new introduced transitions (labeled with letters) using new states. An automaton $\mathcal{S}$ is called *semi-automaton without word-transitions* in case $\Delta \subseteq Q \times (\Sigma \cup \{\varepsilon\}) \times Q$.

If p, q are states in $\mathcal{S}$ and w is a word over Σ, then a *path* in $\mathcal{S}$ from p to q labeled with w is a sequence $p_0 w_1 p_1 \cdots w_m p_m$ where $(p_{i-1}, w_i, p_i) \in \Delta$, $i = 1, \ldots, m$, $p_0 = p$, $p_m = q$, and $w = w_1 \cdots w_m$;

$$L_{\mathcal{S}}(p, q) := \{w \in \Sigma^* \mid \text{ there is a path from } p \text{ to } q \text{ in } \mathcal{S} \text{ labeled with } w\}$$

is a regular language containing all labels of paths from p to q in $\mathcal{S}$. Thus, $L_{\mathcal{S}}(p, q)$ is the regular language accepted by the *finite automaton* $(\Sigma, Q, \{p\}, \Delta, \{q\})$, where $\{p\}$ is the set of initial states and $\{q\}$ is the set of final states.[4]

In order to turn a TBox $\mathcal{T}_C$ of an $\mathcal{ALN}^*$-concept description $C = (A, \mathcal{T}_C)$ into its corresponding semi-automaton $\mathcal{S}_C$, we need to turn the defining concepts in $\mathcal{T}_C$ into a so-called $\mathcal{FL}_0$-normal form. Recall that, with $w = r_1 \cdots r_n$, $\forall w.F$ stands for the concept description $\forall r_1. \cdots. \forall r_n.F$, where $\forall \varepsilon.F := F$.

Definition 4.2.2. *An $\mathcal{ALN}$-concept description D is in $\mathcal{FL}_0$-normal form if it consists of a conjunction of $\mathcal{ALN}$-concept descriptions of the form $\forall w.F$, where F is the top or bottom concept, a (negated) concept name, or a number restriction. An $\mathcal{ALN}$-TBox is in $\mathcal{FL}_0$-normal form if every defining concept in the TBox is in $\mathcal{FL}_0$-normal form.*

Obviously, because the transformation $\forall r.(D \sqcap E) \longrightarrow \forall r.D \sqcap \forall r.E$ on $\mathcal{ALN}$-concept descriptions is equivalence preserving, every $\mathcal{ALN}$-concept description can be turned into its $\mathcal{FL}_0$-normal form (in linear time). In particular, every $\mathcal{ALN}$-TBox can easily be turned into $\mathcal{FL}_0$-normal form.

Definition 4.2.3. *Let $C = (A, \mathcal{T})$ be a cyclic $\mathcal{ALN}$-concept description with $\mathcal{T}$ in $\mathcal{FL}_0$-normal form. Then, define $\mathcal{S}_C := (N_R, Q, \Delta)$ to be the (nondeterministic) semi-automaton of C, where N_R is the set of role names in C; Q consists of $\top$, $\bot$, the set of defined names, the set of (negated) primitive concepts, and the number restrictions in $\mathcal{T}$; and each concept definition $B \doteq \forall w_1.F_1 \sqcap \cdots \forall w_m.F_k$ in $\mathcal{T}$ gives rise to m word-transitions, where the transition from B to F_i is labeled by the word w_i over N_R.*

---

[4] Usually, finite automata do not allow for word-transitions. Just as in the semi-automata case these transitions can however be eliminated. For a comprehensive introduction to finite automata and regular languages see, for example, [HU79].

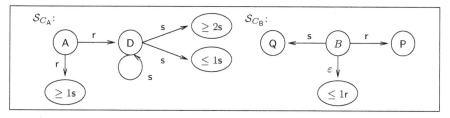

Fig. 4.4. The Automata Corresponding to C_A and C_B.

As an example, the TBoxes $\mathcal{T}_A$ and $\mathcal{T}_B$ defining the descriptions $C_A := (A, \mathcal{T}_A)$ and $C_B := (B, \mathcal{T}_B)$ with

$$\mathcal{T}_A : A \doteq \forall r.D \sqcap \forall r.(\geq 1\,s)$$
$$D \doteq \forall s.D \sqcap \forall s.(\geq 2\,s) \sqcap \forall s.(\leq 1\,s)$$
$$\mathcal{T}_B : B \doteq \forall \varepsilon.(\leq 1\,r) \sqcap \forall r.P \sqcap \forall s.Q$$

give rise to the automata depicted in Figure 4.4 where the states $\top$ and $\bot$ are omitted since they are not reachable from A and B, respectively.

In what follows, we fix a finite set $\mathcal{C}$ consisting of the top-concept, the bottom-concept, primitive concepts and there negation as well as number restrictions. A cyclic $\mathcal{ALN}$-concept description $C = (A, \mathcal{T})$ over $\mathcal{C}$ uses only (negated) primitive concepts and number restrictions that occur in $\mathcal{C}$. For such a concept description we define the regular language

$$L_C(F) := L_{\mathcal{S}_C}(A, F),$$

where $L_C(F) := \emptyset$ if F does not occur in $\mathcal{T}$. Referring to Figure 4.4, $L_{C_A}(\geq 2s)$ corresponds to the regular expression rs*s.

Based on these languages, one can characterize the semantics of cyclic $\mathcal{ALN}^*$-concept descriptions $C = (A, \mathcal{T})$. First recall that the semantics of C is uniquely determined by the interpretation of the primitive concepts and roles in $\mathcal{T}$ since such an interpretation is, by convention, always extended to the (unique) gfp-model of $\mathcal{T}$ and the resulting interpretation of A then determines the one of C. Therefore, we can take every interpretation $\mathcal{I}$ to interpret C since the meaning of defined names in $\mathcal{T}$ is always given by the gfp-model induced by $\mathcal{I}$ when restricted to primitive concepts and roles.

Theorem 4.2.1. *[Küs98] Let $C = (A, \mathcal{T})$ be a cyclic $\mathcal{ALN}$-concept description, let $\mathcal{I}$ be an interpretation, and let $d \in \Delta^{\mathcal{I}}$. Then, $d \in C^{\mathcal{I}}$ if, and only if, for all $F \in \mathcal{C}$: $w \in L_C(F)$ implies $d \in (\forall w.F)^{\mathcal{I}}$.*[5]

---

[5] Note that the language $L_C(\top)$ does not influence the semantics of C since $\forall w.\top \equiv \top$, thus, $d \in (\forall w.\top)^{\mathcal{I}}$ is always satisfied.

This theorem shows that the semantics of a concept C is determined by the regular languages $L_C(F)$. Thus, C is completely specified by its $\mathcal{FL}_0$-*normal form*:

$$D := \bigcap_{F \in \mathcal{C}} \forall L_C(F).F.$$

This representation of C is motivated by the following fact: Viewed as an $\mathcal{ALN}^*$-concept description it is equivalent to C, i.e., $C^{\mathcal{I}} = D^{\mathcal{I}}$ for every interpretation $\mathcal{I}$. This can easily be proved using Theorem 4.2.1 and the fact that according to the semantics of $\mathcal{ALN}^*$-concept descriptions, $D^{\mathcal{I}}$ equals

$$\bigcap_{F \in \mathcal{C}} \bigcap_{w \in L_C(F)} (\forall w.F)^{\mathcal{I}}.$$

The $\mathcal{FL}_0$-normal form shows that for every cyclic $\mathcal{ALN}$-concept description there exists an equivalent $\mathcal{ALN}^*$-concept description.

Conversely, every $\mathcal{ALN}^*$-concept description E can be mapped to an equivalent cyclic $\mathcal{ALN}$-concept description. To see this, we need to define the $\mathcal{FL}_0$-*normal form* of $\mathcal{ALN}^*$-concept descriptions. Roughly speaking, $\mathcal{ALN}^*$-concept descriptions are in $\mathcal{FL}_0$-normal form if they have the same form as D. More precisely, an $\mathcal{ALN}^*$-concept description E (over $\mathcal{C}$) is in $\mathcal{FL}_0$-*normal form* if i) every conjunct in E is of the form $\forall L.F$ (where L is a regular language over N_R and $F \in \mathcal{C}$), and ii) for every $F \in \mathcal{C}$ there exists exactly one such conjunct in E.

Every $\mathcal{ALN}^*$-concept description E can be turned in an equivalent $\mathcal{FL}_0$-normal form: First, exhaustively applying the (equivalence preserving) rule $\forall L.(E_1 \sqcap E_2) \longrightarrow \forall L.E_1 \sqcap \forall L.E_2$ turns E into a concept descriptions that satisfies condition i). Second, exhaustive application of the (equivalence preserving) rule $\forall L.F \sqcap \forall L'.F \longrightarrow \forall(L \cup L').F$ guarantees that for every $F \in \mathcal{C}$ there exists at most one value restriction of the form $\forall L.F$. Finally, conjoining the resulting concept description with $\forall \emptyset.F$ ($\equiv \top$) for all $F \in \mathcal{C}$ not occurring in E yields the desired $\mathcal{FL}_0$-normal form of E.

Now, given some $\mathcal{ALN}^*$-concept description E, let

$$E \equiv \bigcap_{F \in \mathcal{C}} \forall L_E(F).F$$

denote its $\mathcal{FL}_0$-normal form. Since the languages $L_E(F)$ are regular, one can obviously define a cyclic $\mathcal{ALN}$-concept description $C = (A, \mathcal{T})$ with $L_C(F) = L_E(F)$ for all $F \in \mathcal{C}$. Then, with the same argument as before, it follows that C and E are equivalent.

Summarizing, we have shown that there exists a 1-1 correspondence between the $\mathcal{FL}_0$-normal forms of $\mathcal{ALN}^*$-concept descriptions and the ones of cyclic $\mathcal{ALN}$-concept descriptions.

Proposition 4.2.1. *The set of $\mathcal{FL}_0$-normal forms of cyclic $\mathcal{ALN}$-concept descriptions and $\mathcal{ALN}^*$-concept descriptions coincides. Moreover, given a cyclic $\mathcal{ALN}$-concept description C and an $\mathcal{ALN}^*$-concept description E with* *the same $\mathcal{FL}_0$-normal form, i.e., $L_C(F) = L_E(F)$ for all $F \in \mathcal{C}$, then C and E are equivalent.*

This proposition implies that the expressive power of the two logics coincides. As an aside we note that this is no longer the case if cyclic $\mathcal{ALN}$-concept descriptions are interpreted by the lfp-semantics. While this semantics prohibits infinite role chains, they can be required by $\mathcal{ALN}^*$-concept descriptions. The following remark makes this more precise.

Remark 4.2.1. If, in Theorem 4.2.1, $\mathcal{I}$ is considered to be an *lfp-model* of $\mathcal{T}$, then $d \in C^{\mathcal{I}}$ requires, in addition to the conditions already stated in the theorem, that for every infinite path $A =: A_0 w_0 A_1 w_1 \cdots$ in $\mathcal{S}_C$, i.e., $(A_{i-1}, w_i, A_i) \in \Delta$ for every $i \geq 1$, and all $d =: d_0, d_1, \cdots \in \Delta^{\mathcal{I}}$ there exists an $i \geq 1$ with $(d_{i-1}, d_i) \notin w_i^{\mathcal{I}}$. ("Infinite role chains our prohibited.") The $\mathcal{ALN}^*$-concept description $\forall r^*.(\geq 1 r)$, however, requires such an infinite chain for all its instances. Thus, this concept cannot be expressed by cyclic $\mathcal{ALN}$-concept descriptions when interpreted by the lfp-semantics since it would be unsatisfiable.

Subsumption in $\mathcal{ALN}^*$. We now review the characterization of subsumption for cyclic $\mathcal{ALN}$-concept descriptions as proved in [Küs98]. Proposition 4.2.1 allows to directly transfer this result to $\mathcal{ALN}^*$-concept descriptions since the characterization for cyclic $\mathcal{ALN}$-concept description is exclusively based on $\mathcal{FL}_0$-normal forms. Besides the regular languages $L_C(\cdot)$, we need so-called value-restriction sets that encode all value-restrictions subsuming C.

Definition 4.2.4. *Let C be an $\mathcal{ALN}^*$-concept description and F be the top-, bottom-concept, a (negated) concept name, or a number restriction in C. Then, the set $V_C(F) := \{w \in N_R^* \mid C \sqsubseteq \forall w.F\}$ is called the* value-restriction set *of C for F.*

We can immediately conclude that $L_C(F) \subseteq V_C(F)$. However, the reverse inclusion does not hold in general (see below for an example). The characterization of subsumption is a simple consequence of the definition of value-restriction sets.

Theorem 4.2.2. *Let C, D be $\mathcal{ALN}^*$-concept descriptions. Then, $C \sqsubseteq D$ if, and only if, $L_D(F) \subseteq V_C(F)$ for the bottom-concept, all (negated) concept names, and number restrictions F in C and D.*[6]

Proof. Let us first assume that $L_D(F) \subseteq V_C(F)$ for all F. Given $d \in C^{\mathcal{I}}$ for an interpretation $\mathcal{I}$, we want to show $d \in D^{\mathcal{I}}$, i.e., $d \in (\forall w.F)^{\mathcal{I}}$ for every $w \in L_D(F)$. With $w \in L_D(F)$ it follows $w \in V_C(F)$. Thus, $C \sqsubseteq \forall w.F$. This implies $d \in (\forall w.F)^{\mathcal{I}}$.

We prove the only-if direction by contraposition and assume that there exists an F as well as a word $w \in L_D(F) \setminus V_C(F)$. Consequently, by definition

---

[6] Since $V_C(\top) = N_R^*$ the case $F = \top$ need not be considered.

of $V_C(F)$, there exists an interpretation $\mathcal{I}$ and an individual $d \in \Delta^{\mathcal{I}}$ with $d \in C^{\mathcal{I}}$ and $d \notin (\forall w.F)^{\mathcal{I}}$. But then, $d \notin D^{\mathcal{I}}$. This shows, $C \not\sqsubseteq D$.   □

We remark that instead of $L_D(F) \subseteq V_C(F)$ one can also require $V_D(F) \subseteq V_C(F)$.

Corollary 4.2.1. *Let C, D be $\mathcal{ALN}^*$-concept descriptions. Then, $C \sqsubseteq D$ if, and only if, $V_D(F) \subseteq V_C(F)$ for the bottom-concept, all (negated) concept names, and number restrictions F in C and D.*

Proof. Given $V_D(F) \subseteq V_C(F)$ it follows $L_D(F) \subseteq V_C(F)$ because $L_D(F) \subseteq V_D(F)$. Thus, with Theorem 4.2.3 we can conclude $C \sqsubseteq D$.

Conversely, if $C \sqsubseteq D$, then $D \sqsubseteq \forall w.F$ implies $C \sqsubseteq \forall w.F$. This means $V_D(F) \subseteq V_C(F)$.   □

From this corollary, we immediately obtain a characterization of equivalence, which will prove useful in Section 6.2.1.

Corollary 4.2.2. *Let C, D be $\mathcal{ALN}^*$-concept descriptions. Then, $C \equiv D$ if, and only if, $V_D(F) = V_C(F)$ for the bottom-concept, all (negated) concept names, and number restrictions F in C and D.*

In order to use the above theorem or the corollaries to decide subsumption or to solve non-standard inference problems, one needs to show that i) $V_C(F)$ is a regular language and ii) a finite automaton accepting $V_C(F)$ can effectively be computed. In the remainder of this section, we sketch how these (non-trivial) tasks have been accomplished in [Küs98].

We know that $L_C(F)$ is a subset of $V_C(F)$. The example depicted in Figure 4.4 (where the cyclic $\mathcal{ALN}$-concept descriptions can be viewed as $\mathcal{ALN}^*$-concept descriptions) illustrates that the reverse inclusion does not hold in general. It is easy to verify that $C_A \sqsubseteq \forall r.\bot$. But this implies $C_A \sqsubseteq \forall r.(\geq 2s)$, although, $r \notin L_{C_A}(\geq 2s)$. The problem is that $\forall w.\bot$ is subsumed by $\forall w.F$ for all F. Consequently, $V_C(F)$ also contains the set $V_C(\bot)$. In order to distinguish this value-restriction set from others, a new name is introduced.

Definition 4.2.5. *Let C be an $\mathcal{ALN}^*$-concept description. Then $E_C := V_C(\bot) = \{w \in N_R^* \mid C \sqsubseteq \forall w.\bot\}$ is called the set of C-excluding words.*

For the concept description C_A of Figure 4.4, E_{C_A} is the regular language $r\{r,s\}^*$ in case $N_R = \{r,s\}$. In fact, one can show that the sets E_C are always regular. To see this, we need one more notation.

Definition 4.2.6. *Let C be an $\mathcal{ALN}^*$-concept description, $w,v \in N_R^*$, $r_1, \ldots, r_m \in N_R$ with $m \geq 0$, and $w = vr_1 \cdots r_m$. Then, w is v-required by C iff for all i, $1 \leq i \leq m$, there exist positive integers m_i and at-least restrictions $(\geq m_i r_i)$ in C with $vr_1 \cdots r_{i-1} \in L_C(\geq m_i r_i)$ for all i, $1 \leq i \leq m$.*

Note that w may be the empty word and that m may be 0. Thus, the empty word ε is ε-required by any $\mathcal{ALN}^*$-concept description. The intuition underlying the notion of required words is captured in the next lemma.

Lemma 4.2.1. *Assume that $w = vr_1 \cdots r_m$ is v-required by C and that $\mathcal{I}$ is an interpretation with $d \in C^{\mathcal{I}}$ and $(d, e) \in v^{\mathcal{I}}$. Then, e has an $(r_1 \cdots r_m)$-successor in $\mathcal{I}$, i.e., there is an individual f such that $(e, f) \in (r_1 \cdots r_m)^{\mathcal{I}}$.*

In Figure 4.4, all words in the set rs^* are r-required by C_A, since $r \in L_{C_A}(\geq 1 s)$ and $rss^* \subseteq L_{C_A}(\geq 2 s)$.

Using the notion of required words, exclusion can be characterized as follows [Küs98]:

Lemma 4.2.2. *Let C be an $\mathcal{ALN}^*$-concept description. Then, $w \in E_C$ if, and only if,*

1. *there exists a prefix $v \in N_R^*$ of w and a word $v' \in N_R^*$ such that vv' is v-required by C and*
   a) *$vv' \in L_C(\bot)$, or*
   b) *there is a concept name P with $vv' \in L_C(P) \cap L_C(\neg P)$, or*
   c) *there are number restrictions $(\geq l \, r)$ and $(\leq k \, r)$ with $l > k$ and $vv' \in L_C(\geq l \, r) \cap L_C(\leq k \, r)$; or*
2. *there exists a prefix vr of w with $v \in N_R^*$, $r \in N_R$, and $v \in L_C(\leq 0 \, r)$.*

In [Küs98], this lemma is employed to show:

Proposition 4.2.2. *For every $\mathcal{ALN}^*$-concept description C the set E_C of C-excluding words is regular and a finite automaton accepting the words in E_C can be computed in time exponential in the size of C.*

Clearly, if C is an $\mathcal{FL}_0^*$-concept description, then $E_C = \emptyset$. Moreover, if C does not contain number restrictions, (i.e., if C is an $\mathcal{FL}_-^*$-concept descriptions), then a word vv' is v-required by C iff $v' = \varepsilon$. Consequently, together with Lemma 4.2.2, for $\mathcal{FL}_-^*$-concept descriptions C one obtains

$$E_C = L_C(\bot) \cup \bigcup_P (L_C(P) \cap L_C(\neg P)),$$

where P ranges over the concept names of C. Hence, for concept descriptions C that do not allow for number restrictions, automata accepting the set of C-excluding words can be computed in polynomial time. In case of $\mathcal{ALN}^*$-concept descriptions the finite automaton for E_C (roughly speaking) is the powerset automaton of $\mathcal{S}_C$. Up to now, it is an open problem whether this powerset-construction, and thus the exponential blow up, can be avoided.

Finally, we obtain the desired description of the value-restriction sets.

Theorem 4.2.3. *[Küs98] For every $\mathcal{ALN}^*$-concept description C the value-restriction sets are regular and finite automata accepting these sets can be computed in exponential time. More precisely,*

1. *$V_C(\bot) = E_C$;*
2. *$V_C(P) = L_C(P) \cup E_C$ for all concept names P in C;*
3. *$V_C(\neg P) = L_C(\neg P) \cup E_C$ for all negated concept names $\neg P$ in C;*

4. $V_C(\geq m\,r) = \bigcup_{k \geq m} L_C(\geq k\,r) \cup E_C$ *for all at-least restrictions* $(\geq m\,r)$ *in* C *with* $m \geq 1$; *and*

5. $V_C(\leq m r) = \bigcup_{k \leq m} L_C(\leq k r) \cup E_C r^{-1}$ *for all at-most restrictions* $(\leq m r)$ *in* C, *where for a language* L *and a letter* r, $L r^{-1} := \{w \mid wr \in L\}$.

For $\mathcal{FL}_\neg^*$-*concept descriptions* C, *automata accepting the value-restrictions sets can be computed in polynomial time.*

Note that the union in 4. is finite since C contains only a finite number of number restrictions and for number restrictions not contained in C, the sets $L_C(\cdot)$ are empty. In 5., the value-restriction set contains $E_C r^{-1}$ (instead of only E_C) because a value-restriction of the form $\forall w r.\bot$ is subsumed by $\forall w.(\leq 0\,r)$. Nevertheless, $E_C r^{-1} \supseteq E_C$ since $w \in E_C$ implies $wr \in E_C$, and thus $w \in E_C r^{-1}$.

Combining Theorem 4.2.2 and Theorem 4.2.3, it is possible to specify a PSPACE decision algorithm for subsumption of $\mathcal{ALN}^*$-concept descriptions. This algorithm matches the complexity lower bound, which has been shown in [Baa96] for $\mathcal{FL}_0^*$-concept descriptions by reducing the inclusion problem of regular languages to subsumption.

Corollary 4.2.3. *Deciding subsumption of* $\mathcal{FL}_0^*$-, $\mathcal{FL}_\neg^*$-, *and* $\mathcal{ALN}^*$-*concept descriptions is a PSPACE-complete problem.*

The Automata-Theoretic Approach for $\mathcal{ALN}$**-Concept Descriptions.** In [BKBM99], it has been shown that, when applying the automata-theoretic characterization of subsumption to $\mathcal{ALN}$-concept descriptions C, the languages $L_C(\cdot)$ are finite. More importantly, E_C is a language of the form $U \cdot N_R^*$, where U is a finite language, which can be computed in polynomial time. In particular, value-restriction sets of C can be computed in polynomial time. In [BKBM99], automata accepting these languages are called tree-like automata. *Tree-like automata*, when represented as graphs, are trees where some leaves may have self-loops (in order to accept N_R^*). In [BKM98b], it has been pointed out that there is a close connection between tree-like automata and the description trees introduced in Section 4.1. Specifically, deciding inclusion of languages accepted by tree-like automata corresponds to deciding the existence of homomorphisms between $\mathcal{ALN}$-description trees.

4.3 Subsumption in $\mathcal{ALE}$

Similar to $\mathcal{ALNS}$ (Section 4.1), for $\mathcal{ALE}$-concept descriptions one can state tree-based and description-based characterizations of subsumption. Again, throughout this book both characterizations are employed depending on which one is more appropriate.

The tree-based characterization works in three steps. First, concept descriptions are turned into normal forms. Second, these normal forms are translated into description trees. Then, subsumption is characterized in terms of homomorphisms between the description trees. This characterization has originally been introduced in [BKM99] in order to compute least common subsumers of $\mathcal{ALE}$-concept descriptions (see Section 5.3). There are three major differences of this characterization to the one for $\mathcal{ALNS}$: i) Whereas for $\mathcal{ALNS}$, normal forms are defined with respect to description graphs, for $\mathcal{ALE}$ they are defined with respect to concept descriptions. One could also define them on $\mathcal{ALE}$-description trees, though. It is, however, not clear how to define (useful) normal forms directly on $\mathcal{ALNS}$-concept descriptions; ii) the size of $\mathcal{ALE}$-normal forms can grow exponentially in the size of the given concept descriptions, whereas the size of normalized $\mathcal{ALNS}$-description graphs is linearly bounded by the size of the corresponding concept descriptions; iii) in $\mathcal{ALNS}$ there always exists at most one homomorphism into a normalized description graph, whereas this is not the case anymore for $\mathcal{ALE}$-description trees.

The description-based characterization is exclusively based on concept descriptions and, just as for $\mathcal{ALN}$, it only requires the concept descriptions to be in $\forall$-normal form. This kind of characterization turns out to be very useful in order to characterize equivalence between reduced concept descriptions (Section 6.3.2).

4.3.1 A Tree-Based Characterization of Subsumption

We now recall the characterization of subsumption first presented in [BKM99]. For this purpose, we introduce $\mathcal{ALE}$-description trees, define homomorphisms between these trees, and finally state the characterization of subsumption. In addition to the results already established in [BKM99], we introduce the notion of an image and inverse image of a homomorphism and prove some simple properties needed later on in Section 6.3.

$\mathcal{ALE}$**-Description Trees.** Similar to $\mathcal{ALN}$-description trees, nodes are labeled with sets of concept names, and edges are labeled with roles r ($\exists$-edges) or with $\forall r$ ($\forall$-edges).

Definition 4.3.1. *An $\mathcal{ALE}$-description tree is a tree of the form $\mathcal{G} = (N, E, n_0, \ell)$ where*

- *N is a finite set of* nodes *of $\mathcal{G}$;*
- *$E \subseteq N \times (N_R \cup \forall N_R) \times N$ is a finite set of* edges *labeled with role names r ($\exists$-edges) or with $\forall r$ ($\forall$-edges); $\forall N_R := \{\forall r \mid r \in N_R\}$;*
- *n_0 is the root of $\mathcal{G}$;*
- *ℓ is a labeling function* mapping the nodes in N to finite sets $\{P_1, \ldots, P_k\}$ *where each P_i, $1 \leq i \leq k$, is of one of the following forms: $P_i \in N_C$, $P_i = \neg P$ for some $P \in N_C$, or $P_i = \bot$. The empty label corresponds to the top-concept.*

For the sublanguages $\mathcal{EL}$ and $\mathcal{FLE}$ of $\mathcal{ALE}$, description trees are restricted in the obvious way, i.e., $\mathcal{FLE}$-description trees do not allow for $\bot$ or negated concept names in their label and, in addition, $\mathcal{EL}$-description trees do not have $\forall$-edges. All the following notions can be restricted to sublanguages of $\mathcal{ALE}$ in the obvious way.

For $n, m \in N$ and $r \in N_R$ we write $\exists$-edges from n to m labeled r as nrm and $\forall$-edges as $n\forall rm$. For the sake of simplicity, we occasionally write $n \in \mathcal{G}$ instead of $n \in N$; $nrm \in \mathcal{G}$ ($n\forall rm \in \mathcal{G}$) instead of $nrm \in E$ ($n\forall rm \in E$); and $\mathcal{G}(n)$ instead of $\ell(n)$.

A sequence $m_0 r_1 m_1 \cdots r_k m_k$ is a *path* in $\mathcal{G}$ from m_0 to m_k (for short, $m_0 r_1 m_1 \cdots r_k m_k \in \mathcal{G}$) iff $m_{i-1} r_i m_i \in \mathcal{G}$ or $m_{i-1} \forall r_i m_i \in \mathcal{G}$ for all $i = 1, \ldots k$. Such a path is called *rooted* in case m_0 is the root of $\mathcal{G}$. The path is called $\exists$-*path* ($\forall$-*path*) iff $m_{i-1} r_i m_i \in \mathcal{G}$ ($m_{i-1} \forall r_i m_i \in \mathcal{G}$) for all $i = 1, \ldots, k$.

For $n \in N$, m is a *direct successor* of n in $\mathcal{G}$ if there exists $r \in N_R$ with $nrm \in E$ or $n\forall rm \in E$; m is a *successor* of n if there exists a path from n to m. Since we allow for empty paths, n is a successor of itself. Analogously, we define *(direct) predecessors*.

A *subtree* $\mathcal{G}'$ of $\mathcal{G}$ is a description tree consisting of a subset of nodes of $\mathcal{G}$ such that the labels of the nodes in $\mathcal{G}'$ are subsets of the corresponding ones in $\mathcal{G}$; $\mathcal{G}'$ is called *rooted subtree* in case the root of $\mathcal{G}'$ coincides with the one of $\mathcal{G}$. Consider, for example, the tree called $\mathcal{G}(C_{ex})$ depicted in Figure 4.5. A possible rooted subtree of this tree is the one that comprises the nodes n_0, n_1, n_3, n_2, where the label of each of these nodes is empty.

For a node $n \in N$, $\mathcal{G}_n$ denotes the subtree of $\mathcal{G}$ consisting of *all* successors of n in $\mathcal{G}$. The root of $\mathcal{G}_n$ is n and the labels of the nodes in $\mathcal{G}_n$ coincide with the corresponding ones in $\mathcal{G}$.

For a tree $\mathcal{G}$, $|\mathcal{G}|$ denotes its size, i.e., the number of nodes in $\mathcal{G}$ plus the cardinality of every label of nodes in $\mathcal{G}$. The maximal length of a rooted path in $\mathcal{G}$ is referred to by $depth(\mathcal{G})$.

$\mathcal{ALE}$-concept descriptions C are turned into $\mathcal{ALE}$-description trees $\mathcal{G}(C)$ analogously to $\mathcal{ALN}$-concept descriptions: The (negated) concept names and the bottom-concept (if any) on the top-level of C form the label of the root of $\mathcal{G}(C)$; existential restrictions are turned into $\exists$-edges and value restrictions are represented by $\forall$-edges. We will illustrate the translation by an example (see [BKM98a] for a formal definition):

$$C_{ex} := \forall r.(\exists s.Q \sqcap \forall s.\neg Q) \sqcap \exists s.(P \sqcap \exists r.\neg P).$$

The corresponding description tree $\mathcal{G}(C_{ex})$ is depicted in Figure 4.5.

On the other hand, every $\mathcal{ALE}$-description tree $\mathcal{G}$ can be translated into an $\mathcal{ALE}$-concept description $C_{\mathcal{G}}$ ([BKM98a] contains a formal translation). The description tree $\mathcal{G}$ in Figure 4.5 yields the $\mathcal{ALE}$-concept description

$$D_{ex} := C_{\mathcal{G}} = \forall r.(\exists r.P \sqcap \exists r.\neg P) \sqcap (\exists s.\exists r.\neg P).$$

The semantics of $\mathcal{ALE}$-description trees $\mathcal{G}$ is defined by the semantics of their corresponding concept descriptions $C_{\mathcal{G}}$, i.e., $\mathcal{G}^{\mathcal{I}} := (C_{\mathcal{G}})^{\mathcal{I}}$ for every interpreta-

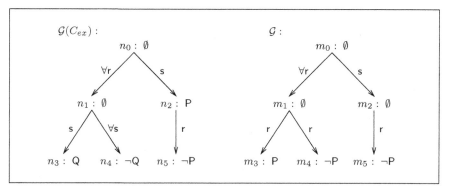

Fig. 4.5. The Description Trees for $\mathcal{G}(C_{ex})$ and $\mathcal{G}$.

tion $\mathcal{I}$. It is easy to verify that the translation of concept descriptions and description trees into one another preserves semantics, i.e., $C \equiv C_{\mathcal{G}(C)}$. Having the semantics for description trees at hand, subsumption between description trees (e.g., $\mathcal{G} \sqsubseteq \mathcal{H}$) or between a concept description and a description tree (e.g., $C \sqsubseteq \mathcal{G}$) is defined in the obvious way.

Finally, we need to introduce an operation on trees which later on is used to describe the instantiation $\sigma(D)$ of a concept pattern D by a substitution σ. Applying σ to D means that certain concept descriptions are "plugged into" D. If D and the images of σ are presented by description trees, then this operation results in attaching trees representing images of σ to certain nodes of D. In what follows, it is described what it means to attach a tree to a certain node of another tree. Given $\mathcal{ALE}$-description trees $\mathcal{G}$ and $\mathcal{H}$ (with disjoint sets of nodes) and a node $n \in \mathcal{G}$, *instantiating $\mathcal{G}$ at node n with $\mathcal{H}$* yields an extension $\mathcal{G}' = (N', E', n_0, \ell')$ of $\mathcal{G} = (N, E, n_0, \ell)$ defined as follows: First, the root of $\mathcal{H}$ is replaced by n, which yields the tree $\mathcal{H}' = (N'', E'', n, \ell'')$. Then,

- $N' := N \cup N''$;
- $E' := E \cup E''$;
- $\ell'(m) := \ell(m)$ for all $m \in N \setminus \{n\}$; $\ell'(m) := \ell''(m)$ for all $m \in N'' \setminus \{n\}$; $\ell'(n) := \ell(n) \cup \ell''(n)$.

Homomorphisms between $\mathcal{ALE}$-Description Trees. Homomorphisms between $\mathcal{ALE}$-description trees are defined in a straightforward manner. As with $\mathcal{ALN}$-description trees, one allows to map a node and all its successors onto an unsatisfiable node, i.e., a node containing $\bot$.

Definition 4.3.2. *A mapping $\varphi : N_H \longrightarrow N_G$ from an $\mathcal{ALE}$-description tree $\mathcal{H} = (N_H, E_H, m_0, \ell_H)$ to an $\mathcal{ALE}$-description tree $\mathcal{G} = (N_G, E_G, n_0, \ell_G)$ is called* homomorphism *if, and only if, the following conditions are satisfied:*

1. *$\varphi(m_0) = n_0$;*
2. *for all $n \in N_H$ we have $\ell_H(n) \subseteq \ell_G(\varphi(n))$ or $\bot \in \ell_G(\varphi(n))$;*

3. for all $vrm \in E_H$, either $\varphi(n)r\varphi(m) \in E_G$, or $\varphi(n) = \varphi(m)$ and $\bot \in \ell_G(\varphi(n))$; and

4. for all $n\forall rm \in E_H$, either $\varphi(n)\forall r\varphi(m) \in E_G$, or $\varphi(n) = \varphi(m)$ and $\bot \in \ell_G(\varphi(n))$.

The second condition says that the label of n is a subset of the one of $\varphi(n)$, unless n is mapped onto an unsatisfiable node.

Isomorphisms between description trees, defined next, are needed when equivalence between concept descriptions is characterized. However, unlike the previous two sections, the characterization itself is postponed to Section 6.3.2 since it requires some more involved investigations regarding reduced concept descriptions.

Definition 4.3.3. Let $\mathcal{G} = (N_G, E_G, n_0, \ell_G)$ and $\mathcal{H} = (N_H, E_H, m_0, \ell_H)$ be $\mathcal{ALE}$-description trees. The mapping φ from N_H onto N_G is called isomorphism from $\mathcal{H}$ onto $\mathcal{G}$ iff

1. φ is a bijection from N_H onto N_G;
2. $\varphi(m_0) = n_0$;
3. for all $n, m \in N_H$ and $r \in N_R$: $nrm \in E_H$ $(n\forall rm \in E_H)$ iff $\varphi(n)r\varphi(m) \in E_G$ $(\varphi(n)\forall r\varphi(m) \in E_G)$;
4. for all $n \in N$: $\ell_H(n) = \ell_G(\varphi(n))$.

Two description trees $\mathcal{G}$ and $\mathcal{H}$ are called *isomorphic* $(\mathcal{G} \cong \mathcal{H}$ for short) if there exists an isomorphism between them. In other words, if $\mathcal{G}$ and $\mathcal{H}$ are isomorphic, then they coincide up to renaming of nodes.

Definition 4.3.4. Let $\mathcal{G} = (N_G, E_G, n_0, \ell_G)$ and $\mathcal{H} = (N_H, E_H, m_0, \ell_H)$ be $\mathcal{ALE}$-description trees, and let φ be an homomorphism from $\mathcal{H}$ into $\mathcal{G}$. Finally, let $\mathcal{H}' = (N', E', n', \ell')$ be a subtree of $\mathcal{H}$. Then, the homomorphic image $\varphi(\mathcal{H}') = (N, E, n, \ell)$ of $\mathcal{H}'$ under φ is defined as follows:

- $N := \varphi(N') := \{m \mid$ there exists a node $m' \in N'$ with $m = \varphi(m')\}$;
- $E := E_G \cap (N \times (N_R \cup \forall N_R) \times N)$;
- $n := \varphi(n')$;

- $\ell(m) := \left(\bigcup\limits_{m' \in \varphi^{-1}(m)} \ell'(m') \right) \cap \ell_G(m)$ for all $m \in N$ where $\varphi^{-1}(m)$ denotes the set $\{m' \mid \varphi(m') = m\}$.

It is easy to prove the following properties of homomorphic images:

Lemma 4.3.1. Let $\mathcal{G}$ and $\mathcal{H}'$ be defined as in the preceding definition. Then,

1. $\varphi(\mathcal{H}')$ is a subtree of $\mathcal{G}$; and
2. φ is a surjective homomorphism from $\mathcal{H}'$ onto $\varphi(\mathcal{H}')$.

In case one only deals with $\mathcal{EL}$- and $\mathcal{FLE}$-description trees, one can dispense with intersecting the union in the definition of $\ell(m)$ with $\ell_G(m)$ (Definition 4.3.4) in order to guarantee 1.: These trees do not contain the bottom-concept such that the subset inclusion of the label of a node and its image must be satisfied. Thus, the label of an image is always a superset of the labels of its inverse images, making it dispensable to intersect the label of the image with the labels of the inverse images. In the $\mathcal{ALE}$ case, however, nodes can be mapped onto nodes containing the bottom-concept regardless of the subset relationships of the labels. Thus, labels of nodes, m', in $\mathcal{H}'$ might contain elements that do not belong to the labels of their images, m. Therefore, in order to guarantee 1., it is necessary to intersect the label of m with that of its inverse images.

Definition 4.3.5. *Let $\mathcal{G} = (N_G, E_G, n_0, \ell_G)$ and $\mathcal{H} = (N_H, E_H, m_0, \ell_H)$ be $\mathcal{ALE}$-description trees, and let $\psi : N_H \longrightarrow N_G$ be a homomorphism from $\mathcal{H}$ into $\mathcal{G}$. Finally, let $\mathcal{G}' = (N', E', n', \ell')$ be some subtree of $\mathcal{G}$ in case ψ is injective, and a rooted subtree in case ψ is not injective. Then, the* inverse image *of $\mathcal{G}'$ under ψ, $\psi^{-1}(\mathcal{G}') = (N, E, n, \ell)$, is defined as follows:*

- *$N := \psi^{-1}(N')$; if $N = \emptyset$, then let $\psi^{-1}(\mathcal{G}')$ be a description tree containing only the root with empty label; otherwise*
- *$E := E_H \cap (N \times (N_R \cup \forall N_R) \times N)$;*
- *$n := \psi^{-1}(n')$;*
- *$\ell(m) := \ell_H(m) \cap \ell'(\psi(m))$ for all $m \in N$.*

If, in the above definition, ψ is not injective and $\mathcal{G}'$ is not a rooted subtree of $\mathcal{G}$, then several nodes in $\mathcal{H}$ might be mapped onto the root of $\mathcal{G}'$. But then, the inverse image of $\mathcal{G}'$ under ψ cannot form a tree. It would rather yield a set of subtrees of $\mathcal{H}$. Obviously, this phenomenon can be avoided if $\mathcal{G}'$ is a rooted subtree of $\mathcal{G}$, or alternatively, ψ is injective. In both cases at most one node in $\mathcal{H}$ can be mapped onto the root of $\mathcal{G}'$. We summarize some simple properties of inverse homomorphisms in the following lemma.

Lemma 4.3.2. *If N as defined in Definition 4.3.5 is not the empty set, then*

1. *$\psi^{-1}(\mathcal{G}')$ is a subtree of $\mathcal{H}$ with root $\psi^{-1}(n')$;*
2. *$\psi(\psi^{-1}(\mathcal{G}'))$ is a rooted subtree of $\mathcal{G}'$;*
3. *in case ψ is injective, $\psi(\psi^{-1}(\mathcal{G}'))$ and $\psi^{-1}(\mathcal{G}')$ are isomorphic.*

Subsumption in $\mathcal{ALE}$. As shown in [BKM99], in order to characterize subsumption of $\mathcal{ALE}$-concept descriptions in terms of homomorphisms between the corresponding description trees, the concept descriptions need to be normalized before translating them into description trees.

Definition 4.3.6. *Let E, F be two $\mathcal{ALE}$-concept descriptions and $r \in N_R$ be a role name. The $\mathcal{ALE}$-normalization rules are defined as follows*

$$\forall r.E \sqcap \forall r.F \longrightarrow \forall r.(E \sqcap F)$$
$$\forall r.E \sqcap \exists r.F \longrightarrow \forall r.E \sqcap \exists r.(E \sqcap F)$$
$$\forall r.\top \longrightarrow \top$$
$$E \sqcap \top \longrightarrow E$$

$$P \sqcap \neg P \quad \longrightarrow \quad \bot, \text{ for each } P \in N_C$$
$$\exists r.\bot \quad \longrightarrow \quad \bot$$
$$E \sqcap \bot \quad \longrightarrow \quad \bot$$

The main idea underlying the normalization rules is to make the knowledge implicitly given by a concept description explicit. For example, the second rule makes explicit the fact that every individual in the extension of $\forall r.E \sqcap \exists r.F$ not only has an r-successor in F but in $E \sqcap F$.

A concept description C is called *normalized* if none of the above normalization rules can be applied at some place in C. Note that the second rule must only be applied once to every pair $\forall r.E$ and $\exists r.F$ in C. The rules should be read modulo commutativity of conjunction; e.g., $\exists r.E \sqcap \forall r.F$ is also normalized to $\exists r.(E \sqcap F) \sqcap \forall r.F$. An unnormalized concept description C can be normalized by exhaustively applying the normalization rules to C. The resulting (normalized) concept description is called *normal form of C*. Since each normalization rule preserves equivalence, the normal form of C is equivalent to C. We refer to $\mathcal{G}_C$ as the description tree corresponding to the normal form of C, i.e., if C' is the normal form of C, then $\mathcal{G}_C := \mathcal{G}(C')$. As pointed out in [BKM99], due to the second rule in Definition 4.3.6, $\mathcal{G}_C$ may grow exponentially in the size of C.

In order to see this point, consider the $\mathcal{ALE}$-concept descriptions C_k, $k \geq 1$, inductively defined by

- $C_1 := \exists r.P \sqcap \exists r.Q$ and
- $C_k := \exists r.P \sqcap \exists r.Q \sqcap \forall r.C_{k-1}$.

As an example, the $\mathcal{ALE}$-description tree $\mathcal{G}_{C_2}$ corresponding to $C_2 = \exists r.P \sqcap \exists r.Q \sqcap \forall r.(\exists r.P \sqcap \exists r.Q)$ is depicted in Figure 4.6. It is easy to show by induction on k that the size of C_k is linear in k, but that the size of $\mathcal{G}_{C_k}$ is at least 2^k.

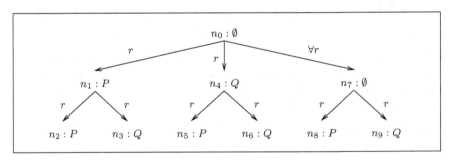

Fig. 4.6. The $\mathcal{ALE}$-Description tree $\mathcal{G}_{C_2}$.

As an aside, it should be noted that there is a close relationship between the normalization rules introduced above and some of the so-called *propagation rules* employed by tableau-based subsumption algorithms, as e.g. in-

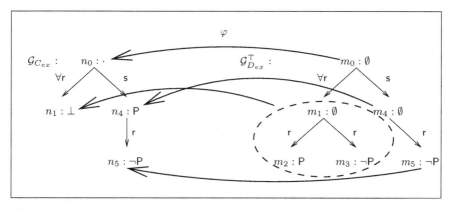

Fig. 4.7. Subsumption for $\mathcal{ALE}$.

troduced in [DHL⁺92] (see also Chapter 2). In particular, after exhaustively applying the propagation rule to the tableau $\{C_2(n_0)\}$, the complete tableau corresponds to $\mathcal{G}_{C_2}$.

Similar to $\mathcal{ALNS}$, if only the rule $\forall r.\top \longrightarrow \top$ is exhaustively applied to a concept description C, then the resulting concept description is called $\top$-*normal form of* C. We refer to $\mathcal{G}_C^\top$ as the description tree corresponding to the $\top$-normal form of C. Note that $\mathcal{G}_C^\top$ is of size linear in C.

Now, subsumption can be characterized in terms of homomorphisms, just as for $\mathcal{ALN}$ (Theorem 4.1.2) and $\mathcal{ALNS}$ (Theorem 4.1.3).

Theorem 4.3.1. *[BKM99] Let C, D be $\mathcal{ALE}$-concept descriptions. Then, $C \sqsubseteq D$ iff there exists a homomorphism from $\mathcal{G}_D^\top$ to $\mathcal{G}_C$.*

It should be noted that the theorem stated in [BKM99] requires a homomorphism originating from $\mathcal{G}_D$ instead of $\mathcal{G}_D^\top$. However, the proof of this theorem [BKM98a] reveals that $\top$-normalization of the subsumer is sufficient. From this proof one can also conclude that the if direction of Theorem 4.3.1 does not require normalization:

Remark 4.3.1. The existence of a homomorphism from a description tree $\mathcal{G}$ into $\mathcal{H}$ implies $\mathcal{H} \sqsubseteq \mathcal{G}$ regardless of whether $\mathcal{G}$ or $\mathcal{H}$ is normalized.

We illustrate the theorem by the concept descriptions C_{ex} and D_{ex} introduced above. The normal form of C_{ex} is $\forall r.\bot \sqcap \exists s.(P \sqcap \exists r.\neg P)$; D_{ex} is already in $\top$-normal form. A homomorphism from $\mathcal{G}_{D_{ex}}^\top$ into $\mathcal{G}_{C_{ex}}$ is depicted in Figure 4.7. By Theorem 4.3.1 we can conclude $C_{ex} \sqsubseteq D_{ex}$. Observe, however, that there is no homomorphism from $\mathcal{G}(D_{ex})$ into $\mathcal{G}(C_{ex})$. This shows that the only-if direction of Theorem 4.3.1 does require the subsumee to be normalized before translating it into its description tree.

In case of $\mathcal{EL}$-concept descriptions, normalization is not necessary since the normalization rules do not change an $\mathcal{EL}$-concept description apart from the fourth rule in Definition 4.3.6. But this rule is taken care of by the translation of concept descriptions into description trees: the top-concept corresponds to the empty label and labels do not contain $\top$. Thus, as an immediate consequence of Theorem 4.3.1, we can derive the following corollary.

Corollary 4.3.1. *Let C, D be $\mathcal{EL}$-concept descriptions. Then, $C \sqsubseteq D$ iff there exists a homomorphism from $\mathcal{G}(D)$ to $\mathcal{G}(C)$.*

In [BKM98a], it has been shown that the existence of homomorphisms between description trees can be decided in time polynomial in the size of the trees. Thus, as a direct consequence of the above corollary we obtain a polynomial time subsumption algorithm for $\mathcal{EL}$-concept descriptions. For $\mathcal{ALE}$, Theorem 4.3.1 only yields an exponential time algorithm because $\mathcal{G}_C$ might grow exponentially in the size of C. Thus, checking for the existence of a homomorphism between $\mathcal{G}_D^\top$ and $\mathcal{G}_C$ is an exponential time algorithm as well (compared to the size of the C and D). This approach of deciding subsumption, however, does not yield an optimal complexity upper bound, since in [DHL$^+$92], subsumption in $\mathcal{ALE}$ has shown to be NP-complete.

4.3.2 A Description-Based Characterization of Subsumption

Analogously to Section 4.1.2, the description-based characterization of subsumption requires the concept descriptions to be in $\forall$-normal form (see Definition 3.2.5). Recall that, if a concept description C is in $\forall$-normal form, then for every $r \in N_R$ there exists at most one value restriction $\forall r.E$ on the top-level of C. We refer to E by $C.r$; $C.r := \top$, if C does not contain a value restriction for r. In the sequel, $\exists r.E \in C$ means that $\exists r.E$ occurs on the top-level of C. Moreover, let $prim(C)$ denote the set of (negated) concept names and the bottom-concept (if any) on the top-level of C. In the following characterization of subsumption we can dispense with most of the normalization rules listed in Definition 4.3.6, because i) unsatisfiability is tested explicitly and ii) the propagation of value restrictions to existential restrictions is taken care of implicitly by the condition 3. in the following theorem. This characterization can easily be derived from Theorem 4.3.1.

Theorem 4.3.2. *Let C, D be two $\mathcal{ALE}$-concept descriptions in $\forall$-normal form. Then, $C \sqsubseteq D$ iff i) $C \equiv \bot$ or ii)*

1. *$prim(D) \subseteq prim(C)$;*
2. *for every $r \in N_R$, $C.r \sqsubseteq D.r$; and*
3. *for every existential restriction $\exists r.E \in D$, there exists an existential restriction $\exists r.F \in C$ such that $C.r \sqcap F \sqsubseteq E$.*

Note that, $prim(\top) = \emptyset$, $\top.r = \top$, and there does not exist an existential restriction on the top-level of $\top$. In particular, all three conditions required above are satisfied in case $D = \top$.

Similar to the characterization of subsumption for $\mathcal{ALN}$-concept descriptions (Theorem 4.1.4), Theorem 4.3.2 cannot directly be turned into a recursive subsumption algorithm because it does not specify how to decide unsatisfiability of $\mathcal{ALE}$-concept descriptions. It is rather used as a tool to prove results on reduced concept descriptions and reduced matchers (Section 6.3).

5. LCS and MSC

In Section 3.1.4, we have summarized the (new) theoretical results on the lcs and the msc. The purpose of this chapter is to provide proofs for the DLs $\mathcal{ALNS}$ (Section 5.1) and $\mathcal{ALN}^*$ (Section 5.2). The lcs in $\mathcal{ALE}$ has been investigated in a thesis by Molitor [Mol00]. In Section 6.3, we therefore cite the results on $\mathcal{ALE}$ without proofs.

5.1 LCS for $\mathcal{ALNS}$-Concept Descriptions

As pointed out in Chapter 3, the lcs was originally introduced as an operation in the context of inductive learning from examples [CBH92], and several papers followed up this lead. The DLs considered were mostly sublanguages of $\mathcal{ALNS}$, the language which will be explored in detail in this section. Cohen et al. [CBH92] proposed an lcs algorithm for a language that allows for concept conjunction and same-as, i.e., the language we call $\mathcal{LS}$. Cohen and Hirsh [CH94a] extended this algorithms to apply to CORECLASSIC, which additionally allows for value restrictions. In [CH94b] they presented an lcs algorithm for $\mathcal{ALN}$. Finally, Frazier and Pitt [FP96] generalized these algorithms to full CLASSIC, which comprised CORECLASSIC and $\mathcal{ALN}$.

All these lcs algorithms are based on the graph-based characterization of subsumption discussed in Section 4.1.1. More precisely, the lcs is computed in three steps: First, the concept descriptions are turned into normalized description graphs. Second, the product of these graphs is determined. Finally, the product graph thus obtained is turned back into a concept description, which represents the lcs of the given concepts.

However, in the contributions mentioned above there is a mismatch between the semantics of attributes underlying the characterization of subsumption, on the one hand, and the lcs algorithms, on the other hand. Whereas the characterizations of subsumption proposed by Borgida and Patel-Schneider [BPS94] requires attributes to be interpreted as total functions, a careful examination of the lcs algorithms reveals that the lcs is computed for DLs with partial attributes. In addition, it turns out that the lcs algorithms do not handle unsatisfiability in a proper manner.

In this section, we show that, as far as computing the lcs for languages with same-as equalities is concerned, there exist significant differences be-

R.Küsters: Non-Standard Inferences in Description Logics, LNAI 2100, pp. 107–152, 2001.
© Springer-Verlag Berlin Heidelberg 2001

tween partial and total attributes. To this end, we investigate the lcs for the languages $\mathcal{ALNS}$ and $\mathcal{LS}$ in detail, where the former language allows for partial attributes and the latter for total ones. It turns out that, for $\mathcal{ALNS}$-concept descriptions, the lcs always exists and that it can be computed by a polynomial time algorithm given two descriptions and by a (necessarily) worst-case exponential time algorithm given a sequence of concept descriptions. (We point the reader to [KB99] for a complete treatment of CLASSIC with attributes interpreted as partial functions.) For $\mathcal{LS}$, things are quite different. The lcs need not exist. Nevertheless, we can provide a polynomial time algorithm for deciding the existence of the lcs, and a (necessarily) worst-case exponential time algorithm for computing the lcs (if any).

5.1.1 The LCS in $\mathcal{ALNS}$

We show that the lcs of two $\mathcal{ALNS}$-concept descriptions can be stated in terms of the product of normalized description graphs.

A similar approach has been chosen in [CH94a] for a sublanguage of $\mathcal{ALNS}$, which only allows for concept names, concept conjunction, value restrictions, and same-as equalities. In particular, unlike full $\mathcal{ALNS}$, this sublanguage does not allow for unsatisfiable concept descriptions. Additionally, the semantics of the description graphs provided in [CH94a] is well-defined only when the graphs are acyclic. This excludes, for example, same-as equalities of the form $(\varepsilon \downarrow \mathsf{spouse} \circ \mathsf{spouse})$.

The Product of Description Graphs. Intuitively, a description graph represents the set of constraints that must be satisfied by all individuals in the extension of the graph. Consequently, the lcs of two descriptions should correspond to the intersection of the set of constraints. As we will see, the product of description graphs provides us with such an intersection.

The product of description graphs $\mathcal{G}_1$, $\mathcal{G}_2$ is defined similar to the product of finite automata. However, special care has to be taken of incoherent nodes, i.e., nodes containing $\bot$. Also, since attributes may occur both in r-edges and a-edges, one needs to take the product between restriction graphs of r-edges, on the one hand, and the original graph $\mathcal{G}_1$ or $\mathcal{G}_2$ (rooted at certain nodes), on the other hand.

Definition 5.1.1. *Let $\mathcal{G}_1 = (N_1, E_1, n_1, \ell_1)$ and $\mathcal{G}_2 = (N_2, E_2, n_2, \ell_2)$ be two description graphs. Then, the product $\mathcal{G} := \mathcal{G}_1 \times \mathcal{G}_2 := (N, E, n_0, \ell)$ of $\mathcal{G}_1$ and $\mathcal{G}_2$ is recursively defined as follows:*

1. $N := N_1 \times N_2$;
2. $n_0 := (n_1, n_2)$;
3. $E := \{((n, n'), a, (m, m')) \mid (n, a, m) \in E_1 \text{ and } (n', a, m') \in E_2\}$;
4. *Let $n \in N_1$ and $n' \in N_2$. If the atoms of n contain $\bot$, then define $\ell(n, n') := \ell_2(n')$ and, analogously, if the atoms of n' contain $\bot$, define $\ell(n, n') := \ell_1(n)$. Otherwise, for $\ell_1(n) = (S_1, H_1)$ and $\ell_2(n') = (S_2, H_2)$, define $\ell(n, n') := (S, H)$ where*

a) $S := S_1 \cap S_2$;

b) $H :=$

$\{(r, min(k_1, k_2), max(l_1, l_2), \mathcal{G}'_1 \times \mathcal{G}'_2) \mid (r, k_1, l_1, \mathcal{G}'_1) \in H_1, \ (r, k_2, l_2, \mathcal{G}'_2) \in H_2\} \cup$

$\{(a, 0, 1, (\mathcal{G}_1)_m \times \mathcal{G}'_2) \mid (n, a, m) \in E_1, \ (a, k_2, l_2, \mathcal{G}'_2) \in H_2\} \cup$

$\{(a, 0, 1, \mathcal{G}'_1 \times (\mathcal{G}_2)_m) \mid (a, k_1, l_1, \mathcal{G}'_1) \in H_1, \ (n', a, m) \in E_2\}$.

According to this definition, if in the tuple (n, n') some node, say n, is incoherent, then the label of (n, n') coincides with the one for n'. The reason for defining the label in this way is that $lcs(\bot, C) \equiv C$ for every concept description C.

Note that $\mathcal{G}$, as defined here, might not be connected, i.e., it might contain nodes that cannot be reached from the root n_0. Even if $\mathcal{G}_1$ and $\mathcal{G}_2$ are connected this can happen because all tuples (n_1, n_2) belong to the set of nodes of $\mathcal{G}$ regardless of whether they are reachable from the root or not. However, as already mentioned in Section 4.1.1 we may assume $\mathcal{G}$ to be connected. Otherwise, nodes that cannot be reached from the root can be removed without changing the semantics of $\mathcal{G}$.

Also note, since the product of two description graphs is again a description graph, the product graph can be translated back into an $\mathcal{ALNS}$-concept descriptions.

Computing the LCS. We now prove the main theorem of this subsection, which states that the product of two description graphs is equivalent to the lcs of the corresponding concept descriptions.

Theorem 5.1.1. *Let C_1 and C_2 be two concept descriptions, and let $\mathcal{G}_1$ and $\mathcal{G}_2$ be the corresponding normalized description graphs. Then, $C_{\mathcal{G}_1 \times \mathcal{G}_2} \equiv lcs(C_1, C_2)$.*

Proof. For the sake of simplicity, let $\mathcal{G}$ denote the product $\mathcal{G}_1 \times \mathcal{G}_2$. In order to show that $\mathcal{G}$ subsumes $\mathcal{G}_1$ and $\mathcal{G}_2$, we rephrase item 4. of Definition 5.1.1 in the following way: We not just define $\ell(n, n')$ to be $\ell_2(n')$ in case the atoms of n contain $\bot$ [and $\ell(n, n')$ to be $\ell_1(n)$ in case the atoms of n' contain $\bot$], but replace the nodes m of the nested graphs in $\ell(n, n')$ by (n, m) [(m, n')], i.e., we add n [n'] as second component for every node.

Then, it is easy to verify that the mapping φ which maps every node of the form (m_1, m_2) in $\mathcal{G}_1 \times \mathcal{G}_2$ to its first component m_1 (second component m_2) is a homomorphism from $\mathcal{G}_1 \times \mathcal{G}_2$ into $\mathcal{G}_1$ ($\mathcal{G}_2$). Thus, $\mathcal{G}$ subsumes both $\mathcal{G}_1$ and $\mathcal{G}_2$.

The more interesting part of the proof is to show that $C_{\mathcal{G}}$ is the *least* common subsumer of C_1 and C_2. We now prove by induction over the size of D, C_1, and C_2 that if D subsumes C_1 and C_2, then D subsumes $C_{\mathcal{G}}$: We distinguish different cases according to Theorem 4.1.3. Let $\mathcal{G}_1 = (N_1, E_1, n_1, \ell_1)$ be the normalized description graph of C_1, $\mathcal{G}_2 = (N_2, E_2, n_2, \ell_2)$ be the normalized description graph of C_2, and $\mathcal{G} = (N, E, n_0, \ell) = \mathcal{G}_1 \times \mathcal{G}_2$. In the following, we assume that $C_1 \sqsubseteq D$ and $C_2 \sqsubseteq D$.

1. If $\mathcal{G}$ is incoherent or $D = \top$, then there is nothing to show.
2. If D is a concept name, $\bot$, or a number-restriction, then by definition of the label of n_0, Remark 4.1.1 implies $\mathcal{G} \sqsubseteq D$. Note that since $\mathcal{G}$ is not necessarily normalized, we need to resort to Remark 4.1.1 instead of Theorem 4.1.3.
3. If $D = v \downarrow w$, then according to Theorem 4.1.3 there exist two rooted paths in $\mathcal{G}_1$ ($\mathcal{G}_2$) labeled v and w, respectively, leading to the same node m_1 (m_2) in $\mathcal{G}_1$ ($\mathcal{G}_2$). Consequently, there are two paths in $\mathcal{G}$ from $n_0 = (n_1, n_2)$ to (m_1, m_2) with label v and w, respectively. By Remark 4.1.1 this means $\mathcal{G} \sqsubseteq D$.
4. If $D = \forall r.C$ where r is a role or an attribute, then one of several cases applies:
   (i) n_1 and n_2 have r-edges with role or attribute r, and restriction graphs $\mathcal{G}_1'$ and $\mathcal{G}_2'$, respectively, such that $\mathcal{G}_1' \sqsubseteq C$ and $\mathcal{G}_2' \sqsubseteq C$;
   (ii) without loss of generality, n_1 has an a-edge pointing to m_1 with attribute r, such that $\mathcal{G}_1' \sqsubseteq C$, where $\mathcal{G}_1' := (\mathcal{G}_1)_{m_1}$; and n_2 has an r-edge with restriction graph $\mathcal{G}_2'$ such that $\mathcal{G}_2' \sqsubseteq C$.
   In both cases (i) and (ii), $(\mathcal{G}_1' \times \mathcal{G}_2') \sqsubseteq C$ follows by induction. Furthermore, by 4b of the definition of $\mathcal{G}$, the node n_0 has an r-edge with role r and restriction graph $\mathcal{G}_1' \times \mathcal{G}_2'$. This implies $\mathcal{G} \sqsubseteq D$.
   (iii) n_1 and n_2 have a-edges with attribute r pointing to nodes m_1 and m_2, respectively. Then, $(\mathcal{G}_1)_{m_1} \sqsubseteq C$ and $(\mathcal{G}_2)_{m_2} \sqsubseteq C$. By induction, we know $(\mathcal{G}_1)_{m_1} \times (\mathcal{G}_2)_{m_2} \sqsubseteq C$. It is easy to see that $\mathcal{G}_{(m_1, m_2)} = (\mathcal{G}_1)_{m_1} \times (\mathcal{G}_2)_{m_2}$. Furthermore, by definition of $\mathcal{G}$ there is an a-edge with attribute r from (n_1, n_2) to (m_1, m_2) in $\mathcal{G}$. Now, Remark 4.1.1 ensures $\mathcal{G} \sqsubseteq D$.
   (iv) without loss of generality, n_1 has no r-edge and no a-edge with role or attribute r. This means $\top \sqsubseteq C$, and thus, $\mathcal{G} \sqsubseteq D$.
5. If $D = C \sqcap E$, then Theorem 4.1.3 implies $\mathcal{G}_1 \sqsubseteq C$ and $\mathcal{G}_2 \sqsubseteq C$. By induction, we can conclude $\mathcal{G} \sqsubseteq C$, and analogously, $\mathcal{G} \sqsubseteq E$. Thus, $\mathcal{G} \sqsubseteq D$.

$\square$

As stated in Section 4.1.1, given an $\mathcal{ALNS}$-concept description, the corresponding normalized description graph can be computed in time polynomial in the size of the concept description. Moreover, it is easy to see that the product of two description graphs can be computed in time polynomial in the size of the graphs. Turning the product graph back into a concept description can be carried out in polynomial time as well. Thus, as a direct consequence of Theorem 5.1.1 we obtain:

Corollary 5.1.1. *The lcs of two $\mathcal{ALNS}$-concept descriptions always exists and can be computed in time polynomial in the size of the concept descriptions.*

This statement does not hold for sequences of concept descriptions. Intuitively, generalizing the lcs algorithm to sequences of, say, n concept descriptions, means computing the product of n description graphs. The following

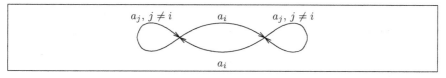

Fig. 5.1. The normalized description graph for D_i, without node labels.

proposition shows that the size of such a product graph may grow exponentially in n. Thus, the lcs computed in this way grows exponentially in the size of the given sequence. However, this does not imply that this exponential blow-up is unavoidable. There might exist a smaller, still equivalent representation of the lcs. Nevertheless, we can show that the exponential growth is inevitable.

Proposition 5.1.1. *For every integer $k \geq 2$ there is a sequence $D_1, \ldots, D_k$ of $\mathcal{ALNS}$-concept descriptions such that the size of every $\mathcal{ALNS}$-concept description equivalent to $lcs(D_1, \ldots, D_k)$ is at least exponential in k and the size of the $D_i's$ is linear in k.*

Proof. For a given k the concept description D_i is defined as follows:[1]

$$D_i := \prod_{j \neq i}(\varepsilon \downarrow a_j) \sqcap \prod_{j \neq i}(a_i \downarrow a_i a_j) \sqcap (\varepsilon \downarrow a_i a_i)$$

where $a_1, \ldots, a_k$ denote attributes. The normalized description graph for D_i is depicted in Figure 5.1. Using Theorem 4.1.3 it is easy to see that $D_i \sqsubseteq v \downarrow w$ iff the number of $a_i's$ in v and the number of $a_i's$ in w are equal modulo 2 where v, w are words over $\{a_1, \ldots, a_k\}$. This implies that

$$D_1, \ldots, D_k \sqsubseteq v \downarrow w \quad \text{iff} \quad \text{for all } 1 \leq i \leq k \text{ the number of } a_i's \quad (5.1)$$
$$\text{in } v \text{ and the number of } a_i's \text{ in } w \text{ are}$$
$$\text{equal modulo 2.}$$

Let $s \subseteq \{1, \ldots, k\}$ be a non-empty set. We define $v_s := a_{i_1} \cdots a_{i_l}$ where $i_1 < \cdots < i_l$ are the elements of s and $w_s := a_{i_1}{}^3 a_{i_2}{}^3 \cdots a_{i_l}{}^3$ with $a_j{}^3 := a_j a_j a_j$. Now let E be the lcs of $D_1, \ldots, D_k$, and let $\mathcal{G}_E$ be the corresponding normalized description graph with root n_0. From (5.1) we know that $E \sqsubseteq v_s \downarrow w_s$ for every $= s \subseteq \{1, \ldots, k\}$, $s \neq \emptyset$. Theorem 4.1.3 implies that the paths from n_0 in $\mathcal{G}_E$ labeled v_s and w_s exist and that they lead to the same node q_s. Assume, there are non-empty subsets s, t of $\{1, \ldots, k\}$, $s \neq t$, such that $q_s = q_t$. This would imply $E \sqsubseteq v_s \downarrow v_t$ in contradiction to (5.1). Thus, $s \neq t$ implies $q_s \neq q_t$. Since there are $2^k - 1$ non-empty subsets of $\{1, \ldots, k\}$, we can conclude that $\mathcal{G}_E$ contains at least $2^k - 1$ nodes. The fact that the size of $\mathcal{G}_E$ is linear in the size of E completes the proof. □

---

[1] This example has first been proposed in [CBH92] to prove a similar result for total attributes.

This proposition shows that algorithms computing the lcs of sequences are necessarily worst-case exponential. Conversely, based on the polynomial time algorithm for the binary lcs operation, an exponential time algorithm can easily be specified employing the following identity $lcs(D_1, \ldots, D_n) \equiv lcs(D_n, lcs(D_{n-1}, lcs(\cdots lcs(D_2, D_1) \cdots))$.

Corollary 5.1.2. *The size of the lcs of sequences of $\mathcal{ALNS}$-concept descriptions can grow exponentially in the size of the sequences and there exists an exponential time algorithm for computing the lcs.*

As pointed out in Section 4.1.1, $\mathcal{ALN}$-concept descriptions can be represented by description *trees*. Exploring the correspondence between $\mathcal{ALN}$-description trees and those description graphs that come from $\mathcal{ALN}$-concept descriptions, the definition of product graphs (Definition 5.1.1) can easily be carried over to products of $\mathcal{ALN}$-description trees. Now, given a sequence of normalized $\mathcal{ALN}$-description trees, it is easy to verify by induction on the size of these trees that the size of the product tree is bounded by the sum (rather than the product as in the general case) of the size of the input trees. Since proving this is routine, we omit the proof. Note, however, that one must make use of the fact that the trees are deterministic, i.e., every node in a normalized tree has, for every role name, at most one outgoing r-edges labeled with this role. This characteristic is crucial in that otherwise subtrees could be doubled leading to an exponential blow-up. Summing up, for $\mathcal{ALN}$-concept descriptions Corollary 5.1.2 can be rephrased as follows:

Corollary 5.1.3. *The size of the lcs of sequences of $\mathcal{ALN}$-concept descriptions can polynomially be bounded in the size of the sequences and there exists a polynomial time algorithm for computing the lcs.*

5.1.2 The LCS in $\mathcal{LS}$

In the previous subsection, attributes were interpreted as partial functions. In this subsection, we show that interpreting attributes as total functions has a major impact on the existence and complexity of the lcs. More precisely, we will look at a sublanguage $\mathcal{LS}$ of $\mathcal{ALNS}$, which only allows for concept conjunction and same-as equalities, but where we have the general assumption that *attributes are interpreted as total functions*.

We restrict our attention to the language $\mathcal{LS}$ in order to concentrate on the changes caused by going from partial to total attributes. However, we strongly conjecture that the results represented here can easily be transfered to $\mathcal{ALNS}$ using description graphs similar to the ones introduced in Section 4.1.1.

First, we shall show that in $\mathcal{LS}$ the lcs of two concept descriptions does not always exist. Then, we will present a polynomial time decision algorithm for the existence of an lcs of two concept descriptions. Finally, it will be shown that if the lcs of two concept descriptions exists, then i) it may be of size exponential in the size of the given concept descriptions and ii) it can be computed in exponential time. Note that the latter result considerably generalizes the original result in [CBH92], which only provides an exponential size for the lcs of a sequence of concept descriptions.

As an aside, we note that, as pointed out in [CBH92], concept descriptions in $\mathcal{LS}$ correspond to finitely generated right-congruences [Eil74]. Moreover, the lcs of two concept descriptions coincides with the intersection of right-congruences. Thus, first, the results presented in this subsection show that the intersection of finitely generated right-congruences is not always finitely generated, and that, second, there is a polynomial time algorithm deciding the existence of a finite generating system for the intersection. In addition, if the intersection can be finitely generated, then the generating system can be computed by a (necessarily) worst-case exponential time algorithm in the size of the generating systems of the given right-congruences.

A useful observation for understanding the proofs in this section is that for total attributes we have $(u \downarrow v) \sqsubseteq (uw \downarrow vw)$ for any $u, w, v \in N_A^*$, where N_A^* is the set of finite words over N_A, the finite set of attribute names. For partial attributes, this statement not true in general.

The Existence of the LCS. We now show that i) the lcs of two $\mathcal{LS}$-concept descriptions does not exist in general, but that ii) there always exist an infinite representation of the lcs, which will be used later on to characterize the existence of the lcs.

To establish the above, we return to the graph-based characterization of subsumption proposed in [BPS94] — the one modified for partial attributes in Section 4.1.1. For an $\mathcal{LS}$-concept description C, let $\mathcal{G}_C$ denote the corresponding normalized description graph, as defined in Section 4.1.1. Also, the semantics of such graphs can be adopted, except that now attributes must be interpreted as total functions.

Since $\mathcal{LS}$ does not contain (negated) concept names and does not allow for value-restrictions, the nodes in $\mathcal{G}_C$ do not contain (negated) concept names or r-edges. Therefore, $\mathcal{G}_C$ can be defined merely by the triple (N, E, n_0) where N is a finite set of nodes, E is a finite set over $N \times N_A \times N$, and n_0 is the root of the graph.

According to [BPS94], subsumption in $\mathcal{LS}$ can be characterized as follows.

Theorem 5.1.2. *Let C, D be $\mathcal{LS}$-concept descriptions, and $\mathcal{G}_C = (N, E, n_0)$ be the normalized description graph of C. Then, $C \sqsubseteq D$ if, and only if, one of the following conditions are satisfied:*

1. *$D = v \downarrow w$ and there exist words $v', w', u \in N_A^*$ such that $v = v'u$, $w = w'u$, and there are rooted paths in $\mathcal{G}_C$ labeled v' and w', respectively, ending at the same node.*
2. *$D = D_1 \sqcap D_2$ and both $\mathcal{G}_C \sqsubseteq D_1$ and $\mathcal{G}_C \sqsubseteq D_2$.*

We should point out that Theorem 5.1.2 differs from Theorem 4.1.3 in that, for total attributes, as considered here, only rooted paths labeled with *prefixes* of v and w must lead to a common node.

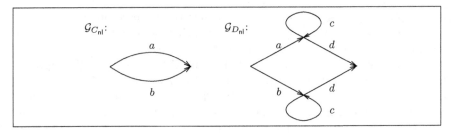

Fig. 5.2. The Normalized Graphs for C_{nl} and D_{nl}.

Theorem 5.1.3. *The lcs for $\mathcal{LS}$-concept descriptions does not exist in general.*[2]

The theorem is proved by the following $\mathcal{LS}$-concept descriptions, for which we show that they do not have an lcs:[3]

$$C_{nl} := a \downarrow b,$$
$$D_{nl} := a \downarrow ac \sqcap b \downarrow bc \sqcap ad \downarrow bd.$$

The graphs for these concepts are depicted in Figure 5.2. The following statement shows that an lcs E of C_{nl} and D_{nl} would satisfy a condition which does not have a "regular structure".

$E \sqsubseteq v \downarrow w$ iff $v = w$ or there exists a nonnegative integer k
and $u \in N_A^*$ such that $v = ac^k du$ and $w = bc^k du$ or vice versa.

In fact, employing Theorem 5.1.2, one can show that no finite description graph can be equivalent to E. However, we omit this elementary proof here, because the absence of the lcs also follows from Theorem 5.1.4, where infinite graphs are used to characterize the existence of an lcs. To state this theorem, we first introduce infinite description graphs and show that there always exists an infinite description graph representing the lcs of two $\mathcal{LS}$-concept descriptions.

An *infinite description graph* $\mathcal{G}$ is defined, like a finite graph, by a triple (N, E, n_0) except that the set of nodes N and the set of edges E may be infinite. As in the finite case, $nvn' \in \mathcal{G}$ means that $\mathcal{G}$ contains a path from n to n' labeled with the word $v \in N_A^*$. The semantics of infinite graphs is defined as in the finite case as well. Furthermore, infinite graphs are translated into concept descriptions as follows: take an (infinite) spanning tree T of $\mathcal{G}$, and, as in the finite case, for every edge of $\mathcal{G}$ not contained in it, add to $C_\mathcal{G}$ a same-as equality. Note that in contrast to the partial attribute case, $C_\mathcal{G}$

---

[2] This result corrects a statement in [CBH92], which claimed that the lcs in $\mathcal{LS}$ always exists. The proposed lcs algorithm, from which this statement was derived, computed however only common subsumers instead of *least* common ones.

[3] "nl" stands for "no lcs".

does not need to contain same-as equalities of the form $v \downarrow v$ since, for total attributes, $v \downarrow v \equiv \top$. Still, $C_{\mathcal{G}}$ might be a concept description with an infinite number of conjuncts (thus, an *infinite concept description*). The semantics of such concept descriptions is defined in the obvious way. Analogously to Lemma 4.1.2, one can show that an (infinite) graph $\mathcal{G}$ and its corresponding (infinite) concept description $C_{\mathcal{G}}$ are equivalent, i.e., $C_{\mathcal{G}} \equiv \mathcal{G}$.

We call an (infinite) description graph $\mathcal{G}$ *deterministic* if, and only if, for every node n in $\mathcal{G}$ and every attribute $a \in N_A$ there exists at most one a-successor for n in $\mathcal{G}$. The graph $\mathcal{G}$ is called *complete* if for every node n in $\mathcal{G}$ and every attribute $a \in N_A$ there is (at least) one a-successor for n in $\mathcal{G}$. Clearly, for a deterministic and complete (infinite) description graph, every path is uniquely determined by its starting point and its label.

Theorem 5.1.2 (which deals with finite description graphs $\mathcal{G}_C$) can be generalized to deterministic and complete (infinite) description graphs $\mathcal{G}$ in a straightforward way. To see this, first note that a (finite) description graph coming from an $\mathcal{LS}$-concept description is normalized iff it is deterministic in the sense just introduced. Analogously, a deterministic infinite graph can be viewed as being normalized. Thus, requiring (infinite) graphs to be deterministic, satisfies the precondition of Theorem 5.1.2. Now, if in addition these graphs are complete, then (unlike the characterization stated in Theorem 5.1.2) it is no longer necessary to consider prefixes of words because a complete graph contains a rooted path for every word. More precisely, if v' and w' lead to the same node, then this is the case for $v = v'u$ and $w = w'u$ as well, thus making it unnecessary to consider the prefixes v' and w' of v and w, respectively. Summing up, we can conclude:

Corollary 5.1.4. *Let $\mathcal{G} = (N, E, n_0)$ be a deterministic and complete (infinite) description graph and $v, w \in N_A^*$. Then,*

$$\mathcal{G} \sqsubseteq v \downarrow w \text{ iff } n_0 v n \in \mathcal{G} \text{ and } n_0 w n \in \mathcal{G} \text{ for some node } n.$$

We shall construct an (infinite) graph representing the lcs of two concept descriptions in $\mathcal{LS}$ as the product of the so-called completed normalized graphs (introduced below). This infinite representation of the lcs will be used later on to characterize the existence of an lcs in $\mathcal{LS}$, i.e., the existence of a finite representation of the lcs.

We now define the completion of a graph. Intuitively, a graph is completed by iteratively adding outgoing a-edges labeled with an attribute a for every node in the graph that does not have such an outgoing a-edge. This process might extend a graph by infinite trees. As an example, the completion of $\mathcal{G}_{C_{nl}}$ (cf. Figure 5.2) is depicted in Figure 5.3 with $N_A = \{a, b, c, d\}$.

Formally, completions are defined as follows: Let $\mathcal{G}$ be an (infinite) description graph. The graph $\mathcal{G}'$ is an *extension* of $\mathcal{G}$ if $\mathcal{G}'$ is obtained from $\mathcal{G}$ by adding a new node $m_{n,a}$ and an edge $(n, a, m_{n,a})$ for every node n in $\mathcal{G}$ and every attribute $a \in N_A$ such that n does not have an outgoing edge labeled a. Now, let $\mathcal{G}^0, \mathcal{G}^1, \mathcal{G}^2, \ldots$ be a sequence of graphs such that $\mathcal{G}^0 = \mathcal{G}$ and $\mathcal{G}^{i+1}$ is an extension of $\mathcal{G}^i$, for $i \geq 0$. If $\mathcal{G}^i = (N_i, E_i, n_0)$, then

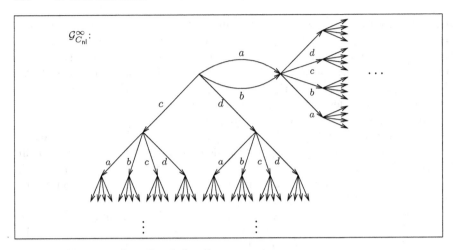

Fig. 5.3. The Complete Graph for C_{nl}.

$$\mathcal{G}^{\infty} := (\bigcup_{i \geq 0} N_i, \bigcup_{i \geq 0} E_i, n_0)$$

is called the *completion* of $\mathcal{G}$. By construction, $\mathcal{G}^{\infty}$ is a complete graph. In addition, if $\mathcal{G}$ is deterministic, then $\mathcal{G}^{\infty}$ is deterministic as well. Finally, it is easy to see that a graph and its extension are equivalent. Thus, by induction, $\mathcal{G}^{\infty} \equiv \mathcal{G}$.

The nodes in $\bigcup_{i \geq 1} N_i$, i.e., the nodes in $\mathcal{G}^{\infty}$ that do not belong to $\mathcal{G}$, are called *tree nodes*; the nodes of $\mathcal{G}$ are called *non-tree nodes*. By construction, for every tree node t in $\mathcal{G}^{\infty}$ there is exactly one direct predecessor of t in $\mathcal{G}^{\infty}$, i.e., there is exactly one node n and one attribute a such that (n, a, t) is an edge in $\mathcal{G}^{\infty}$; n is called *a-predecessor* of t. Furthermore, there is exactly one youngest ancestor n in $\mathcal{G}$ of a tree node t in $\mathcal{G}^{\infty}$: n is the *youngest ancestor* of t if there is a path from n to t in $\mathcal{G}^{\infty}$ which does not contain non-tree nodes except for n. Note that there is exactly one such path from n to t in $\mathcal{G}^{\infty}$. Finally, observe that non-tree nodes have only non-tree nodes as ancestors.

Note that the completion of a normalized description graph is always complete and deterministic.

In the sequel, let C, D be two concept descriptions in $\mathcal{LS}$, $\mathcal{G}_C = (N_C, E_C, n_C)$, $\mathcal{G}_D = (N_D, E_D, n_D)$ be their corresponding normalized graphs, and $\mathcal{G}_C^{\infty}$, $\mathcal{G}_D^{\infty}$ the completions of $\mathcal{G}_C$, $\mathcal{G}_D$. The products

$$\mathcal{G} := \mathcal{G}_C \times \mathcal{G}_D \text{ and } \mathcal{G}_{\infty}^{\times} := \mathcal{G}_C^{\infty} \times \mathcal{G}_D^{\infty}$$

are specified as in Definition 5.1.1. As mentioned below Definition 5.1.1, we may assume $\mathcal{G}$ and $\mathcal{G}_{\infty}^{\times}$ to be connected, i.e., they only contain nodes that are reachable from the root (n_C, n_D). Otherwise, one can remove all those nodes that cannot be reached from the root without changing the semantics of the graphs.

We denote the product $\mathcal{G}_C^\infty \times \mathcal{G}_D^\infty$ by $\mathcal{G}_\infty^\times$ instead of $\mathcal{G}^\infty$ (or $\mathcal{G}_\times^\infty$) because otherwise this graph could be confused with the completion of $\mathcal{G}$. In general, these graphs do not coincide. As an example, take the products $\mathcal{G}_{C_{nl}} \times \mathcal{G}_{D_{nl}}$ and $\mathcal{G}_{C_{nl}}^\infty \times \mathcal{G}_{D_{nl}}^\infty$ (see Figure 5.2 for the graphs $\mathcal{G}_{C_{nl}}$ and $\mathcal{G}_{D_{nl}}$). The former product results in a graph that consists of a root with two outgoing a-edges, one labeled a and the other one labeled b. The product of the completed graphs, on the other hand, is a graph that is obtained as completion of the graph depicted in Figure 5.4 (the infinite trees are omitted for the sake of simplicity).

As an easy consequence of the fact $\mathcal{G}_C \equiv \mathcal{G}_C^\infty$ and Corollary 5.1.4 one can prove the following lemma.

Lemma 5.1.1. $C \sqsubseteq v \downarrow w$ *if, and only if,* $n_C v n \in \mathcal{G}_C^\infty$ *and* $n_C w n \in \mathcal{G}_C^\infty$ *for a node* n *in* $\mathcal{G}_C^\infty$.

But then, by the construction of $\mathcal{G}_\infty^\times$, we know:

Proposition 5.1.2. $C \sqsubseteq v \downarrow w$ *and* $D \sqsubseteq v \downarrow w$ *if, and only if,* $(n_C, n_D)vn \in \mathcal{G}_\infty^\times$ *and* $(n_C, n_D)wn \in \mathcal{G}_\infty^\times$ *for a node* n *in* $\mathcal{G}_\infty^\times$.

In particular, $\mathcal{G}_\infty^\times$ represents the lcs of the concept descriptions C and D in the following sense.

Corollary 5.1.5. *The (infinite) concept description* $C_{\mathcal{G}_\infty^\times}$ *corresponding to* $\mathcal{G}_\infty^\times$ *is the lcs of* C *and* D, *i.e.,* i) $C, D \sqsubseteq C_{\mathcal{G}_\infty^\times}$ *and* ii) $C, D \sqsubseteq E$ *implies* $C_{\mathcal{G}_\infty^\times} \sqsubseteq E$ *for every* $\mathcal{LS}$-*concept description* E.

Characterizing the Existence of an LCS. Let C, D be concept descriptions in $\mathcal{LS}$ and let the graphs $\mathcal{G}_C$, $\mathcal{G}_D$, $\mathcal{G}$, $\mathcal{G}_C^\infty$, $\mathcal{G}_D^\infty$, and $\mathcal{G}_\infty^\times$ be defined as above.

We will show that $\mathcal{G}_\infty^\times$ not only represents a (possibly infinite) lcs of the $\mathcal{LS}$-concept descriptions C and D (Corollary 5.1.5), but that $\mathcal{G}_\infty^\times$ can be used to characterize the existence of a finite lcs. The existence depends on whether $\mathcal{G}_\infty^\times$ contains a finite or an infinite number of so-called same-as nodes.

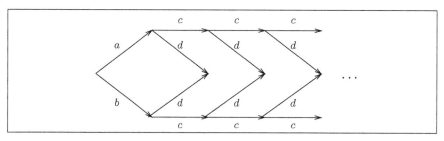

Fig. 5.4. A Subgraph of $\mathcal{G}_{C_{nl}}^\infty \times \mathcal{G}_{D_{nl}}^\infty$.

Definition 5.1.2. *A node n of an (infinite) description graph $\mathcal{H}$ is called a same-as node if there exist two direct predecessors of n in $\mathcal{H}$. (The a-edges leading to n from these nodes may be labeled differently.)*

For example, the graph depicted in Figure 5.4 contains an infinite number of same-as nodes. We will show that this is a sufficient and necessary condition for the (finite) lcs of C_{nl} and D_{nl} *not* to exist.

It is helpful to observe that same-as nodes in $\mathcal{G}_\infty^\times$ are of one of the forms (g, f), (f, t), and (t, f), where g and f are non-tree nodes and t is a tree node. There cannot exist a same-as node of the form (t_1, t_2), where both t_1 and t_2 are tree nodes, since tree nodes only have exactly one direct predecessor, and thus (t_1, t_2) does. Moreover, if $\mathcal{G}_\infty^\times$ has an infinite number of same-as nodes, then it must have an infinite number of same-as nodes of the form (f, t) or (t, f), because there only exist a finite number of nodes in $\mathcal{G}_\infty^\times$ of the form (g, f). For this reason, in the following lemma we only characterize same-as nodes of the form (f, t). (Nodes of the form (t, f) can be dealt with analogously.) To state the lemma, recall that with $n_0 u n_1 v n_2 \in \mathcal{H}$, for some graph $\mathcal{H}$, we describe a path in $\mathcal{H}$ labeled uv from n_0 to n_2 that passes through node n_1 after u (i.e., $n_0 u n_1 \in \mathcal{H}$ and $n_1 v n_2 \in \mathcal{H}$); this is generalized the obvious way to interpret $n_0 u_1 n_1 u_2 n_2 u_3 n_3 \in \mathcal{H}$.

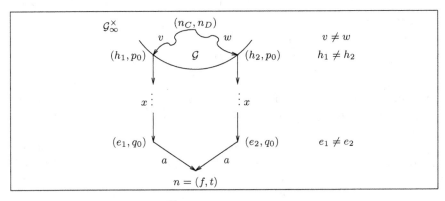

Fig. 5.5. Same-As Nodes in $\mathcal{G}_\infty^\times$.

Lemma 5.1.2. *Given a node f in $\mathcal{G}_C$ and a tree-node t in $\mathcal{G}_D^\infty$, the node $n = (f, t)$ in $\mathcal{G}_\infty^\times$ is a same-as node if, and only if,*

- *there exist nodes (h_1, p_0), (h_2, p_0) in $\mathcal{G}$, $h_1 \neq h_2$;*
- *there exist nodes (e_1, q_0), (e_2, q_0) in $\mathcal{G}_\infty^\times$, where e_1, e_2 are distinct nodes in $\mathcal{G}_C$ and q_0 is a node in $\mathcal{G}_D^\infty$; and*
- *there exists an attribute $a \in N_A$ as well as words $v, w, x \in N_A^*$, $v \neq w$, where N_A is the set of attributes in C,*

such that

$$(n_C, n_D)v(h_1, p_0)x(e_1, q_0)a(f, t) \quad and \quad (n_C, n_D)w(h_2, p_0)x(e_2, q_0)a(f, t)$$

are paths in $\mathcal{G}_\infty^\times$ (see Figure 5.5). For the direct successors (h_1', p_0') and (h_2', p_0') of (h_1, p_0) and (h_2, p_0) in this paths, we, in addition, require p_0' to be a tree node in $\mathcal{G}_D^\infty$.[4]

Proof. The if direction is obvious. For the only-if direction, we assume that n is a same-as node in $\mathcal{G}_\infty^\times$. Let p_0 be the (uniquely determined) youngest ancestor of t in $\mathcal{G}_\infty^\infty$. In particular, p_0 is a node in $\mathcal{G}_D$ and there exists a path $p_0 x q_0 a t$ in $\mathcal{G}_D^\infty$ with $a \in N_A$ and $x \in N_A^*$ such that the direct successor of p_0 in this path is a tree node in $\mathcal{G}_D$.

Since n is a same-as node and t can only be reached via q_0 and the attribute a, there must exist e_1, e_2 in $\mathcal{G}_C$ with $e_1 \neq e_2$ and edges $(e_1, q_0)a(f, t)$, $(e_2, q_0)a(f, t) \in \mathcal{G}_\infty^\times$. Since $\mathcal{G}_\infty^\times$ is connected, there are paths from (n_C, n_D) to (e_1, q_0) and (e_2, q_0). Every path from n_D to q_0 must pass through p_0 and the suffix of the label of this path is x. Consequently, there exist nodes h_1, h_2 in $\mathcal{G}_C$ such that $(h_1, p_0)x(e_1, q_0)a(f, t)$ and $(h_2, p_0)x(e_2, q_0)a(f, t)$ are paths in $\mathcal{G}_\infty^\times$. In particular, xa is a label of a path from h_1 to f in $\mathcal{G}_C$, and the label xa only consists of attributes contained in C. If $h_1 = h_2$, then this, together with the fact that $\mathcal{G}_C$ is deterministic, would imply $e_1 = e_2$. Hence, $h_1 \neq h_2$. Let v, w be the labels of the paths from (n_C, n_D) to (h_1, p_0) and (h_2, p_0), respectively. As $\mathcal{G}$ is deterministic and $h_1 \neq h_2$, it follows that $v \neq w$. □

The main result of this section is stated in the next theorem. As a direct consequence of this theorem, we obtain that there does not exist an lcs in $\mathcal{LS}$ for the concept descriptions C_{nl} and D_{nl} of our example.

Theorem 5.1.4. *The lcs of C and D exists if, and only if, the number of same-as nodes in $\mathcal{G}_\infty^\times$ is finite.*

Proof. We start by proving the only-if direction. For this purpose, we assume that $\mathcal{G}_\infty^\times$ contains an infinite number of same-as nodes, and show that there is no (finite) lcs for C and D in $\mathcal{LS}$.

As argued before, we may assume that $\mathcal{G}_\infty^\times$ contains an infinite number of same-as nodes of the form (f, t) or (t, f), where t is a tree node and f is a non-tree node. More precisely, say $\mathcal{G}_\infty^\times$ contains for every $i \geq 1$ nodes $n_i = (f_i, t_i)$ such that f_i is a node in $\mathcal{G}_C$ and t_i is a tree node in $\mathcal{G}_D^\infty$. According to Lemma 5.1.2, for every same-as node n_i there exist nodes $h_{1,i}, h_{2,i}, e_{1,i}, e_{2,i}$ in $\mathcal{G}_C$, $p_{0,i}$ in $\mathcal{G}_D$, and $q_{0,i}$ in $\mathcal{G}_D^\infty$ as well as $a_i \in N_A$ and $x_i \in N_A^*$ with the properties required in Lemma 5.1.2.

Since $\mathcal{G}_C$ and $\mathcal{G}_D$ are finite description graphs, the number of tuples of the form $h_{1,i}, h_{2,i}, e_{1,i}, e_{2,i}, p_{0,i}, f_i, a_i$ is finite. Thus, there must be an infinite

---

[4] Note that since $\mathcal{G}_\infty^\times$ is deterministic, the successors of (h_1, p_0) and (h_2, p_0) in the two paths must in fact be of the form $(\cdot, p_0')$.

number of indices i yielding the same tuple $h_1, h_2, e_1, e_2, p_0, f, a$. In particular, $h_1 \neq h_2$ and $e_1 \neq e_2$ are nodes in $\mathcal{G}_C$ and there is an infinite number of same-as nodes of the form $n_i = (f, t_i)$. Finally, as in the lemma, let v, w be the label of paths (in $\mathcal{G}$) from (n_C, n_D) to (h_1, p_0) and (h_2, p_0).

Now, assume that there is an lcs E of C and D in $\mathcal{LS}$. According to Corollary 5.1.5, $E \equiv C_{\mathcal{G}_\infty^\times}$. Let $\mathcal{G}_E$ be the finite normalized graph for E with root n'. By Proposition 5.1.2 and Lemma 5.1.2, we know $E \sqsubseteq vx_i a \downarrow wx_i a$. From Theorem 5.1.2 it follows that there are words v', w', and u such that $vx_i a = v'u$ and $wx_i a = w'u$, where the paths in $\mathcal{G}_E$ starting from n' labeled v', w' lead to the same node in $\mathcal{G}_E$.

If $u \neq \varepsilon$, then $u = u'a$ for some word u'. But then, Theorem 5.1.2 ensures $E \sqsubseteq vx_i \downarrow wx_i$. However, by Lemma 5.1.2 we know that the words vx_i and wx_i lead to different nodes in $\mathcal{G}_\infty^\times$, namely, $(e_1, q_{0,i})$ and $(e_2, q_{0,i})$, which, with Proposition 5.1.2, leads to the contradiction $E \equiv \mathcal{G}_\infty^\times \not\sqsubseteq vx_i \downarrow wx_i$. Thus, $u = \varepsilon$.

As a result, for every $i \geq 1$ there exists a node q_i in $\mathcal{G}_E$ such that $n'vx_iaq_i$ and $n'wx_iaq_i$ are paths in $\mathcal{G}_E$. Because $\mathcal{G}_E$ is a finite graph, there exist $i, j \geq 1$, $i \neq j$, with $q_i = q_j$. By Theorem 5.1.2, this implies $E \sqsubseteq vx_i a \downarrow wx_j a$. On the other hand, the path in $\mathcal{G}_\infty^\times$ starting from (n_C, n_D) with label $vx_i a$ leads to the node n_i and the one for $wx_j a$ leads to n_j. Since $n_i \neq n_j$, Proposition 5.1.2 implies $E \equiv \mathcal{G}_\infty^\times \not\sqsubseteq vx_i a \downarrow wx_j a$, which is a contradiction. To sum up, we have shown that there does not exist an lcs of C, D in $\mathcal{LS}$.

We now turn to the proof of the if direction. For this purpose, we assume that $\mathcal{G}_\infty^\times$ has only a finite number of same-as nodes. Note that every same-as node in $\mathcal{G}_\infty^\times$ has only a finite number of direct predecessors. To see this point, two cases are distinguished: i) a node of the form (g_1, g_2) in $\mathcal{G}$ has only predecessors in $\mathcal{G}$; ii) if t is a tree node and g a non-tree node, then a predecessor of (g, t) in $\mathcal{G}_\infty^\times$ is of the form (g', t') where t' is the unique predecessor (tree or non-tree node) of t and g' is a non-tree node. Since the number of nodes in $\mathcal{G}_C$ and $\mathcal{G}_D$ is finite, in both cases we only have a finite number of predecessors. But then, the spanning tree T of $\mathcal{G}_\infty^\times$ coincides with $\mathcal{G}_\infty^\times$ except for a finite number of edges because, if T does not contain a certain edge, then this edge leads to a same-as node. As a result, $C_{\mathcal{G}_\infty^\times}$ is an $\mathcal{LS}$- concept description because it is a finite conjunction of same-as equalities. Finally, Corollary 5.1.5 shows that $C_{\mathcal{G}_\infty^\times}$ is the lcs of C and D. □

If $v \downarrow w$ is a conjunct in $C_{\mathcal{G}_\infty^\times}$, then v and w lead from the root of $\mathcal{G}_\infty^\times$ to a same-as node. As mentioned before, same-as nodes are of one of the three forms $(f, g), (f, t)$, or (t, f), where t is a tree node and f, g are non-tree nodes. Consequently, v and w must be paths in $\mathcal{G}_C$ or $\mathcal{G}_D$ because in a rooted path to a same-as node, in one component one must follow a path in $\mathcal{G}_C$ or $\mathcal{G}_D$. Thus, v and w only contain attributes occurring in C or D.

Corollary 5.1.6. *If the lcs of two $\mathcal{LS}$-concept descriptions C and D exists in $\mathcal{LS}$, then there also exists an equivalent $\mathcal{LS}$-concept description only containing attributes occurring in C or D.*

Therefore, when asking for the existence of an lcs, we can w.o.l.g. assume that the set of attributes N_A is finite. This fact will be used in the following.

Deciding the Existence of an LCS. From the following corollary, we will derive the desired decision algorithm for the existence of the lcs in $\mathcal{LS}$. To state the corollary we need to introduce the regular language $L_{\mathcal{G}_C}(q_1, q_2) := \{w \in N_A^* \mid q_1 w q_2 \in \mathcal{G}_C\}$. Moreover, let aN_A^* denote the set $\{aw \mid w \in N_A^*\}$ for an attribute $a \in N_A$, where N_A is a finite alphabet.

Corollary 5.1.7. $\mathcal{G}_\infty^\times$ *contains an infinite number of same-as nodes if, and only if, either (i) there exist nodes* (h_1, p_0), (h_2, p_0) *in* $\mathcal{G}$ *as well as nodes* f, e_1, e_2 *in* $\mathcal{G}_C$, *and attributes* $a, b \in N_A$ *such that*

1. $h_1 \neq h_2$, $e_1 \neq e_2$;
2. p_0 *does not have a b-successor in* $\mathcal{G}_D$;
3. (e_1, a, f), (e_2, a, f) *are edges in* $\mathcal{G}_C$; *and*
4. $L_{\mathcal{G}_C}(h_1, e_1) \cap L_{\mathcal{G}_C}(h_2, e_2) \cap bN_A^*$ *is an infinite set of words;*

or

(ii) the same statement as (i), but with rôles of C and D switched.

Proof. We first prove the only-if direction. Assume that $\mathcal{G}_\infty^\times$ contains an infinite number of same-as nodes. Then, w.l.o.g., we find the configuration in $\mathcal{G}_\infty^\times$ described in the proof of Theorem 5.1.4. This configuration satisfies the conditions 1. and 3. stated in the corollary. If, for $i \neq j$, the words x_i and x_j coincide, then we can conclude $n_i = n_j$ because $\mathcal{G}_\infty^\times$ is a deterministic graph. However, by definition, $n_i \neq n_j$. Hence, $x_i \neq x_j$. Since N_A is finite, we can, w.l.o.g., assume that all x_i's have $b \in N_A$ as their first letter for some fixed b. Thus, condition 4. is satisfied as well. According to the configuration, the b-successor of $(\cdot, p_0)$ in $\mathcal{G}_\infty^\times$ is of the form $(\cdot, p_0')$ where p_0' is a tree node. Thus, p_0 does not have a b-successor in $\mathcal{G}_D$, which means that condition 2. is satisfied.

We now prove the if direction of the corollary. For this purpose, let $bx \in L_{\mathcal{G}_C}(h_1, e_1) \cap L_{\mathcal{G}_C}(h_2, e_2) \cap bN_A^*$. Since p_0 does not have a b-successor in $\mathcal{G}_D$ it follows that there are tree nodes t, t' in $\mathcal{G}_D^\infty$ such that $p_0 bxtat' \in \mathcal{G}_D^\infty$. Thus, we have $(h_1, p_0)bx(e_1, t)a(f, t') \in \mathcal{G}_\infty^\times$ and $(h_2, p_0)bx(e_2, t)a(f, t') \in \mathcal{G}_\infty^\times$. Since $e_1 \neq e_2$, we can conclude $(e_1, t) \neq (e_2, t)$. This means that (f, t') is a same-as node. Analogously, for $by \in L_{\mathcal{G}_C}(h_1, e_1) \cap L_{\mathcal{G}_C}(h_2, e_2) \cap bN_A^*$ there are tree nodes s, s' in $\mathcal{G}_D^\infty$ such that $p_0 bysas' \in \mathcal{G}_D^\infty$ and (f, s') is a same-as node in $\mathcal{G}_\infty^\times$. Since bx and by both start with b, and the b-successor of p_0 in $\mathcal{G}_D^\infty$ is a tree node, $x \neq y$ implies $s' \neq t'$. Hence, (f, t') and (f, s') are distinct same-as nodes. This shows that if the set $L_{\mathcal{G}_C}(h_1, e_1) \cap L_{\mathcal{G}_C}(h_2, e_2) \cap bN_A^*$ is infinite, $\mathcal{G}_\infty^\times$ must have an infinite number of same-as nodes. □

For given nodes (h_1, p_0), (h_2, p_0) in $\mathcal{G}$, attributes $a, b \in N_A$, and nodes $f, e_1, e_2 \in \mathcal{G}_C$, the conditions 1. to 3. in Corollary 5.1.7 can obviously be checked in time polynomial in the size of the concept descriptions C and D.

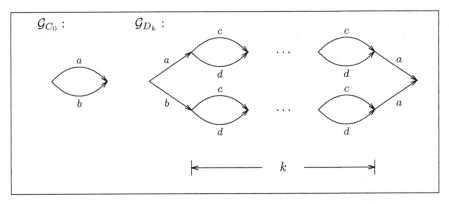

Fig. 5.6. The Normalized Description Graphs for C_0 and D_k.

As for the last condition, note that an automaton accepting the language $L_{\mathcal{G}_C}(h_1, e_1) \cap L_{\mathcal{G}_C}(h_2, e_2) \cap bN_A^*$ can be constructed in time polynomial in the size of C. Furthermore, for a given finite automaton it is decidable in time polynomial in the size of the automaton if it accepts an infinite language (see [HU79] for details). Thus, condition 4. can be tested in time polynomial in the size of C and D as well. Finally, since the size of $\mathcal{G}$ and $\mathcal{G}_C$ is polynomial in the size of C and D, only a polynomial number of configurations need to be tested. Together with Corollary 5.1.7 these complexities provide us with the following corollary.

Corollary 5.1.8. *For given $\mathcal{LS}$-concept descriptions C and D it is decidable in time polynomial in the size of C and D whether the lcs of C and D exists in $\mathcal{LS}$.*

Computing the LCS. In the remainder of this subsection, we first show that the size of the lcs of two $\mathcal{LS}$-concept descriptions may grow exponentially in the size of the concept descriptions, and then present an exponential time lcs algorithm for $\mathcal{LS}$-concept descriptions.

Let us consider the following example, where $N_A := \{a, b, c, d\}$. For an attribute α, let α^k, $k \geq 0$, denote the word $\alpha \cdots \alpha$ of length k. We define

$$C_0 := a \downarrow b,$$

$$D_k := \prod_{i=1}^{k} ac^i \downarrow ad^i \sqcap \prod_{i=1}^{k} bc^i \downarrow bd^i \sqcap ac^k a \downarrow bc^k a.$$

The corresponding normalized description graphs $\mathcal{G}_{C_0}$ and $\mathcal{G}_{D_k}$ are depicted in Figure 5.6. A finite graph representing the lcs of C_0 and D_k with $k = 2$ is depicted in Figure 5.7. It can easily be derived from $\mathcal{G}_{C_0}^\infty \times \mathcal{G}_{D_2}^\infty$.

In the following, we will show that there is no normalized description graph $\mathcal{G}_{E_k}$ (with root n_0) representing the lcs E_k of C_0 and D_k with less than 2^k nodes. Let $x \in \{c, d\}^k$ be a word of length k over $\{c, d\}$ and let $v := axa$,

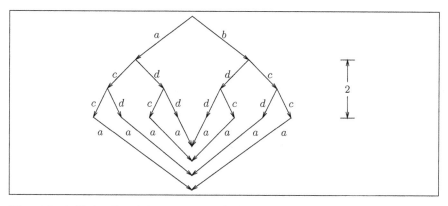

Fig. 5.7. A Finite Graph Representing the lcs of C_0 and D_2.

$w := bxa$. Using the normalized description graphs $\mathcal{G}_{C_0}$ and $\mathcal{G}_{D_k}$ it is easy to see that $C_0 \sqsubseteq v \downarrow w$ and $D_k \sqsubseteq v \downarrow w$. Thus, $E_k \sqsubseteq v \downarrow w$. By Theorem 5.1.2, this means that there are words v', w', u such that $v = v'u$, $w = w'u$, and there are paths from n_0 labeled v' and w' in $\mathcal{G}_{E_k}$ leading to the same node in $\mathcal{G}_{E_k}$. Suppose $u \neq \varepsilon$. Then, Theorem 5.1.2 implies $E_k \sqsubseteq ax \downarrow bx$. But according to $\mathcal{G}_D$, $D \not\sqsubseteq ax \downarrow bx$. Therefore, u must be the empty word ε. This proves that in $\mathcal{G}_{E_k}$ there is a path from n_0 labeled axa for every $x \in \{c, d\}^k$. Hence, there exists a path for every ax. Now, let $y \in \{c, d\}^k$ be such that $x \neq y$. If the paths for ax and ay from n_0 in $\mathcal{G}_{E_k}$ lead to the same node, then this implies $E_k \sqsubseteq ax \downarrow ay$ in contradiction to $C_0 \not\sqsubseteq ax \downarrow ay$. As a result, ax and ay lead to different nodes in $\mathcal{G}_{E_k}$. Since the set $\{c, d\}^k$ contains 2^k words, this shows that $\mathcal{G}_{E_k}$ has at least 2^k nodes. Finally, taking into account that the size of a normalized graph of a concept description in $\mathcal{LS}$ is linear in the size of the corresponding description we obtain the following theorem.

Theorem 5.1.5. *The lcs of two $\mathcal{LS}$-concept descriptions may grow exponentially in the size of the concepts.*

The following (exponential time) algorithm computes the lcs of two $\mathcal{LS}$-concept descriptions in case it exists.

Algorithm 5.1.1

Input: *two $\mathcal{LS}$-concept descriptions C and D for which the lcs exists in $\mathcal{LS}$;*

Output: *lcs of C and D;*

1. *Compute $\mathcal{G}' := \mathcal{G}_C \times \mathcal{G}_D$;*
2. *For every combination*
   - *of nodes (h_1, p_0), (h_2, p_0) in $\mathcal{G} = \mathcal{G}_C \times \mathcal{G}_D$, $h_1 \neq h_2$;*
   - *$a \in N_A$, e_1, e_2, f in $\mathcal{G}_C$, $e_1 \neq e_2$, where (e_1, a, f) and (e_2, a, f) are edges in $\mathcal{G}_C$*

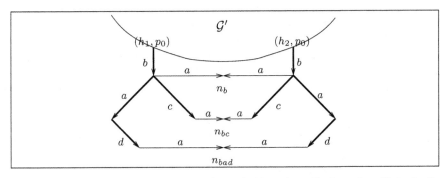

Fig. 5.8. The Extension at the Nodes (h_1, p_0), (h_2, p_0) in $\mathcal{G}'$ where $L = \{b, bc, bad\}$.

extend $\mathcal{G}'$ as follows: Let $\mathcal{G}_{h_1,t}$, $\mathcal{G}_{h_2,t}$ be two trees representing the (finite) set of words in L defined by

$$\left(L_{\mathcal{G}_C}(h_1, e_1) \cap L_{\mathcal{G}_C}(h_2, e_2) \cap \bigcup_{b \notin succ(p_0)} bN_A^* \right) \cup \begin{cases} \{\varepsilon\}, & \text{if } a \notin succ(p_0) \\ \emptyset, & \text{otherwise} \end{cases}$$

where $succ(p_0) := \{b \mid p_0 \text{ has a } b\text{-successor}\}$ and the set of nodes of $\mathcal{G}_{h_1,t}$, $\mathcal{G}_{h_2,t}$, and $\mathcal{G}'$ are disjoint. Now, replace the root of $\mathcal{G}_{h_1,t}$ by (h_1, p_0), the root of $\mathcal{G}_{h_2,t}$ by (h_2, p_0), and extend $\mathcal{G}'$ by the nodes and edges of these two trees. Finally, add a new node n_v for every word v in L, and for each node of the trees $\mathcal{G}_{h_1,t}$ and $\mathcal{G}_{h_2,t}$ reachable from the root of $\mathcal{G}_{h_1,t}$ and $\mathcal{G}_{h_2,t}$ by a path labeled v, add an edge with label a from it to n_v. The extension is illustrated in Figure 5.8.

3. *The same as in step 2, with rôles of C and D switched.*

4. *Compute the normalized graph of $\mathcal{G}'$, which is called $\mathcal{G}'$ again. Then, output the concept description $C_{\mathcal{G}'}$ of $\mathcal{G}'$.*

Proposition 5.1.3. *The translation $C_{\mathcal{G}'}$ of the graph $\mathcal{G}'$ computed by Algorithm 5.1.1 is the lcs E of C and D.*

Proof. It is easy to see that, if there are two path in $\mathcal{G}'$ labeled y_1 and y_2 leading from the root (n_C, n_D) to the same node, then $\mathcal{G}_\infty^\times$ contains such paths as well. Consequently, $(E \equiv) \mathcal{G}_\infty^\times \sqsubseteq \mathcal{G}'$.

Now, assume $E \sqsubseteq y_1 \downarrow y_2$, $y_1 \neq y_2$. By Proposition 5.1.2 we know that there are paths in $\mathcal{G}_\infty^\times$ labeled y_1 and y_2 leading to the same node n. W.l.o.g, we may assume that n is a same-as node in $\mathcal{G}_\infty^\times$. Otherwise, there exist words y_1', y_2', u with $y_1 = y_1'u$, $y_2 = y_2'u$ such that y_1' and y_2' lead to a same-as node. If we can show that $\mathcal{G}'$ contains paths labeled y_1' and y_2' leading to the same node, then by Theorem 5.1.2 this is sufficient for $\mathcal{G}' \sqsubseteq y_1 \downarrow y_2$. So let n be a same-as node. We distinguish two cases:

1. If n is a node in $\mathcal{G} = \mathcal{G}_C \times \mathcal{G}_D$, then the paths for y_1 and y_2 are paths in $\mathcal{G}$. Since $\mathcal{G}$ is a subgraph of $\mathcal{G}'$ this holds true for $\mathcal{G}'$ as well. Hence, $C_{\mathcal{G}'} \sqsubseteq y_1 \downarrow y_2$.

2. Assume n is not a node in $\mathcal{G}$. Then, since n is a same-as node, we know that n is of the form (f, t) or (t, f) where f is a non-tree node and t is a tree node. By symmetry, we may assume that $n = (f, t)$. Now, it is easy to see that there exist nodes h_1, h_2, e_1, e_2 in $\mathcal{G}_C$, p_0 in $\mathcal{G}_D$, and a tree node q_0 in $\mathcal{G}_D^\infty$ as well as $a \in N_A$ and $x, v, w \in N_A^*$ as specified in Lemma 5.1.2 such that $y_1 = vxa$ and $y_2 = wxa$. But then, with $h_1, h_2, e_1, e_2, p_0, f$ and a the preconditions of Algorithm 5.1.1 are satisfied and $x \in L$. Therefore, by construction of $\mathcal{G}'$ there are paths labeled y_1 and y_2, respectively, leading from the root to the same node. □

We note that the product $\mathcal{G}$ of $\mathcal{G}_C$ and $\mathcal{G}_D$ can be computed in time polynomial in the size of C and D. Furthermore, there is only a polynomial number of combinations of nodes (h_1, p_0), (h_2, p_0) in $\mathcal{G}$, e_1, e_2, f in $\mathcal{G}_C$, $a \in N_A$. Finally, the finite automaton for L can be computed in time polynomial in the size of C and D. In particular, the set of states of this automaton can polynomially be bounded in the size of C and D. If L contained a word longer than the number of states, then this implies that the accepting path in the automaton contains a cyclic. But then, the automaton would accept infinite many words, in contradiction to the assumption that L is finite. Thus, the length of all words in L can polynomially be bounded in the size of C and D. Particularly, this means that L contains only an exponential number of words. Trees representing these words can be computed in time exponential in the size of C and D.

Corollary 5.1.9. *If the lcs of two $\mathcal{LS}$-concept descriptions exists, then it can be computed in time exponential in the size of the concept descriptions.*

5.2 LCS and MSC for $\mathcal{ALN}^*$-Concept Descriptions

As pointed out in Section 3.1, the msc of concept descriptions has first been introduced to reduce instance checking to the subsumption problem (see [Neb90a, DLN90, DE92, DLNS94]). Cohen and Hirsh [CH94b] employed the msc operation to abstract from individuals defined in an ABox in order to learn new concept descriptions from examples. In all these cases, the msc has only been approximated since in the considered languages the msc does not exist in general. In Section 3.1, an example of an $\mathcal{ALN}$-ABox was presented demonstrating this.

In this section, we show that, when going from $\mathcal{ALN}$- to $\mathcal{ALN}^*$-concept descriptions, the msc always exists and can effectively be computed. Once one allows for cyclic concept descriptions, the algorithm computing the lcs must also deal with these descriptions.

In the following subsection, we show how the lcs of $\mathcal{ALN}^*$-concept descriptions can be computed. The second subsection then presents an algorithm for computing the msc. As by-product, we obtain decision algorithms for the consistency of ABoxes and the instance problem.

5.2.1 Computing the LCS for $\mathcal{ALN}^*$-Concept Descriptions

Intuitively, the lcs of a collection of concepts describes the largest set of commonalities of these concepts. In $\mathcal{ALN}^*$, all properties of a concept are explicated by its value-restriction sets. Therefore, intuitively the value-restriction sets of the lcs should be intersections of the value-restriction sets of the input concepts. In fact, as a simple consequence of Corollary 4.2.1, we obtain:

Theorem 5.2.1. *Let C, D be $\mathcal{ALN}^*$-concept descriptions. Then, the $\mathcal{ALN}^*$-concept description E is the lcs of C and D if, and only if, $V_E(F) = V_C(F) \cap V_D(F)$ for the bottom-concept, all (negated) concept names, and number restrictions F in C and D.*

Proof. First, assume that E is the lcs of C and D. Then by definition of the lcs we can conclude: $C \sqsubseteq \forall w.F$ and $D \sqsubseteq \forall w.F$ iff $E \sqsubseteq \forall w.F$ for every word $w \in N_A^*$ and every F. But this means, $w \in V_C(F)$ and $w \in V_D(F)$ iff $w \in V_E(F)$. Thus, $V_E(F) = V_C(F) \cap V_D(F)$.

Conversely, assume $V_E(F) = V_C(F) \cap V_D(F)$. Thus, $V_E(F) \subseteq V_C(F)$ and $V_E(F) \subseteq V_D(F)$. By Corollary 4.2.1 this means that $C \sqsubseteq E$ and $D \sqsubseteq E$. Now, let E' be some $\mathcal{ALN}^*$-concept descriptions with $C \sqsubseteq E'$ and $D \sqsubseteq E'$. Then, Corollary 4.2.1 implies $V'_E(F) \subseteq V_C(F) \cap V_D(F)$. But then, $V'_E(F) \subseteq V_E(F)$, and thus, $E \sqsubseteq E'$. This shows that E is the lcs of C and D. $\square$

This theorem can be generalized to sequences of $\mathcal{ALN}^*$-concept descriptions in the obvious way.

An $\mathcal{ALN}^*$-concept description E satisfying the property stated in Theorem 5.2.1 (both for two concepts and sequences of concepts) can be constructed as follows: First, recall that value-restriction sets are regular languages and automata accepting these languages can be computed in time exponential in the size of the given concept descriptions (Theorem 4.2.3). Therefore, automata accepting the intersection of these sets can be computed in exponential time as well. Translating the automata back into TBoxes, yields an $\mathcal{ALN}^*$-concept description E with $L_E(F) = V_C(F) \cap V_D(F)$. Consequently, $V_E(F) \supseteq V_C(F) \cap V_D(F)$, since $L_E(F) \subseteq V_E(F)$. On the other hand, from $L_E(F) \subseteq V_C(F)$ and Theorem 4.2.2 it follows that $C \sqsubseteq E$. But then, Corollary 4.2.3 implies $V_E(F) \subseteq V_C(F)$. The same argument applies to D, which shows $V_E(F) = V_C(F) \cap V_D(F)$.

Corollary 5.2.1. *The lcs of a sequence of $\mathcal{ALN}^*$-concept descriptions can be computed in exponential time and its size is at most exponential in the size of the input descriptions.*

We conjecture that this complexity cannot be avoided, i.e., there does not exist a polynomial time algorithm for computing the lcs in this case. One point supporting this conjecture is that subsumption for $\mathcal{ALN}^*$-concept descriptions is already PSPACE-complete (Corollary 4.2.3). It is, however, not clear how to reduce the subsumption problem (in polynomial time) to the problem of computing the lcs. In fact, if $C \sqsubseteq D$, then the lcs of C and D is equivalent to D, but testing for this equivalence may be as hard as testing for subsumption.

In [YZ91], it has been shown that the size of finite automata accepting the intersection $L_1 \cap \cdots \cap L_n$ of a sequence of regular languages L_i may grow exponentially in the size of the automata accepting the languages L_i.[5] Thus, the size of the lcs of the $\mathcal{ALN}^*$-concept descriptions $C_i := \forall L_i.P$, where P is some concept name, may grow exponentially as well.

Corollary 5.2.2. *The size of the lcs of a sequence of $\mathcal{ALN}^*$-concept descriptions may grow exponentially in the size of the sequence.*

As already mentioned in Section 4.2, value-restriction sets $V_C(\cdot)$ for $\mathcal{ALN}$-concept descriptions are accepted by tree-like automata which can be computed in time polynomial in the size of C. In [BKBM99], it has been shown that the size of the product of sequences of tree-like automata can polynomially be bounded in the size of the input automata. Together with Theorem 5.2.1 this provides us with yet another proof of Corollary 5.1.3.

5.2.2 Computing the MSC for $\mathcal{ALN}^*$-Concept Descriptions

Similar to the previous subsection, the key to computing the msc of an individual a are value-restriction sets, i.e., the set of all words w such that $a \in_{\mathcal{A}} \forall w.F$. The main difficulty lies in showing that these sets are regular languages and that finite automata accepting these sets can be effectively computed. As a by-product, we will obtain decision algorithms for the instance problem. Note that, if $\mathcal{A}$ is inconsistent, then the value-restriction set of a is N_R^*. Therefore, before examining value-restriction sets, we need to characterize the inconsistency of ABoxes.

In this subsection, we restrict our attention to the sublanguage $\mathcal{FLN}^*$ of $\mathcal{ALN}^*$, which does not allow for primitive negation and the bottom-concept. The reasons for this are twofold: First, the main technical problems to be solved already occur for $\mathcal{FLN}^*$. Thus, taking primitive negation

---

[5] Actually, the result in [YZ91] has been shown for deterministic finite automata only. More precisely, for certain classes of languages L_i (which can be accepted by deterministic automata of size n) it has been shown that the size of every deterministic automaton accepting the intersection of the L_i's must have at least n^n states. However, it is not hard to verify that the L_i's can only be excepted by non-deterministic automata of size at least n as well, and that a non-deterministic automaton accepting the intersection must also have n^n states. Thus, the result shown in [YZ91] carries over to the non-deterministic case.

or the bottom-concept into account would only distract us from the actual problems. Second, extending the obtained results to $\mathcal{ALN}^*$ is simple.

Inconsistency of ABoxes. We will now prove an automata-theoretic characterization of the inconsistency of $\mathcal{FLN}^*$-ABoxes. On the one hand, from this characterization we derive decision algorithms and complexity results for inconsistency, and on the other hand, the characterization is needed later on to compute the msc of individuals.

Throughout the section, let $\mathcal{A}$ be an arbitrary but fixed $\mathcal{FLN}^*$-ABox, $I_{\mathcal{A}}$ the set of individuals in $\mathcal{A}$, $a, b, c \in I_{\mathcal{A}}$ individuals in $\mathcal{A}$ and F a concept name or a number-restriction. Recall that, if $\mathcal{I}$ is a model of $\mathcal{A}$, $d, e \in \Delta^{\mathcal{I}}$, $v \in N_R^*$ with $(d, e) \in v^{\mathcal{I}}$ ($dv^{\mathcal{I}}e$ for short), then e is called v-*successor* of d and we refer to a path in $\mathcal{I}$ from d to e labeled v by $dv^{\mathcal{I}}e$. As usual, for $r \in N_A$ and an interpretation $\mathcal{I}$, $r^{\mathcal{I}}(d) := \{e \mid (d, e) \in r^{\mathcal{I}}\}$ denotes the set of r-successors of d in $\mathcal{I}$.

In addition to automata corresponding to cyclic $\mathcal{FLN}$-concept descriptions (see Section 4.2), and thus $\mathcal{FLN}^*$-concept descriptions, we need a semi-automaton corresponding to the role assertions in the ABox $\mathcal{A}$.

Definition 5.2.1. *For an ABox $\mathcal{A}$, the* semi-automaton corresponding to $\mathcal{A}$ *is a triple $(N_R, I_{\mathcal{A}}, \Delta)$, where the states of this automaton are the individual names $I_{\mathcal{A}}$ occurring in $\mathcal{A}$, and the transitions Δ are the role assertions of $\mathcal{A}$, i.e., there is a transition labeled r from a to b iff $r(a, b) \in \mathcal{A}$.*

For individual names a, b occurring in $\mathcal{A}$, the (regular) language $L_a(b)$ is the set of all words labeling paths from a to b in the automaton to $\mathcal{A}$. We say that there is a *role chain in $\mathcal{A}$* from the individual a to b with label u (aub for short) iff $u \in L_a(b)$. Note that $a\varepsilon a$ is also a role chain in $\mathcal{A}$. The set $r_{\mathcal{A}}(a) := \{b \mid r(a, b) \in \mathcal{A}\}$ denotes the set of r-*successors* of a in $\mathcal{A}$.

The notions specified in the following two definitions, which build the basis for all subsequent considerations in this section, represent value-restrictions and number-restrictions that must be satisfied by individuals of $\mathcal{A}$.

Definition 5.2.2. *A* predecessor restriction set *for an individual a and a concept name or number restriction F (w.r.t. an ABox $\mathcal{A}$) is defined by*

$$L_a(F) := \{w \in N_R^* \mid \text{there exists } E(f) \in \mathcal{A} \text{ and a word } u \in L_f(a) \\ \text{such that } uw \in L_E(F)\}.$$

The name of this set is inspired by the fact that all value-restrictions $\forall w.F$ encoded by it are imposed by predecessors f of a. The following lemma shows that a must be an instance of these value-restrictions.

Lemma 5.2.1. *For all words $w \in L_a(F)$, $a \in_{\mathcal{A}} \forall w.F$.*

Proof. Let $\mathcal{I}$ be a model of $\mathcal{A}$. If $w \in L_a(F)$, then there exists $E(f) \in \mathcal{A}$ and a word $u \in L_f(a)$ such that $uw \in L_E(F)$. Let $d \in \Delta^{\mathcal{I}}$ be a w-successor of $a^{\mathcal{I}}$, i.e., $a^{\mathcal{I}}w^{\mathcal{I}}d$. Since $\mathcal{I}$ is a model of $\mathcal{A}$, it follows that $f^{\mathcal{I}}u^{\mathcal{I}}a^{\mathcal{I}}w^{\mathcal{I}}d$ and $f^{\mathcal{I}} \in E^{\mathcal{I}}$. Now, by Theorem 4.2.1, $uw \in L_E(F)$ implies $d \in F^{\mathcal{I}}$, which shows $a^{\mathcal{I}} \in (\forall w.F)^{\mathcal{I}}$. $\qquad\square$

For number restrictions we are, in addition, interested in the maximum and minimum number restrictions an individual and its successors have to satisfy.

Definition 5.2.3. *For $v \in N_R^*$, $r \in N_R$, and an individual a define*

$$c_{a,v}^{\geq r} := max\{n \mid v \in L_a(\geq nr)\} \quad (max(\emptyset) := 0) \text{ and}$$
$$c_{a,v}^{\leq r} := min\{n \mid v \in L_a(\leq nr)\} \quad (min(\emptyset) := \infty)$$

to be the r-number conditions for v-successors of a.

Since the languages $L_a(\geq nr)$ and $L_a(\leq nr)$ are non-empty for only a finite number of number restrictions, the number conditions are well-defined. In every model of $\mathcal{A}$, the number of r-successors of v-successors of a has to satisfy the number conditions.

Lemma 5.2.2. *If $\mathcal{I}$ is a model of $\mathcal{A}$ and $d \in \Delta^{\mathcal{I}}$ with $a^{\mathcal{I}} v^{\mathcal{I}} d$, then $c_{a,v}^{\geq r} \leq |r^{\mathcal{I}}(d)| \leq c_{a,v}^{\leq r}$.*

Proof. To show $c_{a,v}^{\geq r} \leq |r^{\mathcal{I}}(d)|$, we distinguish two cases:

- There exists a non-negative integer n such that $v \in L_a(\geq nr)$ and $n = c_{a,v}^{\geq r}$. According to Lemma 5.2.1, it follows that $a^{\mathcal{I}} \in (\forall v. \geq n\, r)^{\mathcal{I}}$. But then, $a^{\mathcal{I}} v^{\mathcal{I}} d$ implies $d \in (\geq n\, r)^{\mathcal{I}}$, which shows $c_{a,v}^{\geq r} \leq |r^{\mathcal{I}}(d)|$.
- If $c_{a,v}^{\geq r} = 0$, then there is nothing to show.

The statement $c_{a,v}^{\leq r} \geq |r^{\mathcal{I}}(d)|$ can be proved analogously.   □

Finally, similar to the case of cyclic concept descriptions (Definition 4.2.6), certain words might be required by individuals.

Definition 5.2.4. *Let $v, v' \in N_R^*$, $v' = r_1 \cdots r_n$, and $\mathcal{A}$ be an ABox. Then, we say vv' is v-required by the individual a if $c_{a,vr_1 \cdots r_{i-1}}^{\geq r_i} \geq 1$ for all $1 \leq i \leq n$. Moreover, a word w is required by a if there are words v, v' and an individual b in $\mathcal{A}$ such that $w = vv'$, avb is a role chain in $\mathcal{A}$, and v' is ε-required by b.*

The following lemma, which illustrates the meaning of the above definition, is an easy consequence of Lemma 5.2.2.

Lemma 5.2.3. *Let $\mathcal{I}$ be a model of $\mathcal{A}$. If $d \in \Delta^{\mathcal{I}}$, $v, v' \in N_R^*$, $a^{\mathcal{I}} v^{\mathcal{I}} d$, and vv' is v-required by a, then there exists a v'-successor of d in $\mathcal{I}$. If the word v is ε-required by a, then there is a v-successor of a in $\mathcal{I}$.*

With these notions, we are prepared to characterize inconsistency of $\mathcal{FLN}^*$-ABoxes.

Theorem 5.2.2. *The $\mathcal{FLN}^*$-ABox $\mathcal{A}$ is inconsistent if, and only if,*

1. *there exists an individual a in $\mathcal{A}$, $r \in N_R$ such that $|r_{\mathcal{A}}(a)| > c_{a,\varepsilon}^{\leq r}$, or*
2. *there exists an individual a in $\mathcal{A}$, $v \in N_R^*$, and $r \in N_R$ such that v is ε-required by a and $c_{a,v}^{\geq r} > c_{a,v}^{\leq r}$.*

In what follows, we prove Theorem 5.2.2. The if direction is easy to show by contraposition: Let $\mathcal{I}$ be a model of $\mathcal{A}$. Let a be an individual in $\mathcal{A}$ and $r \in N_R$. By Lemma 5.2.2 we know $|r^{\mathcal{I}}(a)| \leq c_{a,\varepsilon}^{\leq r}$. As a consequence of the unique name assumption this means $|r_{\mathcal{A}}(a)| \leq c_{a,\varepsilon}^{\leq r}$, and thus excludes 1. In addition, if there is an individual a in $\mathcal{A}$ and a v ε-required by a, Lemma 5.2.3 implies that a has a v-successor d in $\mathcal{I}$. But then, Lemma 5.2.2 ensures $c_{a,v}^{\geq r} \leq r^{\mathcal{I}}(d) \leq c_{a,v}^{\leq r}$, and thus $c_{a,v}^{\geq r} \leq c_{a,v}^{\leq r}$, excluding 2.

For the only-if direction, we show that, if 1. or 2. do not hold, then it is possible to construct a model of $\mathcal{A}$. For this purpose we need to extend the definitions of predecessor restriction sets and number conditions to arbitrary individuals of the domain of an interpretation $\mathcal{I}$.

Definition 5.2.5. *Let $\mathcal{I}$ be an interpretation and $d \in \Delta^{\mathcal{I}}$. Then, for d and a concept name or number restriction F, a predecessor restriction set w.r.t. $\mathcal{I}$ (and $\mathcal{A}$) is defined by:*

$$L_{d,\mathcal{I}}(F) := \{w \in N_R^* \mid \text{ there exists } E(f) \in \mathcal{A} \text{ and a word } u \in N_R^* \text{ such that } uw \in L_E(F) \text{ and } f^{\mathcal{I}} u^{\mathcal{I}} d\}.$$

Analogously to Lemma 5.2.1 we can show the following.

Lemma 5.2.4. *If $\mathcal{I}$ is a model of $\mathcal{A}$, $d \in \Delta^{\mathcal{I}}$, and F a concept name or number-restriction, then $w \in L_{d,\mathcal{I}}(F)$ implies $d \in (\forall w.F)^{\mathcal{I}}$.*

In the same way, number conditions are generalized.

Definition 5.2.6. *Let $\mathcal{I}$ be an interpretation, $d \in \Delta^{\mathcal{I}}$, and $r \in N_R$. Then, define*

$$c_{d,\mathcal{I}}^{\geq r} := \max\{n \mid \varepsilon \in L_{d,\mathcal{I}}(\geq nr)\} \quad (\max(\emptyset) := 0) \text{ and}$$
$$c_{d,\mathcal{I}}^{\leq r} := \min\{n \mid \varepsilon \in L_{d,\mathcal{I}}(\leq nr)\} \quad (\min(\emptyset) := \infty)$$

to be the r-number conditions of d w.r.t. $\mathcal{I}$.

As an easy consequence of Lemma 5.2.4, the following lemma generalizes Lemma 5.2.2.

Lemma 5.2.5. *If $\mathcal{I}$ is a model of $\mathcal{A}$ and $d \in \Delta^{\mathcal{I}}$, then $c_{d,\mathcal{I}}^{\geq r} \leq |r^{\mathcal{I}}(d)| \leq c_{d,\mathcal{I}}^{\leq r}$.*

The relationship between "predecessor restriction sets" and "number conditions" for ABox individuals on the one hand, and the corresponding generalized notions for elements of an interpretation on the other hand, can be summarized as follows:

Lemma 5.2.6. *Let $\mathcal{I}$ be some model of $\mathcal{A}$, $v \in N_R^*$, $r \in N_R$, and n be a non-negative integer. Then,*

- $L_a(\geq nr) \subseteq L_{a^{\mathcal{I}},\mathcal{I}}(\geq nr)$;
- *if $a^{\mathcal{I}} v^{\mathcal{I}} d$, then $c_{a,v}^{\geq r} \leq c_{d,\mathcal{I}}^{\geq r}$;*
- *if $a^{\mathcal{I}} v^{\mathcal{I}} d$, then $c_{a,v}^{\leq r} \geq c_{d,\mathcal{I}}^{\leq r}$.*

In the next definition so-called canonical interpretations are defined. They are used to show that an ABox is consistent in case neither of the two conditions in Theorem 5.2.2 hold.

Definition 5.2.7. *The* canonical interpretation $\mathcal{I}$ *of* $\mathcal{A}$ *is defined inductively:*

$\mathcal{I}_0$: $\Delta^{\mathcal{I}_0} := I_{\mathcal{A}}$; *for all* $r \in N_R$ *let* $r^{\mathcal{I}_0} := \{(a,b) \mid r(a,b) \in \mathcal{A}\}$.

$\mathcal{I}_{i+1}$: *For all* $r \in N_R$ *and* $d \in \Delta^{\mathcal{I}_i}$ *with* $(c_{d,\mathcal{I}_i}^{\geq r} - |r^{\mathcal{I}_i}(d)|) > 0$, *the domain of* $\mathcal{I}_i$ *is extended by the newly introduced, pairwise distinct individuals* $d_1, \ldots, d_{c_{d,\mathcal{I}_i}^{\geq r} - |r^{\mathcal{I}_i}(d)|}$. *Moreover, these new individuals are added to the set of* r-*successors of* d.

Now, $\mathcal{I}$ *is defined by*

$$\Delta^{\mathcal{I}} := \bigcup_{i \geq 0} \Delta^{\mathcal{I}_i}$$

$$r^{\mathcal{I}} := \bigcup_{i \geq 0} r^{\mathcal{I}_i}$$

$$P^{\mathcal{I}} := \{d \in \Delta^{\mathcal{I}} \mid \varepsilon \in L_{d,\mathcal{I}}(P)\},$$

for all roles $r \in N_R$ *and concept names* P.

The individuals in $\Delta^{\mathcal{I}} \setminus \Delta^{\mathcal{I}_0}$ are called *new elements of* $\mathcal{I}$; the others are called *old*. An individual $e \in \Delta^{\mathcal{I}}$ is *generated in* $\mathcal{I}_k$ if $k = 0$ and $e \in \Delta^{\mathcal{I}_0}$, or if $e \in \Delta^{\mathcal{I}_k} \setminus \Delta^{\mathcal{I}_{k-1}}$ for $k \geq 1$. Note that there is exactly one such $k \geq 0$ for each individual in $\Delta^{\mathcal{I}}$. If $i < j$, then we say that the individuals generated in $\mathcal{I}_j$ are *generated later* than the ones in $\mathcal{I}_i$. For $d, e \in \Delta^{\mathcal{I}}$ and $w \in N_R^*$ we say that $dw^{\mathcal{I}}e$ is a *new role chain* if apart from d this role chain contains only new elements. We summarize important properties of the canonical interpretation in the next lemma. In particular, the last statement establishes the only-if direction of Theorem 5.2.2.

Lemma 5.2.7. *The canonical interpretation* $\mathcal{I}$ *satisfies the following properties:*

1. *Every new element* d *in* $\mathcal{I}$ *has only successors in* $\mathcal{I}$ *that are generated later than* d.
2. *If an element* $d \in \Delta^{\mathcal{I}}$ *has been generated in* $\mathcal{I}_i$ *for some* i, *then all newly generated* r-*successors of* d $(r \in N_R)$ *are generated in* $\mathcal{I}_{i+1}$.
3. *Let* a *be an old individual,* d *be a new individual, and* $w \in N_R^*$ *such that* $a^{\mathcal{I}} w^{\mathcal{I}} d$ *is a new role chain. Then, if* b *is an old individual and* $v \in N_R^*$ *such that* $b^{\mathcal{I}} v^{\mathcal{I}} d$ *is a new role chain, it follows that* $a = b$, $v = w$, *and the role chains* $a^{\mathcal{I}} w^{\mathcal{I}} d$ *and* $b^{\mathcal{I}} v^{\mathcal{I}} d$ *coincide.*
4. *Let* a *be an old individual and* $w \in N_R^*$. *Then, there exists* $d \in \Delta^{\mathcal{I}}$ *with* $a^{\mathcal{I}} w^{\mathcal{I}} d$ *iff* w *is required by* a, *i.e., there are words* $v, v' \in N_R^*$ *as well as an old element* b *such that* avb *is a role chain in* $\mathcal{A}$ *and* v' *is* ε-*required by* b.

5. Let $d \in \Delta^{\mathcal{I}}$ and $r \in N_R$. Then, if $|r^{\mathcal{I}_0}(d)| \leq c_{d,\mathcal{I}}^{\geq r}$, it follows that $|r^{\mathcal{I}}(d)| = c_{d,\mathcal{I}}^{\geq r}$. Note that, actually, $r^{\mathcal{I}_0}(d)$ is only defined for $d \in \Delta^{\mathcal{I}_0}$. In case d is a new individual, we simply declare $|r^{\mathcal{I}_0}(d)| := 0$.

6. If neither 1. nor 2. in Theorem 5.2.2 is holds, then $\mathcal{I}$ is a model of $\mathcal{A}$.

Proof. 1.: If d is generated in $\mathcal{I}_i$, $i \geq 1$, then, by definition, d does not have successors in $\mathcal{I}_i$. Now, 1. follows immediately.

2.: Let $d \in \Delta^{\mathcal{I}_i}$, $i \geq 0$, be generated in $\mathcal{I}_i$ and $r \in N_R$.

Claim: $c_{d,\mathcal{I}_i}^{\geq r} = c_{d,\mathcal{I}_j}^{\geq r}$ for all $j \geq i$.

Proof of the Claim: Since $\mathcal{I}_j$ is an extension of $\mathcal{I}_i$, it follows $L_{d,\mathcal{I}_i}(\geq nr) \subseteq L_{d,\mathcal{I}_j}(\geq nr)$. As an easy consequence, it follows that $c_{d,\mathcal{I}_i}^{\geq r} \leq c_{d,\mathcal{I}_j}^{\geq r}$. On the other hand, let $n = c_{d,\mathcal{I}_j}^{\geq r}$, and thus, $\varepsilon \in L_{d,\mathcal{I}_j}(\geq nr)$. According to the definition of $L_{d,\mathcal{I}_j}(\geq nr)$ there is a concept assertion $E(f) \in \mathcal{A}$, and a word $u \in N_R^*$ such that $u \in L_E(\geq nr)$ and $f^{\mathcal{I}_j}u^{\mathcal{I}_j}d$. The role chain $f^{\mathcal{I}_j}U^{\mathcal{I}_j}d$ cannot contain individuals generated in $\mathcal{I}_k$ for $k > i$; otherwise d would be a successor of an individual generated later than d, in contradiction to 1. Thus, $\varepsilon \in L_{d,\mathcal{I}_i}(\geq nr)$, and hence, $c_{d,\mathcal{I}_i}^{\geq r} \geq c_{d,\mathcal{I}_j}^{\geq r}$. This completes the proof of the claim.

To prove 2., we distinguish two cases:

- First assume $(c_{d,\mathcal{I}_i}^{\geq r} - |r^{\mathcal{I}_i}(d)|) > 0$. Then, by construction, in $\mathcal{I}_{i+1}$ $(c_{d,\mathcal{I}_i}^{\geq r} - |r^{\mathcal{I}_i}(d)|)$ r-successors are generated for d such that $c_{d,\mathcal{I}_i}^{\geq r} = |r^{\mathcal{I}_{i+1}}(d)|$. But then, the claim implies that no new r-successors of d are generated in $\mathcal{I}_j$, $j > i+1$.
- If $(c_{d,\mathcal{I}_i}^{\geq r} - |r^{\mathcal{I}_i}(d)|) \leq 0$, then, because of $r^{\mathcal{I}_i} \subseteq r^{\mathcal{I}_j}$, the claim shows $(c_{d,\mathcal{I}_j}^{\geq r} - |r^{\mathcal{I}_j}(d)|) \leq 0$ for all $j \geq i$. Thus, by construction no r-successors of d are generated.

3.: Statement 3. is a simple consequence of the fact that every new element has exactly one predecessor.

4.: For the if direction of statement 4., assume that w is required by a. Then, there are words $v, v' \in N_R^*$ as well as an old element b such that avb is a role chain in $\mathcal{A}$ and v' is ε-required by b. Let $v' = r_1 \cdots r_n$. By induction over the length of v', the existence of an individual $d_i \in \Delta^{\mathcal{I}_i}$, $0 \leq i \leq n$, such that $b^{\mathcal{I}_i}(r_1 \cdots r_i)^{\mathcal{I}_i}d_i$ can easily be proved. Consequently, $a^{\mathcal{I}}v^{\mathcal{I}}b^{\mathcal{I}}v'^{\mathcal{I}}d$ where $d = d_n$.

For the only-if direction, we first assume that d is an old element. Then, by 1., it follows that awd is a role chain in $\mathcal{A}$, and thus, d is required by a. Now, let d be a new element. Then, there are $v, v' \in N_R^*$, and an old element b such that $w = vv'$, avb is a role chain in $\mathcal{A}$, and $b^{\mathcal{I}}v'^{\mathcal{I}}d$ is a new role chain. Let $v' = r_1 \cdots r_n$, $d_0 := b^{\mathcal{I}}$, $d_n := d$, and $d_1, \ldots, d_{n-1}$ be new elements in $\mathcal{I}$ such that $d_0 r_1^{\mathcal{I}} d_1 r_2^{\mathcal{I}} \cdots r_n^{\mathcal{I}} d_n$ is the new role chain from d_0 to

d_n. According to the construction and 2., we have $(c_{d_i,\mathcal{I}_i}^{\geq r_{i+1}} - |r_{i+1}^{\mathcal{I}_i}(d_i)|) > 0$ for all $0 \leq i < n$. This implies $c_{d_i,\mathcal{I}_i}^{\geq r_{i+1}} \geq 1$ for all $0 \leq i < n$. Thus, for every $0 \leq i < n$ there is a concept assertion $E_i(f_i) \in \mathcal{A}$ and a word $u_i \in N_R^*$ such that $u_i \in L_{E_i}(\geq n_{i+1} \, r_{i+1})$, $n_{i+1} \geq 1$, and $f_i^{\mathcal{I}_i} u_i^{\mathcal{I}_i} d_i$. Because of 3., there exists $v_i \in N_R^*$ such that $u_i = v_i r_1 \cdots r_i$ and $f_i^{\mathcal{I}_i} v_i^{\mathcal{I}_i} d_0 (r_1 \cdots r_i)^{\mathcal{I}_i} d_i$ where $d_0 (r_1 \cdots r_i)^{\mathcal{I}_i} d_i$ is the new role chain in $\mathcal{I}$ from d_0 to d_i and $f_i v_i d_0$ is a role chain in $\mathcal{A}$. This implies $c_{b,r_1 \cdots r_i}^{\geq r_{i+1}} \geq 1$ for all $0 \leq i < n$. Thus, v' is ε-required by b, which shows that $w = vv'$ is required by a.

5.: Let d be an element generated in $\mathcal{I}_i$, $i \geq 0$.

- First assume that d is an old element in $\mathcal{I}$ with $|r^{\mathcal{I}_0}(d)| \leq c_{d,\mathcal{I}}^{\geq r}$. By the claim in the proof of 2., we know $c_{d,\mathcal{I}_0}^{\geq r} = c_{d,\mathcal{I}}^{\geq r}$, and thus, $(c_{d,\mathcal{I}_0}^{\geq r} - |r^{\mathcal{I}_0}(d)|) \geq 0$. In case $(c_{d,\mathcal{I}_0}^{\geq r} - |r^{\mathcal{I}_0}(d)|) = 0$, no r-successors for d are generated (2.). Thus, $|r^{\mathcal{I}}(d)| = c_{d,\mathcal{I}}^{\geq r}$. In case $(c_{d,\mathcal{I}_0}^{\geq r} - |r^{\mathcal{I}_0}(d)|) > 0$, r-successors of d are generated in $\mathcal{I}_1$ such that $c_{d,\mathcal{I}_0}^{\geq r} = |r^{\mathcal{I}_1}(d)|$. By 2. it follows that $|r^{\mathcal{I}_1}(d)| = |r^{\mathcal{I}}(d)| = c_{d,\mathcal{I}}^{\geq r}$.
- Now, let d be a new element generated in $\mathcal{I}_i$ for some $i \geq 1$. By construction, d does not have successors in $\mathcal{I}_i$, and thus, $0 = |r^{\mathcal{I}_0}(d)| \leq c_{d,\mathcal{I}}^{\geq r}$. By statement 2, only in $\mathcal{I}_{i+1}$ r-successors are generated for d with $|r^{\mathcal{I}_{i+1}}(d)| = |r^{\mathcal{I}}(d)| = c_{d,\mathcal{I}_i}^{\geq r}$. By the claim in the proof of 2., we have $c_{d,\mathcal{I}_i}^{\geq r} = c_{d,\mathcal{I}}^{\geq r}$, and thus, $|r^{\mathcal{I}}(d)| = c_{d,\mathcal{I}}^{\geq r}$.

6.: Assume that 1. and 2. in Theorem 5.2.2 do not hold. Let $C(a) \in \mathcal{A}$. We want to show $a^{\mathcal{I}} \in C^{\mathcal{I}}$ for the canonical model $\mathcal{I}$. According to Theorem 4.2.1, we distinguish the following cases:

a) Let $w \in N_R^*$, $d \in \Delta^{\mathcal{I}}$, and P be a concept name such that $a^{\mathcal{I}} w^{\mathcal{I}} d$ and $w \in L_C(P)$. Thus, $\varepsilon \in L_{d,\mathcal{I}}(P)$, which, by definition, implies $d \in P^{\mathcal{I}}$.

b) Let $w \in N_R^*$, $d \in \Delta^{\mathcal{I}}$, and let $(\geq n \, r)$ an at-least restriction with $a^{\mathcal{I}} w^{\mathcal{I}} d$ and $w \in L_C(\geq n \, r)$. Since $\mathcal{I}$ is an extension of $\mathcal{I}_0$, we know $|r^{\mathcal{I}}(d)| \geq |r^{\mathcal{I}_0}(d)|$. But then, 5. implies $|r^{\mathcal{I}}(d)| \geq c_{d,\mathcal{I}}^{\geq r}$. Now, $w \in L_C(\geq n \, r)$ and $a^{\mathcal{I}} w^{\mathcal{I}} d$ imply $\varepsilon \in L_{d,\mathcal{I}}(\geq nr)$, which means $c_{d,\mathcal{I}}^{\geq r} \geq n$, and thus, $|r^{\mathcal{I}}(d)| \geq n$.

c) Let $w \in N_R^*$, $d \in \Delta^{\mathcal{I}}$, and let $(\leq nr)$ be an at-most restriction with $a^{\mathcal{I}} w^{\mathcal{I}} d$ and $w \in L_C(\leq n \, r)$. Assume that $d \notin (\leq n \, r)^{\mathcal{I}}$. Then, $|r^{\mathcal{I}}(d)| > n$. If $d \in \Delta^{\mathcal{I}_0}$, then, by 1., awd is a role chain in $\mathcal{A}$. Thus, $w \in L_C(\leq n \, r)$ means $c_{d,\varepsilon}^{\leq r} \leq n$. But then, $|r^{\mathcal{I}_0}(d)| > n$ is a contradiction to the assumption that 1. in Theorem 5.2.2 is not true. This means that, if $d \in \Delta^{\mathcal{I}_0}$, we can conclude $|r^{\mathcal{I}_0}(d)| \leq n$. In case d is a new individual, then $|r^{\mathcal{I}_0}(d)| \leq n$ follows trivially because $|r^{\mathcal{I}_0}(d)| = 0$. Therefore, given some $d \in \Delta^{\mathcal{I}}$ we may assume $|r^{\mathcal{I}_0}(d)| \leq n$. Since $|r^{\mathcal{I}}(d)| > n$, we know $m := c_{d,\mathcal{I}}^{\geq r} = |r^{\mathcal{I}}(d)| > n$ and 4. shows that w is required by a. Consequently, there is an old individual b as well as $v, v' \in N_R^*$ such that $w = vv'$, avb is a role chain in $\mathcal{A}$, $b^{\mathcal{I}} v'^{\mathcal{I}} d$ is a new role chain in $\mathcal{I}$, and v' is ε-required by b. Moreover, because of $m > 0$ there is a concept assertion $E(f) \in \mathcal{A}$ and a word $u \in L_E(\geq m\, r)$ with $f^{\mathcal{I}} u^{\mathcal{I}} d$. If d is an old individual, then $b = d$, $v' = \varepsilon$, and fud is a role chain in $\mathcal{A}$. Thus, $c_{b,v'}^{\geq r} \geq m > n$. If d is a new individual, then by 3. there is a word u' such that $u = u'v'$ and $f^{\mathcal{I}} u'^{\mathcal{I}} b^{\mathcal{I}} v'^{\mathcal{I}} d$. Again, it follows that $c_{b,v'}^{\geq r} \geq m > n$. On the other hand, the fact that avb is a role chain in $\mathcal{A}$, $b^{\mathcal{I}} v'^{\mathcal{I}} d$, and $w \in L_C(\leq n\, r)$ implies $c_{b,v'}^{\leq r} \leq n < m$. This yields $c_{b,v'}^{\leq r} < c_{b,v'}^{\geq r}$ where v' is ε-required by b, which is a contradiction to the assumption that 2. in Theorem 5.2.2 does not hold.   □

In [Küs98], it has been shown that deciding the unsatisfiability of $\mathcal{FLN}^*$-concept descriptions is a PSPACE-complete problem. Because a $\mathcal{FLN}^*$-concept description C is unsatisfiable if, and only if, the ABox consisting only of the concept assertion $C(a)$ is inconsistent, PSPACE-hardness carries over to the consistency of ABoxes. Theorem 5.2.2 allows to prove a matching upper bound for this problem. The technique used is similar to the one employed in [Küs98].

In what follows, we assume the semi-automaton corresponding to an $\mathcal{FLN}^*$-concept description to be an automaton without word-transitions (see Section 4.2). This corresponds to the fact that the defining concepts in the TBox underlying the $\mathcal{FLN}^*$-concept description are conjunctions of concepts of the form F or $\forall r.F$, where F is a (defined or primitive) concept name or a number restriction in this TBox. Moreover, the set of TBoxes corresponding to the $\mathcal{FLN}^*$-concept description occurring in $\mathcal{A}$ can be conjoined to one TBox $\mathcal{T}_\mathcal{A}$ such that $\mathcal{T}_\mathcal{A}$ contains a defined name for every $\mathcal{FLN}^*$-concept description in $\mathcal{A}$. We denote the semi-automaton corresponding to this TBox by $\mathcal{S}_{\mathcal{T}_\mathcal{A}}$ and the set of states of this automaton, i.e., the concept names and number-restrictions of the TBox, by $\mathcal{C}$.

The following operation takes a subset $\mathcal{F}$ of $\mathcal{C}$ and a word w and returns the set of states reachable via w from $\mathcal{F}$ in $\mathcal{S}_{\mathcal{T}_\mathcal{A}}$:

$$\delta(\mathcal{F}, w) := \{ A \in \mathcal{C} \mid \text{there is a } B \in \mathcal{F} \text{ such that } w \in L_B(A) \}.$$

In order to decide inconsistency of ABoxes, we introduce so-called pre-exclusion sets, where "pre" stands for "predecessor" and stresses the fact that these sets are only determined by predecessor restrictions sets. Intuitively, these sets are subsets of $\mathcal{C}$ that require words leading to conflicting number-restrictions.

Definition 5.2.8. *The set $\mathcal{F}_0 \subseteq \mathcal{C}$ is called* pre-exclusion set *if there exists a word $r_1 \cdots r_n \in N_R^*$, conflicting number-restrictions $(\geq l\, r)$ and $(\leq k\, r)$, $l > k$, and for all $1 \leq i \leq n$, positive integers m_i such that for $\mathcal{F}_i := \delta(\mathcal{F}_0, r_1 \cdots r_i)$, $1 \leq i \leq n$, $(\geq m_i\, r_i) \in \mathcal{F}_{i-1}$ for all $1 \leq i \leq n$ and $(\geq l\, r), (\leq k\, r) \in \mathcal{F}_n$. We denote the set of all pre-exclusion sets by $\mathcal{E}$.*

Deciding whether $\mathcal{F}_0$ is a pre-exclusion set can be carried out by a non-deterministic algorithm that iteratively guesses a role r_i (satisfying certain properties) and computes $\mathcal{F}_i := \delta(\mathcal{F}_{i-1}, r_i)$. The algorithm stops if $\mathcal{F}_{i-1}$ contains conflicting number restrictions or if $i > 2^{|\mathcal{C}|}$. Otherwise, r_i is chosen in such a way that $\mathcal{F}_{i-1}$ has a number restriction $(\geq m_i r_i)$ for some $m_i > 0$. Note that, if $i > 2^{|\mathcal{C}|}$, then among the computed sets $\mathcal{F}_k$, there is at least one set that occurs twice. Thus, by a pumping argument, if there exists a role chain leading to a set containing conflicting number restrictions, then there also exists a shorter one. Obviously, this non-deterministic algorithm requires only polynomial space. Now, using that the class NPSPACE (non-deterministic polynomial space algorithms) coincides with the class PSPACE (deterministic polynomial space algorithms) [Sav70], there also exists a deterministic algorithm which runs in polynomial space.

Lemma 5.2.8. *Deciding whether a given subset of $\mathcal{C}$ (as defined above) is a pre-exclusion set can be carried out using polynomial space in the size of the underlying ABox.*

The set defined next, contains all states in $\mathcal{C}$ that have a given individual as instance.

Definition 5.2.9. *The set*

$$q_a := \{A \in \mathcal{C} \mid E(f) \in \mathcal{A}, L_f(a) \cap L_E(A) \neq \emptyset\}$$

is called the initial set *of the individual a in $\mathcal{A}$.*

It can easily be verified that q_a is computable in polynomial time. Now, the following proposition, which is based on Theorem 5.2.2, will serve as basis for a decision algorithm for the inconsistency of ABoxes.

Proposition 5.2.1. *The $\mathcal{FLN}^*$-ABox $\mathcal{A}$ is inconsistent if, and only if,*

1. *there exists an individual a in $\mathcal{A}$, $r \in N_R$, and $(\leq nr) \in q_a$ with $|r_\mathcal{A}(a)| > n$, or*
2. *there exists an individual a such that $q_a \in \mathcal{E}$.*

Proof. Let us first assume that $\mathcal{A}$ is inconsistent. According to Theorem 5.2.2, we distinguish two cases in order to show 1. and 2. of the proposition.

a) There exists an individual a in $\mathcal{A}$, $r \in N_R$ with $|r_\mathcal{A}(a)| > c^{\leq r}_{a,\varepsilon}$. Thus, there must exist a concept assertion $E(f) \in \mathcal{A}$, a word $w \in L_f(a)$, and an at-most restriction $(\leq n\, r)$ with $w \in L_E(\leq n\, r)$, $n = c^{\leq r}_{a,\varepsilon}$. Consequently, $(\leq n\, r) \in q_a$, proving statement 1. of the proposition.

b) There exists an individual a in $\mathcal{A}$, a word $v = r_1 \cdots r_n \in N_R^*$, and $r \in N_R$ such that v is ε-required by a and $c^{\geq r}_{a,v} > c^{\leq r}_{a,v}$. Thus, there are concept assertions $E_i(f_i) \in \mathcal{A}$, words $w_i \in L_{f_i}(a)$, and positive integers n_i with $w_i r_1 \cdots r_{i-1} \in L_{E_i}(\geq n_i\, r_i)$ for all $1 \leq i \leq n$. Consequently, since $\mathcal{S}_{T_\mathcal{A}}$ is a semi-automaton without word-transitions, there are states $A_i \in \mathcal{C}$ with

$w_i \in L_{E_i}(A_i)$ and $r_1 \cdots r_{i-1} \in L_{A_i}(\geq n_i \, r_i)$ for all $1 \leq i \leq n$. Hence, $A_1, \ldots, A_n \in q_a$ and $(\geq n_i \, r_i) \in \delta(q_a, r_1 \cdots r_{i-1})$. Additionally, there is a concept assertion $E(f) \in \mathcal{A}$, a word $w \in L_f(a)$, and an integer $l = c_{a,v}^{\geq r}$ such that $wv \in L_E(\geq l \, r)$. As before, there exists a state $A \in \mathcal{C}$ with $w \in L_E(A)$ and $v \in L_A(\geq l \, r)$. As a result, $A \in q_a$ and $(\geq l \, r) \in \delta(q_a, v)$. Analogously, for $k = c_{a,v}^{\leq r}$ it can be shown that $(\leq k \, r) \in \delta(q_a, v)$. This shows that q_a is a pre-exclusion set.

We now prove the if direction of the proposition and distinguish the following two cases:

c) There exists an individual a in $\mathcal{A}$, $r \in N_R$, and $(\leq nr) \in q_a$ with $|r_{\mathcal{A}}(a)| > n$. Hence, by definition of q_a, there is a concept assertion $E(f) \in \mathcal{A}$ and a word $w \in L_f(a)$ with $w \in L_E(\leq n \, r)$. This implies $c_{a,\varepsilon}^{\leq r} \leq n$, and thus, $|r_{\mathcal{A}}(a)| > c_{a,\varepsilon}^{\leq r}$. Then, according to Theorem 5.2.2, $\mathcal{A}$ is inconsistent.

d) There exists an individual a with $q_a \in \mathcal{E}$. By definition of $\mathcal{E}$ there exists a word $v = r_1 \cdots r_n \in N_R^*$, conflicting number-restrictions $(\geq l \, r)$ and $(\leq k \, r)$, $l > k$, and for all $1 \leq i \leq n$ there are positive integers m_i such that for $\mathcal{F}_0 := q_a$ and $\mathcal{F}_i := \delta(\mathcal{F}_0, r_1 \cdots r_i)$, $1 \leq i \leq n$, $(\geq m_i r_i) \in \mathcal{F}_{i-1}$ for all $1 \leq i \leq n$ and $(\geq lr), (\leq kr) \in \mathcal{F}_n$. Consequently, there are $A_1, \ldots, A_n$ as well as A^l, A^k in $\mathcal{F}_0 = q_a$ such that $r_1 \cdots r_{i-1} \in L_{A_i}(\geq m_i \, r_i)$ for all $1 \leq i \leq n$ as well as $v \in L_{A^l}(\geq l \, r)$ and $v \in L_{A^k}(\leq k \, r)$. By definition of q_a, there exist concept assertions $E_i(f_i)$, and words $w_i \in L_{f_i}(a)$ for all $1 \leq i \leq n$ as well as concept assertions $E^l(f^l)$, $E^k(f^k)$, and words $w^l \in L_{f^l}(a)$, $w^k \in L_{f^k}(a)$ such that $w_i \in L_{E_i}(A_i)$ as well as $w^l \in L_{E^l}(A^l)$ and $w^k \in L_{E^k}(A^k)$. This means, $w_i r_1 \cdots r_{i-1} \in L_{E_i}(\geq m_i \, r_i)$ for all $1 \leq i \leq n$ as well as $w^l v \in L_{E^l}(\geq l \, r)$ and $w^k v \in L_{E^k}(\leq k \, r)$. Consequently, v is ε-required by a and $c_{a,v}^{\geq r} \geq l > k \geq c_{a,v}^{\leq r}$. By Theorem 5.2.2, it follows that $\mathcal{A}$ is inconsistent. □

Since q_a is computable in polynomial time and it can be decided whether q_a is a pre-exclusion set by a polynomial space algorithm, Proposition 5.2.1 provides us with a complexity upper bound for deciding consistency of ABoxes matching the lower bound stated above.

Corollary 5.2.3. *Deciding the consistency of $\mathcal{FLN}^*$-ABoxes is a PSPACE-complete problem.*

Value-Restriction Sets of Individuals. We will now come to the main challenge of this subsection and show that value-restriction sets are regular sets.

Definition 5.2.10. *For an individual a of an ABox $\mathcal{A}$ and a concept name or a number-restriction F, the value-restriction set is defined as follows:*

$$V_a(F) := \{w \in N_R^* \mid a \in_{\mathcal{A}} \forall w.F\}.$$

By Lemma 5.2.1, we know $L_a(F) \subseteq V_a(F)$. The language $L_a(F)$ corresponds to $L_C(F)$ introduced in Section 4.2, and just as for cyclic concept descriptions, in general, $L_a(F)$ does not represent all value-restrictions a is an instance of, since there might exist a-excluding words.

Definition 5.2.11. *For an ABox $\mathcal{A}$ and an individual a, a word $w \in N_R^*$ with $a \in_{\mathcal{A}} \forall w.\bot$ is called a-excluding.*

Because $a \in_{\mathcal{A}} \forall w.\bot$ implies $a \in_{\mathcal{A}} \forall w.F$ for any concept name and number restriction F, a-excluding words are contained in the value-restriction sets of a. In contrast to excluding words of cyclic concept descriptions, however, it is not possible to describe the set of a-excluding words exclusively by predecessor restriction sets. Specifically, adapting Lemma 4.2.2 to deal with excluding words of individuals by simply substituting $L_C(F)$ with $L_a(\cdot)$ does not yield a complete characterization of a-excluding words. Before we discuss the problems one encounters, we introduce the notion of pre-excluding words, which is derived from Lemma 4.2.2, where "pre" stands for "predecessor" and reflects the fact that only those words are captured that exclude a due to predecessor restriction sets of a.

Definition 5.2.12. *For an individual a, the word $w \in N_R^*$ is called a-pre-excluding if*

1. *there exist $v, v' \in N_R^*$, $r \in N_R$ such that v is a prefix of w, vv' is v-required by a, and $c_{a,vv'}^{\geq r} > c_{a,vv'}^{\leq r}$; or*
2. *there is a prefix vr of w, $v \in N_R^*$, $r \in N_R$, such that $c_{a,v}^{\leq r} = 0$.*

We denote the set of a-pre-excluding words by E_a.

The next lemma shows that E_a is a subset of the set of a-excluding words.

Lemma 5.2.9. *If $w \in E_a$, then $a \in_{\mathcal{A}} (\forall w.\bot)$.*

Proof. Let $w \in E_a$ and $v, v' \in N_R^*$ specified as in Definition 5.2.12, 1. Assume that $\mathcal{I}$ is a model of $\mathcal{A}$ and $d \in \Delta^{\mathcal{I}}$ with $a^{\mathcal{I}} w^{\mathcal{I}} d$. Consequently, there exists an individual $e \in \Delta^{\mathcal{I}}$ such that $a^{\mathcal{I}} v^{\mathcal{I}} e$. By Lemma 5.2.3 we know that there exists a v'-successor $f \in \Delta^{\mathcal{I}}$ of e. According to Lemma 5.2.2 it follows that $c_{a,vv'}^{\geq r} \leq r^{\mathcal{I}}(f) \leq c_{a,vv'}^{\leq r}$, which is a contradiction to $c_{a,vv'}^{\geq r} > c_{a,vv'}^{\leq r}$.

Now let $w \in E_a$, vr prefix of w with $v \in N_R^*$, $r \in N_R$, and $c_{a,v}^{\leq r} = 0$. Assume that $\mathcal{I}$ is a model of $\mathcal{A}$ and $d \in \Delta^{\mathcal{I}}$ with $a^{\mathcal{I}} w^{\mathcal{I}} d$. Consequently, there are individuals e, f such that $a^{\mathcal{I}} v^{\mathcal{I}} e r^{\mathcal{I}} f$. Now, Lemma 5.2.2 yields the contradiction $1 \leq r^{\mathcal{I}}(e) \leq c_{a,v}^{\leq r} = 0$. $\square$

Using that $w \in (E_a r^{-1})$ implies $a \in_{\mathcal{A}} \forall w.(\leq 0\, r)$ we obtain, as an easy consequence of the Lemmas 5.2.9 and 5.2.1 the following statement. Recall that $Lr^{-1} := \{w \mid wr \in L\}$ for $L \subseteq N_R^*$ and $r \in N_R$.

Lemma 5.2.10. *For all a concept name P, at-least restrictions $(\geq n\, r)$, at-most restrictions $(\leq nr)$, individuals a in $\mathcal{A}$, and words $w \in N_R^*$ the following three statements hold:*

- *If $w \in L_a(P) \cup E_a$, then $a \in_{\mathcal{A}} \forall w.P$;*
- *If $w \in \bigcup_{m \geq n} L_a(\geq mr) \cup E_a$, then $a \in_{\mathcal{A}} \forall w.(\geq n\, r)$; and*
- *If $w \in \bigcup_{m \leq n} L_a(\leq mr) \cup (E_a r^{-1})$, then $a \in_{\mathcal{A}} \forall w.(\leq n\, r)$.*

In general, for the statements in Lemma 5.2.10 the reverse implications do not hold. Intuitively, this can be explained as follows: Predecessor restriction sets $L_a(F)$, and thus, pre-exclusion sets only take value restrictions into account that come from predecessors of a. At-most restrictions in the ABox can, however, also require the propagation of value restrictions from successors of a back to a.

Let us first illustrate this phenomenon by a simple example. Assume that the ABox $\mathcal{A}$ consists of the following assertions:

$$r(a, b), \quad (\leq 1\, r)(a), \quad (\forall s.P)(b).$$

It is easy to see that $rs \notin L_a(P) \cup E_a$. However, $(\leq 1\, r)(a)$ ensures that, in any model $\mathcal{I}$ of $\mathcal{A}$, $b^{\mathcal{I}}$ is the only r-successor of $a^{\mathcal{I}}$. Consequently, all $(rs)^{\mathcal{I}}$-successors of $a^{\mathcal{I}}$ are $s^{\mathcal{I}}$-successors of $b^{\mathcal{I}}$, and thus $b^{\mathcal{I}} \in (\forall s.P)^{\mathcal{I}}$ implies $a^{\mathcal{I}} \in (\forall rs.P)^{\mathcal{I}}$. This shows that $rs \in V_a(P)$.

More generally, this problem occurs if concept assertions involving at-most restrictions in the ABox force role chains to use role assertions explicitly present in the ABox. In the example, we were forced to use the assertion $r(a, b)$ when going from $a^{\mathcal{I}}$ to an $(rs)^{\mathcal{I}}$-successor of $a^{\mathcal{I}}$. As a slightly more complex example, we assume that the ABox $\mathcal{A}$ contains the assertions

$$r(a, b), \quad r(a, c), \quad s(b, d), \quad (\leq 2\, r)(a), \quad (\forall r.(\leq 1\, s))(a),$$

and that $s \in L_c(P)$ and $\varepsilon \in L_d(P)$. In a model $\mathcal{I}$ of $\mathcal{A}$, any $(rs)^{\mathcal{I}}$-successor x of $a^{\mathcal{I}}$ is either equal to $d^{\mathcal{I}}$ or an $s^{\mathcal{I}}$-successor of $c^{\mathcal{I}}$. In the former case, $\varepsilon \in L_d(P)$ implies $x \in P^{\mathcal{I}}$, and in the latter case $s \in L_c(P)$ does the same. Consequently, we have $rs \in V_a(P)$, even though $rs \notin L_a(P) \cup E_a$. Here, we are forced to use either the assertions $r(a, b)$ and $r(b, d)$ or the assertion $r(a, c)$ when going from $a^{\mathcal{I}}$ to one of its $(rs)^{\mathcal{I}}$-successors. Since in both cases the obtained successor must belong to $P^{\mathcal{I}}$, a restriction on P must be propagated back to a from the successors of a.

Unfortunately, it is not yet clear how to give a *direct* characterization (as a regular language) of $V_a(P)$ that is based on an appropriate characterization of the set of words in $V_a(P) \setminus (L_a(P) \cup E_a)$ that come from this "backward propagation." Instead, we will describe the complement of $V_a(P)$ as a regular language. Since the class of regular languages is closed under complement, this also shows that $V_a(P)$ is regular.

In the example we have had words (such as rs) with prefixes (r in the examples) that must follow role chains of $\mathcal{A}$ in every model of $\mathcal{A}$. The words defined in the next sets do *not* have such prefixes:

$$N_a := \{\varepsilon\} \cup \bigcup_{\substack{s \in N_{R}, \\ |s_{\mathcal{A}}(a)| < c_{a,\varepsilon}^{\leq s}}} s \cdot N_R^*,$$

$$N_a(\geq l\, r) := \begin{cases} N_a \setminus \{\varepsilon\}, & |r_{\mathcal{A}}(a)| \geq l \\ N_a, & \text{otherwise.} \end{cases}$$

where $s \cdot N_R^* := \{sw \mid w \in N_R^*\}$. Intuitively, a word of the form su belongs to N_a if at-most restrictions in the ABox do not force all s-successors of a to be reached using role assertions explicitly present in the ABox. These words will be used to extend the canonical model of an ABox in such a way that certain instance relationships do not hold. For at-least restrictions $(\geq l\, r)$ it depends on the restriction if the empty word belongs to $N_a(\geq l\, r)$. The reason is that, if $|r_{\mathcal{A}}(a)| \geq l$, then of course $a \in_{\mathcal{A}} (\geq l\, r)$. Therefore in this case $N_a(\geq l\, r)$ does not contain ε since one cannot construct a model where a has less than l r-successors.

Theorem 5.2.3. *Let $\mathcal{A}$ be a consistent $\mathcal{FLN}^*$-ABox, and let b be an individual in $\mathcal{A}$. Moreover, let P be a concept name, $(\geq l\, r)$, $l \geq 1$, be an at-least restriction, and $(\leq l\, r)$, $l \geq 0$, be an at-most restriction. Then,*

$$V_b(P) = \bigcup_{c \in I_{\mathcal{A}}} L_b(c) \cdot (N_c \cap \overline{L_c(P) \cup E_c}),$$

$$V_b(\geq l\, r) = \bigcup_{c \in I_{\mathcal{A}}} L_b(c) \cdot (N_c(\geq l\, r) \cap \overline{\bigcup_{k \geq l} L_c(\geq kr) \cup E_c}),$$

$$V_b(\leq l\, r) = \bigcup_{c \in I_{\mathcal{A}}} L_b(c) \cdot (N_c \cap \overline{\bigcup_{k \leq l} L_c(\leq kr) \cup (E_c r^{-1})}),$$

where for a language $L \subseteq N_R^*$, $\overline{L}$ denotes the complement $N_R^* \setminus L$ of L.

In the sequel, we refer to the right-hand side of the equations by $\overline{V}_b(\cdot)$. The hardest part of the proof of Theorem 5.2.3 is to show $V_b(\cdot) \subseteq \overline{V}_b(\cdot)$. But first, we prove the reverse inclusion relationship. We distinguish three cases:

1. Let $w \in \overline{V}_b(P)$, $\mathcal{I}$ be a model of $\mathcal{A}$ and $d \in \Delta^{\mathcal{I}}$ with $b^{\mathcal{I}} w^{\mathcal{I}} d$. We need to show $d^{\mathcal{I}} \in P^{\mathcal{I}}$. By the definition of $\overline{V}_b(P)$ it follows for every $c \in I_{\mathcal{A}}$, $v, v' \in N_R^*$ with $w = vv'$, bvc role chain in $\mathcal{A}$, and $v' \in N_c$ that $v' \in L_c(P) \cup E_c$. Because of $b^{\mathcal{I}} w^{\mathcal{I}} d$ there exist $c \in I_{\mathcal{A}}$, $v, v' \in N_R^*$ such that $b^{\mathcal{I}} v^{\mathcal{I}} c^{\mathcal{I}} v'^{\mathcal{I}} d$, $w = vv'$ and bvc is a role chain in $\mathcal{A}$. Moreover, if $v' \in s \cdot N_R^*$, for some $s \in N_R$, we can assume that the direct successor of c in the path $c^{\mathcal{I}} v'^{\mathcal{I}} d$ is not an individual in $\mathcal{A}$. But then, $|s^{\mathcal{I}}(c^{\mathcal{I}})| > |s_{\mathcal{A}}(c)|$. By Lemma 5.2.2, $c_{c,\varepsilon}^{\geq s} \leq |s^{\mathcal{I}}(c^{\mathcal{I}})| \leq c_{c,\varepsilon}^{\leq s}$, and thus $|s_{\mathcal{A}}(c)| < c_{c,\varepsilon}^{\leq s}$. This implies $v' \in N_c$. In case v' is the empty word, $v' \in N_c$ by definition. Now, by the assumption, we can infer $v' \in L_c(P) \cup E_c$, and Lemma 5.2.10 implies $d \in P^{\mathcal{I}}$.

2. Let $w \in \overline{V}_b(\geq l r)$, $\mathcal{I}$ be a model of $\mathcal{A}$ and $d \in \Delta^{\mathcal{I}}$ with $b^{\mathcal{I}} w^{\mathcal{I}} d$. We need to show $d^{\mathcal{I}} \in (\geq l\, r)^{\mathcal{I}}$. By definition of $\overline{V}_b(\geq l\, r)$ it follows for every $c \in I_{\mathcal{A}}$, $v, v' \in N_R^*$ with $w = vv'$, bvc role chain in $\mathcal{A}$, and $v' \in N_c(\geq l\, r)$ that $v' \in \bigcup_{k \geq l} L_c(\geq kr) \cup E_c$. As before, because of $b^{\mathcal{I}} w^{\mathcal{I}} d$ there exist $c \in I_{\mathcal{A}}$,

$v, v' \in N_R^*$ such that $b^{\mathcal{I}} v^{\mathcal{I}} c^{\mathcal{I}} v'^{\mathcal{I}} d$, $w = vv'$, and bvc is a role chain in $\mathcal{A}$. Moreover, if $v' \in s \cdot N_R^*$, for some $s \in N_R$, we may assume that the direct successor of c in the path $c^{\mathcal{I}} v'^{\mathcal{I}} d$ is not an individual in $\mathcal{A}$. Then, we can conclude $|s^{\mathcal{I}}(c^{\mathcal{I}})| > |s_{\mathcal{A}}(c)|$. By Lemma 5.2.2, $c_{\bar{c},\varepsilon}^{\geq s} \leq |s^{\mathcal{I}}(c^{\mathcal{I}})| \leq c_{\bar{c},\varepsilon}^{\leq s}$, and thus $|s_{\mathcal{A}}(c)| < c_{\bar{c},\varepsilon}^{\leq s}$. This implies $v' \in N_c(\geq l\, r)$, and thus, $v' \in \bigcup_{k \geq l} L_c(\geq kr) \cup E_c$. In particular, Lemma 5.2.10 shows $d \in (\geq l\, r)^{\mathcal{I}}$. Now assume that $v' = \varepsilon$. If $v' \in N_c(\geq l\, r)$, then again $v' \in \bigcup_{k \geq l} L_c(\geq kr) \cup E_c$, and Lemma 5.2.10 ensures $d \in (\geq l\, r)^{\mathcal{I}}$. If $v' \notin N_c(\geq l\, r)$, then, by definition, it follows that $|r_{\mathcal{A}}(c)| \geq l$. But then, due to the unique name assumption, we can conclude $d \in (\geq l\, r)^{\mathcal{I}}$ as well.

3. Let $w \in \overline{V}_b(\leq l\, r)$, $\mathcal{I}$ be a model of $\mathcal{A}$ and $d \in \Delta^{\mathcal{I}}$ such that $b^{\mathcal{I}} w^{\mathcal{I}} d$. Analogously to 1., we can split up w into the words v and v', and can show $v' \in \bigcup_{k \leq l} L_c(\leq kr) \cup (E_c r^{-1})$. Thus, by Lemma 5.2.10 we have $d \in (\leq l\, r)^{\mathcal{I}}$.

For every identity in Theorem 5.2.3, this shows $\overline{V}_b(\cdot) \subseteq V_b(\cdot)$.

In order to prove the inclusion in the other direction, we need a model $\mathcal{I}'$ of $\mathcal{A}$ such that, if a word w is not an element of $\overline{V}_b(\cdot)$, then $b^{\mathcal{I}'}$ does not satisfy the corresponding value-restriction in $\mathcal{I}'$. Such a model is constructed as an extension of the canonical model $\mathcal{I}$ of $\mathcal{A}$ (see Definition 5.2.7) to $\mathcal{I}(c, v')$ where c and v' are chosen as in the proof of $\overline{V}_b(\cdot) \subseteq V_b(\cdot)$ with $w = vv'$. More precisely, the model is constructed in such a way that there is a role chain from b to some c in $\mathcal{A}$ (labeled v) and a new role chain in $\mathcal{I}(c, v')$ labeled v' leading from c to a new element d which is, say, not contained in the extension of P. In case of at-most restrictions ($\leq l\, r$) we further extend the model to $\mathcal{I}(c, v', r, l{+}1)$ such that d has $l{+}1$ r-successors. The fact that the role chain from c to d only contains new elements (except for c), i.e., elements not contained in $\mathcal{A}$, is crucial since then the value-restrictions that are satisfied by d are determined only by the predecessor restriction sets of c, i.e., "backward propagation" is avoided. The reason why such a new role chain from c to d can be constructed is that $v' \in N_c$, i.e., at-most restrictions do not force the role chain to follow existing role assertions. In the following, the extended canonical model $\mathcal{I}(a, w, r, h)$ is defined where a corresponds to c, w to v' and h to $l{+}1$. Figure 5.9 illustrates the model where for the words u, v, $w = uv$, $v = r_1 \cdots r_n$, and where d_{n+1} corresponds to the aforementioned individual d.

Definition 5.2.13. *Let a be an individual in $\mathcal{A}$, $w \in N_R^*$, and $r \in N_R$. Let $\mathcal{I}$ denote the canonical model of $\mathcal{A}$ (Definition 5.2.7). We define the extended canonical interpretation $\mathcal{I}' = \mathcal{I}(a, w)$ and $\mathcal{I}' = \mathcal{I}(a, w, r, h)$, $h > 0$, of $\mathcal{A}$ inductively as follows.*

$\mathcal{I}_0$: *Let $u \in N_R^*$ be a prefix of w of maximal length such that there exists an individual $d_1 \in \Delta^{\mathcal{I}}$ where $a^{\mathcal{I}} u^{\mathcal{I}} d_1$ is a new role chain in $\mathcal{I}$. Let $v = r_1 \cdots r_n \in N_R^*$, $n \geq 0$, with $w = uv$. Furthermore, let $d_2, \ldots, d_{n+1} \notin \Delta^{\mathcal{I}}$ be new individuals. If $h - |r^{\mathcal{I}}(d_{n+1})| \geq 0$, then let $k := h - |r^{\mathcal{I}}(d_{n+1})|$, otherwise*

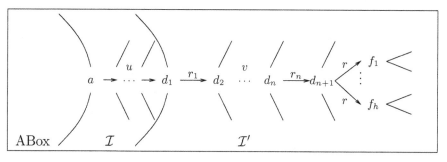

Fig. 5.9. The Extended Canonical Model $\mathcal{I}(a, w, r, h)$.

define $k := 0$. (In case d_{n+1} is a new individual, the set $r^{\mathcal{I}}(d_{n+1})$ is defined to be the empty.) Finally, let $f_1, \ldots, f_k \notin \Delta^{\mathcal{I}} \cup \{d_2, \ldots, d_{n+1}\}$ be new individuals. Now, $\mathcal{I}_0$ is obtained by extending the domain of $\mathcal{I}$ by $d_2, \ldots, d_{n+1}, f_1, \ldots, f_k$ as well as adding (d_i, d_{i+1}) to the extension of r_i for all $1 \le i \le n$ and adding $(d_{n+1}, f_1), \ldots, (d_{n+1}, f_k)$ to the extension of r.

$\mathcal{I}_{i+1}$: For all $s \in N_R$ and $d \in \Delta^{\mathcal{I}_i}$ where $(c^{\ge s}_{d, \mathcal{I}_i} - |s^{\mathcal{I}_i}(d)|) > 0$, the domain of $\mathcal{I}_i$ is extended by the newly introduced, pairwise distinct individuals $e_1, \ldots, e_{c^{\ge s}_{d, \mathcal{I}_i} - |s^{\mathcal{I}_i}(d)|}$. Finally, these new individuals are added to the set of s-successors of d.

Now, $\mathcal{I}'$ is defined by

$$\Delta^{\mathcal{I}'} := \bigcup_{i \ge 0} \Delta^{\mathcal{I}_i},$$

$$s^{\mathcal{I}'} := \bigcup_{i \ge 0} s^{\mathcal{I}_i},$$

$$P^{\mathcal{I}'} := \{d \in \Delta^{\mathcal{I}'} \mid \varepsilon \in L_{d, \mathcal{I}'}(P)\}.$$

We call elements in $\Delta^{\mathcal{I}'} \setminus \Delta^{\mathcal{I}}$ *extension elements*. An individual $e \in \Delta^{\mathcal{I}'}$ is *generated in $\mathcal{I}_k$* if $k = 0$ and $e \in \Delta^{\mathcal{I}_k}$ or if $e \in \Delta^{\mathcal{I}_k} \setminus \Delta^{\mathcal{I}_{k-1}}$ for $k \ge 1$. Note that there is exactly one $k \ge 0$ such that e is generated in $\mathcal{I}_k$. If $i < j$, then we say that the individuals generated in $\mathcal{I}_j$ are *generated later* than the individuals in $\mathcal{I}_i$.

In order to show that $\mathcal{I}'$ is a model of $\mathcal{A}$, the following condition is necessary:

The ABox $\mathcal{A}$ is consistent; $w \notin E_a$ and if $h > 0$, then $wr \notin E_a$; $c^{\le r}_{a,w} \ge h$; and if $w \in s \cdot N_R^*$, then $|s_{\mathcal{A}}(a)| < c^{\le s}_{a, \varepsilon}$ (meaning   (5.2) $w \in N_a$).

Lemma 5.2.11. *Let $\mathcal{I}'$ be the extended canonical interpretation as specified in Definition 5.2.13. Then, the following statements hold:*

1. *Extension elements only have (later generated) extension elements as successors. These successors form a tree.*
2. *For all $d \in \Delta^{\mathcal{I}}$ the following equations are satisfied:*

$$c_{d,\mathcal{I}}^{\geq s} = c_{d,\mathcal{I}'}^{\geq s} = c_{d,\mathcal{I}_i}^{\geq s}, \text{ for all } i \geq 0,$$

$$c_{d,\mathcal{I}}^{\leq s} = c_{d,\mathcal{I}'}^{\leq s} = c_{d,\mathcal{I}_i}^{\leq s}, \text{ for all } i \geq 0.$$

3. *All paths in $\mathcal{I}'$ that lead from an individual in $\mathcal{A}$ to an extension element (or to d_1) have as suffix a path from $a^{\mathcal{I}'}$ to this extension element (or to d_1). Moreover, this suffix can be chosen in such a way that $a^{\mathcal{I}'}$ only occurs at the beginning. It has $a^{\mathcal{I}'} u^{\mathcal{I}'} d_1$ as prefix and is uniquely determined by the extension element.*
4. *The direct successors of d_1 are elements of the set $\Delta^{\mathcal{I}} \cup \{d_2\}$ or, if $w = u$, of $\Delta^{\mathcal{I}} \cup \{f_1, \ldots, f_k\}$.*
5. *For all $d \in \Delta^{\mathcal{I}_i}$, $i \geq 0$, the following identities are true:*

$$c_{d,\mathcal{I}_i}^{\geq s} = c_{d,\mathcal{I}_j}^{\geq s} \text{ for all } j \geq i,$$

$$c_{d,\mathcal{I}_i}^{\geq s} = c_{d,\mathcal{I}'}^{\geq s},$$

$$c_{d,\mathcal{I}_i}^{\leq s} = c_{d,\mathcal{I}_j}^{\leq s} \text{ for all } j \geq i,$$

$$c_{d,\mathcal{I}_i}^{\leq s} = c_{d,\mathcal{I}'}^{\leq s}.$$

6. *For an individual generated in $\mathcal{I}_i$, $i \geq 0$, all later generated direct successors are generated in $\mathcal{I}_{i+1}$.*
7. *Let $d \in \Delta^{\mathcal{I}'}$, $s \in N_R$. Then, if $|s^{\mathcal{I}_0}(d)| \leq c_{d,\mathcal{I}'}^{\geq s}$, then $|s^{\mathcal{I}'}(d)| = c_{d,\mathcal{I}'}^{\geq s}$.*
8. *For $d \in (\Delta^{\mathcal{I}'} \setminus \Delta^{\mathcal{I}}) \cup \{d_1\}$ let $x \in N_R^*$ be the label of the (unique) path from $a^{\mathcal{I}'}$ to d where $a^{\mathcal{I}'}$ only occurs as initial node. Then, $c_{d,\mathcal{I}'}^{\leq s} \geq c_{a,x}^{\leq s}$ and $c_{d,\mathcal{I}'}^{\geq s} \leq c_{a,x}^{\geq s}$, for all $s \in N_R$.*
9. *There is an individual $d \in \Delta^{\mathcal{I}'}$ such that $a^{\mathcal{I}'} w^{\mathcal{I}'} d$ and $|r^{\mathcal{I}'}(d)| \geq h$.*
10. *If the conditions in (5.2) are satisfied, then the extended canonical model $\mathcal{I}'$ is a model of $\mathcal{A}$.*

Proof. 1.: This is an easy consequence of the construction of $\mathcal{I}'$.

2.: Since $\mathcal{I}_i$, $i \geq 0$, and $\mathcal{I}'$ are extensions of $\mathcal{I}$, every path in $\mathcal{I}$ from an individual in $\mathcal{A}$ to d is also a path in $\mathcal{I}_i$, $i \geq 0$, and $\mathcal{I}'$. Thus, $c_{d,\mathcal{I}}^{\geq s} \leq c_{d,\mathcal{I}'}^{\geq s}$ and $c_{d,\mathcal{I}}^{\geq s} \leq c_{d,\mathcal{I}_i}^{\geq s}$ for all $i \geq 0$. On the other hand, because of 1., every path in $\mathcal{I}'$ and $\mathcal{I}_i$ from an individual in $\mathcal{A}$ to d is also a path in $\mathcal{I}$. Consequently, $c_{d,\mathcal{I}}^{\geq s} \geq c_{d,\mathcal{I}'}^{\geq s}$ and $c_{d,\mathcal{I}}^{\geq s} \geq c_{d,\mathcal{I}_i}^{\leq s}$ for all $i \geq 0$. For at-most restrictions the identities can be shown analogously.

3.: By Lemma 5.2.7, 5. for all $d \in \Delta^{\mathcal{I}}$ and $s \in N_R$ we know $|s^{\mathcal{I}}(d)| \geq c_{d,\mathcal{I}}^{\geq s}$. Thus, according to 2., no direct successors for d are generated, and consequently, all extension elements are successors of d_1, and every path from an element in $\Delta^{\mathcal{I}}$ to an extension element has as suffix a path from d_1 to this element. Lemma 5.2.7, 3. implies that every path in $\mathcal{I}'$ from an element in $\mathcal{A}$ to d_1, which by 1. is also a path in $\mathcal{I}$, has as suffix a path from $a^{\mathcal{I}'}$ to d_1. This completes the proof of the first part of 3. The last part of the statement is an easy consequence of Lemma 5.2.7, 3.

4.: From 2. we can deduce that for d_1 no direct successors are generated since $|s^{\mathcal{I}}(d_1)| \geq c_{d_1,\mathcal{I}}^{\geq s} = c_{d_1,\mathcal{I}_i}^{\geq s}$ for all $i \geq 0$. Thus, the only direct successors of d_1 which are extension elements are those defined in $\mathcal{I}_0$, namely, d_2 or $f_1, \ldots, f_k$.

5.: Let b be an individual in $\mathcal{A}$, $v \in N_R^*$, $i \leq j$, and $d \in \Delta^{\mathcal{I}_i}$. Then,

Claim: $b^{\mathcal{I}_i} v^{\mathcal{I}_i} d$ iff $b^{\mathcal{I}_j} v^{\mathcal{I}_j} d$.

Proof of the Claim: For $i = j$ there is nothing to show. Assume that $i < j$. Since $\mathcal{I}_j$ is an extension of $\mathcal{I}_i$, the only-if direction of the claim is trivial. All elements generated in $\mathcal{I}_j$ are, by definition, generated later than those in $\mathcal{I}_i$. Thus, by 1. we can conclude that $b^{\mathcal{I}_j} v^{\mathcal{I}_j} d$ contains no elements generated in $\mathcal{I}_j$, which completes the proof of the if direction.

Now, the identities easily follow from the claim.

6.: Let d be an individual generated in $\mathcal{I}_i$, $i \geq 0$. According to the construction we know $|s^{\mathcal{I}_{i+1}}(d)| \geq c_{d,\mathcal{I}_i}^{\geq s}$. Now 5. implies that no direct successors for d are generated in $\mathcal{I}_j$, $j > i+1$.

7.: Let $|s^{\mathcal{I}_0}(d)| \leq c_{d,\mathcal{I}'}^{\geq s}$ and $d \in \Delta^{\mathcal{I}'}$. Then, there is an integer $i \geq 0$ such that d is generated in $\mathcal{I}_i$. Thus, $|s^{\mathcal{I}_0}(d)| = |s^{\mathcal{I}_i}(d)|$. Using 5., $|s^{\mathcal{I}_0}(d)| \leq c_{d,\mathcal{I}'}^{\geq s}$ implies $|s^{\mathcal{I}_i}(d)| \leq c_{d,\mathcal{I}_i}^{\geq s}$. By construction it follows $|s^{\mathcal{I}_{i+1}}(d)| = c_{d,\mathcal{I}_i}^{\geq s}$, 6. ensures $|s^{\mathcal{I}_{i+1}}(d)| = |s^{\mathcal{I}'}(d)|$, and with 5. we can infer $c_{d,\mathcal{I}_i}^{\geq s} = c_{d,\mathcal{I}'}^{\geq s}$. Consequently, $|s^{\mathcal{I}'}(d)| = c_{d,\mathcal{I}'}^{\geq s}$.

8.: Let $m := c_{d,\mathcal{I}'}^{\leq s}$. If $m = \infty$, we know $m \geq c_{a,x}^{\leq s}$. Assume $m < \infty$. Then, by definition of $c_{d,\mathcal{I}'}^{\leq s}$ there exists a concept assertion $E(f) \in \mathcal{A}$ and a word $y \in N_R^*$ such that $y \in L_E(\leq m\ s)$ and $f^{\mathcal{I}'} y^{\mathcal{I}'} d$. According to 3. we know that $f^{\mathcal{I}'} y^{\mathcal{I}'} d$ has the path $a^{\mathcal{I}'} x^{\mathcal{I}'} d$ as suffix. Consequently, there exists a $y' \in N_R^*$ such that $y = y'x$ and $f^{\mathcal{I}'} y'^{\mathcal{I}'} a^{\mathcal{I}'} x^{\mathcal{I}'} d$. Using 1. and Lemma 5.2.7, 1. the path $f^{\mathcal{I}'} y'^{\mathcal{I}'} a^{\mathcal{I}'}$ is a path in $\mathcal{A}$. Hence, $m \geq c_{a,x}^{\leq s}$. Analogously, we can deduce $c_{d,\mathcal{I}'}^{\geq s} \leq c_{a,x}^{\geq s}$.

9.: This claim is an immediate consequence of the construction of $\mathcal{I}_0$.

10.: By definition of $\mathcal{I}'$ the role assertions in $\mathcal{A}$ are satisfied. Now let $B(b) \in \mathcal{A}$. We need to show $b^{\mathcal{I}'} \in B^{\mathcal{I}'}$ provided that the conditions in (5.2) are satisfied. According to Theorem 4.2.1 we distinguish the following three cases:

Let P be a concept name, $y \in L_B(P)$, $d \in \Delta^{\mathcal{I}'}$ with $b^{\mathcal{I}'} y^{\mathcal{I}'} d$. By definition of $L_{d,\mathcal{I}'}(P)$ it follows $\varepsilon \in L_{d,\mathcal{I}'}(P)$, and hence, $d \in P^{\mathcal{I}'}$.

Now, let $(\geq m\ s)$ be an at-least restriction, $y \in L_B(\geq m\ s)$, $d \in \Delta^{\mathcal{I}'}$ with $b^{\mathcal{I}'} y^{\mathcal{I}'} d$. This implies $c_{d,\mathcal{I}'}^{\geq s} \geq m$. By 7., we can conclude $|s^{\mathcal{I}'}(d)| \geq c_{d,\mathcal{I}'}^{\geq s}$, and thus, $d \in (\geq m\ s)^{\mathcal{I}'}$.

Finally, let $(\leq m\ s)$ be an at-most restriction, $y \in L_B(\leq m\ s)$, $d \in \Delta^{\mathcal{I}'}$ with $b^{\mathcal{I}'} y^{\mathcal{I}'} d$. Assume that $d \notin (\leq m\ s)^{\mathcal{I}'}$, i.e., $|s^{\mathcal{I}'}(d)| > m$. We distinguish the following cases:

(i) Assume $d \in \Delta^{\mathcal{I}} \setminus \{d_1\}$. As a consequence of 1., the path $b^{\mathcal{I}'} y^{\mathcal{I}'} d$ is a path in $\mathcal{I}$. Furthermore, 2. implies $s^{\mathcal{I}'}(d) = s^{\mathcal{I}}(d)$. But then, it follows $b^{\mathcal{I}} \notin B^{\mathcal{I}}$, which means that $\mathcal{I}$ is not a model of $\mathcal{A}$, in contradiction to Lemma 5.2.7, 6.

(ii) Assume $d = d_1$ and $n \geq 1$ (see (iv) for the case $n = 0$). As shown in 4., for d_1 no direct successors are generated. Thus, if $s \neq r_1$, then we have $s^{\mathcal{I}'}(d) = s^{\mathcal{I}}(d)$, and consequently, $d \notin (\leq m\ s)^{\mathcal{I}}$. Furthermore, 1. implies that the path $b^{\mathcal{I}'} y^{\mathcal{I}'} d$ is a path in $\mathcal{I}$. Again, this is a contradiction to the fact that $\mathcal{I}$ is a model of $\mathcal{A}$. Now, assume $s = r_1$. We distinguish two cases:

(I) The word u in Definition 5.2.13 is not the empty word. Then $|s^{\mathcal{I}}(d)| = 0$, because u was chosen to be a maximal prefix of w. We already know that for d_1 no direct successors are generated. Thus, by construction we can conclude $|s^{\mathcal{I}'}(d_1)| = 1$. But then, it follows $m = 0$. By 3. the path $b^{\mathcal{I}'} y^{\mathcal{I}'} d_1$ contains $a^{\mathcal{I}'}$, say $b^{\mathcal{I}'} y'^{\mathcal{I}'} a^{\mathcal{I}'} y''^{\mathcal{I}'} d_1$ where $y = y'y''$ and $b^{\mathcal{I}'} y'^{\mathcal{I}'} a^{\mathcal{I}'}$ is a role chain in $\mathcal{A}$. We can assume y'' to be of minimal length, i.e., the path $a^{\mathcal{I}'} y''^{\mathcal{I}'} d_1$ only contains $a^{\mathcal{I}'}$ as initial node. By 3., this implies $y'' = u$. Consequently, $c_{a,u}^{\leq s} = 0$. Since us is a prefix of w this is a contradiction to $w \notin E_a$.

(II) Assume $u = \varepsilon$. Then, by construction it is $d_1 = a^{\mathcal{I}'}$. By definition of u we know that for d no s-successors were generated in $\mathcal{I}$, i.e., d does not have s-successors in $\mathcal{I}$ which are not individuals in $\mathcal{A}$. This means $|s_{\mathcal{A}}(a)| \geq c_{a,\mathcal{I}}^{\geq s}$. By 2., we have $c_{a,\mathcal{I}}^{\geq s} = c_{a,\mathcal{I}_i}^{\geq s}$ for every $i \geq 0$. This implies that even in $\mathcal{I}'$ no s-successors are generated for d. Then, we can conclude $|s^{\mathcal{I}_0}(d)| = |s^{\mathcal{I}'}(d)| = |s_{\mathcal{A}}(a)|+1$. By the assumption (5.2), it is $|s_{\mathcal{A}}(a)| < c_{a,\varepsilon}^{\leq s}$. Furthermore, by 8. we know $c_{a,\varepsilon}^{\leq s} \leq c_{a,\mathcal{I}'}^{\leq s}$. This shows $|s^{\mathcal{I}'}(d)| \leq c_{a,\mathcal{I}'}^{\leq s}$. Additionally, using $b^{\mathcal{I}'} y^{\mathcal{I}'} d$, $y \in L_B(\leq m\ s)$, and $B(b) \in \mathcal{A}$ it follows $c_{a,\mathcal{I}'}^{\leq s} \leq m$. But then, $|s^{\mathcal{I}'}(d)| \leq m$, in contradiction to the assumption.

(iii) Assume $d \in \{d_2, \ldots, d_n\}$. We distinguish two cases:

(I) Assume $s \neq r_i$ and $d = d_i$ where $2 \leq i \leq n$. By construction we know $|s^{\mathcal{I}_0}(d)| = 0$. Now 7. implies $|s^{\mathcal{I}'}(d)| = c_{d,\mathcal{I}'}^{\geq s} > m$. On the other hand, as in (ii), (II) we can conclude $c_{d,\mathcal{I}'}^{\leq s} \leq m$. Let $a^{\mathcal{I}'} x^{\mathcal{I}'} d$ be the suffix of $b^{\mathcal{I}'} y^{\mathcal{I}'} d$ as stipulated in 8. Then, by 8., $c_{a,x}^{\leq s} \leq c_{d,\mathcal{I}'}^{\leq s}$ and $c_{a,x}^{\geq s} \geq c_{d,\mathcal{I}'}^{\geq s}$. Consequently, $c_{a,x}^{\leq s} \leq m < c_{a,x}^{\geq s}$. Also, since x is uniquely determined, x is a prefix of w. Hence, $w \in E_a$, in contradiction to the assumption.

(II) Now, let $s = r_i$ and $d = d_i$ where $2 \leq i \leq n$. If $|s^{\mathcal{I}_0}(d)| \leq c_{d,\mathcal{I}'}^{\geq s}$, then we can proceed as in (iii), (I). Now, assume $|s^{\mathcal{I}_0}(d)| > c_{d,\mathcal{I}'}^{\geq s}$. Since $|s^{\mathcal{I}_0}(d)| = 1$, we know $c_{d,\mathcal{I}'}^{\geq s} = 0$. But then, $c_{d,\mathcal{I}_i}^{\geq s} = 0$ for all $i \geq 0$, and no direct s-successors of d are generated. Hence, $|s^{\mathcal{I}'}(d)| = 1$. Using $|s^{\mathcal{I}'}(d)| > m$ it follows $m = 0$. By 3., the path $b^{\mathcal{I}'} y^{\mathcal{I}'} d_i$ is of the form $b^{\mathcal{I}'} y'^{\mathcal{I}'} a^{\mathcal{I}'} y''^{\mathcal{I}'} d_i$ where $y = y'y''$ and $y'' = ur_1 \cdots r_{i-1}$. Consequently, $c_{a,ur_1 \cdots r_{i-1}}^{\leq r_i} = 0$. Since $ur_1 \cdots r_i$ is a prefix of w, this is a contradiction to $w \notin E_a$.

(iv) Assume $d = d_{n+1}$.

(I) If $s \neq r$, then this leads us to a contradiction as in (iii), (I).

(II) Let us assume that $s = r$. We consider two cases.

(a) Let $|r^{\mathcal{I}_0}(d)| \leq c_{d,\mathcal{I}'}^{\geq r}$. Then, by 7. we know $|r^{\mathcal{I}'}(d)| = c_{d,\mathcal{I}'}^{\geq r} > m$. On the other hand, as in (ii), (II) we can infer $c_{d,\mathcal{I}'}^{\leq s} \leq m$. Analogously to (iii), (I), this leads to a contradiction.

(b) Let $|r^{\mathcal{I}_0}(d)| > c_{d,\mathcal{I}'}^{\geq r}$. Since $c_{d,\mathcal{I}'}^{\geq r} = c_{d,\mathcal{I}_i}^{\geq r}$ for all $i \geq 0$ (5.), no r-successors are generated for d. Hence, $|r^{\mathcal{I}'}(d)| = |r^{\mathcal{I}_0}(d)|$. We distinguish two more cases.

(A) Assume $|r^{\mathcal{I}_0}(d)| = h > m$. According to 8., we know $c_{d,\mathcal{I}'}^{\leq r} \geq c_{a,w}^{\leq r}$. Moreover, as in (ii),(II) it is $c_{d,\mathcal{I}'}^{\leq r} \leq m$. On the other hand, by assumption (5.2) we have $c_{a,w}^{\leq r} \geq h$. Thus, $h > m \geq c_{d,\mathcal{I}'}^{\leq r} \geq c_{a,w}^{\leq r} \geq h$, which is a contradiction.

(B) Now, suppose $|r^{\mathcal{I}_0}(d)| > h$. By construction this implies $r^{\mathcal{I}}(d) = r^{\mathcal{I}_0}(d)$, $d = d_1 \in \Delta^{\mathcal{I}}$, and $a^{\mathcal{I}} u^{\mathcal{I}} d$. Since $\mathcal{I}$ is a model of $\mathcal{A}$, we know by Lemma 5.2.2 that (*) $c_{a,u}^{\geq r} \leq |r^{\mathcal{I}}(d)| \leq c_{a,u}^{\leq r}$. As above $c_{d,\mathcal{I}'}^{\leq r} \leq m$. Then 8. means $c_{a,u}^{\leq r} \leq m$, in contradiction to (*) and $|r^{\mathcal{I}}(d)| > m$.

(v) Assume $d \in \{f_1, \ldots, f_k\}$. By construction, $|s^{\mathcal{I}_0}(d)| = 0$. Thus, 7. implies $|s^{\mathcal{I}'}(d)| = c_{d,\mathcal{I}'}^{\geq s}(> m)$. As above we have $c_{d,\mathcal{I}'}^{\leq s} \leq m$. According to 8., we know $c_{a,ur}^{\leq s} \leq c_{d,\mathcal{I}'}^{\leq s}$ and $c_{a,ur}^{\geq s} \geq c_{d,\mathcal{I}'}^{\geq s}$. Hence, $c_{a,ur}^{\leq s} < c_{a,ur}^{\geq s}$. Consequently, $ur \in E_a$, in contradiction to (5.2).

(vi) Suppose $d \in \Delta^{\mathcal{I}'} \setminus (\Delta^{\mathcal{I}} \cup \{d_2, \ldots, d_{n+1}, f_1, \ldots, f_k\})$. By construction we know $|s^{\mathcal{I}_0}| = 0$. Thus, 7. means $|s^{\mathcal{I}'}(d)| = c_{d,\mathcal{I}'}^{\geq s}(> m)$. As above we have $c_{d,\mathcal{I}'}^{\leq s} \leq m$. According to 8., there exists a word y' such that $c_{a,y'}^{\leq s} \leq c_{d,\mathcal{I}'}^{\leq s}$ and $c_{a,y'}^{\geq s} \geq c_{d,\mathcal{I}'}^{\geq s}$. Consequently, $c_{a,y'}^{\geq s} > c_{a,y'}^{\leq s}$. By construction of $\mathcal{I}'$ the word y' is of the form $y' = v'v''$ where v' is a prefix of w (in case of $h = 0$) or wr (in case of $h > 0$) of maximal length, and $a^{\mathcal{I}'} v'^{\mathcal{I}'} gv''^{\mathcal{I}'} d$ with $g \in \{d_2, \ldots, d_{n+1}, f_1, \ldots, f_k\}$ (The element d_1 is not contained in this set because of 4.) Let $v'' = q_1 \cdots q_l$, $l \geq 1$, and $e_1, \ldots, e_{l-1}$ elements with $e_0 q_1^{\mathcal{I}'} e_1 \cdots q_l^{\mathcal{I}'} e_l$ where $e_0 := g$ and $e_l := d$. By 6., the element e_j, $0 \leq j \leq l$, is generated in $\mathcal{I}_j$. Thus, for $0 \leq j \leq l - 1$ we have $(c_{e_j,\mathcal{I}_j}^{\geq q_{j+1}} - |q_{j+1}(e_j)|) > 0$. In particular, it follows $c_{e_j,\mathcal{I}_j}^{\geq q_{j+1}} \geq 1$, and with

8., this implies $c_{a,v'q_1\cdots q_j}^{\geq q_{j+1}} \geq 1$ for all $0 \leq j \leq l-1$. Consequently, $v'v''$ is v'-required by a and $c_{a,v'v''}^{\geq s} > c_{a,v'v''}^{\leq s}$. This is a contradiction to the fact that $w \notin E_a$ ($h = 0$) or $wr \notin E_a$ ($h > 0$). $\qquad\square$

Now, we can proceed with the proof of Theorem 5.2.3 and show $V_b(\cdot) \subseteq \overline{V}_b(\cdot)$. We consider each of the three types of inclusions separately.

1. Assume $w \notin \overline{V}_b(P)$. Then, there is a $c \in I_A$, v, v' such that $w = vv'$, $v \in L_b(c)$, and $v' \in N_c \cap \overline{L_c(P)} \cup E_c$. But then, by Lemma 5.2.11, $\mathcal{I}' = \mathcal{I}(c, v')$ is a model of $\mathcal{A}$ since the conditions in (5.2) are satisfied. In addition, there is an element $d = d_{n+1}$ such that $b^{\mathcal{I}'} v^{\mathcal{I}'} c^{\mathcal{I}'} v'^{\mathcal{I}'} d$. Assume $d \in P^{\mathcal{I}'}$, i.e., $\varepsilon \in L_{d,\mathcal{I}'}(P)$. Consequently, there is a concept assertion $E(f) \in \mathcal{A}$ and a word $u \in N_R^*$ such that $u \in L_E(P)$ and $f^{\mathcal{I}'} u^{\mathcal{I}'} d$. Since $d = d_{n+1}$, the path $f^{\mathcal{I}'} u^{\mathcal{I}'} d$ is of the form $f^{\mathcal{I}'} u'c^{\mathcal{I}'} v'^{\mathcal{I}'} d$ where $fu'c$ is a role chain in $\mathcal{A}$ (Lemma 5.2.11, 3.). Hence, $v' \in L_c(P)$, which is a contradiction. This implies $d \notin P^{\mathcal{I}'}$, and thus, $b^{\mathcal{I}'} \notin (\forall w.P)^{\mathcal{I}'}$.

2. Assume $w \notin \overline{V}_b(\geq l\, r)$, $l > 0$. Then, there is a $c \in I_A$, v, v' such that $w = vv'$, $v \in L_b(c)$, and $v' \in N_c(\geq lr) \cap \overline{\bigcup_{k \geq l} L_c(\geq kr)} \cup E_c$. But then, by Lemma 5.2.11, $\mathcal{I}' = \mathcal{I}(c, v')$ is a model of $\mathcal{A}$ since the conditions in (5.2) are satisfied. In addition, there exists an element $d(= d_{n+1})$ such that $b^{\mathcal{I}'} v^{\mathcal{I}'} c^{\mathcal{I}'} v'^{\mathcal{I}'} d$ where $c^{\mathcal{I}'}$ occurs only as initial node in $c^{\mathcal{I}'} v'^{\mathcal{I}'} d$. Assume $d \in (\geq l\, r)^{\mathcal{I}'}$, i.e., $|r^{\mathcal{I}'}(d)| \geq l$. We consider two cases.

   a) Suppose $|r_A(d)| \geq l$. Then, $d \in I_A$. Moreover, by construction of $\mathcal{I}'$ and since $d = d_{n+1}$ it follows $d = c$ and $v' = \varepsilon$. But then, $v' = \varepsilon \in N_c(\geq l\, r)$ yields $|r_A(d)| < l$, in contradiction to the assumption.

   b) Assume $|r^{\mathcal{I}'}(d)| \geq l$ and $|r_A(d)| < l$. If $d \in \Delta^{\mathcal{I}}$, then no r-successors are generated for d in $\mathcal{I}'$ (Lemma 5.2.11, 2.), i.e. $r^{\mathcal{I}'}(d) = r^{\mathcal{I}}(d)$. On the other hand, r-successors are generated for d in $\mathcal{I}$ because of $|r^{\mathcal{I}'}| \geq l$ and $|r_A(d)| < l$. In particular, $|r^{\mathcal{I}}(d)| = c_{d,\mathcal{I}}^{\geq r}$ (Lemma 5.2.7, 5.), and by Lemma 5.2.11, 2. this means $|r^{\mathcal{I}'}(d)| = c_{d,\mathcal{I}'}^{\geq r}$. If d is an extension element in $\mathcal{I}'$, then we have $|r^{\mathcal{I}_0}(d)| = 0$ since $d = d_{n+1}$. Again, it follows $|r^{\mathcal{I}'}(d)| = c_{d,\mathcal{I}'}^{\geq r}$ (Lemma 5.2.11, 7.). According to Lemma 5.2.11, 8., we know $c_{c,v'}^{\geq r} \geq c_{d,\mathcal{I}'}^{\geq r}$. Hence, $c_{c,v'}^{\geq r} \geq l$. Consequently, there exists a $k \geq l$ with $v' \in L_c(\geq kr)$, which is a contradiction.

   Thus, we have shown $|r^{\mathcal{I}'}(d)| < l$, and $b^{\mathcal{I}'} \notin (\forall w.(\geq l\, r))^{\mathcal{I}'}$.

3. Assume $w \notin \overline{V}_b(\leq l\, r)$. Then, there exists $c \in I_A$ and words $v, v' \in N_R^*$ with $w = vv'$, $v \in L_b(c)$, and $v' \in N_c \cap \overline{\bigcup_{k \leq l} L_c(\leq kr)} \cup (E_c r^{-1})$. But then, by Lemma 5.2.11, $\mathcal{I}' = \mathcal{I}(c, v', r, l+1)$ is a model of $\mathcal{A}$ since the conditions in (5.2) are satisfied. (Observe that, $c_{c,v'}^{\leq r} \leq l$ would imply $v' \in L_c(\leq kr)$ for some $k \leq l$, in contradiction to $v' \in \overline{\bigcup_{k \leq l} L_c(\leq kr)}$.) Also, there exists an element $d(= d_{n+1})$ with $b^{\mathcal{I}'} v^{\mathcal{I}'} c^{\mathcal{I}'} v'^{\mathcal{I}'} d$ and $|r^{\mathcal{I}'}(d)| \geq l+1$ (Lemma 5.2.11, 9.). This shows $d \notin (\leq l\, r)^{\mathcal{I}'}$. Hence, $b^{\mathcal{I}'} \notin (\forall w.(\leq l\, r))^{\mathcal{I}'}$.

This completes the proof of Theorem 5.2.3.

It remains to show that value-restrictions sets are regular languages. By Theorem 5.2.3, it is sufficient to prove that the sets $L_c(F)$, N_c, and E_c are regular.

Lemma 5.2.12. *Predecessor restriction sets are regular languages and automata accepting them can be computed in polynomial time in the size of* $\mathcal{A}$.

Proof. It is easy to see that predecessor restriction sets for concept names or number-restrictions F are obtained as finite union of regular languages:

$$L_a(F) = \bigcup_{\substack{E(f) \in A \\ A \in C \\ L_f(a) \cap L_E(A) \neq \emptyset}} L_A(F)$$

where C is the set of states in $\mathcal{S}_{\mathcal{T}_A}$ (page 134). (This representation of $L_a(F)$ uses the fact that the semi-automaton $\mathcal{S}_{\mathcal{T}_A}$ does not contain word-transitions.) Thus, predecessor restriction sets are regular languages. Clearly, an automaton accepting the union of the regular languages $L_A(F)$ can be computed in polynomial time. $\square$

Obviously, the sets N_c and $N_c(\geq nr)$ are regular. In order to prove that finite automata accepting these languages can be constructed in time polynomial in the size of $\mathcal{A}$, it suffices to show that number conditions can be computed in polynomial time: By Lemma 5.2.12, a finite automaton accepting $L_c(\geq nr)$ can be constructed in polynomial time. Also, testing $v \in L_c(\geq nr)$ can be carried out in time polynomial in the size of v and $\mathcal{A}$. The number of at-least restrictions in $\mathcal{A}$ is linear in the size of $\mathcal{A}$. Thus, computing $max\{n \mid v \in L_c(\geq nr)\}$ is a polynomial time problem. The same is true for $c_{c,v}^{\leq r}$.

Lemma 5.2.13. *Finite automaton accepting the regular languages N_c and $N_c(\geq nr)$ can be computed in time polynomial in the size of* $\mathcal{A}$.

Finally, we have to show that E_c is regular. For this purpose, we construct a finite automaton accepting E_c using the following notion.

Definition 5.2.14. *The word w reaches a pre-exclusion set starting from c if there exists a prefix v of w such that $\delta(q_c, v) \in \mathcal{E}$.*

Now an alternative description of the set E_c of pre-excluding words is:

Lemma 5.2.14. *Let $w \in N_R^*$. Then, $w \in E_c$ if, and only if,*

1. *starting from c a pre-exclusion set is reachable by w; or*
2. *there exists a prefix vr of w with $v \in N_R^*$, $r \in N_R$ such that $(\leq 0 r) \in \delta(q_c, v)$.*

Proof. In order to prove the only-if direction, let $w \in E_c$. We distinguish two cases:

a) There exist $v, v' \in N_R^*$, $r \in N_R$ such that v is a prefix of w, vv' is v-required by c, and $c_{c,vv'}^{\geq r} > c_{c,vv'}^{\leq r}$. Similar to 2. in the proof of Proposition 5.2.1, one can show that for $\mathcal{F}_i := \delta(q_c, vr_1 \cdots r_i)$, $0 \leq i \leq n$, it holds that $(\geq m_i \, r_i) \in \mathcal{F}_{i-1}$ for all $1 \leq i < n$ where $m_i \geq 1$ and $v' = r_1 \cdots r_n$. Moreover, for $l := c_{c,vv'}^{\geq r}$ and $k := c_{c,vv'}^{\leq r}$ we can conclude $(\geq l \, r), (\leq k \, r) \in \mathcal{F}_n$. Thus, $\mathcal{F}_0$ is a pre-exclusion set that is reachable by v starting from c. This means that also w reaches a pre-exclusion set starting from c.

b) There exists a prefix vr of w, $v \in N_R^*$, $r \in N_R$, such that $c_{c,v}^{\leq r} = 0$. As in 2. in the proof of Proposition 5.2.1 it can be shown that $(\leq 0 \, r) \in \delta(q_c, v)$.

In order to show the if direction we assume that w satisfies condition 1. or 2.

c) There is a prefix v of w such that $\delta(q_c, v) \in \mathcal{E}$. By definition of $\mathcal{E}$, there exists a word $v' = r_1 \cdots r_n \in N_R^*$, conflicting number-restrictions $(\geq l \, r)$ and $(\leq k \, r)$, $l > k$, and for all $1 \leq i \leq n$ there are positive integers m_i such that for $\mathcal{F}_0 := \delta(q_c, v)$ and $\mathcal{F}_i := \delta(\mathcal{F}_0, r_1 \cdots r_i)$, $1 \leq i \leq n$, it holds that $(\geq m_i \, r_i) \in \mathcal{F}_{i-1}$ for all $1 \leq i \leq n$, and $(\geq l \, r), (\leq k \, r) \in \mathcal{F}_n$. Consequently, there are $A_1, \ldots, A_n$ as well as A^l, A^k in q_c such that $vr_1 \cdots r_{i-1} \in L_{A_i}(\geq m_i \, r_i)$ for all $1 \leq i \leq n$ as well as $vv' \in L_{A^l}(\geq l \, r)$ and $vv' \in L_{A^k}(\leq k \, r)$. By definition of q_c there are concept names and number restrictions E_i, individuals f_i, and words w_i for all $1 \leq i \leq n$ as well as concept names and number restrictions E^l, E^k, individuals f^l, f^k, and words w^l, w^k such that $E_i(f_i) \in \mathcal{A}$, $f_i w_i c$ is a role chain in $\mathcal{A}$, and $w_i \in L_{E_i}(A_i)$ as well as $E^l(f^l) \in \mathcal{A}$, $f^l w^l c$ is a role chain in $\mathcal{A}$, $w^l \in L_{E^l}(A^l)$, and $E^k(f^k) \in \mathcal{A}$, $f^k w^k c$ is a role chain in $\mathcal{A}$, $w^k \in L_{E^k}(A^k)$. This means, $w_i vr_1 \cdots r_{i-1} \in L_{E_i}(\geq m_i \, r_i)$ for all $1 \leq i \leq n$ as well as $w^l vv' \in L_{E^l}(\geq l \, r)$ and $w^k vv' \in L_{E^k}(\leq k \, r)$. Consequently, vv' is v-required by c and $c_{c,vv'}^{\geq r} \geq l > k \geq c_{c,vv'}^{\leq r}$. Thus, $w \in E_c$.

d) There exists a prefix vr of w where $v \in N_R^*$, $r \in N_R$ with $(\leq 0 \, r) \in \delta(q_c, v)$. Thus, there is $A \in q_c$ such that $v \in L_A(\leq 0 \, r)$. As before by definition of q_c it can be shown $c_{c,v}^{\leq r} \leq 0$. This means, $w \in E_c$.   □

Lemma 5.2.14 allows us to construct a powerset automaton of $\mathcal{S}_{T_A}$ accepting E_c.

Definition 5.2.15. *Let $\mathcal{S}_{T_A} = (N_R, \mathcal{C}, \Delta)$ denote the semi-automaton corresponding to the ABox $\mathcal{A}$ (see Page 134) and let c be an individual in $\mathcal{A}$. Then, the powerset automaton $\mathcal{P}(\mathcal{A}, c)$ of $\mathcal{S}_{T_A}$ and c is defined by $\mathcal{P}(\mathcal{A}, c) := (N_R, \widehat{\mathcal{C}}, \widehat{q}, \widehat{\delta})$ where*

- $\widehat{\mathcal{C}} := \{\mathcal{F} \subseteq \mathcal{C} \mid \delta(q_c, w) = \mathcal{F} \text{ for some } w \in N_R^*\}$ *(set of states), and*
- $\widehat{q} := q_c$ *(initial state), and*
- $\widehat{\delta}(\mathcal{F}, r) := \delta(\mathcal{F}, r) \in \widehat{\mathcal{C}}$ *for $\mathcal{F} \in \widehat{\mathcal{C}}$ and $r \in N_R$ (set of transitions).*[6]

With the help of Lemma 5.2.14, it can easily be verified that the finite automaton $\mathcal{S}_c$, defined in the following definition, accepts the language E_c:

---

[6] Note that we do not incorporate final states.

Definition 5.2.16. *The finite automaton $\mathcal{S}_c$ is obtained from the powerset automaton $\mathcal{P}(\mathcal{A}, c)$ of $\mathcal{S}_{T_\mathcal{A}}$ by adding q as a final state of the automaton. Moreover, i) for every pre-exclusion set $\mathcal{F} \subseteq \mathcal{C}$ in $\mathcal{S}_c$ we add a transition $(\mathcal{F}, \varepsilon, q)$ and ii) for every state $\mathcal{F} \subseteq \mathcal{C}$ in $\mathcal{S}_c$ and at-most restriction $(\leq 0 \, r)$ in $\mathcal{A}$ with $(\leq 0 \, r) \in \mathcal{F}$ we add the transition $(\mathcal{F}, r, q)$. Finally, q has a self-loop (q, r, q) for every $r \in N_R$.*

This non-deterministic automaton can easily be turned into an equivalent deterministic automaton: The transitions $(\mathcal{F}, \varepsilon, q)$ from pre-exclusion sets $\mathcal{F}$ to q are deleted. Instead, pre-exclusion sets are defined to be final states and all outgoing edges of these sets are replaced by self-loops (for all role names). Moreover, if for some set $\mathcal{F} \subseteq \mathcal{C}$ there is a transition $(\mathcal{F}, r, q)$, then all transitions of the form $(\mathcal{F}, r, \mathcal{F}')$ for some $\mathcal{F}' \subseteq \mathcal{C}$ are deleted.

As an immediate consequence of this construction we obtain the desired statement on pre-exclusion sets.

Lemma 5.2.15. *The set E_c is regular and a (deterministic) automata accepting this set can be constructed in time exponential in the size of $\mathcal{A}$.*

Having a (deterministic) automaton for E_c at hand, a (deterministic) automaton for the language $E_c r^{-1}$ can easily be constructed as well. Also, a deterministic automaton for the language $L_a(P) \cup E_c$ can be derived from the (deterministic) automaton to E_c by turning all states $\mathcal{F}$ with $P \in \mathcal{F}$ into final states (in addition to the already existing ones). In the same way, one gains deterministic automata for $\bigcup_{k \geq l} L_c(\geq kr) \cup E_c$ and $\bigcup_{k \leq l} L_c(\leq kr) \cup (E_c r^{-1})$, i.e., states containing $(\geq k \, r)$, $\overline{k} \geq l$, and $(\leq k \, r)$, $k \leq \overline{l}$, respectively, are defined to be final states. Consequently, the complements of these languages are accepted by interchanging non-final and final states in these automata. Together with Theorem 5.2.3, this shows that for the complement of value-restriction sets (non-deterministic) automata can be computed in exponential time. Applying the powerset construction to these automata and interchanging non-final and final states provides us with automata accepting the value-restriction sets (see [HU79] for a description of the powerset construction of finite automata).

Corollary 5.2.4. *Value-restriction sets are regular languages and (deterministic) finite automata accepting these sets can be computed in double exponential time in the size of the underlying ABox.*

Up to now, it is an open problem whether this double exponential blow-up of automata accepting value-restriction sets can be avoided.

Deciding the Instance Problem. Similar to Theorem 4.2.2, instance can be characterized in terms of inclusions of value-restriction sets.

Theorem 5.2.4. *Let C be an $\mathcal{FLN}^*$-concept description and b be an individual name in $\mathcal{A}$, then $b \in_\mathcal{A} C$ if, and only if, $L_C(F) \subseteq V_b(F)$, for all concept names and number restrictions F in $\mathcal{A}$.*

Proof. We first assume that $L_C(F) \subseteq V_b(F)$ for all concept names and number restrictions F. By Theorem 4.2.1, we need to show that $w \in L_C(F)$ implies $b \in_\mathcal{A} \forall w.F$. Let $w \in L_C(F)$. The assumption says that $w \in V_b(F)$. But then, $b \in_\mathcal{A} \forall w.F$.

Now, assume that there exists a concept name or a number restriction F and a word $w \in L_C(F) \setminus V_b(F)$. This means $b \notin_\mathcal{A} \forall w.F$. On the other hand, by Theorem 4.2.1, $w \in L_C(F)$ implies $b \notin_\mathcal{A} C$. $\square$

Following the lines of Corollary 4.2.1, Theorem 5.2.4 can be rephrased as follows:

Corollary 5.2.5. *Let C be an $\mathcal{FLN}^*$-concept description and b be an individual name in $\mathcal{A}$, then $b \in_\mathcal{A} C$ if, and only if, $V_C(F) \subseteq V_b(F)$, for all concept names and number restrictions F in $\mathcal{A}$.*

Proof. Since $L_C(F) \subseteq V_C(F)$, the if direction follows immediately with Theorem 5.2.4.

For the only-if direction assume $b \in_\mathcal{A} C$ and let $w \in V_C(F)$. But then, $C \sqsubseteq \forall w.F$, and thus $b \in_\mathcal{A} \forall w.F$, which means $w \in V_b(F)$. This shows $V_C(F) \subseteq V_b(F)$. $\square$

In order to decide instance we only have to test the inclusions stated in Theorem 5.2.4. This can be accomplished by testing emptiness of the languages $L_C(F) \cap \overline{V_b(F)}$. As shown before, an automaton accepting $\overline{V_b(F)}$ can be computed in exponential time, and hence, this is true for automata accepting $L_C(F) \cap \overline{V_b(F)}$. Since for arbitrary (non-deterministic) automata, emptiness can be decided in time linear in the size of the input automaton, in our case emptiness can be checked in time exponential in the size of the ABox and the size of the concept C. Due to a result established by Baader [Baa96], we know that instance checking in $\mathcal{FLN}^*$-ABoxes is at least PSPACE-hard.

Corollary 5.2.6. *The instance problem for $\mathcal{FLN}^*$-ABoxes is PSPACE-hard and can be decided by an exponential time algorithm.*

Whether and how the gap between this lower and upper complexity bound can be closed is an open problem.

Computing the Msc. The msc of an individual must be subsumed by all value-restrictions the individual is an instance of. Since we already have defined such sets, namely, the value-restriction sets, it is easy to prove the following theorem using the Theorems 5.2.4 and 4.2.2.

Theorem 5.2.5. *Let $\mathcal{A}$ be an $\mathcal{FLN}^*$-ABox, C be an $\mathcal{FLN}^*$-concept description, and b be an individual in $\mathcal{A}$. Then, C is a msc of b if, and only if, $V_C(F) = V_b(F)$ for all concept names and number restrictions F.*

Note that if $\mathcal{A}$ is inconsistent, then $C \equiv \bot$ is the most specific concept of b.

An $\mathcal{FLN}^*$-concept description E that satisfies the property stated in Theorem 5.2.5 is one with $L_E(F) = V_b(F)$. As stated in Corollary 5.2.4, automata accepting the value-restriction sets can be computed in double exponential time. Translating the automata back into TBoxes yields the desired $\mathcal{FLN}^*$-concept description E.

To prove a complexity lower bound for the msc computation, consider the following ABox:

$$r(a, a_1), \ldots, r(a, a_k), \; (\leq k \, r),$$
$$(\forall L_1.P)(a_1), \ldots, (\forall L_k.P)(a_k),$$

where $L_1, \ldots, L_k$ are regular languages and P is a concept name. Then, it is not hard to verify that

$$msc(a) \equiv (\leq k \, r) \sqcap (\geq k \, r) \sqcap \forall \{r\} \cdot (L_1 \cap \cdots \cap L_k).P.$$

Now, just as for the lcs (Section 5.2.1), using that the size of finite automata accepting the intersection of a sequence of regular languages may grow exponentially [YZ91], it follows that the size of the msc of a may grow exponentially as well. Summing up, we obtain the following complexity lower and upper bounds.

Corollary 5.2.7. *Most specific concepts for individuals defined in $\mathcal{FLN}^*$-ABoxes always exist and can be computed in double exponential time in the size of the ABox. Moreover, the size of the msc (applied to one individual) may grow exponentially in the size of the underlying ABox.*

As an aside, we note that, for cyclic $\mathcal{FLN}^*$-concept descriptions interpreted by the lfp-semantics or descriptive semantics, the msc need not exist. In this respect, the gfp-semantics we have employed in this book to interpret cyclic $\mathcal{FLN}$-concept descriptions (which then yields a 1-1 correspondence between these and $\mathcal{FLN}^*$-concept descriptions as shown in Section 4.2) seems to be more appropriate than either of the other semantics.

Example 5.2.1. Let $\mathcal{A}$ be the ABox consisting of the assertions

$$r(a, a), (\leq 1 \, r)(a).$$

Because of $a \in_{\mathcal{A}} \forall w.(\geq 1 \, r) =: C_w$ for all $w \in r^*$, the msc C_a of a must be subsumed by C_w. But then, as an easy consequence of Remark 4.2.1, C_a is unsatisfiable when interpreted by the lfp-semantics. Thus, with respect to the lfp-semantics there does not exist a msc of a. Since C_a is unsatisfiable for the lfp-semantics, for the description semantics there exists a model of C_a, namely the lfp-model, where the extension of C_a is the empty set. But then, with the descriptive semantics, C_a cannot have a as an instance either.

5.3 LCS for $\mathcal{ALE}$-Concept Descriptions

Conceptually, the lcs of $\mathcal{ALE}$-concept descriptions can be computed in the same way as the lcs of $\mathcal{ALNS}$-concept descriptions. That is, the lcs of $\mathcal{ALE}$-concept descriptions is obtained as the product of the corresponding normalized description trees. These products are defined analogously to the product of $\mathcal{ALNS}$-description graphs (Definition 5.1.1). Again, special care has to be taken w.r.t. unsatisfiable nodes.

Algorithms for the lcs of $\mathcal{ALE}$-concept descriptions and their complexity have first been investigated in [BKM99]. For the sake of completeness, we will cite the main results and otherwise point the reader to [BKM98a] for complete proofs.[7] Nevertheless, we will come back to the lcs of $\mathcal{ALE}$-concept descriptions in Section 6.3 as it plays an important rôle when matching $\mathcal{ALE}$-concept descriptions.

Theorem 5.3.1. *The lcs, $lcs(C_1, \ldots, C_k)$, of a sequence $C_1, \ldots, C_k$ of $\mathcal{ALE}$-concept descriptions always exists and can be computed in time exponential in the size of the sequence. The size of the lcs may grow exponentially in the size of the sequence (even if the length k of the sequence is fixed with $k \geq 2$).*

The exponential blow-up of the lcs can be illustrated by the following example. Let D_2 be the $\mathcal{ALE}$-concept description $\exists r.(P \sqcap Q \sqcap \exists r.(P \sqcap Q))$. Then, the lcs E_2 of C_2 (see Page 102) and D_2 is $\exists r.(P \sqcap \exists r.P \sqcap \exists r.Q) \sqcap \exists r.(Q \sqcap \exists r.P \sqcap \exists r.Q)$, thus $\mathcal{G}(E_2)$ is a binary tree of depth 2 with only containing $\exists$-edges. When generalizing this example to C_k and D_k one can show that the size of every concept description equivalent to the lcs E_k of C_k and D_k can only exponentially be bounded in k.

For $\mathcal{EL}$-concept descriptions one obtains a polynomial upper bound for the size of the lcs of sequences with fixed length. The main reason is that $\mathcal{EL}$-concept descriptions do not need to be normalized before turning them into description trees. However, for sequences of arbitrary length, the exponential blow-up cannot be avoided [BKM98a].

Corollary 5.3.1. *The lcs of a sequence of $\mathcal{EL}$-concept descriptions always exists and can be computed in time exponential in the size of the sequence. The size of the lcs may grow exponentially in the size of the sequence. However, if the number of concepts in the sequence is fixed, then their exists a polynomial upper bound for the size of the lcs.*

---

[7] We only cite the results here since the lcs in $\mathcal{ALE}$ is investigated in a thesis my Molitor citeMolitor-PhDThesis-2000.

6. Matching

In this chapter, the results on matching already summarized in Section 3.2.5 are proved. As in the previous two chapters, this is done in three separate sections containing proofs for $\mathcal{ALNS}$, $\mathcal{ALN}^*$, and $\mathcal{ALE}$ (as well as sublanguages thereof).

6.1 Matching in $\mathcal{ALNS}$

The first matching algorithms in DLs have been introduced by Borgida and McGuinness [BM96, McG96] for sublanguages of CLASSIC and a language that extends $\mathcal{ALN}$ by existential restrictions. The main drawback of their algorithms is that they cannot be applied to arbitrary patterns and that, due to an incomplete treatment of the existential restriction as well as the top- and bottom-concept, they are incomplete even if patterns are in the required normal form. The first complete matching algorithm has been presented by Baader and Narendran [BN98] for the language $\mathcal{FL}_0$, which later on was extended to an algorithm for $\mathcal{FL}_\neg$ [BBM98].

In this section, we present sound and complete algorithms for $\mathcal{ALNS}$-matching problems modulo subsumption and equivalence.

We first show that deciding the solvability of $\mathcal{ALNS}$-matching problems is a PSPACE-hard problem for matching modulo equivalence and that there exists a polynomial time decision algorithm for matching modulo subsumption. The main result of this section is that solvable $\mathcal{ALNS}$-matching problems always have a least matcher, which can be computed by an exponential time algorithm. Remarkably, this result follows from a general schema applicable to languages for which, among others, the lcs must always exist. In particular, the schema shows that computing the lcs is an important operation when determining the least matcher. Being able to compute least matchers in $\mathcal{ALNS}$ provides us with an exponential time decision algorithm for matching modulo equivalence. Moreover, since a set containing a least matcher is minimal i-complete this proves that minimal i-complete sets can be computed in exponential time as well. As discussed in Section 3.2.3, for $\mathcal{ALNS}$-matching problems it is not clear how to define d-minimal matchers, i.e., matchers that are free of redundancies. For this reason, in $\mathcal{ALNS}$, only the algorithm computing least matchers is presented.

R.Küsters: Non-Standard Inferences in Description Logics, LNAI 2100, pp. 153–227, 2001.
© Springer-Verlag Berlin Heidelberg 2001

For the sublanguage $\mathcal{ALN}$ of $\mathcal{ALNS}$, however, matching becomes much easier both computationally and conceptually. In particular, it turns out that, in $\mathcal{ALN}$, least matchers can be computed in polynomial time. Moreover, from given least matchers one can derive the minimal d-complete set of matchers.

6.1.1 Deciding the Solvability of Matching Problems

As pointed out in Section 4.1.1, subsumption in $\mathcal{ALNS}$ and $\mathcal{ALN}$ can be decided in polynomial time. Thus, as a direct consequence of Lemma 3.2.3, we obtain the following computational complexity for matching modulo subsumption.

Corollary 6.1.1. *Solvability of $\mathcal{ALNS}$- and $\mathcal{ALN}$-matching problems modulo subsumption can be decided by a polynomial time algorithm.*

The main technical problem tackled in this subsection is to show that matching modulo equivalence in $\mathcal{ALNS}$ is a PSPACE-hard problem. In the following subsection, we then prove a computational upper bound for the solvability of matching modulo equivalence. Specifically, we will show that every solvable $\mathcal{ALNS}$-matching problem has a least matcher, which can be computed in exponential time. Hence, a matching problem is solvable if, and only if, the least matcher solves the problem. Consequently, we obtain the following computational lower and upper bounds for deciding the solvability of matching modulo equivalence.

Corollary 6.1.2. *Solvability of $\mathcal{ALNS}$-matching problems modulo equivalence is a PSPACE-hard problem, which can be decided in exponential time.*

Up to now, it is an open problem whether this problem is actually PSPACE-complete. As we will see in the following subsection, for $\mathcal{ALN}$-matching problems the least matchers can be computed in polynomial time. Thus, for this restricted class we can state the following tighter complexity bounds.

Corollary 6.1.3. *Solvability of $\mathcal{ALN}$-matching problems modulo equivalence can be decided by a polynomial time algorithm.*

In order to establish the hardness result stated in Corollary 6.1.2, the emptiness problem for the intersection of languages accepted by a sequence of deterministic finite automata is reduced to the problem of deciding the solvability of $\mathcal{ALNS}$-matching problems modulo equivalence. The former problem has been shown to be PSPACE-complete by Kozen [Koz77]. Recall that given a sequence of k finite deterministic automata $\mathcal{A}_1, \dots, \mathcal{A}_k$ over the same finite input alphabet Σ, the problem asks whether there exists a word $x \in \Sigma^*$ such that $x \in L(\mathcal{A}_i)$ for all $i = 1, \dots, k$, where $L(\mathcal{A}_i)$ denotes the regular language accepted by $\mathcal{A}_i$. The PSPACE-hardness proof proposed by Kozen reveals that one only needs to consider deterministic finite automata with one initial state and one final state. We may also assume w.l.o.g. that the languages accepted by these automata are not empty.

In the sequel, let $\mathcal{A}_1, \ldots, \mathcal{A}_k$ be deterministic finite automata with only one initial state and one finite state, respectively. For this sequence of automata we will define an $\mathcal{ALNS}$-matching problem modulo equivalence that is solvable if, and only if, the language $L(\mathcal{A}_1) \cap \cdots \cap L(\mathcal{A}_k)$ is not empty.

The finite alphabet Σ denotes the set of attributes of this matching problem. A deterministic finite automaton $\mathcal{A}$ can be viewed as normalized $\mathcal{ALNS}$-description graph $\mathcal{G}_\mathcal{A}$ where the nodes of $\mathcal{G}_\mathcal{A}$ represent the states of $\mathcal{A}$ and the a-edges of $\mathcal{G}_\mathcal{A}$ stand for the transitions of $\mathcal{A}$; the set of atoms and r-edges of nodes of $\mathcal{G}_\mathcal{A}$ are empty. The initial state of $\mathcal{A}$ corresponds to the root of $\mathcal{G}_\mathcal{A}$. Note that $\mathcal{G}_\mathcal{A}$ specified in this way is in fact normalized because $\mathcal{A}$ is deterministic. We define $C_\mathcal{A}$ to be the concept description $C_{\mathcal{G}_\mathcal{A}}$ corresponding to $\mathcal{G}_\mathcal{A}$. Finally, let $\mathcal{G}_\mathcal{A}^F$ denote the description graph obtained from $\mathcal{G}_\mathcal{A}$ when adding the concept name F to the atoms of the node in $\mathcal{G}_\mathcal{A}$ that represents the final state of $\mathcal{A}$. We refer to the corresponding concept description by $C_\mathcal{A}^F$.

The main idea underlying this construction is stated in the following lemma. Recall that, for $w = a_1 \cdots a_l$, the concept description $\forall w.F$ is an abbreviation for $\forall a_1.\cdots.\forall a_l.F$.

Lemma 6.1.1. $C_\mathcal{A}^F \sqsubseteq \forall w.F$ iff $w \in L(\mathcal{A})$.

Proof. Since $\mathcal{G}_\mathcal{A}^F \equiv C_\mathcal{A}^F$, Lemma 4.1.7 ensures that $\mathcal{G}_\mathcal{A}^F \cong \mathcal{G}_{(C_\mathcal{A}^F)}$.

Now, according to Theorem 4.1.3, $w \in L(\mathcal{A})$ together with the construction of $\mathcal{G}_\mathcal{A}^F$ implies $C_\mathcal{A}^F \sqsubseteq \forall w.F$.

On the other hand, if $C_\mathcal{A}^F \sqsubseteq \forall w.F$, then Theorem 4.1.3 ensures that there is a rooted path in $\mathcal{G}_\mathcal{A}^F$ labeled w leading to a node with F in its atoms. By construction of $\mathcal{G}_\mathcal{A}^F$ this means that there is an accepting path for w in $\mathcal{A}$, and hence, $w \in L(\mathcal{A})$. $\square$

Now, the emptiness problem can be reduced to the solvability of matching modulo equivalence as explained next. We first recall that, according to Lemma 3.2.4, every system of matching problems modulo equivalence can easily be turned into a single matching problem modulo equivalence. So instead of a single matching problem, for the reduction it suffices to provide a system of matching problems.

Proposition 6.1.1. *The language* $L(\mathcal{A}_1) \cap \cdots \cap L(\mathcal{A}_k)$ *is non-empty if, and only if, the following matching problem has a solution:*

$$\{C_{\mathcal{A}_1}^F \equiv^? X \sqcap C_{\mathcal{A}_1}, \ldots, C_{\mathcal{A}_k}^F \equiv^? X \sqcap C_{\mathcal{A}_k}\}.$$

Proof. Let $w \in \Sigma^*$ be a word in the intersection of the languages $L(\mathcal{A}_i)$. We define $\sigma(X) := \forall w.F$ and want to show that σ solves the matching problem. If w is accepted by $\mathcal{A}_i$, then this means that, starting from the initial state of $\mathcal{A}_i$, there exists a path in $\mathcal{A}_i$ labeled w leading to the final state of $\mathcal{A}$. Consequently, the normalized description graph for $\forall w.F \sqcap C_{\mathcal{A}_i}$ is isomorphic to $\mathcal{G}_{\mathcal{A}_i}^F$. But then, $C_{\mathcal{A}_i}^F \equiv \sigma(X) \sqcap C_{\mathcal{A}_i}$, which means that σ is a solution of the matching problem.

Let us now turn to the if direction and assume that σ is a solution of the matching problem. W.l.o.g., $\sigma(X)$ is a finite conjunction of concept descriptions of the form $\forall w.E$ where E is $\bot$, $\top$, a (negated) concept name, a number restriction, or a same-as equality. Since by assumption $L(\mathcal{A}_1) \neq \emptyset$, we know that there exists a word $w' \in \Sigma^*$ with $C_{\mathcal{A}_1}^F \sqsubseteq \forall w'.F$. Consequently, (*) $C_{\mathcal{A}_1}^F \equiv \sigma(X) \sqcap C_{\mathcal{A}_1} \sqsubseteq \forall w'.F$. By construction, it is easy to see that if $\sigma(X) \not\sqsubseteq \forall w.F$ for all $w \in \Sigma^*$, then (*) cannot be true. In the following, let us fix some w with $\sigma(X) \sqsubseteq \forall w.F$. Since σ solves the matching problem, it follows that $C_{\mathcal{A}_i}^F \sqsubseteq \forall w.F$ for all i, and thus Lemma 6.1.1 implies $w \in L(\mathcal{A}_i)$ for all i. Hence, $w \in L(\mathcal{A}_1) \cap \cdots \cap L(\mathcal{A}_k)$.   □

The complexity lower bound stated in Corollary 6.1.2 is a direct consequence of Proposition 6.1.1. Moreover, the matching problem in Proposition 6.1.1 shows that, for a solution σ, $\sigma(X)$ must contain a concept description of the form $\forall w.F$ where $w \in L(\mathcal{A}_1) \cap \cdots \cap L(\mathcal{A}_k)$. We now show that the minimal length of words in these intersections may grow exponentially in the size of the automata. As a direct consequence, we then obtain the following corollary.

Corollary 6.1.4. *The size of matchers of $\mathcal{ALNS}$-matching problems modulo equivalence may grow exponentially in the size of the matching problem.*

To show that the minimal length of words in the intersection $L(\mathcal{A}_1) \cap \cdots \cap L(\mathcal{A}_k)$ may explode, consider deterministic automata $\mathcal{A}_i$, $i \geq 1$, which consist of a cycle of length i, i.e., $\mathcal{A}_i$ contains the transitions (q_{j-1}, a, q_j) for every $1 \leq j \leq i$. In addition, we add the transition (q_{i-1}, b, q) and define q_0 to be the initial state and q to be the final state of $\mathcal{A}_i$. Now, let $p_1, \ldots, p_k$ be the first k prime numbers. Then, it is easy to see that the word $w = a^{(p_1 \cdots p_k)-1}b$ belongs to the intersection $L(\mathcal{A}_{p_1}) \cap \cdots \cap L(\mathcal{A}_{p_k})$ and that it is of minimal length with this property. From the Prime Number Theorem [Kor82] it follows for the ith prime number p_i that $p_i \leq i \cdot log\, i$. Thus, the size of the sequence $\mathcal{A}_{p_1}, \ldots, \mathcal{A}_{p_k}$ is bounded by $k^2 \cdot log\, k$. The length of w is $p_1 \cdots p_k$. Since $p_i \geq 2$ for every $i \geq 1$, it follows that the size of w grows exponentially in k.

6.1.2 Computing Minimal i-Complete Sets

For solvable $\mathcal{ALNS}$-matching problems, there always exists a least matcher σ, i.e., if σ' is a matcher, then $\sigma \sqsubseteq_s \sigma'$. We will prove this result in two steps. First, a general schema for computing least matchers is presented, in which those properties of a language are identified that are sufficient to guarantee the existence of least matchers. In a second step, based on this schema we show how to compute least matchers in $\mathcal{ALNS}$. Being able to compute least matchers provides us with an algorithm for computing minimal i-complete sets since a set consisting of a least matcher only is minimal i-complete.

A Schema for Matching Value-Restrictions. The following schema for computing least matchers is applicable to those description logics $\mathcal{L}$ known from the literature which i) allow for concept conjunction and value-restrictions and ii) satisfy three conditions, which are introduced now.

Let $\Sigma := N_R \cup N_A$ denote the set of role and attribute names and let C denote some $\mathcal{L}$-concept description. For $w \in \Sigma^*$ we define C_w to be the least concept description in $\mathcal{L}$ such that $C \sqsubseteq \forall w.C_w$, i.e., if $C \sqsubseteq \forall w.E$ for an $\mathcal{L}$-concept description E, then $C_w \sqsubseteq E$. Now, the three conditions $\mathcal{L}$ must obey are the following:

1. The lcs of $\mathcal{L}$-concept descriptions always exists;
2. for every $\mathcal{L}$-concept description C and $w \in \Sigma^*$, C_w always exists;
3. for all $\mathcal{L}$-concept descriptions E, F, and all $w \in \Sigma^*$, $E \sqsubseteq F$ implies $\forall w.E \sqsubseteq \forall w.F$.

$$(6.1)$$

The matching problems we are interested in are of the form

$$C \equiv^? D \qquad (6.2)$$

where D is a concept pattern with variables only occurring in the scope of value-restrictions, i.e., D is of the form

$$D = D' \sqcap \prod_{i=1}^{l} \forall W_i.X_i \qquad (6.3)$$

where D' is some $\mathcal{L}$-concept description, X_i, $1 \leq i \leq k$, are concept variables, and for all $1 \leq i \leq k$, W_i is a finite subset of Σ^*. The concept pattern $\forall W_i.X_i$ is an abbreviation for the conjunction $\prod_{w \in W_i} \forall w.X_i$.

Note that every $\mathcal{ALNS}$-matching problem can be turned into this form without changing the set of solutions. However, for example, $\mathcal{ALE}$-matching problems (Section 6.3), where variables can also occur in the scope of existential restrictions, do not always fit into this form.

The schema for solving matching problems of the form just introduced is now stated in the following theorem.

Theorem 6.1.1. *Let $\mathcal{L}$ be a language that satisfies the conditions listed in (6.1). Then, the matching problem $C \equiv^? D$ as specified in (6.2) has a solution if, and only if, the substitution*

$$\sigma(X_i) := lcs(C_w \mid w \in W_i),$$

$1 \leq i \leq k$, solves the problem. In addition, in case $C \equiv^? D$ is solvable, σ is a least matcher. Note that because of the first two conditions in (6.1), σ is well-defined.

Proof. The if direction is trivial. For the only-if direction let σ' be a matcher of $C \equiv^? D$, i.e., $C \equiv \sigma'(D)$. This implies $C \sqsubseteq \forall w.\sigma'(X_i)$ for any $w \in W_i$. By definition of C_w we know $C_w \sqsubseteq \sigma'(X_i)$. Now, the definition of $\sigma(X_i)$ ensures

$$\sigma(X_i) \sqsubseteq \sigma'(X_i),$$

and thus, because of condition (6.1), 3., $\sigma(D) \sqsubseteq \sigma'(D) \equiv C$.

Conversely, from $C \equiv \sigma'(D)$ we can infer $C \sqsubseteq D'$, and by definition of C_w, $w \in W_i$, we know $C \sqsubseteq \forall w.C_w$. Since $C_w \sqsubseteq \sigma(X_i)$ for every $w \in W_i$, it follows that $C \sqsubseteq \forall W_i.\sigma(X_i)$. Together, this implies $C \sqsubseteq \sigma(D)$.

Finally, the proof reveals that σ is a least matcher because $\sigma(X_i) \sqsubseteq \sigma'(X_i)$ for every matcher σ'. □

The theorem shows that if i) a language $\mathcal{L}$ satisfies the conditions listed in (6.1), ii) for any two $\mathcal{L}$-concept descriptions the lcs can be computed effectively, and iii) for any C and $w \in \Sigma^*$ the concept C_w is computable, then the following algorithm decides the solvability of $\mathcal{L}$-matching problems of the form (6.2) and returns the least matcher in case the problem is solvable.

Algorithm 6.1.1

Input: *$\mathcal{L}$-matching problem $C \equiv^? D$ of the form (6.2) and $\mathcal{L}$ satisfies (6.1).*

Output: *"No" if the matching problem cannot be solved;*
the least matcher if the matching problem has a solution.

1. *Compute the candidate matcher σ,*

$$\sigma(X_i) := lcs(C_w \mid w \in W_i), 1 \le i \le k.$$

2. *If $C \equiv \sigma(D)$, then return σ else "No".*

Although, Theorem 6.1.1 implies that every solvable $\mathcal{L}$-matching problem has a least matcher, this is no longer the case if $\mathcal{L}$ does not satisfy (6.1), say, if in $\mathcal{L}$ the lcs need not exist in general. For instance, let $\mathcal{L}$ denote the language which extends $\mathcal{LS}$ by value restrictions. Recall that $\mathcal{LS}$ is the language that only allows for concept conjunction and same-as equalities where attributes are interpreted as total functions. Let C_1 and C_2 be arbitrary concept descriptions in $\mathcal{LS}$, r_1 and r_2 be two distinct role names, and X be a concept variable. Then, a solution for the $\mathcal{L}$-matching problem

$$\forall r_1.C_1 \sqcap \forall r_2.C_2 \equiv^? \forall r_1.C_1 \sqcap \forall r_2.C_2 \sqcap \forall \{r_1, r_2\}.X \tag{6.4}$$

is $\sigma(X) := \top$. On the other hand, it is easy to see that a least matcher σ of this problem must map X on the lcs of C_1 and C_2 in $\mathcal{LS}$. But as we have shown in Section 5.1.2, the lcs need not exist in $\mathcal{LS}$. Hence, although the problem is solvable, it need not have a least matcher.

Computing Least Matchers in $\mathcal{ALNS}$. Clearly, every $\mathcal{ALNS}$-matching problem can be turned into an equivalent matching problem of the form (6.3), where equivalent matching problems are those with the same set of solutions. From Section 5.1.1 we already know that in $\mathcal{ALNS}$ the lcs always exists and that it can be computed effectively. Moreover, from the characterization of subsumption (Theorem 4.1.3) it is clear that in $\mathcal{ALNS}$ condition (6.1), 3. holds. Thus, in order to employ Algorithm 6.1.1 for computing least matchers in $\mathcal{ALNS}$, the only thing left to show is that the concept descriptions C_w always exist and that they can be computed effectively.

As we will see, C_w can be computed using the normalized description graph $\mathcal{G}_C$ of C. Roughly speaking, C_w corresponds to the subgraph of $\mathcal{G}_C$ rooted at the node that one reaches when following the path in $\mathcal{G}_C$ along w.

Definition 6.1.1. *Let C be an $\mathcal{ALNS}$-concept description and let $\mathcal{G}_C = (N, E, n_0, \ell)$ be its normalized description graph. Then, for $w \in (N_R \cup N_A)^*$, the graph $(\mathcal{G}_C)_w$ is defined by induction on the length of w as follows:*

1. $w = \varepsilon$: $(\mathcal{G}_C)_\varepsilon := \mathcal{G}_C$;
2. $w = r$ *where r is a role:*
   a) $(\mathcal{G}_C)_r := \mathcal{G}(\bot)$ *if n_0 has $\bot$ in its atoms; or*
   b) $(\mathcal{G}_C)_r := \mathcal{G}'$ *if n_0 has an r-edge of the form $(r, m, M, \mathcal{G}')$; or*
   c) $(\mathcal{G}_C)_r := \mathcal{G}(\top)$ *otherwise;*
3. $w = a$ *where a is an attribute:*
   a) $(\mathcal{G}_C)_a := \mathcal{G}(\bot)$ *if n_0 has $\bot$ in its atoms; or*
   b) $(\mathcal{G}_C)_a := (N, E, n', \ell)$ *if $(n_0, a, n') \in E$; or*
   c) $(\mathcal{G}_C)_a := \mathcal{G}'$ *if n_0 has an r-edge of the form $(a, m, M, \mathcal{G}')$; or*
   d) $(\mathcal{G}_C)_a := \mathcal{G}(\top)$ *otherwise;*
4. $(\mathcal{G}_C)_{rw} := ((\mathcal{G}_C)_r)_w$ *for $r \in N_R \cup N_A$.*

Note that $(\mathcal{G}_C)_w$ is well-defined since with $\mathcal{G}_C$ all subgraphs of $\mathcal{G}_C$ are normalized. In particular, every node has at most one outgoing edge (r-edge or a-edge) labeled with a particular role or attribute.

The items 2. and 3., (a) of Definition 6.1.1 are motivated by the following equivalences: If n_0 contains $\bot$, then this means $C \equiv \bot$. Hence, for every w, $C_w \equiv \bot$. The following lemma shows that $(\mathcal{G}_C)_w$ does indeed provide us with the desired concept description C_w.

Lemma 6.1.2. *Let C be an $\mathcal{ALNS}$-concept description and $w \in (N_R \cup N_A)^*$. Then,*

$$(\mathcal{G}_C)_w \equiv C_w.$$

Proof. The proof is by induction on the length of w. Let $\mathcal{G}_C = (N, E, n_0, \ell)$ denote the normalized description graph of C.

1. $w = \varepsilon$: Obviously, $C_\varepsilon \equiv C \equiv (\mathcal{G}_C)_\varepsilon$.
2. $w = r$, $r \in N_R$: (a) if the atoms of n_0 contain $\bot$, then this means $\mathcal{G}_C \equiv C \equiv \bot$, and thus, $C_r \equiv \bot \equiv (\mathcal{G}_C)_r$. (b) If n_0 contains an r-edge with role r and restriction graph $\mathcal{G}'$, then according to Theorem 4.1.3, $C \sqsubseteq \forall r.F$ implies $\mathcal{G}' \sqsubseteq F$ for every $\mathcal{ALNS}$-concept description F. Hence, $(\mathcal{G}_C)_r = \mathcal{G}' \equiv C_r$. (c) Otherwise, Theorem 4.1.3 ensures $C_r \equiv \top$, and again, $(\mathcal{G}_C)_r = \mathcal{G}(\top) \equiv \top \equiv C_r$.
3. $w = a$, $a \in N_A$. (a) see 2.,(a). (b) If n_0 has an a-edge pointing to n' labeled a, then with Theorem 4.1.3, $C \sqsubseteq \forall a.F$ implies $(N, E, n', \ell) \sqsubseteq F$ for every $\mathcal{ALNS}$-concept description F. Thus, $(\mathcal{G}_C)_a = (N, E, n', \ell) \equiv C_a$. The cases (c) and (d) can be dealt with like 2., (b) and 2., (c), respectively.
4. $w = rw'$ where $r \in (N_R \cup N_A)$: Assume that $C \sqsubseteq \forall rw'.F \equiv \forall r.(\forall w'.F)$ for some $\mathcal{ALNS}$-concept description F. Then, $C_r \sqsubseteq \forall w'.F$. By definition, $(C_r)_{w'} \sqsubseteq F$. This shows that $C_{rw'} \equiv (C_r)_{w'}$. From the previous cases, we know that $C_r \equiv (\mathcal{G}_C)_r$. As mentioned, $(\mathcal{G}_C)_r$ is a normalized graph. But then, with Lemma 4.1.7, we can conclude, $\mathcal{G}_{C_r} \cong (\mathcal{G}_C)_r$. Consequently, the induction hypothesis yields $(C_r)_{w'} \equiv ((\mathcal{G}_C)_r)_{w'} = (\mathcal{G}_C)_{rw'}$. Hence, $C_{rw'} \equiv (\mathcal{G}_C)_{rw'}$. $\qquad\square$

Lemma 6.1.2 establishes that, for a given $\mathcal{ALNS}$-concept description and $w \in \Sigma^*$, C_w can be computed in time polynomial in the size of C and w since: i) $\mathcal{G}_C$ can be computed by a polynomial time algorithm, ii) $(\mathcal{G}_C)_w$ can be determined in time linear in the length of w for a given $\mathcal{G}_C$, and iii) $(\mathcal{G}_C)_w$ can be turned into an equivalent concept description in polynomial time.

Taking into account that the lcs of sequences of $\mathcal{ALNS}$-concept descriptions can be computed by an exponential time algorithm (Corollary 5.1.2), Algorithm 6.1.1 runs in time exponential in the size of the given $\mathcal{ALNS}$-matching problem. Moreover, using Lemma 3.2.2, Algorithm 6.1.1 can also be applied to matching problems modulo subsumption.

We also note that, due to Corollary 6.1.4, the size of least matchers may grow exponentially in the size of the matching problem. However, if we restrict Algorithm 6.1.1 to $\mathcal{ALN}$-matching problems, then according to Corollary 5.1.3 the lcs can be computed in polynomial time. Thus, for $\mathcal{ALN}$ we obtain a polynomial time matching algorithm.

These complexity results are summarized in the following corollary.

Corollary 6.1.5. *For $\mathcal{ALNS}$-matching problems (both modulo equivalence and subsumption):*

1. *there exists an exponential time algorithm that decides the solvability of the problem and returns a least matcher (and thus, a minimal i-complete set) in case the problem is solvable;*
2. *the size of least matchers may grow exponentially in the size of the matching problem.*

For $\mathcal{ALN}$-matching problems (both modulo equivalence and subsumption):

1. *there exists a polynomial time algorithm that decides the solvability of the problem and returns a least matcher (and thus, a minimal i-complete set) in case the problem is solvable;*
2. *the size of least matchers can polynomially be bounded in the size of the matching problem.*

6.1.3 Computing Minimal d-Complete Sets

In the previous section, we have dealt with the problem of computing least matchers, and thus, also, with computing minimal i-complete sets for matching problems of the form $C \sqsubseteq^? D$. As discussed in Section 3.2.3, this is the first step towards computing minimal sets of i-minimal and reduced matchers. In this subsection, we show how to carry out the second step, namely, computing minimal d-complete sets for matching modulo equivalence. More precisely, we restrict our investigations to the sublanguage $\mathcal{ALN}$ of $\mathcal{ALNS}$, since up to now d-minimality is not defined for the more general case (see Section 3.2.3 for a description of the problems one encounters for $\mathcal{ALNS}$). Recall that minimal d-complete sets of matchers consist of all d-minimal (i.e., reduced) matchers in $\forall$-normal form up to s-equivalence. Roughly speaking, we will show that given a least matcher σ for a matching problem modulo equivalence, all d-minimal matchers can be derive from σ by removing redundant parts.

If a matcher σ is reduced, then $\sigma(X)$ is reduced for all variables X. Therefore, before we can turn our attention to reduced matchers, reduced concept descriptions need to be studied more thoroughly.

Reduced $\mathcal{ALN}$-Concept Descriptions. In Section 3.2.3 it was claimed that equivalent and reduced $\mathcal{ALN}$-concept descriptions in $\forall$-normal form coincide up to the following equational theory $\mathsf{AC}\bot$:

$$\text{(A)} \qquad E_1 \sqcap (E_2 \sqcap E_3) = (E_1 \sqcap E_2) \sqcap E_3$$
$$\text{(C)} \qquad E_1 \sqcap E_2 = E_2 \sqcap E_1$$
$$(\bot) \qquad \forall r.\bot = (\leq 0\, r).$$

Recall that concept descriptions E and F coincide modulo $\mathsf{AC}\bot$ ($E =_{\mathsf{AC}\bot} F$ for short) if E and F coincide up to associativity and commutativity of concept conjunction and up to the substitution of $\forall r.\bot$ with $(\leq 0\, r)$ and vice versa. Later on, $\mathsf{AC}\bot$-equivalence is also used for substitutions: $\tau =_{\mathsf{AC}\bot} \sigma$ iff $\tau(X) =_{\mathsf{AC}\bot} \sigma(X)$ for every variable X.

Before we can establish the claimed connection between $\equiv$ and the equational theory $\mathsf{AC}\bot$, it is necessary to characterize reduced $\mathcal{ALN}$-concept descriptions. By the definition of reduced $\mathcal{ALN}$-concept descriptions (see Definition 3.2.4) and using Theorem 4.1.4, the proof of the following proposition is routine. As usual, $E \in C$ means that E occurs on the top-level of C.

Proposition 6.1.2. *An $\mathcal{ALN}$-concept description C in $\forall$-normal form is reduced if, and only if, the following conditions are satisfied:*

- *If $C \equiv \bot$, then $C = \bot$; otherwise*
- *every (negated) concept name occurs at most ones on the top-level of C; unless $C = \top$, $\top$ does not occur on the top-level of C;*
- *for every role name r, there exists at most one at-least restriction $(\geq n\, r)$ and one at-most restriction $(\leq m\, r)$ on the top-level of C (we even know $n \leq m$ since otherwise C would be unsatisfiable); there does not exist an at least restriction $(\geq 0\, r) \in C$;*
- *C has at most one of the concepts $(\leq 0\, r)$ and $\forall r.\bot$ on its top-level;*
- *for every value restriction $\forall r.E \in C$, E is reduced and $E \neq \top$.*

Theorem 4.1.4 together with this characterization of reduced concept descriptions, allows to us prove the desired statement.

Theorem 6.1.2. *Let E and F be reduced $\mathcal{ALN}$-concept descriptions in $\forall$-normal form. Then, $E \equiv F$ if, and only if, $E =_{\mathsf{AC}\bot} F$.*

Proof. The if direction of this theorem is obvious. Now, for the only-if direction assume that $E \equiv F$. If $E \equiv F \equiv \bot$, then $E = F = \bot$. In particular, $E =_{\mathsf{AC}\bot} F$.

In the following, let us assume that $E \equiv F \not\equiv \bot$. First, Theorem 4.1.4 ensures $prim(E) = prim(F)$. By Proposition 6.1.2, we know that every (negated) concept name in $prim(E)$ occurs at most ones on the top-level of E and F.

Second, with Theorem 4.1.4 we can conclude $min_r(E) = min_r(F)$. If $min_r(E) \neq 0$, then $(\geq (min_r(E))\, r) \in E$ and $(\geq (min_r(E))\, r) \in F$ by definition of $min_r(E)$. Again, by Proposition 6.1.2, $(\geq (min_r(E))r)$ is the only at-least restrictions for r on the top-level of E and F. In case $min_r(E) = 0$, neither E nor F contains an at-least restriction for r on its top-level.

Third, we know $max_r(E) = max_r(F)$. i) If $max_r(E) = 0$, then $E, F \sqsubseteq \forall r.\bot$, and therefore, $E.r \equiv F.r \equiv \bot$. This means $(\leq 0\, r) \in E$ or there exists a value restriction $\forall r.E' \in E$ with $E' \equiv \bot$. In the latter case, the fact that E is reduced implies $E' = \bot$. Thus, either $(\leq 0\, r) \in E$ or $\forall r.\bot \in E$. The same is true for F. ii) If $max_r(E) = \infty$, then neither E nor F contains an at-most restriction on r. iii) If $max_r(E)$ is a positive integer, then $(\leq (max_r(E))r) \in E$ and $(\leq (max_r(E))\, r) \in F$. Also, there are no other at-most restrictions on r on the top-level of E and F.

Finally, Theorem 4.1.4 ensures $E.r \equiv F.r$. The case $E.r \equiv \bot$ has been dealt with above. If $E.r \equiv F.r \equiv \top$, then by Proposition 6.1.2 neither E nor F has a value restriction for r on its top-level. Now assume $E.r \equiv F.r \not\equiv \bot$ and $E.r \equiv F.r \not\equiv \top$. Consequently, there exist value restrictions $\forall r.E' \in E$ and $\forall r.F' \in F$ with $E.r = E'$ and $F.r = F'$. According to Proposition 6.1.2, E' and F' are reduced. Now, induction yields $E' =_{\mathsf{AC}\bot} F'$.

From the above, it easily follows that $E =_{\mathsf{AC}\bot} F$. $\qquad\square$

Proposition 6.1.2 can also serve as basis for a polynomial time algorithm that, given an $\mathcal{ALN}$-concept description C in $\forall$-normal form, returns an equivalent and reduced subdescription $C\backslash\top$ of C:[1]

Algorithm 6.1.2

Input: *$\mathcal{ALN}$-concept description C in $\forall$-normal form.*

Output: *$C\backslash\top$, i.e., an $\mathcal{ALN}$-concept concept description satisfying:*
i) $C\backslash\top \equiv C$; ii) $C\backslash\top$ is reduced; and iii) $C\backslash\top \preceq_d C$.

1. *If $C \equiv \bot$, then return $\bot$; otherwise proceed along the following steps:*
2. *remove all multiple occurrences of (negated) concept names and the top-concept on the top-level of C;*
3. *for every r, remove those at-least [at-most] restrictions of the form $(\geq k\, r) \in C$ [$(\leq k\, r) \in C$] such that there exists an at-least [at-most] restriction $(\geq l\, r) \in C$ [$(\leq l\, r) \in C$] with $l > k$ [$l < k$];*
4. *for every r, remove $(\geq 0\, r)$ if it occurs on the top-level of C;*
5. *for every value restriction $\forall r.E \in C$, replace E by $E\backslash\top$; if $E\backslash\top = \top$, then remove $\forall r.(E\backslash\top)$;*
6. *if both $(\leq 0\, r) \in C$ and $\forall r.\bot \in C$, then remove $\forall r.\bot$.*

Note that in the last step of this algorithm one also could have removed $(\leq 0\, r)$ instead of $\forall r.\bot$. So syntactically, $C\backslash\top$ is not uniquely determined. However, Theorem 6.1.2 ensures that it is uniquely determined modulo $\mathsf{AC}\bot$. As a corollary of Algorithm 6.1.2, we obtain the following.

Corollary 6.1.6. *Given an $\mathcal{ALN}$-concept description C, an equivalent and reduced subdescription $C\backslash\top$ of C can be computed in polynomial time.*

As an aside, we note that $C\backslash\top$ can also be computed via the normalized description tree $\mathcal{G}_C$ of C by translating $\mathcal{G}_C$ back into a concept description. Although the translation is almost identical to the one presented in Section 4.1.1 (for $\mathcal{ALNS}$-concept descriptions), slight modifications are necessary in order to guarantee $C_{\mathcal{G}_C}$ to be a reduced concept description. For example, if (n_0, r, m, M, n) is an outgoing r-edge of the root n_0 of $\mathcal{G}_C$ and $M = 0$, then this r-edge should be translated as $(\leq 0 r)$ rather than $(\leq M r) \sqcap (\geq m r) \sqcap \forall r.C_{\mathcal{G}_n}$ as done in Section 4.1.1.

In Section 3.2.3, it has been mentioned that reduced matchers are the smallest representatives of their equivalence class (w.r.t. $\equiv$). Recall that the size $|C|$ of $\mathcal{ALN}$-concept descriptions $|C|$ is inductively defined by:

- $|\top| := |\bot| := |A| := |\neg A| := 1$ for all concept names A;
- $|(\leq n\, r)| := |(\geq n\, r)| := 2 + \lceil log(n+1) \rceil$ (binary encoding of n);

---

[1] This notation is motivated by reduced $\mathcal{ALE}$-concept descriptions discussed in Section 6.3.2 where $E\backslash F$ refers to an $\mathcal{ALE}$-concept description E which is reduced w.r.t. the concept F.

- $|\forall r.E| := 1 + |E|$;
- $|E \sqcap F| := |E| + |F|$.

By employing Theorem 6.1.2, we are now able to prove this claim. First, note that by definition $|(\leq 0\, r)| = |\forall r.\bot|$. Consequently, for some (not necessarily reduced) $\mathcal{ALN}$-concept descriptions E and F, $E =_{\mathsf{AC\bot}} F$ implies $|E| = |F|$. Now, if E is a reduced $\mathcal{ALN}$-concept description in $\forall$-normal form and $F \equiv E$, then turning F into its $\forall$-normal form yields an equivalent description F' with $|F'| \leq |F|$. Moreover, $|F'\backslash\top| \leq |F'|$ and by Theorem 6.1.2 we know $F'\backslash\top =_{\mathsf{AC\bot}} E$. Consequently, $|F| \geq |F'| \geq |F'\backslash\top| = |E|$.

Corollary 6.1.7. *If E is a reduced $\mathcal{ALN}$-concept description in $\forall$-normal form, then $F \equiv E$ implies $|E| \leq |F|$ for all $\mathcal{ALN}$-concept descriptions F.*

Deriving Reduced Matchers from the Least Matcher. We now show how the minimal d-complete set of matchers for $C \equiv^? D$ can be derived from a given least matcher of this problem.

The simple example $\forall r.A \equiv^? \forall r.(X \sqcap Y)$ shows that merely reducing the images of σ does not yield a reduced matcher. In fact, although σ with $\sigma(X) = \sigma(Y) = A$ is a least matcher, just taking $\sigma(X)\backslash\top$ and $\sigma(Y)\backslash\top$ as new images of X and Y, respectively, does not provide us with a reduced matcher. We rather reobtain σ.

The reason for this phenomenon is that although reducing $\sigma(X)$ eliminates the redundancies in $\sigma(X)$, redundancies between images of variables and the concept pattern are not taken care of. In the example, one can eliminate A in one of the variables since A is still contained in the other variable. In Section 3.2.3, we have also considered an example where redundancies were due to interactions between the image of a variable and the pattern.

Roughly speaking, the idea behind our approach is that the minimal d-complete set can be obtained by computing the set of so-called σ-reduced matchers where σ is a least matcher.

Definition 6.1.2. *Let σ be a matcher. Then, τ is called σ-reduced matcher if τ is a reduced matcher with $\tau \preceq_d \sigma$.*

Since for a given $\mathcal{ALN}$-concept description the number of possible subdescriptions can exponentially be bounded in the size of the concept, the number of σ-reduced matchers can exponentially be bounded in the size of the matching problem as well since, according to Corollary 6.1.5, the size of a least matcher can polynomially be bounded in the size of the matching problem. As regards computability, the fact that a) checking whether a given τ is a matcher of $C \equiv^? D$ is a polynomial time problem, and b) testing whether τ is reduced can be carried out in polynomial time, yields the following complexity result.

Lemma 6.1.3. *Given a least matcher σ of size polynomially bounded in the size of the matching problem, the set of σ-reduced matchers can be computed by an exponential time algorithm.*

The main technical problem we are faced with is to show that the set of σ-reduced matchers in fact provides us with a minimal d-complete set. Unfortunately, as illustrated by the following example, this is not true in general: Let C be the $\mathcal{ALN}$-concept description

$$\forall r.\bot \sqcap \forall s.(\geq 7\, r)$$

and D be the $\mathcal{ALN}$-concept pattern

$$\forall r.((\leq 1\, r) \sqcap X) \sqcap \forall s.((\geq 7\, r) \sqcap X).$$

The least matcher σ of the problem $C \equiv^? D$ maps X to $(\geq 7\, r)$. In fact, σ is already reduced. Thus, the only σ-reduced matcher is σ itself. However, matchers of the form $\tau(X) := (\geq k\, r)$ with $2 \leq k \leq 6$ are also reduced. Since they are not s-equivalent, they must belong to the minimal d-complete set of matchers.

Although, as shown by the previous example, the set of σ-reduced matchers does not provide us with the entire minimal d-complete set, roughly speaking, we can show: Given some τ from the minimal d-complete set of matchers, there exists a reduced matcher ν obtained from τ by replacing some number restrictions by more specific ones such that $\nu \preceq_d \sigma$. That is, the set of σ-reduced matchers coincides with the minimal d-complete set except for some matchers with less specific number restrictions.

Let E and F be $\mathcal{ALN}$-concept descriptions. Then, E is called $\mathcal{N}$-subdescription of F ($E \preceq_{\mathcal{N}} F$ for short) if E is obtained from F by replacing (some) number restrictions in F by more specific ones. We generalize this ordering to matchers in the usual way: $\nu \preceq_{\mathcal{N}} \sigma$ iff $\nu(X) \preceq_{\mathcal{N}} \sigma(X)$ for all variables X.

With this notation, the above idea can be stated more formally as follows: Let σ be the least matcher of $C \equiv^? D$ in $\forall$-normal form with $\sigma(X)$ reduced for all X. Then, for every reduced matcher τ of $C \equiv^? D$ in $\forall$-normal form there exists a σ-reduced matcher ν with $\nu \preceq_{\mathcal{N}} \tau$. The following theorem additionally introduces a matcher ν' since, for instance, $\tau(X)$ may contain $\forall r.\bot$ whereas $\sigma(X)$ contains $(\leq 0\, r)$ instead; ν' also takes care of associativity and commutativity of conjunction.

Theorem 6.1.3. *Let $C \equiv^? D$ be an $\mathcal{ALN}$-matching problem, and let σ be a least matcher of this problem such that $\sigma(X)$ is a reduced $\mathcal{ALN}$-concept description in $\forall$-normal form. Now, let τ be some reduced matcher in $\forall$-normal form. Then, there exist reduced matchers ν and ν' with $\nu \preceq_{\mathcal{N}} \tau$, $\nu =_{\mathsf{AC}\bot} \nu'$, and $\nu' \preceq_d \sigma$.*

Proof. Since σ is a least matcher, we know $\sigma(X) \sqsubseteq \tau(X)$ for all variables X in D.

First, assume $\tau(X) \equiv \bot$. Thus, since $\tau(X)$ is reduced, $\tau(X) = \bot$. From this, we can conclude $\sigma(X) \equiv \bot$, and thus $\sigma(X) = \bot$. In this case, we define $\nu(X) := \nu'(X) := \bot$. Obviously,

$$\sigma(X) \sqsubseteq \nu(X) \equiv \nu'(X) \sqsubseteq \tau(X), \ \nu(X) \preceq_{\mathcal{N}} \tau(X),$$
$$\nu(X) =_{\mathsf{ACL}} \nu'(X), \text{ and } \nu'(X) \preceq_d \sigma(X). \tag{6.5}$$

Now, assume $\tau(X) \not\equiv \bot$. Also, assume $\sigma(X) \equiv \bot$. Then, define $\sigma'(X) := \bot$ and $\sigma'(Y) := \tau(Y)$ for all Y, $Y \neq X$. Hence, $\sigma \sqsubseteq_s \sigma' \sqsubseteq_s \tau$, which yields $C \equiv \sigma(D) \sqsubseteq \sigma'(D) \sqsubseteq \tau(D) \equiv C$. In other words, σ' is a matcher. But then, $\sigma' \prec_d \tau$ contradicts the assumption that τ is reduced. Consequently, $\sigma(X) \not\equiv \bot$. In the sequel, we will construct $\nu(X)$ and $\nu'(X)$ for the case where $\tau(X) \not\equiv \bot$ and $\sigma(X) \not\equiv \bot$ such that (6.5) is satisfied.

Since $\sigma(X) \sqsubseteq \tau(X)$, Theorem 4.1.4 ensures $prim(\sigma(X)) \supseteq prim(\tau(X))$. Since both $\sigma(X)$ and $\tau(X)$ are reduced, every element in $prim(\cdot)$ occurs exactly once in $\sigma(X)$ and $\tau(X)$, respectively. We define $\nu(X)$ and $\nu'(X)$ in such a way that $prim(\nu(X)) := prim(\nu'(X)) := prim(\tau(X))$ and every (negated) concept name in $prim(\tau(X))$ occurs exactly once on the top-level of $\nu(X)$ and $\nu'(X)$.

If $(\geq k \ r) \in \tau(X)$, then by Theorem 4.1.4 it follows that there exists exactly one restriction $(\geq l \ r) \in \sigma(X)$, with $l \geq k$. We require $\nu(X)$ and $\nu'(X)$ to contain $(\geq l \ r)$ on their top-level.

If $(\leq k r) \in \tau(X)$, then by Theorem 4.1.4 it follows that $l := max_r(\sigma(X)) \leq k$. If $l = 0$, then either $(\leq 0 \ r) \in \sigma(X)$ or $\forall r.\bot \in \sigma(X)$. In the former case, we define $\nu(X)$ and $\nu'(X)$ to contain $(\leq 0 \ r)$ on their top-level. In the latter case, we define $\nu(X)$ to contain $(\leq 0 \ r)$ and $\nu'(X)$ to contain $\forall r.\bot$. If $l > 0$, then both $(\leq l \ r) \in \nu(X)$ and $(\leq l \ r) \in \nu'(X)$ is required.

From the cases considered so far (base cases), it follows that, if $\tau(X)$ does not have value restrictions on its top-level, then for $\nu(X)$ and $\nu'(X)$ thus defined (6.5) is satisfied.

If $\forall r.E \in \tau(X)$, Theorem 4.1.4 guarantees that $\sigma(X).r \sqsubseteq E$. Let us first assume that $E \equiv \bot$. Thus, since $\tau(X)$ is reduced, $E = \bot$. Then, either $(\leq 0 \ r) \in \sigma(X)$ or $\forall r.\bot \in \sigma(X)$. In the latter case, we define both $\nu(X)$ and $\nu'(X)$ to contain $\forall r.\bot$. In the former case, $\nu(X)$ shall contain $\forall r.\bot$ whereas $\nu'(X)$ contains $(\leq 0 \ r)$ instead.

If $E \not\equiv \bot$, then we know that there exists $\forall r.E' \in \sigma(X)$ with $E' \sqsubseteq E$. The two concepts E', E now take the rôle of $\sigma(X)$ and $\tau(X)$ in the base case. Note that by assumption both concepts are reduced. Moreover, the construction of $\nu(X)$ and $\nu'(X)$ in the base case only made use of the fact that $\tau(X)$ is reduced, but did not use the stronger statement that τ is reduced. Thus, we can indeed apply the induction hypothesis to E and E', which provides us with concepts E'' and E''' satisfying $E' \sqsubseteq E'' \equiv E''' \sqsubseteq E$, $E'' \preceq_{\mathcal{N}} E$, $E'' =_{\mathsf{ACL}} E'''$, and $E''' \preceq_d E'$. Having E'' and E''' at hand, we define $\nu(X)$ and $\nu'(X)$ to have $\forall r.E''$ and $\forall r.E'''$ on their top-level, respectively.

As a result, we have constructed ν and ν' in such a way that (6.5) is satisfied for any reduced matcher τ in $\forall$-normal form. In particular, we can conclude that $\nu \preceq_{\mathcal{N}} \tau$, $\nu =_{\mathsf{ACL}} \nu'$, and $\nu' \preceq_d \sigma$. We can also infer that ν and ν' are matchers since $C \equiv \sigma(D) \sqsubseteq \nu(D) \equiv \nu'(D) \sqsubseteq \tau(D) \equiv C$. From $\nu \preceq_{\mathcal{N}} \tau$ and the fact that τ is reduced it follows that ν is reduced: If some (negated) concept name, number restriction, or value restriction can be removed from ν or if some expression in ν can be replaced by $\bot$, then these changes could be performed on τ as well, in contradiction to the fact that τ is reduced. Finally, given that ν is reduced, $\nu =_{\mathsf{AC}\bot} \nu'$ guarantees that ν' is reduced as well. $\qquad\qquad\qquad\qquad\qquad\qquad\qquad\qquad\qquad\qquad\qquad\qquad\qquad\quad\Box$

Matchers in the set of σ-reduced matchers only contain number restrictions contained in σ. On the other hand, the previous example shows that reduced matchers τ might also introduce new number restrictions. However, if we can prove that (a) the integers of number restrictions in τ are bounded by the maximum integer that occurs in number restrictions of C or D and that (b) τ cannot introduce number restrictions on roles not contained in C or D, then by Theorem 6.1.3 the minimal d-complete set of matchers can be effectively derived from the set of σ-reduced matchers.

Statement (b) immediately follows from Theorem 6.1.3 and the fact that a least matcher can be chosen in such a way that it does not introduce new roles, like the least matchers computed by Algorithm 6.1.1.

In order to prove (a) we need the following characterization of unsatisfiable $\mathcal{ALN}$-concept descriptions, where for a node n in an $\mathcal{ALN}$-description tree, $min_r(n) := max\{m \mid n$ has an outgoing r-edge of the form $(n, r, m, M, n')\}$; $min_r(n) := 0$ if such an r-edges do not exist; $max_r(n)$ is defined analogously.

Lemma 6.1.4. *Let C be an $\mathcal{ALN}$-concept description. Then, $C \equiv \bot$ iff the description tree $\mathcal{G}(C) = (N, E, n_0, \ell)$ contains a rooted path leading to a node n such that i) for every r-edge (n', s, m, M, n'') on this path, $min_s(n') \geq 1$ and ii) $\bot \in \ell(n)$, $P, \neg P \in \ell(n)$ for some P, or $max_r(n) < min_r(n)$ for some r.*

The if direction of this lemma is trivial. The only-if direction follows from the normalization rules listed on Page 80. A closer look at these rules reveals that an $\mathcal{ALN}$-description tree $\mathcal{G}(C)$ is only normalized to the bottom-concept, if $\mathcal{G}(C)$ contains the setting described in Lemma 6.1.4. Now, given this lemma, (a) is shown in the following lemma.

Lemma 6.1.5. *Let τ be a reduced matcher of $C \equiv^? D$ in $\forall$-normal form. Let l be the maximal integer occurring in number restrictions of C and D; $l := 0$ if there is no number restriction in C or D. Then, for every integer k occurring in some number restriction in τ, $k \leq l$.*

Proof. Let σ be a least matcher in $\forall$-normal form with $\sigma(X)$ reduced for all X in D. Then the proof of Theorem 6.1.3 shows that all integers in at-least restrictions in τ are bounded by the maximum integer occurring in some at-least restriction in σ. If σ is computed by Algorithm 6.1.1 using the computation of the lcs according to Theorem 5.1.1, then it can easily be verified that all integers in number restrictions in σ are bounded by l. Thus, for k occurring in some at-least restriction in τ, we can infer $k \leq l$.

Now, assume that $(\leq k\,r)$, $k \neq 0$, $k > l$, occurs in τ. In the following, let E denote the $\forall$-normal form of $\tau(D)$. If we can show that removing every occurrence of $(\leq k\,r)$ in E yields a concept description equivalent to C, then obviously removing $(\leq k\,r)$ in τ still provides us with a matcher, in contradiction to the assumption that τ is reduced.

First, assume $C \equiv E \equiv \bot$. Then, $\mathcal{G}(E)$ contains a rooted path as described in Lemma 6.1.4 leading to an incoherent node. Clearly, removing $(\leq k\,r)$ everywhere in E still guarantees the existence of such a path: First, at-least restrictions along the rooted path are still contained in $\mathcal{G}(E)$, and second, the final node the rooted path is leading to is still incoherent because by definition of k the at-most restriction $(\leq k r)$ cannot cause any inconsistencies. Consequently, E thus obtained is still unsatisfiable.

Now, assume $C \equiv E \not\equiv \bot$. Then, Theorem 4.1.4 ensures that $prim(C) = prim(E)$, $max_r(C) = max_r(E)$, and $min_r(C) = min_r(E)$. Obviously, when deleting $(\leq k r)$ on the top-level of E, these identities are still satisfied. Moreover, Theorem 4.1.4 implies $C.r \equiv E.r$. By induction, removing $(\leq k\,r)$ from $E.r$ still yields a description equivalent to $C.r$.

Thus, removing every occurrence of $(\leq k r)$ in E provides us with a concept description equivalent to C. $\qquad\square$

Since the size of the matching problem $C \equiv^? D$ is measured based on a binary encoding of the integers in number restrictions, the cardinality of the set of number restrictions with integers bounded by l (as defined in Lemma 6.1.5) and with roles occurring in C or D is at most exponential in the size of the matching problem. Consequently, according to Theorem 6.1.3, the set of σ-reduced matchers need only be augmented by an exponential number of reduced matchers in order to obtain the (entire) minimal d-complete set of matchers.

The example

$$\forall r.(A_1 \sqcap \cdots \sqcap A_k) \equiv^? \forall r.(X_1 \sqcap \cdots \sqcap X_k)$$

illustrates that the cardinality of the minimal d-complete set of matchers can in fact be of size exponential in the size of the matching problem since, for every permutation π of $\{1, \ldots, k\}$, the matcher $\sigma_\pi(X_i) := A_{\pi(i)}$, among others, must belong to the minimal d-complete set.

Corollary 6.1.8. *Given an $\mathcal{ALN}$-matching problem modulo equivalence:*

1. *a minimal d-complete set can be computed in exponential time;*
2. *the cardinality of the set can grow exponentially in the size of the matching problem;*
3. *the size of every matcher in this set can be bounded polynomially.*

Given an $\mathcal{ALN}$-matching problem $C \sqsubseteq^? D$, a least matcher σ can be computed in polynomial time (Corollary 6.1.5). Then, for the problem $\sigma(D) \equiv D$ we know that the minimal d-complete set can be computed in exponential time (Corollary 6.1.8). Consequently, we have shown the following results for computing the set of "interesting" matchers in $\mathcal{ALN}$.

Corollary 6.1.9. *Given an $\mathcal{ALN}$-matching problem (modulo subsumption or equivalence), the minimal set of i-minimal and reduced matchers (as specified in Definition 3.2.7) can be computed in time exponential in the size of the matching problem.*

6.2 Matching in $\mathcal{ALN}^*$

The main objective of this section is to show that, just as for $\mathcal{ALNS}$, solvable matching problems in $\mathcal{ALN}^*$ always have a least matcher, which can be computed effectively. In particular, this provides us with a decision algorithm for the solvability of matching problems and it also solves the problem of computing minimal i-complete sets as every set of matchers containing a least matcher is i-complete. In addition, we will show that the problem of deciding the solvability of $\mathcal{ALN}^*$-matching problems (modulo subsumption and equivalence) is PSPACE-hard. The problem of computing d-complete sets of matchers remains open since, as pointed out in Section 3.2.3, it is not even clear how to define reduced matchers in $\mathcal{ALN}^*$.

To accomplish the above, matching is reduced to solving a system of formal language equations such that a matching problem has a solution if, and only if, the corresponding equation system is solvable. This approach has first been proposed in [BN98] for $\mathcal{FL}_0$-matching problems. Following up this lead, in [BKBM99] the results have been extended to $\mathcal{ALN}$-matching problems. In all these works, the formal equation systems were defined over finite languages. In contrast, $\mathcal{ALN}^*$-matching problems lead to equations over regular (instead of finite) languages. Interestingly, such equations have also been studied by Leiss [Lei95, Lei99]. However, he does not provide complexity results for solving them. In this respect, the results obtained for matching in $\mathcal{ALN}^*$ and its sublanguages make contributions in this direction as well.

This section is organized as follows. We first investigate the complexity of deciding the solvability of $\mathcal{ALN}^*$-matching problems and present the reduction of matching to solving formal language equations. We then show how to compute least matchers as certain candidate solutions of such equations.

6.2.1 Deciding the Solvability of Matching

For $\mathcal{ALN}^*$-concept descriptions C and D, the matching problem $C \sqsubseteq^? D$ has a solution if, and only if, $C \sqsubseteq D$. On the other hand, according to Lemma 3.2.3, deciding the solvability of $\mathcal{ALN}^*$-matching problems modulo subsumption can be reduced to deciding subsumption. Therefore, by Corollary 4.2.3 we obtain the following tight complexity bound for matching modulo subsumption.

Corollary 6.2.1. *The problem of deciding the solvability of $\mathcal{ALN}^*$-matching problems modulo subsumption is PSPACE-complete.*

Baader [Baa96] has shown that even testing subsumption for $\mathcal{FL}_0^*$-concept description is a PSPACE-complete problem. Thus, this complexity carries over to matching modulo subsumption as well.

Unfortunately, for matching modulo equivalence things are much more involved. Clearly, just as for matching modulo subsumption, deciding the solvability of $\mathcal{ALN}^*$-matching problems modulo equivalence is a PSPACE-hard problem. However, until now it remains to prove a matching upper bound. The only decision algorithm so far is the one that computes a candidate solution (least matcher) and checks whether it actually solves the problem. In Section 6.2.2, we will present a double exponential time algorithm for computing such a candidate solution in $\mathcal{ALN}^*$. For languages that do not allow for number restrictions, like $\mathcal{FL}_0^*$ and $\mathcal{FL}_\neg^*$, it is possible to come up with an exponential time algorithm. Still, this only suffices to show the following rough complexity bounds:

Corollary 6.2.2. *The problem of deciding the solvability of matching problems modulo equivalence in $\mathcal{FL}_0^*$, $\mathcal{FL}_\neg^*$, and $\mathcal{ALN}^*$ is PSPACE-hard and can be carried out by an EXPSPACE-algorithm for $\mathcal{FL}_0^*$ and $\mathcal{FL}_\neg^*$, and by a 2EXPSPACE-algorithm for $\mathcal{ALN}^*$.*

In the remainder of this subsection, we show how matching modulo equivalence can be reduced to solving formal language equations. On the one hand, these equations form the basis for the matching algorithm presented in Section 6.2.2. On the other hand, by building a bridge between matching and formal language equations, results in one field can contribute to new ones in the other. We will come back to this issue at the end of this subsection.

For the reduction, we proceed in two steps. First, it is shown that, if a matching problem has a solution, then there also exists a solution that does not introduce new concept names or number restrictions. Second, matching is reduced to solving a system of formal language equations, where there is an equation in this system for the bottom-concept as well as for each of the (negated) concept names and number restrictions occurring in the given matching problem. The first step ensures that no equations for new concept names or number restrictions need to be considered.

Lemma 6.2.1. *The matching problem $C \equiv^? D$ for an $\mathcal{ALN}^*$-concept description C and an $\mathcal{ALN}^*$-concept pattern D has a solution if, and only if, it has a solution that does not introduce new concept names or number restrictions.*

Proof. The if direction is trivial. For the only-if direction, we distinguish two cases, depending on whether the new concept is a concept name or a number restriction.

(1) Assume that σ is a matcher which introduces a concept name P that does not occur in C or D. Let σ' be the substitution obtained from σ by replacing every occurrence of P in σ by $\bot$. Obviously, this implies $\sigma' \sqsubseteq_s \sigma$, i.e., $\sigma'(X) \sqsubseteq \sigma(X)$ for every variable X in D, and thus $\sigma'(D) \sqsubseteq \sigma(D) \equiv C$. It remains to show that $\sigma'(D) \sqsupseteq C$. Let F be a (negated) concept name or a number restriction with $F \neq P$. Then, $L_{\sigma'(D)}(F) = L_{\sigma(D)}(F)$. Because of $C \equiv \sigma(D)$, we know $L_{\sigma(D)}(F) \subseteq V_C(F)$, and thus $L_{\sigma'(D)}(F) \subseteq V_C(F)$. By construction of σ', we know $L_{\sigma'(X)}(\bot) = L_{\sigma(X)}(\bot) \cup L_{\sigma(X)}(P)$ for every X in D. Again, because of $C \equiv \sigma(D)$, it follows that $L_{\sigma(D)}(\bot) \subseteq V_C(\bot)$ and $L_{\sigma(D)}(P) \subseteq V_C(P)$. By our assumption on P, $L_C(P) = \emptyset$, and thus, $V_C(P) = \emptyset \cup E_C$ (Theorem 4.2.3). Consequently, $L_{\sigma(D)}(P) \subseteq E_C$, which shows $L_{\sigma'(D)}(\bot) \subseteq E_C$. To sum up, we have shown that $L_{\sigma'(D)}(F) \subseteq V_C(F)$ for the bottom-concept, all (negated) concept names, and number restrictions in C and $\sigma'(D)$. Now, Theorem 4.2.2 ensures $C \sqsubseteq \sigma'(D)$. For a new introduced negated concept name $\neg P$, a matcher σ' can be constructed in the same way. If σ introduces more than one new (negated) concept name, then we simply iterate our construction.

(2) Assume that σ introduces an at-least restriction $(\geq k\ s)$ which does not occur in C or D. In order to construct a matcher σ' that does not contain this at-least restriction, we distinguish two cases:

a) There exists an at-least restriction $(\geq h\ s)$ in C with $h > k$ and there is no $h' < h$ with this property, i.e., we choose the 'least' at-least restriction on s in the set of at-least restrictions occurring in C that is 'greater' than $(\geq k\ s)$ (in the sense that the number h occurring in this restriction is larger than k). We obtain σ' by replacing $(\geq k\ s)$ in σ by $(\geq h\ s)$. Obviously, σ' defined in this way, is a more specific matcher than σ, i.e., $\sigma' \sqsubseteq_s \sigma$, and thus, $\sigma'(D) \sqsubseteq \sigma(D) \equiv C$. It remains to show $\sigma'(D) \sqsupseteq C$. Let F be the bottom-concept, a (negated) concept name or a number restriction with $F \neq (\geq h\ s)$. Then, $L_{\sigma'(D)}(F) = L_{\sigma(D)}(F)$. As in (1) we can conclude $L_{\sigma'(D)}(F) \subseteq V_C(F)$. By construction of σ', we have $L_{\sigma'}(\geq h\ s) = L_{\sigma(D)}(\geq h\ s) \cup L_{\sigma(D)}(\geq k\ s)$. As before, we know $L_{\sigma(D)}(\geq hs) \subseteq V_C(\geq hs)$ and $L_{\sigma(D)}(\geq k\ s) \subseteq V_C(\geq ks)$. Since $L_C(\geq ks) = \emptyset$, by definition of h we can conclude $L_{\sigma(D)}(\geq k\ s) \subseteq V_C(\geq h\ s)$. Consequently, $L_{\sigma'(D)}(\geq h\ s) \subseteq V_C(\geq h\ s)$. To sum up, we have shown that $L_{\sigma'(D)}(F) \subseteq V_C(F)$ for the bottom-concept, all (negated) concept names, and number restrictions in C and $\sigma'(D)$. By Theorem 4.2.2, this means $C \sqsubseteq \sigma'(D)$.

b) If there does not exist a greater at-least restriction $(\geq hs)$ in C for $(\geq ks)$, then σ' is obtained from σ by replacing all occurrences of $(\geq k\ s)$ in σ by $\bot$. Then, as in (1) one can show that σ' is a matcher of the problem.

If more than one new at-least restriction is introduced by σ, then the argument presented above can again be iterated.

For at-most restrictions $(\leq ks)$ one chooses the greatest at-most restriction on s in C that is less than $(\leq k\ s)$. If there is no such at-most restriction, again, $(\leq k\ s)$ is replaced by $\bot$. With this construction, the proof proceeds as for at-least restrictions.   □

In order to define the system of formal language equations corresponding to the matching problem $C \equiv^? D$, we need some notation. First, let $\mathcal{C}$ denote the set of (negated) concept name and number restrictions occurring in C and D, and let $\mathcal{C}_\bot$ be the set $\mathcal{C} \cup \{\bot\}$. If $N_X = \{X_1, \dots, X_l\}$ are the variables in D, then in the system of formal language equations we use the following set of variables: $\mathcal{X}_{C,D} := \bigcup_{F \in \mathcal{C}_\bot} N_{X,F}$ where $N_{X,F} := \{X_{1,F}, \dots, X_{l,F}\}$, i.e., for every F a copy $X_{i,F}$ of the variable X_i is introduced. These variables stand for regular languages over N_R.

Every assignment $\{X \mapsto L_X \mid X \in \mathcal{X}_{C,D}\}$ of the variables to regular languages L_X, yields a substitution σ such that $L_{\sigma(X_i)}(F) = L_{X_{i,F}}$. On the other hand, a substitution σ induces the assignment $\{X_{i,F} \mapsto L_{\sigma(X_i)}(F)\}$.

If the variables in D are considered to be concept names, then D can be viewed as concept description and the definition of the sets $L_D(X_i)$ and $V_D(F)$ carries over from concept descriptions to patterns. In particular, $V_D(F)$ can be characterized as in Theorem 4.2.3. For the sake of simplicity, given $X_{i,F} \in N_{X,F}$ we define $L_D(X_{i,F}) := L_D(X_i)$.

For a concept name or an at-least restriction F we define $E_C(F)$ to be the set E_C. In case F is an at-most restriction of the form $(\leq n\ r)$, then $E_C(F) := E_C r^{-1}$. Finally, for a given assignment of the variables in $\mathcal{X}_{C,D}$, the operator $E_D(\mathcal{X}_{C,D})$ is defined to be the set $E_{\sigma(D)}$, where σ is the substitution induced by the assignment.

Now, the following equations correspond to the matching problem $C \equiv^? D$:

$$(\bot)\quad E_C = E_D(\mathcal{X}_{C,D}),$$

and for every $F \in \mathcal{C}$:

$$(F)\quad V_C(F) = V_D(F) \cup E_C(F) \cup \bigcup_{X \in N_{X,F}} L_D(X) \cdot X.$$

Note that the equations for different F's are independent of each other, i.e., they do not share any variables. Only the equation $(\bot)$ contains all the variables in $\mathcal{X}_{C,D}$. This equation is satisfied if the substitution σ induced by the assignment of the variables in $\mathcal{X}_{C,D}$ satisfies $E_C = E_{\sigma(D)}$. Thus, $(\bot)$ uses a significant more complex operator, namely $E_D(\mathcal{X}_{C,D})$, than the other equations, which basically use union and concatenation.

Roughly speaking, the idea behind this equation system is as follows: For a given solution of this system, i.e., an assignment of the variables in $\mathcal{X}_{C,D}$ which satisfies the equations, the right-hand side of the equations correspond to the value-restriction sets $V_{\sigma(D)}(F)$ of $\sigma(D)$, where σ is the substitution induced by the assignment. Then, since the assignment solves the equation system, we have $V_C(F) = V_{\sigma(D)}(F)$ for all $F \in \mathcal{C}_\bot$, which by Corollary 4.2.2 implies $C \equiv \sigma(D)$. More precisely, the equation $(\bot)$ ensures that $E_C = E_{\sigma(D)}$, and thus $V_C(\bot) = V_{\sigma(D)}(\bot)$. Therefore, E_C ($E_C r^{-1}$ for at-most restrictions) can already be added on the right-hand side in the equation (F), since E_C must be a subset of $V_{\sigma(D)}(F)$. Of course, adding E_C on the right-hand side of $(\bot)$ would not make sense, since then the equation $(\bot)$ would always hold. The purpose of the equation $(\bot)$ is rather to guarantee $E_C = E_{\sigma(D)}$.

It is tempting to think that the equation $(\bot)$ can be stated analogously to the other equations as

$$(*)\quad E_C = V_D(\bot) \cup \bigcup_{X \in N_{X,\bot}} L_D(X) \cdot X.$$

Of course, unlike the equations (F), $F \in C$, E_C may not occur on the right-hand side. However, the following example shows that in $(\bot)$ it is necessary to take *all* variables in $\mathcal{X}_{C,D}$ into account because the combination of assignments might cause inconsistencies that cannot be expressed by assignments for the variables in $N_{X,\bot}$, e.g., assignments for P and $\neg P$. The example is taken from [BKBM99], where the restricted case of matching $\mathcal{ALN}$-concept patterns against $\mathcal{ALN}$-concept descriptions has been considered.

Example 6.2.1. We consider the problem of matching the pattern

$$D_{\mathrm{ex}} := (\forall r.(X_1 \sqcap X_2)) \sqcap (\forall s.X_1) \sqcap (\forall t.X_2)$$

against the description

$$C_{\mathrm{ex}} := (\forall r.\bot) \sqcap (\forall s.P) \sqcap (\forall t.\neg P).$$

Obviously, this matching problem can be solved by simply replacing X_1 by P and X_2 by $\neg P$. Indeed, the corresponding assignment $X_{1,P} := X_{2,\neg P} := \{\varepsilon\}$ and $X_{1,\neg P} := X_{2,P} := X_{1,\bot} := X_{2,\bot} := \emptyset$ solves the equations (P) and $(\neg P)$:

(P)$\quad \{s\} \cup \{r\} \cdot N_R^* = \emptyset \cup \{r\} \cdot N_R^* \cup \{r,s\} \cdot X_{1,P} \cup \{r,t\} \cdot X_{2,P},$

(¬P)$\quad \{t\} \cup \{r\} \cdot N_R^* = \emptyset \cup \{r\} \cdot N_R^* \cup \{r,s\} \cdot X_{1,\neg P} \cup \{r,t\} \cdot X_{2,\neg P},$

where $E_{C_{\mathrm{ex}}} = \{r\} \cdot N_R^*$, $V_{C_{\mathrm{ex}}}(P) = \{s\} \cup \{r\} \cdot N_R^*$, $V_{C_{\mathrm{ex}}}(\neg P) = \{t\} \cup \{r\} \cdot N_R^*$, $L_{D_{\mathrm{ex}}}(X_1) = \{r,s\}$, and $L_{D_{\mathrm{ex}}}(X_2) = \{r,t\}$. The assignment specified above also solves the equation $(\bot)$: $\sigma(X_1) = \forall\{\varepsilon\}.P \sqcap \forall\emptyset.\neg P$ and $\sigma(X_2) = \forall\emptyset.P \sqcap \forall\{\varepsilon\}.\neg P$. Thus, $\sigma(D_{\mathrm{ex}}) \equiv \forall\{r,s\}.P \sqcap \forall\{r,t\}.\neg P$, which implies $E_{\sigma(D_{\mathrm{ex}})} = \{r\} \cdot N_R^* = E_{C_{\mathrm{ex}}}$. But there does not exist an assignment of the variables $X_{1,\bot}$ and $X_{2,\bot}$ that would satisfy the equation $(*)$, which in our example is $\{r\} \cdot N_R^* = \emptyset \cup \{r,s\} \cdot X_{1,\bot} \cup \{r,t\} \cdot X_{2,\bot}$.

The reason for the problem exhibited by this example is that the value-restriction $\forall r.\bot$ required by the description cannot directly be generated from the pattern by insertion of $\bot$, but instead by an interaction of P and $\neg P$ in the instantiated pattern.

The following theorem shows that matching can indeed be reduced to the formal language equations stated above.

Theorem 6.2.1. *Let C be an $\mathcal{ALN}^*$-concept description and D an $\mathcal{ALN}^*$-concept pattern. Then, the matching problem $C \equiv^? D$ has a solution if, and only if, the system of formal language equations (F), $F \in \mathcal{C}_\perp$, is solvable.*

Proof. Let σ be some substitution that only contains (negated) concept names and number restrictions in C. Now, for $X \in N_X$, let σ' be obtained from σ by defining $L_{\sigma'(X)}(\geq n\, r)$ to be the set

$$\bigcup_{m \geq n} L_{\sigma(X)}(\geq m\, r).$$

Analogously, let $L_{\sigma'(X)}(\leq n\, r)$ be the set

$$\bigcup_{m \leq n} L_{\sigma(X)}(\leq m\, r).$$

Finally, define $L_{\sigma'(X)}(F) := L_{\sigma(X)}(F)$ for all (negated) concept names and the bottom concept F. Then, for σ' and $n \geq m$ the inclusions $L_{\sigma'(X)}(\geq nr) \subseteq L_{\sigma'(X)}(\geq m\, r)$ and $L_{\sigma'(X)}(\leq nr) \supseteq L_{\sigma'(X)}(\leq m\, r)$ are satisfied. In particular, this means $\bigcup_{m \geq n} L_{\sigma'(X)}(\geq m\, r) = L_{\sigma'(X)}(\geq nr)$ and $\bigcup_{m \leq n} L_{\sigma'(X)}(\leq m\, r) = L_{\sigma'(X)}(\leq n\, r)$. In addition, because $n \geq m$ implies $(\geq n\, r) \sqsubseteq (\geq m\, r)$ and $(\leq m\, r) \sqsubseteq (\leq n\, r)$, we can conclude that $\sigma(X) \equiv \sigma'(X)$ for all variables $X \in N_X$, and thus $\sigma(D) \equiv \sigma'(D)$. This means that, if σ is a matcher of the problem $C \equiv^? D$, then so is σ'.

Now, let σ be some substitution that only uses (negated) concept names and number restrictions in C and that satisfies the following inclusions: $(*)$ $L_{\sigma(X)}(\geq n\, r) \subseteq L_{\sigma(X)}(\geq m\, r)$ and $L_{\sigma(X)}(\leq n\, r) \supseteq L_{\sigma(X)}(\leq m\, r)$ for $n \geq m$. Recall that σ induces the following assignment of the variables in $\mathcal{X}_{C,D}$: $\{X \mapsto L_X \mid X \in \mathcal{X}_{C,D}\}$, where $L_X := L_{\sigma(X_i)}(F)$ for $X = X_{i,F}$, $F \in \mathcal{C}_\perp$. Together with $(*)$ and Theorem 4.2.3, it is easy to see that

$$V_{\sigma(D)}(F) = V_D(F) \cup E_{\sigma(D)}(F) \cup \bigcup_{X \in N_{X,F}} L_D(X) \cdot L_X.$$

for every $F \in \mathcal{C}$. But then, Corollary 4.2.2 implies that $C \equiv \sigma(D)$ if, and only if,

$$(\perp)' \quad E_C = E_{\sigma(D)},$$

and for every $F \in \mathcal{C}$:

$$(F)' \quad V_C(F) = V_D(F) \cup E_C(F) \cup \bigcup_{X \in N_{X,F}} L_D(X) \cdot L_X.$$

We are now ready to prove the only-if direction of the theorem. Let σ be some matcher of the problem $C \equiv^? D$. According to Lemma 6.2.1, we can assume that σ only contains (negated) concept names and number restriction in $\mathcal{C}$. Then, as proved above, we can construct a matcher σ' such that the assignment of the variables induced by σ' satisfies the equation system.

To prove the if direction, let $\{X \mapsto L_X \mid X \in \mathcal{X}_{C,D}\}$ be some solution of the equation system (F), $F \in \mathcal{C}_\perp$. We show that then the corresponding substitution σ solves the matching problem. To this end, we construct a new assignment $\{X \mapsto L'_X \mid X \in \mathcal{X}_{C,D}\}$ with $L'_{X_{i,F}} := L_{X_{i,F}}$ for all (negated) concept names and the bottom concept F, $L'_{X_{i,(\geq n\,r)}} := \bigcup_{m \geq n} L_{X_{i,(\geq m\,r)}}$, and $L'_{X_{i,(\leq n\,r)}} := \bigcup_{m \leq n} L_{X_{i,(\leq m\,r)}}$. Clearly, with this assignment the equations (F), for (negated) concept names and the bottom concept F, are still satisfied because the assignments of the variables in these equations are unchanged. Following the characterization of $V_C(F)$ for number restrictions F (cf. Theorem 4.2.3), it is easy to see that the equations for number restrictions are satisfied as well. To show that the $(\perp)$ equation also holds, let σ' denote the substitution corresponding to the new assignment. As above, we can conclude $\sigma(X) \equiv \sigma'(X)$ for all $X \in N_X$, i.e., $\sigma \equiv_s \sigma'$. By definition of the operator $E_D(\mathcal{X}_{C,D})$ and since σ is the substitution corresponding to the solution $\{X \mapsto L_X \mid X \in \mathcal{X}_{C,D}\}$ of the equation system, we know that $E_C = E_{\sigma(D)}$. Moreover, $\sigma \equiv_s \sigma'$ implies $\sigma(D) \equiv \sigma'(D)$, and hence $E_{\sigma'(D)} = E_{\sigma(D)} = E_C$. Thus, the new assignment is a solution of the equation system as well. By construction, $L'_{X_{i,(\geq n\,r)}} \subseteq L'_{X_{i,(\geq m\,r)}}$ and $L'_{X_{i,(\leq n\,r)}} \supseteq L'_{X_{i,(\leq m\,r)}}$ for all $n \geq m$. Thus, σ' satisfies $(*)$. As shown above, for such a substitution it holds $C \equiv \sigma'(D)$ iff the corresponding assignment solves the equation system. Since the equation system is in fact solved by the assignment, we can conclude that σ' is a matcher of the problem $C \equiv^? D$. Finally, using $\sigma \equiv_s \sigma'$ it immediately follows that σ is a matcher as well. $\square$

Leiss [Lei95, Lei99] has introduced and investigated, among others, equations of the form

$$L = M_1 \cdot X_1 \cup \cdots \cup M_n \cdot X_n \cup M$$

where $L, M_1, \ldots, M_n$ are regular languages and where the equation asks for substitutions of the variables X_i by regular languages. The equations (F), $F \in \mathcal{C}$, introduced above exactly fit this pattern. Although Leiss shows that the solvability of these languages is decidable, he does not provide complexity results. Nevertheless, obviously the problem is PSPACE-hard since deciding equality of regular languages is PSPACE-hard. Moreover, from results shown in the theory of set constraints [AKVW93] it follows that the solvability can be decided by an EXPTIME-algorithm in case variables can be substituted by arbitrary (i.e., possibly irregular) languages. The next subsection reveals that least solutions (w.r.t. set inclusion) of such equations can grow exponentially in the size of the equation and that there is a EXPSPACE-algorithm computing them.

In [Lei99], also more general equations of the form

$$L_1 \cdot X_1 \cup \cdots \cup L_n \cdot X_n \cup L = M_1 \cdot X_1 \cup \cdots \cup M_n \cdot X_n \cup M$$

have been examined where variables are allowed on both sides of the equation. In case the languages L, M, L_i, and M_i are finite and the variables stand for finite languages as well, solving these equations corresponds to the problem of unifying $\mathcal{FL}_0$-concept descriptions (see Section 3.2.1). In [BN98], it has been shown that deciding the solvability of such unification problems is an EXPTIME-complete problem. Unification of $\mathcal{FL}_0^*$-concept descriptions corresponds to solving the above equations in case of regular languages (as opposed to only finite ones). From results shown in [AKVW93], it follows that this problem is in EXPTIME, again under the assumption that variables can be substituted by arbitrary languages.

The complexity results mentioned above are presented here to demonstrate that investigations on matching and unification problems can contribute to the field of formal language equations. Conversely, although matching and unification have not yet benefited from results on language equations, the close connection between these areas might become fruitful in the future.

6.2.2 Computing Minimal i-Complete Sets

The solvability of a system of formal language equations (F), $F \in \mathcal{C}_\perp$, can be decided by testing whether a certain candidate solution solves the equations. Such a solution will then yield the least matcher, and thus, a minimal i-complete set of the corresponding matching problem $C \equiv^? D$.

In order to define candidate solutions, we need to define the inverse concatenation of formal languages: Let L_1, L_2 be some subsets of N_R^*. Then, the *inverse concatenation* $L_1 \stackrel{\cdot}{:} L_2$ of L_1 and L_2 is defined to be the set

$$L_1 \stackrel{\cdot}{:} L_2 := \{w \in N_R^* \mid L_1 \cdot \{w\} \subseteq L_2\}.$$

Now, the assignment

$$\{X \mapsto \widehat{L}_X\} \tag{6.6}$$

is called *candidate solution* of the system (F), $F \in \mathcal{C}_\perp$ where for $X = X_{i,F}$

$$\widehat{L}_X := L_D(X) \stackrel{\cdot}{:} V_C(F).$$

Lemma 6.2.2. *The system of equations (F), $F \in \mathcal{C}_\perp$, has a solution if, and only if, the candidate solution (6.6) solves the system. Moreover, if the system is solvable, then the substitution corresponding to the candidate solution is a least matcher.*

Proof. We start with showing the first part of the lemma. The if direction is trivial. Now, let $\{X_{i,F} \mapsto L_{i,F}\}$ be a solution of the equation system. First, we consider the case $F \in \mathcal{C}$. By definition of the equations (F) it follows: $V_C(F) \supseteq L_D(X_{i,F}) \cdot w$ for every $w \in L_{i,F}$. But then, $w \in \widehat{L}_{X_{i,F}}$, and thus, $L_{i,F} \subseteq \widehat{L}_{X_{i,F}}$. Therefore, we can conclude that with the candidate solution the left-hand side in the equations (F), $F \in \mathcal{C}$, is a subset of the right-hand side. The inclusion in the other direction follows from the simple facts that the system is solvable (and thus, $V_D(F) \cup E_C(F) \subseteq V_C(F)$) and that $V_C(F) \supseteq L_D(X) \cdot \widehat{L}_X$ for every $X \in N_{X,F}$.

It remains to show that the candidate solution solves the equation $(\bot)$. Let σ be the substitution that corresponds to the assignment $\{X_{i,F} \mapsto L_{i,F}\}$. From the proof of Theorem 6.2.1 it follows that then σ is a matcher of the problem $C \equiv^? D$. Let $w \in L_{i,\bot}$. Then, $\sigma(D) \sqsubseteq \forall vw.\bot$ for all $v \in L_D(X_{i,\bot})$. Since $\sigma(D) \equiv C$, we can conclude $vw \in E_C = V_C(\bot)$. Thus, $L_{i,\bot} \subseteq \widehat{L}_{X_{i,\bot}}$. Let $\widehat{\sigma}$ be the substitution corresponding to the candidate solution. Since, $L_{i,F} \subseteq \widehat{L}_{X_{i,F}}$ for every $i = 1, \ldots, l$ and $F \in \mathcal{C}_\bot$, Theorem 4.2.2 implies $\widehat{\sigma}(X) \sqsubseteq \sigma(X)$ for every $X \in N_X$. In particular, this shows that $\widehat{\sigma}(D) \sqsubseteq \sigma(D)$. Consequently, $E_C = E_{\sigma(D)} \subseteq E_{\widehat{\sigma}(D)}$.

We now show that $C \sqsubseteq \widehat{\sigma}(D)$. If this is the case, then $\widehat{\sigma}(D) \sqsubseteq \forall w.\bot$ implies $C \sqsubseteq \forall w.\bot$, and thus $E_{\widehat{\sigma}(D)} \subseteq E_C$, which completes the first part of the proof. Since the equations (F) for $F \in \mathcal{C}$ are satisfied by the candidate solution, we know that $L_{\widehat{\sigma}(D)}(F) \subseteq V_C(F)$. Moreover, because $E_C = E_{\sigma(D)}$, it follows that $L_D(\bot) \subseteq E_C$. The sets $\widehat{L}_{X_{i,\bot}}$ are defined such that $L_D(X_{i,\bot}) \cdot \widehat{L}_{X_{i,\bot}} \subseteq E_C = V_C(\bot)$. Finally, note that $L_{\widehat{\sigma}(D)}(\bot) = L_D(\bot) \cup \bigcup_{i=1,\ldots,l} L_D(X_i) \cdot \widehat{L}_{X_{i,\bot}}$. Thus, $L_{\widehat{\sigma}(D)}(\bot) \subseteq E_C$. By Theorem 4.2.2, we can now infer $C \sqsubseteq \widehat{\sigma}(D)$.

Finally, we show that $\widehat{\sigma}$ is the least matcher of the matching problem $C \equiv^? D$. Let σ' be some matcher. The proof of Lemma 6.2.1 reveals that there exists a matcher $\sigma \sqsubseteq_s \sigma'$ that does not introduce new (negated) concept names or number restrictions. The proof of the first part of Lemma 6.2.2 shows that $\widehat{\sigma} \sqsubseteq_s \sigma$. Thus, $\widehat{\sigma} \sqsubseteq_s \sigma'$.   □

As an immediate consequence of Theorem 6.2.1 and Lemma 6.2.2, we obtain the following corollary.

Corollary 6.2.3. *Let C be an $\mathcal{ALN}^*$-concept description and D an $\mathcal{ALN}^*$-concept pattern. Then, the matching problem $C \equiv^? D$ has a solution if, and only if, the substitution corresponding to the candidate solution (6.6) is a matcher of this problem. In case the problem is solvable, this substitution is the least matcher of the matching problem.*

From Corollary 6.2.3 we can conclude that the following algorithm decides the solvability of the matching problem $C \equiv^? D$ and returns the least matcher in case the problem is solvable: a) Compute a substitution σ corresponding to the candidate solution of the equation system of $C \equiv^? D$, and b) check whether C and $\sigma(D)$ are equivalent: return σ if this is the case and "No" otherwise.

We already know that step b) can be carried out by a PSPACE-algorithm in the size of C and $\sigma(D)$ (Corollary 4.2.3). To perform step a), according to Lemma 6.2.2 we need to construct a finite automaton for the inverse concatenation of regular languages. We will now show how this can be achieved.

Let L_1, L_2 be regular languages over N_R. If $(N_R, Q_2, I_2, \Delta_2, F_2)$ is the (non-deterministic) finite automaton accepting L_2, then we refer to the language accepted by the automaton $(N_R, Q_2, I, \Delta_2, F)$ by $L_2(I, F)$ where $I \subseteq Q$ is the set of initial states and $F \subseteq Q$ is the set of finite states of this automaton. In order to construct an automaton accepting the inverse concatenation $L_1 \stackrel{.}{.} L_2$ of L_1 and L_2, we need the set

$$\mathcal{I} := \{I \subseteq Q_2 \mid L_1 \subseteq L_2(I_2, I)\}.$$

Lemma 6.2.3.

$$L_1 \stackrel{.}{.} L_2 = \bigcup_{I \in \mathcal{I}} \bigcap_{q \in I} L_2(\{q\}, F_2).$$

Proof. We first show that the right-hand side of the identity is contained in the left one. To this end, let $I \in \mathcal{I}$ and $w \in \bigcap_{q \in I} L_2(\{q\}, F_2)$. For all $v \in L_1$ we must show $vw \in L_2$. By definition of $\mathcal{I}$, we know $v \in L_2(I_2, I)$. Thus, there exists a $q \in I$ with $v \in L_2(I_2, \{q\})$. Consequently, $vw \in L_2(I_2, \{q\}) \cdot L_2(\{q\}, F_2) \subseteq L_2$.

Conversely, assume that $w \in L_1 \stackrel{.}{.} L_2$. We define $I := \{q \mid$ there exists $v \in L_1$ with $v \in L_2(I_2, \{q\}), w \in L_2(\{q\}, F_2)\}$. By definition, for every $q \in I$, $w \in L_2(\{q\}, F_2)$. Thus, if $I \in \mathcal{I}$, then this shows that w is contained in the right-hand side of the identity stated by the lemma. In order to show $I \in \mathcal{I}$, let $v \in L_1$. We want to show $v \in L_2(I_2, I)$. Since $w \in L_1 \stackrel{.}{.} L_2$, we know $vw \in L_2$. Thus, there exists $q \in Q_2$ with $v \in L_2(I_2, \{q\})$ and $w \in L_2(\{q\}, F_2)$. But then $q \in I$, and thus, $v \in L_2(I_2, I)$.   □

Since deciding the inclusion problem for regular languages is a PSPACE-complete problem, the set $\mathcal{I}$ can be computed in exponential time in the size of automata for L_1 and L_2. Given a set $I \in \mathcal{I}$, the automaton for $\bigcap_{q \in I} L_2(\{q\}, F_2)$ is the product automaton of the automata to $L_2(\{q\}, F_2)$. Thus, it can also be computed in exponential time. As an immediate consequence of Lemma 6.2.3, we obtain the following corollary.

Corollary 6.2.4. *Let L_1, L_2 be regular languages. Then, an automaton accepting the inverse concatenation $L_1 \stackrel{.}{.} L_2$ of L_1 and L_2 can be computed in time exponential in the size of (non-deterministic) finite automata for L_1 and L_2.*

The size of the automaton constructed for $L_1 \stackrel{.}{.} L_2$ may grow exponentially in the size of the automata for L_1 and L_2. The following example shows that this cannot be avoided.

Example 6.2.2. Let $L_1 := \{r_1, \ldots, r_n\}$ be a set of letters not contained in N_R. Moreover, let L_2 be the regular language $(r_1 \cdot L_1') \cup \cdots \cup (r_n \cdot L_n')$ where the L_i' are regular languages over N_R. Now, it is easy to see that $L_1 \stackrel{.}{.} L_2 = L_1' \cap \cdots \cap L_n'$. As shown in [YZ91], the size of automata accepting this intersection may grow exponentially in the size of the sequence of automata accepting $L'_1, \ldots, L'_n$.[2]

A similar argument can directly be employed for matching problems. Obviously, for least matchers σ of matching problems of the form

$$\forall((r_1 \cdot L'_1) \cup \cdots \cup (r_n \cdot L'_n)).P \equiv^? \forall((r_1 \cdot L'_1) \cup \cdots \cup (r_n \cdot L'_n)).P \sqcap \forall\{r_1, \ldots, r_n\}.X$$

it follows that $\sigma(X) \equiv \forall(L'_1 \cap \cdots \cap L'_n).P$. Thus, σ grows exponentially in the size of the given matching problem.

Since, according to Theorem 4.2.3, automata accepting value-restriction sets $V_C(F)$ can be computed in time polynomial in the size of a $\mathcal{FL}^*_-$-concept description C (and in exponential time for $\mathcal{ALN}^*$-concept descriptions), Corollary 6.2.4 shows that candidate solutions for matching problems $C \equiv^? D$ can be computed in (double) exponential time. In particular, this provides us with a (double) exponential upper bound for the size of candidate solutions. As mentioned, given a candidate solution, one can decide whether the corresponding substitution solves the matching problem using a PSPACE-algorithm for deciding equivalence in $\mathcal{ALN}^*$ (Corollary 4.2.3). Since the equivalence problem may already be of size (double) exponential in the size of the matching problem, checking whether the candidate solution solves the matching problem can thus be carried out by an algorithm using (double) exponential space. The following theorem summarizes these complexity results.

Theorem 6.2.2. *Let C be an $\mathcal{FL}^*_-$-concept description ($\mathcal{ALN}^*$-concept descriptions) and D be an $\mathcal{FL}^*_-$-concept pattern ($\mathcal{ALN}^*$-concept pattern). Then, it can be decided by an EXPSPACE-algorithm (2EXPSPACE-algorithm) whether the matching problem $C \equiv^? D$ has a solution. In case it is solvable, a least matcher, and thus, a minimal i-complete set, can be constructed in (double) exponential time. The size of the least matcher may grow exponentially in the size of the matching problem.*

As an immediate consequence of Lemma 3.2.2, we obtain the following corollary. For the growth of least matchers, however, one needs to consider the matching problem $\forall((r_1 \cdot L'_1) \cup \cdots \cup (r_n \cdot L'_n)).P \sqsubseteq^? \forall\{r_1, \ldots, r_n\}.X$ instead of the one proposed for matching modulo equivalence.

Corollary 6.2.5. *Let $C \sqsubseteq^? D$ be a solvable $\mathcal{FL}^*_-$-matching problem modulo subsumption ($\mathcal{ALN}^*$-matching problem). Then, the least matcher of this problem (and thus, a minimal i-complete set) can be constructed in (double) exponential time. Its size may grow exponentially in the size of the matching problem.*

---

[2] As already mentioned on Page 127, although the result shown in [YZ91] only applies to deterministic automata, it can easily be generalized to the nondeterministic case.

Up to now, it is not clear how to gain tighter upper bounds for the size of least matchers and the complexity of the decision problem for matching modulo equivalence.

The automata-theoretic approach for solving matching problems presented here for $\mathcal{ALN}^*$ has first been developed in [BKBM99] to tackle $\mathcal{ALN}$-matching problems. In this restricted case, computing least matchers can be carried out by polynomial time algorithms, a result that has also been shown in Section 6.1 using the graph-based approach.

6.3 Matching in $\mathcal{ALE}$

It will be shown that deciding the solvability of $\mathcal{ALE}$-matching problems both modulo equivalence and subsumption is NP-complete. Thus, although from the computational point of view matching in $\mathcal{ALE}$ is not harder than matching in $\mathcal{ALNS}$ and $\mathcal{ALN}^*$, conceptually we are faced with the problem that solvable matching problems no longer need to have least matchers. More precisely, the cardinality of minimal i-complete sets as well as the size of i-minimal matchers may grow exponentially in the size of the given $\mathcal{ALE}$-matching problem. As for minimal d-complete sets, although the cardinality may grow exponentially, the size of d-minimal matchers can be polynomially bounded in the size of the matching problem.

This section is organized as follows: We first explore the problem of matching for the sublanguage $\mathcal{EL}$ of $\mathcal{ALE}$. Then, in the following subsections the results for $\mathcal{EL}$ are extended to $\mathcal{FLE}$ and $\mathcal{ALE}$. For all these languages, we first characterize equivalence of reduced concept descriptions. Building upon this characterization, we then prove complexity upper and lower bounds for deciding the solvability of matching problems. Finally, algorithms for computing minimal i-complete and d-complete sets of matchers are presented.

Matching in $\mathcal{EL}$ is investigated separately in order to present the main ideas underlying our results, and at first, to avoid the rather involved techniques and proofs necessary for the extensions of $\mathcal{EL}$. Moreover, since subsumption in $\mathcal{EL}$ is a polynomial time problem, the complexity results for $\mathcal{EL}$ show that matching is a hard problem on its own and that this complexity is not due to the complexity of subsumption. Finally, unlike the standard decision problems (like subsumption), matching does not a priori allow to transfer complexity results for one language to sublanguages thereof since the set of possible solutions changes.

6.3.1 Matching in $\mathcal{EL}$

The main focus of this subsection lies in developing algorithms for matching in $\mathcal{EL}$ and investigating their complexity. All results will later on be extended to $\mathcal{FLE}$ and $\mathcal{ALE}$. However, one exception is the algorithm for computing minimal d-complete sets of matchers. On the one hand, for $\mathcal{FLE}$ and $\mathcal{ALE}$ a naïve algorithm computing d-complete sets is proposed, which only exploits the fact that the size of d-minimal matchers can be polynomially bounded. For $\mathcal{EL}$, on the other hand, a much more sophisticated algorithm is presented.

Equivalence of $\mathcal{EL}$-Concept Descriptions. Before we turn our attention to matching, we need to show that equivalence of reduced $\mathcal{EL}$-concept descriptions can be characterized in terms of isomorphisms between the corresponding description trees. (Recall that, intuitively, reduced concept descriptions are those descriptions without redundancies, as formalized in Definition 3.2.4.) This result is important in different respects: First, it shows what was already claimed in Section 3.2.3, namely, that equivalent and reduced concept descriptions are uniquely determined up to commutativity and associativity of concept conjunction. In particular, the uniqueness carries over to the minimal set of i-minimal and reduced matchers specified in Definition 3.2.7. Second, the characterization can be employed to prove complexity results for deciding the solvability of matching problems. Finally, understanding the equivalence between reduced concept descriptions is indispensable in the context of computing minimal rewritings [BKM00], i.e., minimal representations of concept descriptions modulo an underlying TBox (see also Section 3.4).

Theorem 6.3.1. *Let C, D be reduced $\mathcal{EL}$-concept descriptions. Then, $C \equiv D$ if, and only if, $\mathcal{G}(C) \cong \mathcal{G}(D)$.*

We postpone the proof of Theorem 6.3.1 to Proposition 6.3.2, since the proposition provides us with a stronger statement. Note that two concept descriptions with isomorphic description trees do not necessarily coincide syntactically, but only up to commutativity and associativity of conjunction, since labels and outgoing $\exists$-edges of nodes are not ordered. Thus, Theorem 6.3.1 can also be phrased as follows, where AC denotes the equation theory introduced in Section 3.2.3.

Corollary 6.3.1. *Let C, D be reduced $\mathcal{EL}$-concept descriptions. Then, $C \equiv D$ if, and only if, $C =_{\mathsf{AC}} D$.*

An inductive description of reduced concept descriptions is given in the subsequent proposition. Recall that $E \in C$ means that E occurs on the top-level of C.

Proposition 6.3.1. *Let C be an $\mathcal{EL}$-concept description. Then, C is reduced if, and only if,*

- *every concept name on the top-level of C only occurs once; unless $C = \top$, $\top \notin C$;*
- *for two distinct existential restrictions $\exists r.E, \exists r.F \in C$ we have $E \not\sqsubseteq F$; and*
- *for all existential restrictions $\exists r.E \in C$, E is reduced.*

From this characterization one can immediately derive a polynomial time algorithm that, given an $\mathcal{EL}$-concept description C, returns an equivalent and reduced subdescription $C \setminus \top$ of C. Note that, due to Theorem 6.3.1, it makes sense to refer to *the* reduced concept $C \setminus \top$.

In order to see that reduced concepts are the smallest representatives of their equivalence class, we prove the following stronger version of Theorem 6.3.1.

Proposition 6.3.2. *Let C and D be $\mathcal{EL}$-concept descriptions such that C is reduced, and let $\mathcal{G}(C) = (N, E, n_0, \ell)$ and $\mathcal{G}(D) = (N', E', n'_0, \ell')$ be the corresponding $\mathcal{EL}$-description trees. Then, $C \equiv D$ implies that every homomorphism ψ from $\mathcal{G}(C)$ into $\mathcal{G}(D)$ is an injective homomorphism and for all $n \in N$, $\mathcal{G}(C)_n \equiv \mathcal{G}(D)_{\psi(n)}$.*

Proof. Let $r \in N_R$, $(n_0, r, n_1) \in E$, and ψ be a homomorphism from $\mathcal{G}(C)$ into $\mathcal{G}(D)$. Corollary 4.3.1 implies that $\mathcal{G}(C)_{n_1} \sqsupseteq \mathcal{G}(D)_{\psi(n_1)}$. Assume that the subsumption relation is strict. Since $C \equiv D$, by Corollary 4.3.1 there exists a node $n_2 \in N$, $(n_0, r, n_2) \in E$ with $\mathcal{G}(D)_{\psi(n_1)} \sqsupseteq \mathcal{G}(C)_{n_2}$. Clearly, $n_1 \neq n_2$. But then, $\mathcal{G}(C)_{n_1} \sqsupset \mathcal{G}(C)_{n_2}$ is a contradiction to the fact that C is reduced. Thus, $\mathcal{G}(C)_{n_1} \equiv \mathcal{G}(D)_{\psi(n_1)}$. By induction this proves that, for all $n \in N$, $\mathcal{G}(C)_n \equiv \mathcal{G}(D)_{\psi(n)}$. Note that, if C is reduced, then so is $C_{\mathcal{G}(C)_n}$ for all $n \in N$.

It remains to show that ψ is injective. Assume, there exist $n_1, n_2 \in N$, $n_1 \neq n_2$, with $\psi(n_1) = \psi(n_2)$. Since ψ is a homomorphism, it follows that there exists a node n' such that $(n', r, n_1), (n', r, n_2) \in E$. From the above we know, $\mathcal{G}(C)_{n_1} \equiv \mathcal{G}(C)_{n_2} \equiv \mathcal{G}(D)_{\psi(n_1)}$, which is a contradiction to the fact that C is reduced. $\qquad\square$

From this proposition, Theorem 6.3.1 can be derived as follows: Let C and D be reduced $\mathcal{EL}$-concept descriptions, and let ψ be a homomorphism from $\mathcal{G}(C)$ into $\mathcal{G}(D)$, and ψ' be a homomorphism from $\mathcal{G}(D)$ into $\mathcal{G}(C)$. According to the proposition, ψ and ψ' are injective. In particular, the number of nodes in $\mathcal{G}(C)$ coincides with the number of nodes in $\mathcal{G}(D)$. Thus, ψ and ψ' are surjective. It remains to show that for every $n \in \mathcal{G}(C)$, the label of n in $\mathcal{G}(C)$ and the one of $\psi(n)$ in $\mathcal{G}(D)$ coincide. This can easily be achieved by induction on the depth of $\mathcal{G}(C)$.

Obviously, $|C \setminus \top| \leq |C|$. More generally, reduced concepts are the minimal representation of their equivalence class. In fact, if $E \equiv C$, then there exists a homomorphism ψ from $\mathcal{G}(C \setminus \top)$ into $\mathcal{G}(E)$. Proposition 6.3.2 says that ψ is injective, and thus, $|C \setminus \top| = |\mathcal{G}(C \setminus \top)| \leq |\mathcal{G}(E)| \leq |E|$.

Corollary 6.3.2. *For every $\mathcal{EL}$-concept description C, the equivalent and reduced subdescription $C \setminus \top$ of C can be computed in polynomial time and it is the smallest $\mathcal{EL}$-concept description equivalent to C, i.e., for every $\mathcal{EL}$-concept description E, $E \equiv C$ implies $|C \setminus \top| \leq |E|$.*

Deciding Solvability of Matching in $\mathcal{EL}$. Since subsumption of $\mathcal{EL}$-concept descriptions is a polynomial time problem [BKM98a], as a direct consequence of Lemma 3.2.3 we obtain the following complexity result for matching modulo subsumption.

Corollary 6.3.3. *The solvability of $\mathcal{EL}$-matching problems modulo subsumption can be decided by a polynomial time algorithm.*

The main technical problem is to show that deciding the solvability of $\mathcal{EL}$-matching problems modulo equivalence is an NP-complete problem.

In order to prove that there exists a non-deterministic polynomial time decision algorithm, it is sufficient to show that every solvable $\mathcal{EL}$-matching problem has a matcher that is i) polynomially bounded in the size of the matching problem and ii) uses only concept names and role names already contained in the matching problem. An NP-algorithm then guesses a substitution σ of size polynomially bounded in the size of the matching problem and checks whether σ solves the matching problem. At the end of this subsection, we will describe a more sophisticated decision algorithm, which significantly prunes the search space for candidate matchers.

Theorem 6.3.2. *If the $\mathcal{EL}$-matching problem $C \equiv^? D$ is solvable, then there exists a matcher of size polynomial in the size of the matching problem that only uses concept names and role names already contained in the matching problem.*

In what follows, we construct such a matcher σ, given some matcher σ' of $C \equiv^? D$. Due to Corollary 6.3.2, we can w.l.o.g. assume that C is reduced. Otherwise we consider the problem $C \backslash \top \equiv^? D$.

According to Corollary 4.3.1, $C \equiv \sigma'(D)$ implies that there exists a homomorphism ψ from $\mathcal{G}(C)$ into $\mathcal{G}(\sigma'(D))$. By Proposition 6.3.2 and since C is reduced, ψ must be injective.

Before constructing σ, we need some more notation. In order to present concept patterns by description trees, description trees are extended to allow variables in the labels of their nodes. Then, given some concept pattern D, its corresponding description tree $\mathcal{G}(D)$ is defined as in the case of simple concept descriptions. We will also consider homomorphisms from description trees $\mathcal{H}$ containing variables into those trees $\mathcal{G}$ without variables. These homomorphisms ignore variables in the inclusion condition between labels. More precisely, in the second condition of Definition 4.3.2, $\ell_H(n) \subseteq \ell_G(\varphi(n))$ is replaced by

$$\ell_H(n) \setminus N_X \subseteq \ell_G(\varphi(n)). \tag{6.7}$$

For a variable X in the concept pattern D, $N_D(X) := \{m \in \mathcal{G}(D) \mid X \in \mathcal{G}(D)(m)\}$ denotes the set of all nodes in $\mathcal{G}(D)$ with X in their label. For a substitution σ', we call a description tree $\mathcal{G}$ *instantiation* of $\mathcal{G}(D)$ *by* σ' if $\mathcal{G}$ is obtained by instantiating $\mathcal{G}(D)$ for every node $m \in N_D(X)$ and every variable X in D by (a copy of) $\mathcal{G}(\sigma'(X))$.[3] Such a copy is called $\mathcal{G}_{\sigma'(X),m}$ where the root of $\mathcal{G}_{\sigma'(X),m}$ is defined to be m. Now, it is easy to prove the following lemma.

Lemma 6.3.1. $\mathcal{G}(\sigma'(D))$ *is isomorphic to the instantiation of* $\mathcal{G}(D)$ *by* σ'. *In particular,* $\mathcal{G}(D)$ *is isomorphic to a subtree of* $\mathcal{G}(\sigma'(D))$ *when ignoring the variables occurring in* $\mathcal{G}(D)$.

Usually, we therefore consider $\mathcal{G}(\sigma'(D))$ itself to be the instantiation of $\mathcal{G}(D)$ by σ'.

Now, σ is defined as follows:

$$\sigma(X) := \bigsqcap_{\substack{m \in N_D(X) \\ \psi^{-1}(m) \neq \emptyset}} C_{\psi^{-1}(\mathcal{G}_{\sigma'(X),m})}$$

for every variable X in D.

The idea behind this construction is as follows: First, recall that the tree $\psi^{-1}(\mathcal{G}_{\sigma'(X),m})$ is isomorphic to $\psi(\psi^{-1}(\mathcal{G}_{\sigma'(X),m}))$, which is a rooted subtree of $\mathcal{G}_{\sigma'(X),m}$ (Lemma 4.3.2). Thus, $\psi^{-1}(\mathcal{G}_{\sigma'(X),m})$ describes those parts of $\mathcal{G}_{\sigma'(X),m}$ that belong to the image $\psi(\mathcal{G}(C))$ of ψ. Now, conjoining these parts for every variables X and every occurrence of X in D, as done in the definition of $\sigma(X)$, guarantees that ψ is still a homomorphism from $\mathcal{G}(C)$ into $\mathcal{G}(\sigma(D))$, and hence, $\sigma(D) \sqsubseteq C$. On the other hand, $\sigma(X)$ is built from subdescriptions of $\sigma'(X)$, which implies $\sigma' \sqsubseteq_s \sigma$, and consequently, $C \equiv \sigma'(D) \sqsubseteq \sigma(D)$ (Lemma 3.2.1). The following two lemmas provide formal proofs supporting this intuition.

Lemma 6.3.2. $\sigma \sqsupseteq_s \sigma'$.

Proof. Let m be a node in $N_D(X)$. By Lemma 4.3.1, ψ is a homomorphism from $\psi^{-1}(\mathcal{G}_{\sigma'(X),m})$ onto $\psi(\psi^{-1}(\mathcal{G}_{\sigma'(X),m}))$, which, according to Lemma 4.3.2, is a rooted subtree of $\mathcal{G}_{\sigma'(X),m}$. This shows that $C_{\psi^{-1}(\mathcal{G}_{\sigma'(X),m})} \sqsupseteq \mathcal{G}_{\sigma'(X),m} \equiv \sigma'(X)$. Hence, $\sigma(X) \sqsupseteq \sigma'(X)$. □

As a direct consequence of Lemma 3.2.1, we can deduce $\sigma(D) \sqsupseteq \sigma'(D) \equiv C$.

Lemma 6.3.3. $\sigma(D) \sqsubseteq C$.

Proof. We show that there exists a homomorphism from $\mathcal{G}(C)$ into $\mathcal{G}$ where $\mathcal{G}$ is a graph satisfying $\mathcal{G} \sqsupseteq \sigma(D)$, which by Corollary 4.3.1 completes the proof of the lemma.

Let $\mathcal{G}$ be the description tree obtained by instantiating $\mathcal{G}(D)$ as follows: For every variable X in D and node $m \in N_D(X)$, instantiate $\mathcal{G}(D)$ by $\psi(\psi^{-1}(\mathcal{G}_{\sigma'(X),m}))$ at m. Now, it is easy to see that ψ is a homomorphism from $\mathcal{G}(C)$ into $\mathcal{G}$ since ψ is a homomorphism from $\mathcal{G}(C)$ into $\mathcal{G}(\sigma'(D))$. (Section 6.3.3 contains a more detailed proof for $\mathcal{FLE}$).

---

[3] See also Section 4.3.1.

Finally, observe that, for $m \in N_D(X)$, $\psi^{-1}(\mathcal{G}_{\sigma'(X),m})$ is isomorphic to the tree $\psi(\psi^{-1}(\mathcal{G}_{\sigma'(X),m}))$ (see Lemma 4.3.2). Therefore, $\mathcal{G}$ is (isomorphic to) a rooted subtree of $\mathcal{G}(\sigma(D))$. Thus, $\mathcal{G} \sqsupseteq \sigma(D)$.   □

Lemma 6.3.2 and 6.3.3 imply that σ is a matcher of the problem $C \equiv^? D$. Moreover, by construction, $\sigma(X)$ is built only from identifiers (i.e., concept names and roles) in C. Therefore, in order to complete the proof of Theorem 6.3.2, it remains to be shown that the size of σ is polynomially bounded in the size of the matching problem. This is a consequence of the following lemma.

Lemma 6.3.4. *For every variable X in D, the size of $\sigma(X)$ is linearly bounded in the size of C.*

Proof. Let $m \in N_D(X)$ and $\psi^{-1}(m) \neq \emptyset$. We know that $\psi^{-1}(\mathcal{G}_{\sigma'(X),m})$ is a subtree of $\mathcal{G}(C)$. Furthermore, for different m's one obtains disjoint subtrees, since ψ is injective.   □

NP-hardness of the solvability of $\mathcal{EL}$-matching problems modulo equivalence is shown by a reduction of SAT [GJ79].

Let $\phi = p_1 \wedge \cdots \wedge p_l$ be a propositional formula in conjunctive normal form and let $\{x_1, \ldots, x_k\}$ be the propositional variables of this problem. For these variables, we introduce the concept variables $\{X_1, \ldots, X_k, \overline{X}_1, \ldots, \overline{X}_k\}$. Furthermore, we need concept names A and B as well as the role names r, r', s, s'.

First, we specify a matching problem $C_k \equiv^? D_k$ that encodes the truth values of the k propositional variables:

$$C_0 := \top,$$
$$C_{i+1} := \exists r'.A \sqcap \exists r'.B \sqcap \exists r.C_i,$$
$$D_0 := \top,$$
$$D_{i+1} := \exists r'.X_{i+1} \sqcap \exists r'.\overline{X}_{i+1} \sqcap \exists r.D_i.$$

The matchers of the problem $C_k \equiv^? D_k$ are exactly the substitutions that replace X_i by (a concept equivalent to) A and $\overline{X}_i$ by (a concept equivalent to) B (corresponding to $x_i = true$) or vice versa (corresponding to $x_i = false$).

In order to encode ϕ, we introduce a concept pattern D_{p_i} for each conjunct p_i. For example, if $p_i = x_1 \vee \overline{x}_2 \vee x_3 \vee \overline{x}_4$, then $D_{p_i} := X_1 \sqcap \overline{X}_2 \sqcap X_3 \sqcap \overline{X}_4 \sqcap B$. The whole formula is then represented by the matching problem $C'_l \equiv^? D'_l$, where

$$C'_0 := \top,$$
$$C'_{i+1} := \exists s'.(A \sqcap B) \sqcap \exists s.C'_i,$$
$$D'_0 := \top,$$
$$D'_{i+1} := \exists s'.D_{p_{i+1}} \sqcap \exists s.D'_i.$$

This matching problem ensures that, among the (negated) variables in D_{p_i}, at least one must be replaced by (a concept equivalent to) A. This corresponds to the fact that, within one conjunct p_i, there must be at least one propositional variable that evaluates to *true*. Note that we need the concept B in D_{p_i} to cover the case where all variables in D_{p_i} are substituted with A.

We combine the two matching problems introduced above into a single problem $C_k \sqcap C'_l \equiv^? D_k \sqcap D'_l$. It is easy to verify that ϕ is satisfiable if, and only if, this matching problem is solvable. Together with the upper bound this proves:

Corollary 6.3.4. *Deciding the solvability of $\mathcal{EL}$-matching problems modulo equivalence is an NP-complete problem.*

Computing i-Minimal Matchers in $\mathcal{EL}$. Recall from Section 3.2.3 that (minimal) i-complete sets are those sets containing at least (exactly) one i-minimal matcher for every i-equivalence class of i-minimal matchers.

For solvable $\mathcal{ALNS}$- as well as $\mathcal{ALN}^*$-matching problems there always exist least matchers. As a result, for these languages it is sufficient to compute such a least matcher in order to obtain a (minimal) i-complete set. As already mentioned in Section 3.2.3, for $\mathcal{EL}$ such a least matcher need no longer exist. For instance, substituting X with A or B in the $\mathcal{EL}$-matching problem $\exists r.A \sqcap \exists r.B \sqsubseteq^? \exists r.X$ yields two i-incomparable, i-minimal matchers. Thus, for $\mathcal{EL}$, minimal i-complete sets may contain more than one element.

As discussed in Section 3.2.3, the task of computing minimal i-complete sets for an $\mathcal{EL}$-matching problem modulo subsumption can be split into two subtasks.

1. Compute an s-complete set of the problem.
2. Filter out a minimal i-complete set from the set computed in the first step.

According to Remark 3.2.1, the second step can be carried out by a polynomial time algorithm in the size of the given s-complete set using an oracle for deciding subsumption. Thus, let us turn to the first task.

Computing s-Complete Sets in $\mathcal{EL}$. The matching algorithm presented in the sequel solves the problem of computing s-complete sets for $\mathcal{EL}$-matching problems modulo equivalence; thus, in view of Lemma 3.2.2, it solves a more general problem than the one we actually need to solve. However, when replacing the last line of the algorithm in Figure 6.1 by $\mathcal{C} := \mathcal{C} \cup \{\sigma\}$, i.e., removing the test, one obtains an algorithm which is directly tailored to matching modulo subsumption. We shall come back to this point later on. The matching algorithm described in Figure 6.1 computes homomorphism originating from the tree $\mathcal{G}(D)$, which may contain variables. Recall that these homomorphisms need only obey the modified inclusion relationship between labels specified in (6.7).

> **Input:** $\mathcal{EL}$-matching problem $C \equiv^? D$
> **Output:** s-complete set $\mathcal{C}$ of matchers for $C \equiv^? D$
>
> $\mathcal{C} := \emptyset$
> For all homomorphisms φ from $\mathcal{G}(D) = (N, E, m_0, \ell)$ into $\mathcal{G}(C)$
> $\quad$ Define σ by $\sigma(X) := lcs(C_{(\mathcal{G}(C))_{\varphi(m)}} \mid X \in \ell(m))$
> $\quad\quad$ for all variables X in D
> $\quad$ If $C \sqsupseteq \sigma(D)$ then $\mathcal{C} := \mathcal{C} \cup \{\sigma\}$

Fig. 6.1. The $\mathcal{EL}$-Matching Algorithm.

Before the soundness of this algorithm is proved formally, we first provide some intuition of how the algorithm works: It first tries to construct substitutions σ such that $C \sqsubseteq \sigma(D)$, i.e., there exists a homomorphism from $\mathcal{G}(\sigma(D))$ into $\mathcal{G}(C)$. In a second step, it checks which of the computed substitutions really solve the matching problem, i.e., also satisfy $C \sqsupseteq \sigma(D)$. (As already mentioned, we will see that for a matching problem modulo subsumption, this second step can be dispensed with.) The first step is achieved by first computing all homomorphisms from $\mathcal{G}(D)$ into $\mathcal{G}(C)$. The remaining problem is that a variable X may occur more than once in D. Thus, we cannot simply define $\sigma(X)$ as $C_{(\mathcal{G}(C))_{\varphi(m)}}$ where m is such that X occurs in the label of m. Since there may exist several nodes m with this property, we take the lcs of the corresponding parts of C. The reason for taking the *least* common subsumer is that we want to compute substitutions that are as small as possible w.r.t. $\sqsubseteq_s$. An algorithm for computing the lcs of $\mathcal{EL}$-concepts has been described in [BKM99] (see also Section 5.3).

Before proving the soundness of our matching algorithm, we illustrate the algorithm by the example depicted in Figure 6.2 (see also Section 3.2.3 where the example has first been introduced).

There are six homomorphisms from $\mathcal{G}(D_{ex})$ into $\mathcal{G}(C_{ex})$. We consider the ones mapping m_i onto n_i for $i = 0, 1, 2$, and m_3 onto n_3 or m_3 onto n_4, which we denote by φ_1 and φ_2, respectively. The homomorphism φ_1 yields the substitution σ_1:

$$\sigma_1(X) := lcs\{C_{\mathcal{G}(C_{ex})_{n_1}}, C_{\mathcal{G}(C_{ex})_{n_2}}\} \equiv \mathsf{W} \sqcap \exists hc.(\mathsf{W} \sqcap \mathsf{P}),$$
$$\sigma_1(Y) := lcs\{C_{\mathcal{G}(C_{ex})_{n_2}}, C_{\mathcal{G}(C_{ex})_{n_3}}\} \equiv \quad\quad \mathsf{W} \sqcap \mathsf{D},$$

whereas φ_2 yields the substitution σ_2:

$$\sigma_2(X) := lcs\{C_{\mathcal{G}(C_{ex})_{n_1}}, C_{\mathcal{G}(C_{ex})_{n_2}}\} \equiv \mathsf{W} \sqcap \exists hc.(\mathsf{W} \sqcap \mathsf{P}),$$
$$\sigma_2(Y) := lcs\{C_{\mathcal{G}(C_{ex})_{n_2}}, C_{\mathcal{G}(C_{ex})_{n_4}}\} \equiv \quad\quad \mathsf{W}.$$

For σ_1, the test $C \sqsupseteq \sigma_1(D)$ is successful, but for σ_2 the test fails. Therefore, only σ_1 belongs to the computed set $\mathcal{C}$. In fact, the last test also fails for the substitutions computed for the remaining four homomorphisms.

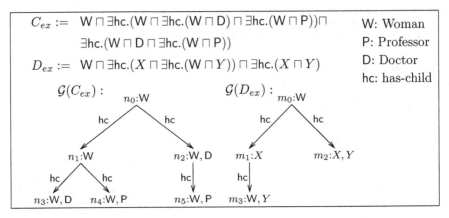

Fig. 6.2. $\mathcal{EL}$-Concept Description and Pattern, and their $\mathcal{EL}$-Description Trees.

Soundness of the $\mathcal{EL}$-Matching Algorithm. For the set $\mathcal{C}$ computed by the matching algorithm (Figure 6.1), we need to verify two properties: First, the substitutions in $\mathcal{C}$ are matchers for the given matching problem. Second, $\mathcal{C}$ is s-complete, i.e., for every matcher σ' of $C \equiv^? D$, there exists a matcher $\sigma \in \mathcal{C}$ such that $\sigma \sqsubseteq_s \sigma'$. We will split the proof into two lemmas. The first lemma says that, for every substitution σ computed by the algorithm, $\sigma(D)$ is guaranteed to subsume C.

Lemma 6.3.5. *Let φ be a homomorphism from $\mathcal{G}(D)$ into $\mathcal{G}(C)$, and let σ be the corresponding substitution, as specified by the matching algorithm in Figure 6.1. Then, $C \sqsubseteq \sigma(D)$.*

Proof. Let X be a variable in D and, as before, let $N_D(X)$ be defined as the set of nodes in $\mathcal{G}(D)$ with X in their label. For $m \in N_D(X)$ define $n := \varphi(m) \in \mathcal{G}(C)$. From the definition of σ it follows that $C_{\mathcal{G}(C)_n} \sqsubseteq \sigma(X)$. Thus, according to Corollary 4.3.1, there exists a homomorphism from $\mathcal{G}(\sigma(X))$ into $\mathcal{G}(C)_n$.

As stated by Lemma 6.3.1, $\mathcal{G}(\sigma(D))$ can be viewed as instantiation of $\mathcal{G}(D)$ by σ. It is then easy to see that φ can be extended to an homomorphism from $\mathcal{G}(\sigma(D))$ into $\mathcal{G}(C)$. By Corollary 4.3.1, this means $C \sqsubseteq \sigma(D)$.   □

Now, let σ' be a matcher of $C \equiv^? D$. This implies $C \sqsubseteq \sigma'(D)$. By Corollary 4.3.1, there exists a homomorphism φ' from $\mathcal{G}(\sigma(D'))$ into $\mathcal{G}(C)$. When deleting the variables in $\mathcal{G}(D)$, then $\mathcal{G}(D)$ is a subtree of $\mathcal{G}(\sigma'(D))$. Thus, restricting φ' to the nodes of $\mathcal{G}(D)$ yields a homomorphism φ from $\mathcal{G}(D)$ into $\mathcal{G}(C)$. For all variables X in D, let $\sigma(X) := lcs(C_{\mathcal{G}(C)_{\varphi(m)}} \mid X \in \ell(m))$ be defined as in the matching algorithm in Figure 6.1.

Lemma 6.3.6. $\sigma \sqsubseteq_s \sigma'$.

Proof. We have to verify $\sigma(X) \sqsubseteq \sigma'(X)$ for every variable X in D. Let X be a variable in D, $N_D(X)$ be defined as above, $\mathcal{G}(D) = (N, E, n_0, \ell)$, $m \in N_D(X)$, and $\varphi(m) = n$. Restricting φ' to the description tree $\mathcal{G}(\sigma'(D))_m$ provides us with a homomorphism from $\mathcal{G}(\sigma'(D))_m$ into $\mathcal{G}(C)_n$. Since $X \in \ell(m)$, $\mathcal{G}(\sigma'(D))_m$ contains a rooted subtree corresponding to $\sigma'(X)$. Consequently, there exists a homomorphism from $\mathcal{G}(\sigma'(X))$ into $\mathcal{G}(C)_n$, which shows $C_{\mathcal{G}(C)_n} \sqsubseteq \sigma'(X)$. Thus, $\sigma(X) \sqsubseteq \sigma'(X)$. $\qquad\square$

With these two lemmas at hand the soundness of the matching algorithm can be derived as follows: If $\sigma \in \mathcal{C}$ is a substitution computed by the matching algorithm, then by Lemma 6.3.5 we know $C \sqsubseteq \sigma(D)$. In addition, the test $C \sqsupseteq \sigma(D)$ at the end of the matching algorithm ensures $C \equiv \sigma(D)$, which shows that σ is a matcher of the matching problem $C \equiv^? D$.

Now, let σ' be some matcher of $C \equiv^? D$, and let σ be defined as specified above Lemma 6.3.6. Then, Lemma 6.3.6 implies $\sigma \sqsubseteq_s \sigma'$. Hence, $\sigma(D) \sqsubseteq \sigma'(D)$. According to its definition, σ is one of the substitutions computed by the matching algorithm in Figure 6.1 before the test in the last line. It remains to be shown that σ survives this test. By Lemma 6.3.5 we can infer $C \sqsubseteq \sigma(D)$. Thus, we have $\sigma(D) \sqsubseteq \sigma'(D) \equiv C \sqsubseteq \sigma(D)$, which means $C \equiv \sigma(D)$. Consequently, σ belongs to $\mathcal{C}$. Additionally, $\sigma \sqsubseteq_s \sigma'$ shows that $\mathcal{C}$ is s-complete. To sum up, we have shown that the matching algorithms specified above is correct in the following sense:

Theorem 6.3.3. *The algorithm depicted in Figure 6.1 computes s-complete sets of matchers for $\mathcal{EL}$-matching problems modulo equivalence.*

Finally, note that the proofs of the Lemmas 6.3.5 and 6.3.6 do not make use of the fact that the algorithm in Figure 6.1 checks $C \sqsupseteq \sigma(D)$. Also, for Lemma 6.3.6 it suffices to require $C \sqsubseteq \sigma'(D)$. Thus, as regards matching modulo subsumption, one can dispense with the test in the last line of the algorithm in Figure 6.1 and immediately add σ to $\mathcal{C}$.

Theorem 6.3.4. *The algorithm depicted in Figure 6.1 computes s-complete sets of matchers for matching modulo subsumption when the last line of the algorithm is replaced by $\mathcal{C} := \mathcal{C} \cup \{\sigma\}$.*

Complexity of Computing s-Complete and i-Complete Sets. There are two different aspect to consider. First, the size of (minimal) s-complete (i-complete) sets. Second, the complexity of algorithms computing these sets.

The size of complete sets can be measured both in terms of their cardinality and in terms of the space needed to represented the sets. The following example shows that the cardinality of (minimal) complete sets may grow exponentially in the size of the matching problem.

Example 6.3.1. Let C_k be the $\mathcal{EL}$-concept description

$$\prod_{i=1}^{k} \exists r.(\prod_{j=1}^{k} \exists r.(A_i \sqcap B_j)$$

and D_k be the $\mathcal{EL}$-concept pattern

$$\prod_{i=1}^{k} \exists r.\exists r.X_i.$$

For the $\mathcal{EL}$-matching problem $C \sqsubseteq^? D$ and a word $w := a_1 \cdots a_k \in \{1, \ldots, k\}^k$, the substitution $\sigma_w(X_i) := A_i \sqcap B_j$ for $a_i = j$ is an i-minimal and s-minimal matcher because all matchers the algorithm in Figure 6.1 computes are of the form $\sigma(X_i) = A_{i'} \sqcap B_j$ for some $1 \le i', j \le k$. Obviously, σ_w is i-minimal and s-minimal among these matchers. Thus, σ_w belongs to a minimal s-complete and a minimal i-complete set derived from the s-complete set computed by the algorithm. Furthermore, for different words w one obtains i-incomparable and s-incomparable matchers. Finally, for the problem $C \equiv^? C \sqcap D$ the σ_w's are s-incomparable, s-minimal matchers. Since there are k^k such words, we can derive the following corollary from the example.

Corollary 6.3.5. *1. For $\mathcal{EL}$-matching problems modulo equivalence, the cardinality of (minimal) s-complete sets of matchers may grow exponentially in the size of the matching problem.*

2. For $\mathcal{EL}$-matching problems modulo subsumption, the cardinality of (minimal) s-complete and i-complete sets of matchers may grow exponentially in the size of the matching problem.

Note that, by definition, a minimal i-complete set for matching problems modulo equivalence contains at most one matcher.

The next example demonstrates that even the size of a single matcher in s-complete and i-complete sets may grow exponentially in the size of the matching problem.

Example 6.3.2. In [BKM99], it has been shown that there exists a sequence $E_1, \ldots, E_k$ of $\mathcal{EL}$-concept descriptions such that the size of $lcs(E_1, \ldots, E_k)$ grows exponentially in the size of $E_1, \ldots, E_k$. Let C_k' be the $\mathcal{EL}$-concept description

$$\exists r_1.E_1 \sqcap \cdots \sqcap \exists r_k.E_k$$

and D_k' be the $\mathcal{EL}$-concept pattern

$$\exists r_1.X \sqcap \cdots \sqcap \exists r_k.X.$$

Clearly, for an i-minimal or s-minimal matcher σ of the matching problem $C_k' \sqsubseteq^? D_k'$, $\sigma(X) \equiv lcs(E_1, \ldots, E_k)$. This still holds for s-minimal matchers of the problem $C_k' \equiv^? C_k' \sqcap D_k'$. As an immediate consequence of the example one obtains the following corollary.

Corollary 6.3.6. *1. For $\mathcal{EL}$-matching problems modulo equivalence, the size of s-minimal matchers may grow exponentially in the size of the matching problem.*

2. For $\mathcal{EL}$-matching problems modulo subsumption, the size of s-minimal and i-minimal matchers may grow exponentially in the size of the matching problem.

Using the matching algorithm depicted in Figure 6.1, we can prove exponential upper bounds for the size of complete sets: The number of mappings from a description tree $\mathcal{G}(D)$ into $\mathcal{G}(C)$ is exponential in the size of the description trees. Since the size of these trees is linear in the size of the matching problem $C \equiv^? D$ $(C \sqsubseteq^? D)$, we can conclude that the cardinality of an s-complete (i-complete) set of matchers computed by our matching algorithm is at most exponential in the size of the matching problem.

As shown in [BKM99], the size of the lcs of a sequence of $\mathcal{EL}$-concept descriptions can exponentially be bounded in the size of the sequence. Thus, the size of every substitution computed by the matching algorithm is at most exponential as well.

Corollary 6.3.7. *1. For $\mathcal{EL}$-matching problems modulo equivalence*
  a) the cardinality of (minimal) s-complete sets of matchers can exponentially be bounded in the size of the matching problem; and
  b) the size of s-minimal matchers can exponentially be bounded in the size of the matching problem.
2. For $\mathcal{EL}$-matching problems modulo subsumption
  a) the cardinality of (minimal) s-complete and i-complete sets of matchers can exponentially be bounded in the size of the matching problem; and
  b) the size of s-minimal and i-minimal matchers can exponentially be bounded in the size of the matching problem.

Note that, due to Theorem 6.3.2, the size of matchers in minimal i-complete sets for matching problems modulo equivalence can polynomially be bounded in the size of the matching problem. Our matching algorithm might compute bigger matchers though.

We now explore the computational complexity of the algorithm in Figure 6.1 (and its adapted version for matching modulo subsumption). Subsumption of $\mathcal{EL}$-concept descriptions can be decided by a polynomial time algorithm [BKM99]. As already mentioned, the size of a substitution σ computed by our matching algorithm is at most exponential in the size of the matching problem. Thus, $C \sqsupseteq \sigma(D)$ can be decided in time exponential in the size of the matching problem $C \equiv^? D$. Since the lcs of a sequence of $\mathcal{EL}$-concept descriptions can be computed in time exponential in the size of the sequence [BKM99], it is easy to see that the loop body of the algorithm in Figure 6.1 runs in exponential time. As mentioned above, there exists only an exponential number of mappings from $\mathcal{G}(D)$ into $\mathcal{G}(C)$. Given a mapping, it can be decided in time polynomial in the size of the matching problem whether it is a homomorphism. Consequently, our algorithm runs in time exponential in the size of the matching problem. According to Remark 3.2.1, given an s-complete set computed by the matching algorithm in Figure 6.3, a minimal s-complete (i-complete) set can be derived in time exponential in the size of the matching problem using a polynomial time subsumption algorithm for $\mathcal{EL}$-concept descriptions.

Corollary 6.3.8. *A (minimal) s-complete and i-complete set of matchers for an $\mathcal{EL}$-matching problem (both modulo equivalence and modulo subsumption) can be computed in time exponential in the size of the matching problem.*

Computing d-Minimal Matchers in $\mathcal{EL}$. After having investigated the problem of computing minimal i-complete sets, we now turn to the problem of computing minimal d-complete sets of matchers for matching modulo equivalence, i.e., the set of all d-minimal matchers up to s-equivalence (Definition 3.2.9).

Our results will reveal that the size of d-minimal matchers can polynomially be bounded in the size of the matching problem. Consequently, a naïve algorithm for computing the set of d-minimal matchers can simply enumerate all matchers up to the polynomial bound and only return those matchers that are d-minimal. However, such an algorithm would not be of much practical use. Therefore, here a much more sophisticated algorithm is developed building on a close relationship between reduced and s-maximal matchers. More precisely, we will show that the set of reduced matchers coincides with the one of s-maximal matchers if the variables are mapped onto reduced concept descriptions. Consequently, minimal d-complete sets can be computed as follows.

1. Compute the set of all s-maximal matchers up to s-equivalence;
2. reduce the images of the matchers computed in the first step.

By Corollary 6.3.2, given an $\mathcal{EL}$-concept description E, the corresponding reduced concept description $E\backslash\top$ can be computed in polynomial time in the size of E. Thus, reducing the images of matchers, as required in the second step of our algorithm, can be done in time polynomial in the size of the set computed in the first step.

In the sequel, we will first establish the correlation between reduced and s-maximal matchers. Then, an algorithm for computing s-maximal matchers is presented. Finally, we investigate the complexity of this algorithm.

S-Maximal and Reduced Matchers. Formally, the relationship between reduced and s-maximal matchers can be stated as follows.

Theorem 6.3.5. *Let $C \equiv^? D$ be an $\mathcal{EL}$-matching problem. Then, a matcher σ of this problem is reduced if, and only if, σ is s-maximal and $\sigma(X)$ is reduced for all variables X in D.*

The proof of the if direction of this theorem is rather easy to see: The main observation to use is that, for $\mathcal{EL}$-concept descriptions E, F, $E \preceq_d F$ implies $F \sqsubseteq E$, which is easy to verify by the definition of subdescription (Definition 3.2.3). Now, let σ be an s-maximal matcher with reduced images. Assume that σ is not reduced. Then, there exists a matcher τ with $\tau \prec_d \sigma$. In particular, there exists a variable X with $\tau(X) \prec_d \sigma(X)$. As above, we know $\tau \sqsupseteq_s \sigma$. Since $\sigma(X)$ is reduced, by Theorem 6.3.1 we can conclude $\tau(X) \sqsupseteq \sigma(X)$. Thus, $\tau \sqsupseteq_s \sigma$, which is a contradiction to the fact that σ is s-maximal. This completes the proof of the if direction.

The only-if direction is much more involved. Let σ be a reduced matcher. Then, by definition of reduced matchers, the images of the variables are reduced. It remains to show that σ is s-maximal. We lead the assumption that σ' is a matcher with $\sigma' \sqsupseteq_s \sigma$ to a contradiction.

The problem is that for $\mathcal{EL}$-concept descriptions E', F', $E' \sqsubseteq F'$ does not necessarily imply $F' \preceq_d E'$, e.g.,

$$E' := \exists r.(A \sqcap B) \text{ and } F' := \exists r.A \sqcap \exists r.B.$$

Otherwise, one could immediately lead the assumption $\sigma' \sqsupseteq_s \sigma$ to a contradiction.

From $\sigma' \sqsupseteq_s \sigma$ it follows that there exists a variable X in D with $\sigma'(X) \sqsupseteq \sigma(X)$. Let the substitution σ'' be defined as $\sigma''(X) := \sigma'(X)$ and $\sigma''(Y) := \sigma(Y)$ for all $Y \neq X$. Then, $C \equiv \sigma(D) \sqsubseteq \sigma''(D) \sqsubseteq \sigma'(D) \equiv C$. Thus, σ'' is also a matcher with $\sigma'' \sqsupseteq_s \sigma$. Therefore, we may assume that σ and σ' coincide on all variables, except on X. The core of the proof is to show that, for $\sigma(X)$ and $\sigma'(X)$, the phenomenon shown above for E', F' cannot occur. For this reason, we modify $\sigma'(X)$ in such a way that eventually the difference of $\sigma(X)$ and $\sigma'(X)$ corresponds to the one of E' and F', which then will lead to a contradiction with $C \equiv \sigma(D)$.

First, by Theorem 4.3.2, $\sigma'(X) \sqsupseteq \sigma(X)$ implies that $prim(\sigma'(X)) \subseteq prim(\sigma(X))$. We claim $prim(\sigma(X)) = prim(\sigma'(X))$. If a concept name P is in $prim(\sigma(X))$ but not in $prim(\sigma'(X))$, then one could delete P in $\sigma(X)$, which yields a substitution σ'' with $C \equiv \sigma(D) \sqsubseteq \sigma''(D) \sqsubseteq \sigma'(D) \equiv C$, i.e., σ'' is a matcher, and $\sigma''(X) \prec_d \sigma(X)$, which is a contradiction to the fact that σ is reduced.

Consequently, by Theorem 4.3.2, $\sigma'(X) \sqsupseteq \sigma(X)$ implies that there exists an existential restriction

$$\exists r.F \in \sigma(X) \text{ with } \sigma'(X) \not\sqsubseteq \exists r.F.$$

By an argument similar to the one above, we may assume that $\sigma'(X)$ and $\sigma(X)$ coincide on all existential restrictions but the ones for r. In the following, let

$$\exists r.F'_1, \ldots, \exists r.F'_l$$

be the existential restrictions for r on the top-level of $\sigma'(X)$ and

$$\exists r.F_1, \ldots, \exists r.F_k$$

the ones for $\sigma(X)$.

Again employing Theorem 4.3.2, from $\sigma'(X) \sqsupseteq \sigma(X)$ we can infer that there exists a mapping φ from $\{1, \ldots, l\}$ into $\{1, \ldots, k\}$ such that, for all $i \in \{1, \ldots, l\}$, $F_{\varphi(i)} \sqsubseteq F_i'$. We claim that φ is surjective. If φ is not surjective, then there exists a $j \in \{1, \ldots, k\}$ with $j \notin image(\varphi)$. Let σ'' be the substitution obtained from σ by removing the existential restriction $\exists r.F_j$ from $\sigma(X)$. Then, similar to the previous argument for $prim$, one can conclude that σ'' is still a matcher for $C \equiv^? D$, which again is a contradiction to the fact that σ is reduced and $\sigma'' \prec_d \sigma$. Thus, φ must be surjective.

Let x be the element in $\{1, \ldots, k\}$ with

$$F_x = F,$$

where F is defined as above. For $i \in \{1, \ldots, l\}$ and $\varphi(i) = x$ we know $F_x \sqsubset F_i'$ since $\sigma'(X) \not\sqsubseteq \exists r.F$. Let $\varphi^{-1}(x) =: \{l_1, \ldots, l_y\}$ be the set of all elements in $\{1, \ldots, l\}$ that are mapped onto x under φ. Since φ is surjective this set is not empty. Let σ'' be the substitution that coincides with σ, except that in $\sigma''(X)$ the existential restriction $\exists r.F_x$ is replaced by $\exists r.F_{l_1}' \sqcap \cdots \sqcap \exists r.F_{l_y}'$. Then, from $\sigma(X) \sqsubseteq \sigma''(X) \sqsubseteq \sigma'(X)$ it follows that σ'' is a matcher. Moreover, $\sigma''(X) \not\sqsubseteq \exists r.F$ because otherwise (Theorem 4.3.2) there must exist an existential restriction, say $\exists r.F'$, on the top-level of $\sigma''(X)$ with $F' \sqsubseteq F$. However, since σ is reduced, we know $F_i \not\sqsubseteq F_j$ for all $i, j \in \{1, \ldots, k\}$, $i \neq j$. Thus, the restriction $\exists r.F'$ in $\sigma''(X)$ cannot be some of the existential restriction also contained on the top-level of $\sigma(X)$. But then, F' must be one of the descriptions F_{l_j}', $j \in \{1, \ldots, l\}$, in contradiction to $F \sqsubset F_{l_j}'$. Consequently, from $\sigma(X) \sqsubseteq \exists r.F$ it follows that $\sigma'' \sqsupseteq_s \sigma$. Therefore, we may continue in the proof with σ'' instead of σ'. In what follows, let $\sigma' := \sigma''$. Note that, for σ' thus obtained, the difference between $\sigma'(X)$ and $\sigma(X)$ exactly corresponds to the one between E' and F' described above. We will now show that this contradicts to the fact that σ is a matcher.

Since $C \equiv \sigma'(D)$, there is a homomorphism ψ from $\mathcal{G}(C \backslash \top)$ into $\mathcal{G}(\sigma'(D))$. Let $N_D(Y)$ and $\mathcal{G}_{\sigma'(Y),m}$ be defined as above Lemma 6.3.1. As usual, $\mathcal{G}(\sigma'(D))$ is considered to be the instantiation of $\mathcal{G}(D)$ by σ'.

The following lemma says that not all of the existential restrictions $\exists r.F_{l_j}'$ can be removed from $\sigma'(X)$ if one wants to keep the property that ψ is a homomorphism from $\mathcal{G}(C \backslash \top)$ into $\mathcal{G}(\sigma'(D))$. For $m \in N_D(X)$ and X defined above, let $m_1, \ldots, m_y$ be the direct successors of m in $\mathcal{G}(\sigma'(D))$ with $C_{(\mathcal{G}_{\sigma'(X),m})_{m_j}} = F_{l_j}'$ (modulo commutativity and associativity of concept conjunction).

Lemma 6.3.7. *There exists a node* $m \in N_D(X)$, $j \in \{1, \ldots, y\}$, *and* $n' \in \mathcal{G}(C \backslash \top)$ *with* $\psi(n') = m_j$.

Proof. Assume that there does not exist such a node m. Let σ'' be the substitution obtained by removing all existential restrictions $\exists r.F'_{l_i}$ in $\sigma'(X)$. Then, $\sigma'' \prec_d \sigma$, $\sigma(X) \sqsubseteq \sigma''(X)$, and thus $\sigma(D) \sqsubseteq \sigma''(D)$. If ψ was still a homomorphism from $\mathcal{G}(C \backslash \top)$ into $\mathcal{G}(\sigma''(D))$, where $\mathcal{G}(\sigma''(D))$ is, w.l.o.g., considered to be a rooted subtree of $\mathcal{G}(\sigma'(D))$, then $C \sqsupseteq \sigma''(D)$. Thus, σ'' is a matcher, which is a contradiction to the fact that σ is reduced and $\sigma'' \prec_d \sigma$. $\square$

We will now show that ψ can be modified in such a way that it is a homomorphism from $\mathcal{G}(C \backslash \top)$ into $\mathcal{G}(\sigma(D))$ which does not have the properties shown in Proposition 6.3.2. From this it follows that $C \not\equiv \sigma(D)$, a contradiction. The modification of ψ is defined as follows. If, for all $m \in N_D(X)$, the subtrees with root m_i and the edges leading to these nodes in $\mathcal{G}(\sigma'(D))$ are deleted and replaced by one direct r-successor m' with a subtree corresponding to $F = F_x$, then the resulting tree is the one for $\sigma(D)$. Since $F'_{l_i} \sqsupseteq F$, the nodes n' in $\mathcal{G}(C \backslash \top)$ mapped on some m_i can now be mapped on m' and for successors of n' one can modify ψ in such a way that ψ is a homomorphism from $\mathcal{G}(C \backslash \top)_{n'}$ into $\mathcal{G}(\sigma(D))_{m'}$. This yields a homomorphism from $\mathcal{G}(C \backslash \top)$ into $\mathcal{G}(\sigma(D))$. However, for m, j, n' as defined in Lemma 6.3.7 and the r-successor m' of m we know by construction that $\psi(n') = m'$, and for some j, $\mathcal{G}(C \backslash \top)_{n'} \sqsupseteq F'_{l_j} \sqsupseteq F \equiv \mathcal{G}(\sigma(D))_{m'}$. Then, with Proposition 6.3.2, we can conclude that $C \not\equiv \sigma(D)$, a contradiction. This completes the proof of Theorem 6.3.5.

Computing s-Maximal Matchers. According to Lemma 3.2.5, computing all s-maximal matchers up to s-equivalence corresponds to computing minimal s-co-complete sets. In what follows, we present an algorithm that computes s-co-complete sets. Given such a set, a *minimal* s-co-complete set can easily be computed along the lines of Remark 3.2.1.

In the proof of Theorem 6.3.2 we have shown that, given a matcher σ' of $C \equiv^? D$, a matcher σ of size polynomial in the size of the matching problem can be constructed with $\sigma' \sqsubseteq_s \sigma$. Consequently, the size of s-maximal matcher can polynomially be bounded. This exhibits that, in order to compute all s-maximal matchers (up to s-equivalence), it is sufficient to enumerate all substitutions of size polynomially bounded in the size of the matching problem and filter out the ones that do not solve the problem or that are not s-maximal. This can obviously be done by an exponential time algorithm.

Clearly, such an algorithm is not of practical use. For this reason, we present an algorithm which cuts down the space of potential matchers significantly. Roughly speaking, this algorithm for computing s-co-complete sets is the dual version of the one in Figure 6.1, which computes s-complete sets. The duality occurs at three places of the algorithm.

– The algorithm in Figure 6.1 computes homomorphisms from $\mathcal{G}(D)$ into $\mathcal{G}(C)$, whereas now (partial) homomorphisms from $\mathcal{G}(C)$ into $\mathcal{G}(D)$ are considered;

– for computing s-complete sets, possible matchers σ are constructed based on the lcs of concepts; now, σ is built from conjunctions of concepts;[4]
– the algorithm in Figure 6.1 ensures that $\sigma(D) \sqsupseteq C$ and needs to check $\sigma(D) \sqsubseteq C$, whereas now the algorithm guarantees $\sigma(D) \sqsubseteq C$ but checks $\sigma(D) \sqsupseteq C$.

In the sequel, we specify the algorithm for computing s-co-complete sets in detail. The idea behind the algorithm is as follows: As mentioned, we consider partial homomorphisms φ from $\mathcal{G}(C)$ into $\mathcal{G}(D)$ in the sense that i) certain nodes of $\mathcal{G}(C)$ need not be mapped onto nodes of $\mathcal{G}(D)$; and ii) for certain nodes the inclusion condition between labels need not hold. Now, substitutions σ are defined such that the parts of $\mathcal{G}(C)$ not mapped by φ and the labels violating the inclusion condition are covered by the concepts substituted for the variables in D. For this reason, a partial homomorphism implicitly associates with each variable a set of concepts that must be covered by this variable. (Note that, for a given partial homomorphism, there are different ways of associating concepts with variables.) In particular, the substitutions σ are defined in such a way that φ can be extended to a total homomorphism from $\mathcal{G}(C)$ into $\mathcal{G}(\sigma(D))$. Thus, the construction guarantees $\sigma(D) \sqsubseteq C$. More precisely, φ and σ will be constructed as follows. If a node n in $\mathcal{G}(C)$ is mapped onto a node n' in $\mathcal{G}(D)$ where the label of n' contains a variable X, then some rooted subtree $\mathcal{G}$ of $\mathcal{G}(C)_n$ need not be mapped by φ. This subtree is then part of one conjunct in the substitution for X. Other conjuncts may come from multiple occurrences of X in $\mathcal{G}(D)$. If the label of n' contains more than one variable, then only parts of $\mathcal{G}$ are substituted for X. One only needs to make sure that the substitutions for the variables in n' "cover" $\mathcal{G}$.

In the following definition, partial homomorphisms are specified more rigorously.

Definition 6.3.1. *For the $\mathcal{EL}$-concept description C and the $\mathcal{EL}$-concept pattern D let $\mathcal{G}(C) = (N_C, E_C, n_C, \ell_C)$ and $\mathcal{G}(D) = (N_D, E_D, n_D, \ell_D)$ be the corresponding description trees. Then, φ is a partial homomorphism from $\mathcal{G}(C)$ into $\mathcal{G}(D)$ if, and only if,*

– φ *is a partial mapping from N_C into N_D;*
– $n_C \in dom(\varphi)$ *and* $\varphi(n_C) = n_D$*;*
– $n \notin dom(\varphi)$ *implies that for all (direct) successors m of n in $\mathcal{G}(C)$, $m \notin dom(\varphi)$;*
– *If* $m \in dom(\varphi)$, $n \notin dom(\varphi)$, *and* $mrn \in E_C$ *for some role r, then* $\ell_D(\varphi(m))$ *contains a variable;*
– *for all* $n, m \in dom(\varphi)$, $nrm \in E_C$ *implies* $\varphi(n)r\varphi(m) \in E_D$;

---

[4] As mentioned in Section 3.1.1, the set of equivalence classes of $\mathcal{EL}$-concept descriptions together with the subsumption relationship forms a lattice (since $\mathcal{EL}$ allows for concept conjunction and the lcs always exists). In this lattice, the lcs of concepts is the supremum of the concepts and the conjunction is their infimum.

Input: $\mathcal{EL}$-matching problem $C \equiv^? D$ with C reduced
(otherwise take $C \backslash \top$ instead of C)
Output: s-co-complete set $\mathcal{C}$ of matchers for $C \equiv^? D$

$\mathcal{C} := \emptyset$
For all partial homomorphisms φ from $\mathcal{G}(C)$ into $\mathcal{G}(D)$
   For all tuples (n, X), $n \in N_\varphi^X$ and X variable in D
      guess rooted subtrees $\mathcal{G}_n^X$ of $\mathcal{G}_n$ such that $\mathcal{G}_n \sqsupseteq \underset{\substack{X \\ n \in N_\varphi^X}}{\sqcap} \mathcal{G}_n^X$

   For all variables X define $\sigma(X) := \underset{n \in N_\varphi^X}{\sqcap} C_{\mathcal{G}_n^X}$

   If $\sigma(D) \sqsupseteq C$, then $\mathcal{C} := \mathcal{C} \cup \{\sigma\}$.

Fig. 6.3. An Algorithm for Computing s-Co-complete Sets.

- If $n \in dom(\varphi)$ and $n \notin N_\varphi$, then $\ell_C(n) \subseteq \ell_D(\varphi(n))$ where $N_\varphi := \{n \in dom(\varphi) \mid \ell_D(\varphi(n))$ contains a variable$\}$.

For the matching problem $C_{ex} \equiv^? D_{ex}$ (cf. Figure 6.2), $\varphi := \{n_0 \mapsto m_0, n_1 \mapsto m_1, n_2 \mapsto m_2, n_3 \mapsto m_3\}$, where $\varphi(n_4)$ and $\varphi(n_5)$ are undefined, is an example of a partial homomorphism from $\mathcal{G}(C_{ex})$ into $\mathcal{G}(D_{ex})$.

In order to specify the algorithm, we need some more notation. For every $n \in N_\varphi$ (for N_φ see Definition 6.3.1), the subtree $\mathcal{G}_n = (N_n, E_n, n, \ell_n)$ of $\mathcal{G}(C)$ contains those parts of $\mathcal{G}(C)_n$ that need to be covered by the variables in $\ell_D(\varphi(n))$:

- $N_n := \{n\} \cup \{m \mid m$ is a (not necessarily direct) successor of n in $\mathcal{G}(C)$
                        with $m \notin dom(\varphi)\}$;
- $E_n := E_C \cap (N_n \times N_R \times N_n)$;
- $\ell_n(m) := \ell_C(m)$ for all $m \in N_n \backslash \{n\}$ and $\ell_n(n) := \ell_C(n) \backslash \ell_D(\varphi(n))$.

Furthermore, for a variable X we need the subset $N_\varphi^X := \{n \in dom(\varphi) \mid X \in \ell_D(\varphi(n))\}$ of N_φ.

Now, the algorithm for computing s-co-complete sets is depicted in Figure 6.3. Of course, the algorithm must compute every possible guess $\mathcal{G}_n^X$. Thus, in general, for one partial homomorphism several candidate matchers σ are computed.

The assumption that C is reduced has been made for two reasons: First, it simplifies the proof of soundness of the algorithm. Second, it reduces the number of homomorphisms, and thus, the number of computed matchers.

Before going into the soundness proof of the algorithm, we illustrate the algorithm by our example problem $C_{ex} \equiv^? D_{ex}$. Let φ be the partial homomorphism already defined. Then, $\mathcal{G}_{n_1} \equiv \mathsf{W} \sqcap \exists \mathsf{hc}.(\mathsf{W} \sqcap \mathsf{P})$, $\mathcal{G}_{n_2} \equiv \mathsf{W} \sqcap \mathsf{D} \sqcap \exists \mathsf{hc}.(\mathsf{W} \sqcap \mathsf{P})$, and $\mathcal{G}_{n_3} \equiv \mathsf{D}$. Thus, the algorithm can choose the trees $\mathcal{G}_n^X$ as follows: $\mathcal{G}_{n_1}^X \equiv \mathcal{G}_{n_2}^X \equiv \mathsf{W} \sqcap \exists \mathsf{hc}.(\mathsf{W} \sqcap \mathsf{P})$, $\mathcal{G}_{n_2}^Y \equiv \mathsf{D}$, and $\mathcal{G}_{n_3}^Y \equiv \mathsf{D}$.

Obviously, $\mathcal{G}_{n_1} \equiv C_{\mathcal{G}_{n_1}^X}$, $\mathcal{G}_{n_2} \equiv C_{\mathcal{G}_{n_2}^X} \sqcap C_{\mathcal{G}_{n_2}^Y}$, and $\mathcal{G}_{n_3} \equiv C_{\mathcal{G}_{n_3}^Y}$. Finally, the resulting substitution $\sigma := \{X \mapsto \mathsf{W} \sqcap \exists \mathrm{hc}.(\mathsf{W} \sqcap \mathsf{P}), Y \mapsto \mathsf{D}\}$ satisfies $\sigma(D) \sqsupseteq C$. Thus, σ is a matcher in the computed s-co-complete set. As an aside we note that σ coincides with the i-minimal and reduced matcher we obtained in Section 3.2.3.

Soundness of the Algorithm. Let $C \equiv^? D$ be an $\mathcal{EL}$-matching problem where C is reduced. We need to show (i) that every substitution $\sigma \in \mathcal{C}$ computed by the algorithm solves $C \equiv^? D$, and (ii) that $\mathcal{C}$ is indeed s-co-complete, i.e., for every matcher σ' of $C \equiv^? D$ there exists a matcher $\sigma \in \mathcal{C}$ with $\sigma \sqsupseteq_s \sigma'$.

In order to show (i), let $\sigma \in \mathcal{C}$. By definition of the algorithm, we know $\sigma(D) \sqsupseteq C$. Assume that σ is constructed with respect to the partial homomorphism φ. Now, the idea is to extend φ to a total homomorphism from $\mathcal{G}(C)$ into a tree $\mathcal{G}$ that contains $\mathcal{G}(D)$ as rooted subtree such that $\mathcal{G} \sqsupseteq \sigma(D)$. The tree $\mathcal{G}$ is defined as follows: for every X and node $n \in N_\varphi^X$ instantiate $\varphi(n)$ in $\mathcal{G}(D)$ by $\mathcal{G}_n^X$. Then, the condition $\mathcal{G}_n \sqsupseteq \sqcap_{X;n \in N_\varphi^X} \mathcal{G}_n^X$ ensures that φ can be extended to $\mathcal{G}_n$ for every $n \in N_\varphi$. But then, φ is a total homomorphism from $\mathcal{G}(C)$ into $\mathcal{G}$. Thus, $\mathcal{G}(C) \sqsupseteq \mathcal{G}$. By construction of σ, we know $\mathcal{G} \sqsupseteq \sigma(D)$. This yields $C \equiv \mathcal{G}(C) \sqsupseteq \sigma(D)$. Hence, σ solves the matching problem.

To prove (ii), let σ' be a matcher for $C \equiv^? D$. We prove that there exists a run of the algorithm in Figure 6.3, such that $\mathcal{C}$ contains a substitution σ with $\sigma \sqsupseteq \sigma'$.

Let the set $N_D(X)$ and the subtree $\mathcal{G}_{\sigma'(X),m} = (N_{X,m}, E_{X,m}, m, \ell_{X,m})$ of $\mathcal{G}(\sigma'(D))$ for a variables X in D and $m \in N_D(X)$ be defined as above Lemma 6.3.1. Since C is reduced, we know that there exists an injective homomorphism ψ from $\mathcal{G}(C) = (N_C, E_C, n_C, \ell_C)$ into $\mathcal{G}(\sigma'(D))$ (Proposition 6.3.2). We define a partial homomorphism φ from $\mathcal{G}(C)$ into $\mathcal{G}(D)$ as follows:

$$- \; dom(\varphi) := N_C \setminus \left(\bigcup_{\substack{X,m \\ m \in N_D(X)}} \psi^{-1}(N_{X,m} \setminus \{m\}) \right);$$

$- \; \varphi(n) := \psi(n)$ for all $n \in dom(\varphi)$.

It is easy to verify that φ is a partial homomorphism from $\mathcal{G}(C)$ into $\mathcal{G}(D)$. For $n \in N_\varphi^X$ we define $\mathcal{G}_n^X$ to be the description tree $\psi^{-1}(\mathcal{G}_{\sigma'(X),\varphi(n)})$, where we eliminate those concept names from the label of the root n of this tree that belong to $\ell_D(\varphi(n))$. We claim

$$\mathcal{G}_n \equiv \bigcap_{\substack{X \\ n \in N_\varphi^X}} \mathcal{G}_n^X.$$

Proof of the Claim: By definition of φ, we know that $\mathcal{G}_n$ is obtained by merging the trees $\psi^{-1}(\mathcal{G}_{\sigma'(X),\varphi(n)})$ for every X with $n \in N_\varphi^X$ where again in the label of n the concept names in $\ell_D(\varphi(n))$ are eliminated. Thus, $\mathcal{G}_n$ is obviously equivalent to the conjunction as stated above.

Now, define $\sigma(X) := \bigsqcap_{n \in N_\varphi^X} C_{\mathcal{G}_n^X}$ as in the algorithm. Let $\tau(X)$ be the conjunction defined above Lemma 6.3.2 (which is called $\sigma(X)$ there). Since $N_\varphi^X \subseteq N_D(X)$ and $\mathcal{G}_n^X$ is a rooted subtree of $\psi^{-1}(\mathcal{G}_{\sigma'(X),\varphi(n)})$, we can conclude $\sigma(X) \sqsupseteq \tau(X)$. By Lemma 6.3.2, it follows that $\tau(X) \sqsupseteq \sigma'(X)$, and thus $\sigma(X) \sqsupseteq \sigma'(X)$. In particular, $\sigma(D) \sqsupseteq \sigma'(D) \equiv C$. This shows that $\sigma \in \mathcal{C}$ and $\sigma \sqsupseteq_s \sigma'$, which completes the proof of soundness of the algorithm in Figure 6.3.

Complexity of Computing (Minimal) d-Complete Sets. The algorithm depicted in Figure 6.3 runs, like the naïve one, obviously in exponential time. As mentioned earlier, given an s-co-complete set, a *minimal* s-co-complete set can be computed in time polynomial in the size of the s-co-complete set, and thus, exponentially in the size of the matching problem. Finally, by Theorem 6.3.5, from such a minimal s-co-complete set one obtains a minimal d-complete set by computing equivalent and reduced concept descriptions for the images of every matcher in the s-co-complete set, which again can be carried out in time exponential in the size of the matching problem. The example

$$\exists r.A_1 \sqcap \cdots \sqcap \exists r.A_k \equiv^? \exists r.X_1 \sqcap \cdots \sqcap \exists r.X_k$$

shows that the cardinality of (minimal) d-complete sets can in fact grow exponentially in the size of the matching problem. Fortunately, the size of d-minimal matchers can be polynomially bounded in the size of the matching problem since, according to Theorem 6.3.5, the set of d-minimal matchers corresponds to the set of s-maximal matchers with reduced images, and, as shown above, the size of s-maximal matchers can be polynomially bounded.

Corollary 6.3.9. *For an $\mathcal{EL}$-matching problem modulo equivalence, a (minimal) d-complete set can be computed by an exponential time algorithm. Since the size of these sets may grow exponentially, this complexity upper bound is tight. The size of d-minimal matchers can be polynomially bounded in the size of the matching problem.*

Note that computing minimal d-complete sets is performed on matching problems of the form $\sigma(D) \equiv^? D$ where σ is an i-minimal matcher, which according to Corollary 6.3.6 may already be of size exponential in the size of the originally problem $C \sqsubseteq^? D$.

Also, observe that an s-co-complete set is only empty if the matching problem is not solvable. Thus, the algorithm in Figure 6.3 can be used as a non-deterministic polynomial time decision algorithm for the solvability of $\mathcal{EL}$-matching problems modulo equivalence. Such an algorithm would i) guess a partial homomorphism from $\mathcal{G}(C)$ into $\mathcal{G}(D)$, ii) guess subtrees $\mathcal{G}_n^X$ of $\mathcal{G}_n$ that satisfy the condition, and iii) check $\sigma(D) \sqsupseteq C$. This certainly provides us with a decision algorithm which is significantly improved compared to the naïve one presented above (see below Corollary 6.3.3).

6.3.2 Equivalence of $\mathcal{ALE}$-Concept Descriptions

In this and the following subsections, we generalize the techniques and results of Section 6.3.1 to $\mathcal{ALE}$. We first show that equivalence of $\mathcal{ALE}$-concept descriptions can be characterized in terms of isomorphisms between description trees of reduced concept descriptions. Just as for $\mathcal{EL}$, this result is important in different respects: First, as already stated in Section 3.2.3, it shows that equivalent and reduced concept descriptions syntactically coincide up to commutativity and associativity of concept conjunction (i.e., modulo the equation theory AC). Applied to matching, this means that the minimal set of i-minimal and reduced matchers (Definition 3.2.7) is uniquely determined modulo AC. Second, we will employ the characterization in order to prove complexity results for deciding the solvability of matching problems. Finally, the characterization is used in the context of computing minimal rewritings [BKM00], i.e., minimal representations of concept descriptions modulo an underlying TBox (see Section 3.4). All results presented in this subsection carry over to $\mathcal{FLE}$ when adapting the definitions appropriately.

E-Reduced $\mathcal{ALE}$-Concept Descriptions. The definition of reduced $\mathcal{ALE}$-concept descriptions (see Definition 3.2.4) intuitively means that reduced concepts do not contain redundancies. From the definition of reduced concept descriptions it follows that unsatisfiable subexpressions in concept descriptions must be made explicit by substituting them with the bottom-concept. In addition, since $\exists r.C \equiv \exists r.C \sqcap \exists r.D$ if $C \sqsubseteq D$, it is clear that reduced concept descriptions must not contain comparable existential restrictions (w.r.t. subsumption). Finally, concepts of the form $\forall r.C \sqcap \exists r.D$ are only reduced if D does not describe properties that are also described in C. For example, the description $\forall r.A \sqcap \exists r.(A \sqcap B)$ is not reduced because removing A in the existential restriction yields an equivalent concept description. Thus, although both conjuncts are reduced on their own, together with $\forall r.A$ the restriction $\exists r.(A \sqcap B)$ is not reduced anymore. This leads us to the following notion.

Definition 6.3.2. *Let F, E be $\mathcal{ALE}$-concept descriptions. Then, F is called E-reduced if there does not exist a strict subdescription F' of F ($F' \prec_d F$) with $F' \sqcap E \equiv F \sqcap E$.*

In the example, $\exists r.(A \sqcap B)$ is *not* $(\forall r.A)$-reduced.

Clearly, a concept description is reduced if, and only if, it is $\top$-reduced. The next lemma supports the intuition that, if a concept description is reduced with respect to some concept, then also with respect to a more general one.

Lemma 6.3.8. *Let F, E, H be $\mathcal{ALE}$-concept descriptions. If F is E-reduced, then $E \sqsubseteq H$ implies that F is also H-reduced.*

Proof. Assume that there exists a concept F' with $F' \prec_d F$ and $F' \sqcap H \equiv F \sqcap H$. Then, $F' \sqcap E \sqcap H \equiv F \sqcap E \sqcap H$, which (because of $E \sqsubseteq H$) implies $F' \sqcap E \equiv F \sqcap E$, in contradiction to the assumption that F is E-reduced. $\square$

The following proposition gives some deeper insight into the properties of E-reduced concepts. We use the notations $prim(C)$, $C.r$, and $\exists r.D \in C$ in the sense introduced in Section 4.3.2.

Proposition 6.3.3. *Let F and E be $\mathcal{ALE}$-concept descriptions in $\forall$-normal form. Then, F is E-reduced if, and only if, the following conditions are satisfied:*

1. *If $E \sqcap F \equiv \bot$, then $F = \bot$;*
2. *$prim(E) \cap prim(F) = \emptyset$; and every (negated) concept name on the top-level of F occurs exactly ones; unless $F = \top$, $\top \notin F$;*
3. *for all distinct existential restrictions $\exists r.F_1, \exists r.F_2 \in F$: $E.r \sqcap F.r \sqcap F_1 \not\sqsubseteq F_2$;*
4. *for all existential restrictions $\exists r.F' \in F$, $\exists r.E' \in E$: $E.r \sqcap F.r \sqcap E' \not\sqsubseteq F'$;*
5. *for all $r \in N_R$, a) $E.r \not\sqsubseteq F.r$ or b) there is no value restriction for r on the top-level of F;*
6. *for all $r \in N_R$, $F.r$ is $E.r$-reduced;*
7. *for all existential restrictions $\exists r.F' \in F$, F' is $(E.r \sqcap F.r)$-reduced.*

Proof. For the only-if direction, it is very easy to see that, if one of the conditions required above is not satisfied, then F is not E-reduced.

Let us thus turn to the if direction, and assume that Conditions 1.–7. are satisfied. Moreover, let F' be a concept description with $F' \preceq_d F$ and $E \sqcap F' \equiv E \sqcap F$. We want to show $F' = F$.

If $E \sqcap F \equiv \bot$, then condition 1. implies $F = \bot$. But then $F' = F$ since no concept description can be a strict subdescription of $\bot$.

Now, consider the case where $E \sqcap F \equiv E \sqcap F' \not\equiv \bot$. Theorem 4.3.2 implies that $prim(E) \cup prim(F) = prim(E) \cup prim(F')$. We also know that $prim(E)$ and $prim(F)$ are disjoint and $prim(F') \subseteq prim(F)$. Thus, $prim(F') = prim(F)$.

By the assumption $F' \preceq_d F$, we know $F'.r \preceq_d F.r$ for all roles r. Moreover, Theorem 4.3.2 ensures $E.r \sqcap F.r \equiv E.r \sqcap F'.r$. Since $F.r$ is $E.r$-reduced (Condition 6.), we know by induction $F'.r = F.r$.

Now, let $\exists r.F_1 \in F$ be an existential restriction on the top-level of F. Together with $E \sqcap F \equiv E \sqcap F'$, Theorem 4.3.2 implies that a) there exists an existential restriction $\exists r.F_1' \in F'$ with $E.r \sqcap F.r \sqcap F_1' \sqsubseteq F_1$ (recalling $F'.r = F.r$) or b) there exists an existential restriction $\exists r.E' \in E$ with $E.r \sqcap F.r \sqcap E' \sqsubseteq F_1$. Because of Condition 4., the case b) cannot occur. Analogously, for F_1' i) there exists an existential restriction $\exists r.F_2 \in F$ with $E.r \sqcap F.r \sqcap F_2 \sqsubseteq F_1'$ or ii) there exists an existential restriction $\exists r.E'' \in E$ with $E.r \sqcap F.r \sqcap E'' \sqsubseteq F_1'$. Now, ii) implies $E.r \sqcap F.r \sqcap E'' \sqsubseteq E.r \sqcap F.r \sqcap F_1$ in contradiction to Condition 4. Then, from i) and Condition 3. we can conclude $F_1 = F_2$. In particular, $E.r \sqcap F.r \sqcap F_1 \equiv E.r \sqcap F.r \sqcap F_1'$.

Now, assume that some existential restriction on the top-level of F has been removed from F to obtain F', then the number of existential restrictions on the top-level of F' is smaller than the number of existential restrictions on the top-level of F. Hence, using what has just been proved, there exist two different existential restrictions $\exists r.F_1, \exists r.F_2 \in F$ and one existential restriction $\exists r.F_1' \in F'$ with $E.r \sqcap F.r \sqcap F_1 \equiv E.r \sqcap F.r \sqcap F_2 \equiv E.r \sqcap F.r \sqcap F_1'$, in contradiction to Condition 3. Thus, no existential restriction of F can have been removed to obtain F'. In particular, for every $\exists r.F_1 \in F$ there exists an existential restriction $\exists r.F_1' \in F'$ with $F_1' \preceq_d F_1$. Again, Condition 3. ensures that $E.r \sqcap F.r \sqcap F_1 \equiv E.r \sqcap F.r \sqcap F_1'$. Finally, with Condition 7. and $F_1' \preceq_d F_1$ we can deduce $F_1' = F_1$.

To sum up, we have shown $F = F'$.   □

In order to establish the main theorem of this subsection, namely the characterization of equivalence of reduced concepts, we need to prove that two concepts that are equivalent modulo a given concept and reduced w.r.t. that concept must in fact be equivalent.

Lemma 6.3.9. *Let C, D, E be $\mathcal{ALE}$-concept descriptions in $\forall$-normal from. If $E \sqcap C \equiv E \sqcap D$ and C, D are E-reduced, then $C \equiv D$.*

Proof. If $E \sqcap C \equiv E \sqcap D \equiv \bot$, then we know $C = D = \bot$. Now, assume $E \sqcap C \equiv E \sqcap D \not\equiv \bot$.

i) By Proposition 6.3.3, we know that $prim(C)$ and $prim(D)$ are disjoint from $prim(E)$. Then, Theorem 4.3.2 implies $prim(C) = prim(D)$.

ii) Let $r \in N_R$. By Proposition 6.3.3, 6., $C.r, D.r$ are $E.r$-reduced. Moreover, with Theorem 4.3.2 we can conclude $E.r \sqcap C.r \equiv E.r \sqcap D.r$. Then, by induction, it follows that $C.r \equiv D.r$.

iii) By Theorem 4.3.2, we know that for every existential restriction $\exists r.D' \in D$ a) there exists an existential restriction $\exists r.C' \in C$ with $E.r \sqcap D.r \sqcap C' \sqsubseteq E.r \sqcap D.r \sqcap D'$ (recalling $C.r \equiv D.r$) or b) there exists an existential restriction $\exists r.E' \in E$ with $E.r \sqcap D.r \sqcap E' \sqsubseteq E.r \sqcap D.r \sqcap D'$. However, since D is E-reduced, by Proposition 6.3.3 b) cannot occur. Analogously, for $\exists r.C'$ there exists an existential restriction $\exists r.D'' \in D$ such that $E.r \sqcap D.r \sqcap D'' \sqsubseteq E.r \sqcap D.r \sqcap C'$. Since D is E-reduced, we can conclude that $D' = D''$. Therefore, $E.r \sqcap D.r \sqcap D' \equiv E.r \sqcap D.r \sqcap C'$. By Proposition 6.3.3, 7., D' is $(E.r \sqcap D.r)$-reduced and C' is $(E.r \sqcap C.r)$-reduced. Since $E.r \sqcap D.r \equiv E.r \sqcap C.r$, Lemma 6.3.8 implies that C' is also $(E.r \sqcap D.r)$-reduced. Now, induction yields $C' \equiv D'$. Analogously, by symmetry, for every existential restriction $\exists r.C' \in C$ there exists an existential restriction $\exists r.D' \in D$ with $D' \equiv C'$.

Finally, from i), ii), and iii) it follows that $C \equiv D$.   □

As a corollary of the following theorem, we can deduce that, as already mentioned in Section 3.2.3, equivalent and reduced $\mathcal{ALE}$-concept descriptions syntactically coincide modulo AC.

Theorem 6.3.6. *Let C, D, E be $\mathcal{ALE}$-concept descriptions in $\forall$-normal form where C, D are E-reduced. Then, $C \equiv D$ if, and only if, $\mathcal{G}(C) \cong \mathcal{G}(D)$.*

Proof. The if direction of the statement is trivial. We proceed by proving the only-if direction. If $E \sqcap C \equiv \bot$, then by Proposition 6.3.3 $C = \bot$. As a consequence, $D \equiv \bot$, but then $E \sqcap D \equiv \bot$ implies $D = \bot$, which shows $\mathcal{G}(C) \cong \mathcal{G}(D)$.

Now, assume that $E \sqcap C \equiv E \sqcap D \not\equiv \bot$. The proof proceeds by induction on the depths of the quantifiers of C, D and E. We inductively construct an isomorphism from $\mathcal{G}(C)$ onto $\mathcal{G}(D)$.

i) Since $C \equiv D \not\equiv \bot$, Theorem 4.3.2 implies $prim(C) = prim(D)$. Thus, mapping the root of $\mathcal{G}(C)$ to the root of $\mathcal{G}(D)$ satisfies the isomorphism conditions at the roots.

ii) From Theorem 4.3.2 we can conclude that, for every $r \in N_R$, $C.r \equiv D.r$. By Proposition 6.3.3, $C.r$, $D.r$ are $E.r$-reduced. Thus, induction yields $\mathcal{G}(C.r) \cong \mathcal{G}(D.r)$. Consequently, we can extend the isomorphism from i) to the value restrictions.

iii) Theorem 4.3.2 also implies that, for every existential restriction $\exists r.D' \in D$ there exists an existential restriction $\exists r.C' \in C$ such that $D.r \sqcap C' \sqsubseteq D.r \sqcap D'$, recalling $D.r \equiv C.r$. Analogously, for C' there exists an existential restriction $\exists r.D'' \in D$ with $D.r \sqcap D'' \sqsubseteq D.r \sqcap C'$. Hence, $D.r \sqcap D'' \sqsubseteq D.r \sqcap D'$, and adding $E.r$, $E.r \sqcap D.r \sqcap D'' \sqsubseteq E.r \sqcap D.r \sqcap D'$. Since D is E-reduced, it follows that $D' = D''$. Therefore, $E.r \sqcap D.r \sqcap C' \equiv E.r \sqcap D.r \sqcap D'$. By Proposition 6.3.3, C' is $(E.r \sqcap C.r)$-reduced and D' is $(E.r \sqcap D.r)$-reduced. From Lemma 6.3.8 we can conclude that D' is also $(E.r \sqcap C.r)$-reduced. Then, employing Lemma 6.3.9 we obtain $C' \equiv D'$. Again, induction yields $\mathcal{G}(C') \cong \mathcal{G}(D')$. Since C is E-reduced, we know that for D' there is exactly one C' equivalent to D'. Analogously, for every existential restriction $\exists r.C' \in C$ there exists exactly one existential restriction $\exists r.D' \in D$ with $C' \equiv D'$. This means that there exists a bijection, mapping every existential restriction $\exists r.D'$ in D to a restriction $\exists r.C'$ in C with $D' \equiv C'$.

From i), ii), and iii) it follows that $\mathcal{G}(C) \cong \mathcal{G}(D)$.   □

Computing Reduced $\mathcal{ALE}$-Concept Descriptions. In the following, we show that every $\mathcal{ALE}$-concept description C can be turned into an equivalent $\top$-reduced, and thus reduced concept, which by Theorem 6.3.6 is uniquely determined modulo AC. More generally, we show how to compute E-reduced concept descriptions.

Definition 6.3.3. *Let F, E, and H be $\mathcal{ALE}$-concept descriptions in $\forall$-normal form. Then, H is called the E-reduced concept of F ($F\backslash E$ for short) if, and only if, H is E-reduced and $H \sqcap E \equiv F \sqcap E$.*

If H' is also an E-reduced concept of F, then with $H'\sqcap E \equiv H\sqcap E \equiv F\sqcap E$ and Lemma 6.3.9 it follows that $H' \equiv H$. Moreover, Theorem 6.3.6 guarantees that H and H' coincide modulo AC. Therefore, it makes sense to refer to *the* E-reduced concept of F.

The following proposition is an easy consequence of Proposition 6.3.3. It states that $F\backslash E$ can be obtained by removing those parts of F that are redundant w.r.t. E.

Proposition 6.3.4. *Let F, E, and H be $\mathcal{ALE}$-concept descriptions in $\forall$-normal form. Then, H is the E-reduced concept of F if, and only if,*

$H = \bot$ *in case $E \sqcap F \equiv \bot$; otherwise*

1. *$prim(H) = prim(F) \setminus prim(E)$; and every concept name on the top-level of H only occurs ones; unless $H = \top$, $\top \notin H$;*
2. *for all $r \in N_R$, $H.r = F.r \setminus E.r$ and H does not have a value restriction for r on its top-level if $H.r = \top$;*
3. *for all $r \in N_R$, let $\exists r.H_1, \ldots, \exists r.H_q \in H$, $\exists r.F_1, \ldots, \exists r.F_k \in F$ as well as $\exists r.E_1, \ldots, \exists.E_l \in E$ be all existential restrictions on the top-level of H, F, and E, respectively. Then, there exists a subset $\{C_1, \ldots, C_q\}$ of $\{F_1, \ldots, F_k\}$ such that*
   a) *there do not exist $j_1, j_2 \in \{1, \ldots, q\}$, $j_1 \neq j_2$, with $E.r \sqcap F.r \sqcap C_{j_1} \sqsubseteq C_{j_2}$;*
   b) *there does not exist $i \in \{1, \ldots, l\}$ and $j \in \{1, \ldots, q\}$ with $E.r \sqcap F.r \sqcap E_i \sqsubseteq C_j$;*
   c) *for all $i \in \{1, \ldots, k\}$ a) there exists $j \in \{1, \ldots, q\}$ with $E.r \sqcap F.r \sqcap C_j \sqsubseteq F_i$ or b) there exists $j \in \{1, \ldots, l\}$ with $E.r \sqcap F.r \sqcap E_j \sqsubseteq F_i$; and*
   d) *for all $j \in \{1, \ldots, q\}$, $H_j = C_j \setminus (E.r \sqcap F.r)$.*

From this proposition one can easily derive a polynomial time algorithm (with an oracle for subsumption) that computes $F \setminus E$. The main challenge is to compute the set $\{C_1, \ldots, C_q\}$ efficiently. This can be done by iteratively removing those F_i's that do not satisfy the conditions (a) and (b). Then, the remaining F_i's form the desired set. We summarize this and other simple properties of $F \setminus E$ in the following lemma.

Lemma 6.3.10.   1. *$F \setminus E$ is uniquely determined modulo AC.*
2. *$F \setminus E \preceq_d F$.*
3. *$|F \setminus E| \leq |F|$ where, as usual, $|\cdot|$ denotes the size of a concept.*
4. *$F \setminus \top \equiv F$.*
5. *$F \setminus E$ can be computed by a polynomial time algorithm with an oracle for deciding subsumption.*

As an easy consequence, for $\top$-reduction we obtain the following corollary.

Corollary 6.3.10. *Let F be an $\mathcal{ALE}$-concept description in $\forall$-normal form. Then, the reduced and equivalent subdescription $F \setminus \top$ of F can be computed in polynomial time using an oracle for subsumption. For all $\mathcal{ALE}$-concept descriptions F', $F \equiv F'$ implies $|F \setminus \top| \leq |F'|$.*

Proof. The first part of the corollary is a direct consequence of Lemma 6.3.10. It remains to show $|F \setminus \top| \leq |F'|$ for all $F' \equiv F$. First, note that turning a concept into its $\forall$-normal form decreases the size of the concept. Therefore, we can assume that F' is in $\forall$-normal form. But now $F \setminus \top \equiv F' \setminus \top \equiv F$ implies $|F \setminus \top| = |F' \setminus \top| \leq |F'|$.   □

In the following subsections, we will need a stronger version of Theorem 6.3.6, where only one concept description is reduced. For this purpose, the notion $\perp$-extension is introduced: Let C be an $\mathcal{ALE}$-concept description. Then, the $\perp$-*extension* $C_\perp$ of C denotes the $\mathcal{ALE}$-concept description obtained from C by adding $\perp$ at all positions in C such that the resulting concept description is equivalent to C. In other words, in $C_\perp$ unsatisfiable subexpressions are made explicit. Analogously, $\perp$-extensions $\mathcal{G}_\perp$ of description trees $\mathcal{G}$ are defined.

Proposition 6.3.5. *Let C, D be equivalent $\mathcal{ALE}$-concept descriptions in $\forall$-normal form and let C be reduced. Then, there exists an injective homomorphism from $\mathcal{G}(C)$ into $\mathcal{G}(D_\perp)(= \mathcal{G}(D)_\perp)$.*

Proof. By Theorem 6.3.6, we know that there exists an isomorphism ψ from $\mathcal{G}(C)$ onto $\mathcal{G}(D\backslash\top)$. By Lemma 6.3.10, $D\backslash\top$ is a subdescription of D. But then, $\mathcal{G}(D\backslash\top)$ must be a rooted subtree of $\mathcal{G}(D_\perp)$. Consequently, ψ is an injective homomorphism from $\mathcal{G}(C)$ into $\mathcal{G}(D_\perp)$.   □

Since inconsistency cannot be expressed by $\mathcal{FLE}$-concept descriptions, the above proposition can be simplified when dealing with $\mathcal{FLE}$-concept descriptions in that $D_\perp$ is replaced by D.

6.3.3 Deciding the Solvability of Matching in $\mathcal{FLE}$

As an immediate consequence of Lemma 3.2.3 and the fact that subsumption in $\mathcal{FLE}$ is NP-complete [DHL$^+$92], we obtain the following complexity bounds for matching modulo subsumption.

Corollary 6.3.11. *Deciding the solvability of $\mathcal{FLE}$-matching problems modulo subsumption is NP-complete.*

Clearly, matching modulo equivalence is also NP-hard. The main contribution of this subsection is to show a matching complexity upper bound. More precisely, just as for $\mathcal{EL}$, it will be proved that, for solvable matching problems of the form $C \equiv^? D$, there always exists a matcher of size polynomially bounded in the size of the matching problem. Then, an NP-decision algorithm can simply guess a candidate matcher of this bounded size and check whether it actually solves the problem.

The reason why we consider $\mathcal{FLE}$ separately from $\mathcal{ALE}$ is twofold. First, as mentioned, results for one language not necessarily carry over to sublanguages. Second, the proof for $\mathcal{FLE}$ differs from the one for $\mathcal{ALE}$ in that, for $\mathcal{FLE}$, matchers can always be built from conjunctions of subdescriptions of C. Although for $\mathcal{ALE}$ we can establish a polynomial upper bound for the size of matchers, no further information about the structure of the matchers is known. We conjecture that, with the additional information gained for $\mathcal{FLE}$, it is possible to specify an algorithm for computing d-complete sets similar to the one for $\mathcal{EL}$ in Section 6.3.1. This would also yield an improved decision algorithm for the solvability of matching modulo equivalence as it significantly prunes the search space for candidate matchers.

The proof for $\mathcal{FLE}$ makes heavy use of reduced concept descriptions in $\forall$-normal form. Therefore, as a first step towards proving the complexity upper bound, we need to introduce so-called $\forall$-mappings that turn description trees into their $\forall$-normal from.

The $\forall$-Mapping. Recall that, on concept descriptions, the $\forall$-rule is of the form

$$\forall r.E \sqcap \forall r.F \longrightarrow \forall r.(E \sqcap F).$$

Applied to a description tree $\mathcal{G} := (N, E, n, \ell)$, this rule results in merging certain nodes of $\mathcal{G}$: Let n, n_1, n_2 be nodes of $\mathcal{G}$ and $r \in N_R$ with $n \forall r n_1, n \forall r n_2 \in E$. Now, applying the $\forall$-rule to n requires to *merge* n_1 and n_2, i.e. a new node $n_1 \otimes n_2$ with label $\ell(n_1) \cup \ell(n_2)$ is constructed and in all edges of $\mathcal{G}$, n_1 and n_2 are replaced by $n_1 \otimes n_2$. Just as for concepts, $\mathcal{G}$ is in $\forall$-*normal form* if the $\forall$-rule cannot be applied.

As just described, the $\forall$-rule takes $\mathcal{G}$ into a new tree $\mathcal{G}'$ where two nodes of $\mathcal{G}$ are merged. This induces a homomorphism from $\mathcal{G}$ into $\mathcal{G}'$ where n_1 and n_2 are mapped onto $n_1 \otimes n_2$ in $\mathcal{G}'$ and all other nodes are mapped onto themselves.

Exhaustively applying the $\forall$-rule to $\mathcal{G}$ induces a sequence $\varphi_1, \ldots, \varphi_k$ of homomorphisms such that $\varphi := \varphi_k \circ \cdots \circ \varphi_1$ is a homomorphism from $\mathcal{G}$ into the $\forall$-normal form of $\mathcal{G}$; φ is called the $\forall$-*mapping* of $\mathcal{G}$. Important properties of φ are summarized in the following lemma.

Lemma 6.3.11.   *1. φ is a homomorphism from $\mathcal{G}$ into the $\forall$-normal form of $\mathcal{G}$.*

2. If $\mathcal{H}$ is a subtree of $\mathcal{G}$, then $\varphi(\mathcal{H})$ is the $\forall$-normal form of $\mathcal{H}$; in particular, $\varphi(\mathcal{H}) \equiv \mathcal{H}$.

3. If the subtree $\mathcal{H}$ of $\mathcal{G}$ is in $\forall$-normal form, then $\varphi(\mathcal{H})$ is isomorphic to $\mathcal{H}$.

NP-Completeness of Matching Modulo Equivalence. The main result of this subsection is summarized in the following theorem, from which an NP-decision algorithm for the solvability of $\mathcal{FLE}$-matching problems modulo equivalence can immediately be derived.

Theorem 6.3.7. *If the $\mathcal{FLE}$-matching problem $C \equiv^? D$ is solvable, then there exists a matcher of size polynomially bounded in the size of the matching problem, which only uses concept names and role names already contained in the matching problem.*

Just as for $\mathcal{EL}$, we construct a matcher σ polynomially bounded in the size of the matching problem (using only identifiers in C) from a given matcher σ' of $C \equiv^? D$. Without loss of generality, we may assume that $\sigma'(X)$ is in $\forall$-normal form for every variable X in D. We also assume that C is reduced; otherwise consider the problem $C \backslash \top \equiv^? D$.

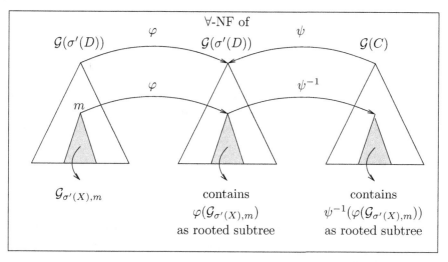

Fig. 6.4. The $\forall$-Mapping φ and the Injective Homomorphism ψ.

Let φ denote the $\forall$-mapping from $\mathcal{G}(\sigma'(D))$ onto its $\forall$-normal form. Then, according to Proposition 6.3.5, there exists an injective homomorphism ψ from $\mathcal{G}(C)$ into $\varphi(\mathcal{G}(\sigma'(D)))$.

As usual, let $N_D(X) := \{m \in \mathcal{G}(D) \mid X \in \mathcal{G}(D)(m)\}$ denote the set of nodes in $\mathcal{G}(D)$ with X in their label and let $\mathcal{G}_{\sigma'(X),m}$ be a copy of $\mathcal{G}(\sigma'(X))$ with m as its root. According to Lemma 6.3.1, the description tree $\mathcal{G}(D)$ can be viewed as rooted subtree of $\mathcal{G}(\sigma'(D))$, where $\mathcal{G}(\sigma'(D))$ is obtained by instantiating $\mathcal{G}(D)$ at $m \in N_D(X)$ with a $\mathcal{G}_{\sigma'(X),m}$.

Now, σ is defined as follows:

$$\sigma(X) := \prod_{m \in N_D(X)} C_{\psi^{-1}(\varphi(\mathcal{G}_{\sigma'(X),m}))}$$

for every variable X in D. The construction is illustrated in Figure 6.4.

As in the case of $\mathcal{EL}$ (Section 6.3.1), $\sigma(X)$ is defined as a conjunction of subdescriptions of C. This means that, if an $\mathcal{FLE}$-matching problem has a solution, then this solution can be constructed from subdescriptions of C.

The main difference between $\mathcal{FLE}$ and $\mathcal{EL}$ is that now σ is defined according to the $\forall$-normal form of $\sigma'(D)$. This is necessary to guarantee the existence of ψ. The image $\psi(\mathcal{G}(C))$ of ψ identifies those parts of the $\forall$-normal form of $\mathcal{G}(\sigma'(D))$, i.e., $\varphi(\mathcal{G}(\sigma'(D)))$, that together are equivalent to C. Intuitively, $\sigma(X)$ is defined such that the $\forall$-normal form of $\mathcal{G}(\sigma(D))$ covers these parts of $\varphi(\mathcal{G}(\sigma'(D)))$.

Just as for $\mathcal{EL}$, we first show that σ is more general than σ'.

Lemma 6.3.12. $\sigma \sqsupseteq_s \sigma'$.

Proof. Let $m \in N_D(X)$. By Lemma 4.3.1, we know that ψ is a homomorphism from $\psi^{-1}(\varphi(\mathcal{G}_{\sigma'(X),m}))$ into $\psi(\psi^{-1}(\varphi(\mathcal{G}_{\sigma'(X),m})))$, which, according to

Lemma 4.3.2, is a rooted subtree of $\varphi(\mathcal{G}_{\sigma'(X),m})$. Thus, ψ is a homomorphism from $\psi^{-1}(\varphi(\mathcal{G}_{\sigma'(X),m}))$ into $\varphi(\mathcal{G}_{\sigma'(X),m})$. Then, Remark 4.3.1 implies $\psi^{-1}(\varphi(\mathcal{G}_{\sigma'(X),m})) \sqsupseteq \varphi(\mathcal{G}_{\sigma'(X),m})$. According to Lemma 6.3.11, $\varphi(\mathcal{G}_{\sigma'(X),m})$ is equivalent to $\mathcal{G}_{\sigma'(X),m}$, and by definition, $\mathcal{G}_{\sigma'(X),m} \equiv \sigma'(X)$. This shows that $C_{\psi^{-1}(\varphi(\mathcal{G}_{\sigma'(X),m}))} \sqsupseteq \mathcal{G}_{\sigma'(X),m} \equiv \sigma'(X)$, and hence, $\sigma(X) \sqsupseteq \sigma'(X)$.   □

As a direct consequence, Lemma 3.2.1 ensures $\sigma(D) \sqsupseteq \sigma'(D) \equiv C$. The subsumption relationship in the other direction is stated in the following lemma.

Lemma 6.3.13. $\sigma(D) \sqsubseteq C$.

Proof. Since $\sigma'(X)$ is in ∀-normal form, from Lemma 6.3.11 we can conclude that, for every $m \in N_D(X)$, $\varphi(\mathcal{G}_{\sigma'(X),m})$ is isomorphic to $\mathcal{G}_{\sigma'(X),m}$. Furthermore, Lemma 4.3.2 ensures that $\psi(\psi^{-1}(\varphi(\mathcal{G}_{\sigma'(X),m}))$ is a rooted subtree of $\varphi(\mathcal{G}_{\sigma'(X),m})$, and thus isomorphic to a rooted subtree of $\mathcal{G}_{\sigma'(X),m}$. In the sequel, we will call this subtree $\mathcal{G}_{X,m}$ and refer to the isomorphism from $\mathcal{G}_{X,m}$ onto the corresponding subtree in $\varphi(\mathcal{G}_{\sigma'(X),m})$ by $\psi_{X,m}$. Hence,

$$\mathcal{G}_{X,m} = \psi_{X,m}^{-1}(\psi(\psi^{-1}(\varphi(\mathcal{G}_{\sigma'(X),m})))).$$

Note that $\psi_{X,m}(n) = \varphi(n)$ for every $n \in \mathcal{G}_{X,m}$.

Let $\mathcal{G}$ be the description tree obtained from $\mathcal{G}(D)$ as follows:

For every X and $m \in N_D(X)$ instantiate $\mathcal{G}(D)$ at m by $\mathcal{G}_{X,m}$.

By construction, $\mathcal{G}$ is a rooted subtree of $\mathcal{G}(\sigma'(D))$. We will prove that ψ is a homomorphism from $\mathcal{G}(C)$ into $\varphi(\mathcal{G})$. If this is the case, then Remark 4.3.1 implies that $\mathcal{G}(C) \sqsupseteq \varphi(\mathcal{G})$. Moreover, observe that for, $m \in N_D(X)$, $C_{\psi^{-1}(\varphi(\mathcal{G}_{\sigma'(X),m}))}$ is equivalent to the tree $\psi(\psi^{-1}(\varphi(\mathcal{G}_{\sigma'(X),m})))$ (see Lemma 4.3.2), which is a rooted subtree of $\varphi(\mathcal{G}_{\sigma'(X),m})$, and which is isomorphic to $\mathcal{G}_{X,m}$. Thus, $C_{\psi^{-1}(\varphi(\mathcal{G}_{\sigma'(X),m}))} \equiv \mathcal{G}_{X,m}$. As an immediate consequence of the definition of σ and the definition of $\mathcal{G}$ we then obtain $\mathcal{G} \sqsupseteq \mathcal{G}(\sigma(D))$. Summing up, we have $C \equiv \mathcal{G}(C) \sqsupseteq \varphi(\mathcal{G}) \equiv \mathcal{G} \sqsupseteq \mathcal{G}(\sigma(D)) \equiv \sigma(D)$.

Thus, in order to complete the prove it remains to show that ψ is a homomorphism from $\mathcal{G}(C)$ into $\varphi(\mathcal{G})$. To do so, we first show that the image of ψ is a subset of the nodes of $\varphi(\mathcal{G})$. Second, we prove that ψ preserves the edge relationships of $\mathcal{G}(C)$. Finally, it is shown that the label condition imposed on homomorphism is satisfied.

1. Let $n \in \mathcal{G}(C)$. If there exists a node $n' \in \mathcal{G}(D)$ with $\varphi(n') = \psi(n)$, then, as $n' \in \mathcal{G}$, we know $\psi(n) \in \varphi(\mathcal{G})$. In case there does not exist a node $n' \in \mathcal{G}(D)$ with $\varphi(n') = \psi(n)$, then there exists a variable X in D and a node $m \in N_D(X)$ as well as $n' \in \mathcal{G}_{\sigma'(X),m}$ with $\varphi(n') = \psi(n)$. Hence, $\psi(\psi^{-1}(\varphi(n')) = \psi(n)$. Therefore, $\psi_{X,m}^{-1}(\psi(n))$ is an element of $\mathcal{G}_{X,m}$, and thus of $\mathcal{G}$. Also, $\varphi(\psi_{X,m}^{-1}(\psi(n))) = \psi(n) \in \varphi(\mathcal{G})$. This shows that $\psi(n) \in \varphi(\mathcal{G})$ for every $n \in \mathcal{G}(C)$.

2. Let $n, w \in \mathcal{G}(C)$, $r \in N_R$, and $nrw \in \mathcal{G}(C)$. We know that ψ is a homomorphism from $\mathcal{G}(C)$ into $\varphi(\mathcal{G}(\sigma'(D)))$. Therefore, $\psi(n)r\psi(m) \in \varphi(\mathcal{G}(\sigma'(D)))$. As verified above, $\psi(n), \psi(m) \in \varphi(\mathcal{G})$ and $\mathcal{G}$ is a rooted subtree of $\mathcal{G}(\sigma'(D))$. Consequently, $\psi(n)r\psi(m) \in \varphi(\mathcal{G})$. The same can be shown for $\forall$-edges of $\mathcal{G}(C)$.

3. It remains to show that $\mathcal{G}(C)(n) \subseteq \varphi(\mathcal{G})(\psi(n))$ for every node $n \in \mathcal{G}(C)$. Assume that $A \in \mathcal{G}(C)(n)$. We know $\mathcal{G}(C)(n) \subseteq \varphi(\mathcal{G}(\sigma'(D)))(\psi(n))$. By the definition of homomorphic images (Definition 4.3.4), there exists a node $n' \in \mathcal{G}(\sigma'(D))$ with $\varphi(n') = \psi(n)$ and $A \in \mathcal{G}(\sigma'(D))(n')$. If $n' \in \mathcal{G}(D)$ and $A \in \mathcal{G}(D)(n')$, then, as $\mathcal{G}$ extends $\mathcal{G}(D)$, it follows that $A \in \mathcal{G}(n')$, and therefore, $A \in \varphi(\mathcal{G})(\varphi(n'))$. Otherwise, there exists a variable X in D and $m \in N_D(X)$ as well as $n' \in \mathcal{G}_{\sigma'(X),m}$ with $\varphi(n') = \psi(n)$ and $A \in \mathcal{G}_{\sigma'(X),m}(n')$. As a result, $A \in \varphi(\mathcal{G}_{\sigma'(X),m})(\varphi(n'))$. Together with $A \in \mathcal{G}(C)(n)$, this implies $A \in \psi^{-1}(\varphi(\mathcal{G}_{\sigma'(X),m}))(n)$. Therefore, $A \in \psi(\psi^{-1}(\varphi(\mathcal{G}_{\sigma'(X),m})))(\psi(n))$. Consequently, $A \in \mathcal{G}_{X,m}(\psi_{X,m}^{-1}(\psi(n))$, which shows that $A \in \varphi(\mathcal{G}_{X,m})(\psi(n))$. Thus, $A \in \varphi(\mathcal{G})(\psi(n))$. □

From Lemma 6.3.12 and 6.3.13 we can conclude that σ is a matcher of the problem $C \equiv^? D$. Moreover, by construction, σ only uses identifiers occurring in C. In order to complete the proof of Theorem 6.3.7, it remains to show that the size of σ is polynomially bounded in the size of the matching problem.

Lemma 6.3.14. *For every variable X in D, the size of $\sigma(X)$ is polynomially bounded in the size of C.*

Proof. By Lemma 4.3.2, we know that $\psi^{-1}(\varphi(\mathcal{G}_{\sigma'(X),m}))$ is a subtree of $\mathcal{G}(C)$. Thus, $C_{\psi^{-1}(\varphi(\mathcal{G}_{\sigma'(X),m}))}$ is linearly bounded in the size of C. This shows that $\sigma(X)$ is bounded by the product $|D| \cdot |C|$. □

Together with the already known hardness result, Theorem 6.3.7 yields the following computational complexity for matching modulo equivalence.

Corollary 6.3.12. *Deciding the solvability of $\mathcal{FLE}$-matching problems modulo equivalence is NP-complete.*

6.3.4 Deciding the Solvability of Matching in $\mathcal{ALE}$

In this subsection, we investigate the complexity of deciding the solvability of matching problems in $\mathcal{ALE}$. Due to unsatisfiable concept descriptions, the proofs become more involved. However, just as for $\mathcal{EL}$ and $\mathcal{FLE}$, the computational complexity of subsumption in $\mathcal{ALE}$ immediate carries over to matching modulo subsumption.

Corollary 6.3.13. *The problem of deciding the solvability of $\mathcal{ALE}$-matching problems modulo subsumption is NP-complete.*

Of course, matching modulo equivalence is NP-hard too. Again, the main difficulty is to show that this problem can be decided by a non-deterministic polynomial time algorithm. Similar to $\mathcal{EL}$ and $\mathcal{FLE}$, we obtain this complexity upper bound as follows: Given some matcher σ', we construct a matcher σ of size polynomially bounded in the size of the matching problem. Then, as a direct consequence, we can derive a (naïve) NP-decision algorithm for the solvability of matching problems modulo equivalence. For $\mathcal{EL}$ and $\mathcal{FLE}$, such a matcher σ has been built as a conjunction of subdescriptions of C. For $\mathcal{ALE}$, however, it is not clear whether there always exists such a matcher. Therefore, we define $\sigma(X)$ as a certain subdescription of $\sigma'(X)$. In this construction, an important step is to show that an unsatisfiable concept contains a "small" unsatisfiable subexpression. For this reason, we introduce the notion of "traces". Throughout this subsection, by "subexpression of C" we mean a subdescription of C (Definition 3.2.3) where none of the parts of C can be replaced by $\bot$. Thus, a subexpression of C is literally obtained from C by removing some parts of C.

Traces and Unsatisfiable Concepts. We shall show that, for every unsatisfiable concept description C, there exists an unsatisfiable subexpression C' of C of size polynomially bounded in the role depth $depth(C)$ of C.

A first characterization of unsatisfiable $\mathcal{ALE}$-concept descriptions is due to results by Donini et al. [DHL$^+$92]. In their work, a tableau-based algorithm is employed to test unsatisfiability. One can simulate their approach by applying the following so-called *p-rule* ('p' for propagation) to concept descriptions (see also Definition 4.3.6):

$$\forall r.E \sqcap \exists r.F \longrightarrow \forall r.E \sqcap \exists r.(F \sqcap E).$$

A concept description is in *p-normal form* if the p-rule cannot be applied (in the same sense as stated for the rules in Definition 4.3.6). A concept description can be turned into p-normal form by exhaustively applying the p-rule. The p-rule can be applied directly to description trees as well. If $m_0 r m_1, m_0 \forall r m_2$ are edges in $\mathcal{G}$, then applying the p-rule means instantiating $\mathcal{G}$ at m_1 with a copy of $\mathcal{G}_{m_2}$. Now, analogously to concept descriptions, a description tree is in p-normal form if the p-rule cannot by applied. Also, every description tree can be turned into p-normal form by exhaustively applying the p-rule. We denote the p-normal form of $\mathcal{G}(C)$ by $\mathcal{G}^p(C)$.

Based on the results in [DHL$^+$92], it is easy to see that unsatisfiability can be described in terms of the existence of certain $\exists$-paths in $\mathcal{G}^p(C)$.

Lemma 6.3.15. *Let C be an $\mathcal{ALE}$-concept description. Then, $C \equiv \bot$ iff $\mathcal{G}^p(C)$ contains a rooted $\exists$-path p of length less or equal $depth(C)$ such that the last node of p has i) $\bot$ or ii) P and $\neg P$ in its label for some concept name P.*

Such an $\exists$-path corresponds to a role chain in an ABox leading to contradictory assertions $x : \bot$, or $x : P$ and $x : \neg P$ (also called *clash*).

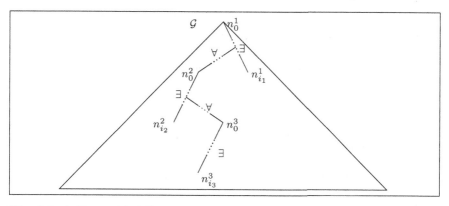

Fig. 6.5. A Trace with 3 Segments.

Recall that we are interested in a "small" unsatisfiable subexpression of an unsatisfiable concept C. According to Lemma 6.3.15, the p-normal form of such a subdescription of C should contain an $\exists$-path leading to an unsatisfiable label. The question is which parts of C are necessary to obtain such a path. We now define so-called traces, which exactly describe those parts of a concept description that contribute to $\exists$-paths in the p-normal form of a concept description. Intuitively, a trace of a graph $\mathcal{G}$ consists of segments of $\exists$-paths in $\mathcal{G}$ which are connected via $\forall$-paths such that the propagation of value restrictions onto existential restrictions results in a contiguous $\exists$-path. The following formal definition of traces is illustrated in Figure 6.5. In the sequel, $\neg N_C := \{\neg A \mid A \in N_C\}$ denotes the set of negated concept names.

Definition 6.3.4. *Let $\mathcal{G} = (N, E, n_0, \ell)$ be an $\mathcal{ALE}$-description tree and L be a finite subset of $N_C \cup \neg N_C \cup \{\bot\}$. Then, a trace t of the tree $\mathcal{G}$ labeled $r_1^1 \cdots r_{i_1}^1 \cdots r_1^l \cdots r_{i_l}^l L$ is a tuple $(\bar{t}, \cdot^t)$ where $\bar{t}$ is a sequence*

$$n_0^1, \ldots, n_{i_1}^1, \ldots, n_0^l, \ldots, n_{i_l}^l$$

of nodes of $\mathcal{G}$ and $\cdot^t$ is a mapping that takes every $A \in L$ to a node A^t in $\mathcal{G}$ such that

1. *$n_0^1 = n_0$;*
2. *for all $j = 1, \ldots l$, $n_0^j r_1^j \cdots r_{i_j}^j n_{i_j}^j$ is an $\exists$-path in $\mathcal{G}$;*
3. *for all $j = 2, \ldots, l$ there exists an $x \in \{1, \ldots, j{-}1\}$ and a $y \in \{0, \ldots, i_x{-}1\}$ such that there exists a $\forall$-path in $\mathcal{G}$ from n_y^x to n_0^j labeled $r_{y+1}^x \cdots r_{i_x}^x r_1^{x+1} \cdots r_{i_{j-1}}^{j-1}$; and*
4. *for all $A \in L$, the following holds: i) $A \in \ell(A^t)$ and ii) there exists an $x \in \{1, \ldots, l\}$ and a $y \in \{0, \ldots, i_x\}$ such that there is a $\forall$-path from n_y^x to A^t in $\mathcal{G}$ labeled $r_{y+1}^x \cdots r_{i_l}^l$ in case $y < i_x$ and $r_1^{x+1} \cdots r_{i_l}^l$ otherwise. Note that, if $x = l$ and $y = i_x$, then the $\forall$-path is labeled with the empty word ε.*

We write $n \in t$ if n occurs in $\bar{t}$ or in the image of $\cdot^t$. The trace t as defined above is said to consist of l segments of the form $n_0^j, \ldots, n_{i_j}^j$. As an example of a trace, consider the description tree depicted in Figure 4.6. The sequence n_0, n_1, n_7, n_8 together with $P^t := n_8$ defines a trace in $\mathcal{G}_{C_2}$ labeled $rr\{P\}$ with 2 segments.

In order to state the desired relationship between $\exists$-paths in p-normalized trees and traces in the corresponding unnormalized trees, we need the following notations: Let L be a finite subset of $N_C \cup \neg N_C \cup \{\bot\}$. Then, a rooted $\exists$-path in $\mathcal{G}$ labeled $r_1 \cdots r_k L$ stands for a rooted $\exists$-path in $\mathcal{G}$ labeled $r_1 \cdots r_k$ where the label of the last node in the path has L as subset. Such a rooted $\exists$-path can be viewed as a trace with one segment.

Lemma 6.3.16. *Let $\mathcal{G}$ be an $\mathcal{ALE}$-description tree and $\mathcal{G}^p$ its p-normal form. Then, $\mathcal{G}^p$ contains a rooted $\exists$-path labeled $r_1 \cdots r_k L$ iff there exists a trace in $\mathcal{G}$ labeled $r_1 \cdots r_k L$.*

Proof. The if-direction of the statement is easy to prove by induction on the number of segments l of the trace. For the only-if direction, assume that $\mathcal{G}_0, \mathcal{G}_1, \ldots, \mathcal{G}_z$ with $\mathcal{G}_0 := \mathcal{G}$ and $\mathcal{G}_z := \mathcal{G}^p$ denote the sequence of graphs obtained when turning $\mathcal{G}$ into its p-normal form $\mathcal{G}^p$.

We now show that, if $\mathcal{G}_{i+1}$ contains a trace labeled $r_1 \cdots r_k L$, then $\mathcal{G}_i$ contains such a trace. By induction, this implies that, for every trace in $\mathcal{G}_z$, there exists a trace in $\mathcal{G}_0$ with the same label. In particular, for a rooted $\exists$-path in $\mathcal{G}^p$ labeled $r_1 \cdots r_k L$ there exists a trace in $\mathcal{G}$ with the same label.

Let $\mathcal{G}_{i+1} = (N_{i+1}, E_{i+1}, n_0, \ell_{i+1})$ be obtained from $\mathcal{G}_i = (N_i, E_i, n_0, \ell_i)$ by applying the p-rule at $m_0 \in \mathcal{G}_i$ with $m_0 r m_1, m_0 \forall r m_2 \in \mathcal{G}_i$. This means that $\mathcal{G}_{i+1}$ is obtained by instantiating $\mathcal{G}_i$ at m_1 by a copy $\mathcal{G}'$ of $(\mathcal{G}_i)_{m_2}$. In what follows, we call the nodes in $\mathcal{G}'$, except for its root, *new* nodes. All other nodes in $\mathcal{G}_{i+1}$ are called *old*. The node a new node originates from is called *corresponding old node*.

Now, let t be a trace in $\mathcal{G}_{i+1}$ labeled $r_1 \cdots r_k L$. We prove that there exists a trace in $\mathcal{G}_i$ with the same label. We distinguish two cases:

1. t only contains old nodes:
   a) If $m_1 \notin t$, then, obviously, t is a trace in $\mathcal{G}_i$ since old nodes only have old nodes as their predecessors. Furthermore, the labels of the nodes in t coincide for $\mathcal{G}_i$ and $\mathcal{G}_{i+1}$.
   b) Assume $m_1 \in t$. We define a new trace t' as follows: The sequence of t' coincides with the one for t. If, for $A \in L$, A is not in the label of $\ell_i(m_1)$, but $A^t = m_1$, then $A^{t'} := m_2$; $\cdot^{t'}$ coincides with $\cdot^t$ on all other elements of L. It is easy to see that t' thus defined is a trace in $\mathcal{G}_i$ with label $r_1 \cdots r_k L$.
2. Assume that t contains new nodes m. First, we consider the case where L is the empty set. Then, m must belong to one of the segments, i.e., there exists $x \in \{1, \ldots, l\}$ and $y \in \{0, \ldots, i_x\}$ with $m = n_y^x$. We choose x to be minimal and for this x we assume that y is minimal as well, i.e.,

we choose the first segment x of t containing a new node and within this segment we choose the first new node. Again, two cases are distinguished:

a) If m is connected to its predecessor by a $\forall$-edge, then, by definition of $\mathcal{G}_{i+1}$ and m, there must exist an $\forall$-path from m_1 to m. But then it is easy to verify that replacing the new nodes by their corresponding old ones yields a trace in $\mathcal{G}_i$ labeled $r_1 \cdots r_k L$.

b) If m is connected to its predecessor by an $\exists$-edge, then, because of the minimality of x and y, the predecessor must be m_1. Now, a new trace is constructed as follows. The xth segment is pruned to end with m_1. We introduce an additional segment after this segment containing m_2, m, and all successors of m previously belonging to the xth segment in t. In this and all subsequent segments, all new nodes are replaced by their corresponding old nodes. It is not hard to prove that the resulting trace is a trace in $\mathcal{G}_i$ labeled $r_1 \cdots r_k L$.

If L is not the empty set, then in either case replacing every new node A^t, $A \in L$, by its corresponding old node yields a trace labeled $r_1 \cdots r_k L$ in $\mathcal{G}_i$. Note that there cannot exist an $A \in L$ with $A^t = m_1$ since the rooted path to A^t must have the same length as the one to $n_{i_l}^l$. But since t contains new nodes and new nodes only occur after m_1, the path to $n_{i_l}^l$ is longer than the one to m_1. Therefore, the problem dealt with in 1.,(b) cannot occur here. $\square$

A trace t of $\mathcal{G}$ induces a rooted subtree $\mathcal{G}_t$ of $\mathcal{G}$ in the following way.

Definition 6.3.5. *Let t be a trace in $\mathcal{G}$ labeled $r_1 \cdots r_k L$. Then, $\mathcal{G}_t$ is defined to be a subtree of $\mathcal{G}$ containing all nodes of t and their predecessors. For a node $n \in \mathcal{G}_t$, its label $\mathcal{G}_t(n)$ is defined as follows:*

$$A \in \mathcal{G}_t(n) \text{ iff there exists } A \in L \text{ with } A^t = n.$$

Obviously, $\mathcal{G}_t$ contains t as a trace and the size of $\mathcal{G}_t$ is polynomially bounded in the size of the label $r_1 \cdots r_k L$ of t. As an immediate consequence of Lemma 6.3.16 we obtain:

Corollary 6.3.14. *Let t be a trace in $\mathcal{G}$ labeled $r_1 \cdots r_k L$. Then, $\mathcal{G}_t^p$ contains a rooted $\exists$-path labeled $r_1 \cdots r_k L$.*

An unsatisfiable subexpression C' of C now corresponds to $\mathcal{G}_t$ where t is a trace in $\mathcal{G}(C)$ which induces the $\exists$-path in $\mathcal{G}^p(C)$ that leads to a clash.

Theorem 6.3.8. *Let C be an $\mathcal{ALE}$-concept description. Then, $C \equiv \bot$ if, and only if, there exists an subexpression C' of C of size polynomially bounded in $depth(C)$ such that $C' \equiv \bot$.*

Proof. The if direction of the theorem is trivial. Let us assume that C is unsatisfiable. Define $\mathcal{G} := \mathcal{G}(C)$. Then, by Lemma 6.3.15, $\mathcal{G}^p$ contains a rooted $\exists$-path labeled $r_1 \cdots r_k L$ where $L = \{\bot\}$ or $L = \{P, \neg P\}$ for some concept name P. According to Lemma 6.3.16, $\mathcal{G}$ contains a trace t labeled $r_1 \cdots r_k L$. By Corollary 6.3.14, we know that $\mathcal{G}_t$ is an unsatisfiable rooted subtree of $\mathcal{G}$. We define C' to be the subexpression $C_{\mathcal{G}_t}$ of C.

It remains to show that the size of $\mathcal{G}_t$ (and thus C') is polynomially bounded in the size of C. First, note that L is a set of cardinality at most two. Thus, the size of the label $r_1 \cdots r_k L$ is linear in k. Moreover, $k \leq depth(C)$ by Lemma 6.3.15. Finally, as mentioned above, the size of $\mathcal{G}_t$ is polynomially bound in the size of the label of t. Thus, the size of C' is polynomially bounded in $depth(C)$.   □

NP-Completeness of Matching in $\mathcal{ALE}$. We now prove the following theorem:

Theorem 6.3.9. *If the $\mathcal{ALE}$ matching problem $C \equiv^? D$ is solvable, then there exists a matcher of size polynomially bounded in the size of the matching problem which only uses concept names and role names already contained in the matching problem.*

First, we show that for solvable matching problems there always exist matchers where the role depth of the image of every variable is restricted by the role depth of C. For this purpose, we prove a more general statement, which will be used later on as well.

Proposition 6.3.6. *For every matcher τ of the $\mathcal{ALE}$-matching problem $C \equiv^? D$, there exists a matcher τ' such that $\tau'(X)$ is a subdescription of $\tau(X)$ with $depth(\tau'(X)) \leq depth(C)$ for all variables X in D and $\tau'(X)$ only contains identifiers already used in C.*

Proof. First, every $\tau(X)$ can be turned into $\top$-normal form, which yields a matcher τ'' of $C \equiv^? D$ with $\tau(X) \equiv \tau''(X)$ and $\tau''(X)$ subdescription of $\tau(X)$ for all variables X in D. Since, $C \equiv \tau''(D)$, by Theorem 4.3.1 we know that there exists a homomorphism φ from $\mathcal{G}^\top_{\tau''(D)}$ into $\mathcal{G}_C$. According to Lemma 6.3.1, $\mathcal{G}(\tau''(D))$ is the instantiation of $\mathcal{G}(D)$ by τ''. Since $\tau''(X)$ is in $\top$-normal form, the copies of $\mathcal{G}(\tau''(X))$ in $\mathcal{G}^\top_{\tau''(D)}$ remain unchanged in case $\tau''(X) \neq \top$ when going from $\mathcal{G}(\tau''(D))$ to $\mathcal{G}^\top_{\tau''(D)}$. Now, by the definition of a homomorphism, it is easy to see that every node n in (a copy of) $\mathcal{G}(\tau''(X))$ which is reached by a rooted path in $\mathcal{G}(\tau''(X))$ of length greater $depth(\mathcal{G}_C)(\leq depth(C))$ must be mapped by φ on a node m in $\mathcal{G}_C$ with $\bot$ in its label. But then, also the predecessor n' of n must be mapped on m. Consequently, in $\mathcal{G}(\tau''(X))$ the label of n' can be replaced by $\bot$ and one can remove the subtrees of n'. The same is true if n' has an outgoing edge labeled by a role name not used in C. Furthermore, if a node n' in $\mathcal{G}(\tau''(X))$ contains a (negated) concept name not used in C, then this node must also be mapped on a node in $\mathcal{G}_C$ containing $\bot$. Again, the label of n' can be replaced by $\bot$ and one can remove the subtrees of n'. Modifying $\mathcal{G}(\tau''(X))$ in this way provides us with the description tree for $\tau'(X)$ of the desired matcher τ'.   □

Now, let σ' be a matcher of $C \equiv^? D$ with $depth(\sigma'(X)) \leq depth(C)$ such that $\sigma'(X)$ only contains identifiers already used in C. We assume C to be reduced as otherwise one can consider $C \backslash \top \equiv^? D$ instead. Also, w.l.o.g., we may assume that $\sigma'(X)$ is in $\forall$-normal form for every variable X in D. In the following, we will turn σ' into a new matcher σ of size polynomially bounded in the size of the matching problem $C \equiv^? D$. More precisely, our proof proceeds in two steps:

1. We define a rooted subtree $\mathcal{G}$ of $\mathcal{G}(\sigma'(D))$ of size polynomially bounded in the size of the matching problem $C \equiv^? D$ such that $\mathcal{G} \sqsubseteq C$; we are guaranteed to have $\mathcal{G} \sqsupseteq \mathcal{G}(\sigma'(D))(\equiv C)$ since $\mathcal{G}$ is a rooted subtree of $\mathcal{G}(\sigma'(D))$. Intuitively, $\mathcal{G}$ comprises only those parts of $\mathcal{G}(\sigma'(D))$ that are necessary to ensure $\mathcal{G} \sqsubseteq C$.
2. Using $\mathcal{G}$, we define $\sigma(X)$ by keeping only those parts of $\sigma'(X)$ that are sufficient to guarantee that $\mathcal{G}$ is a rooted subtree of $\mathcal{G}(\sigma(D))$.

Then, since $\mathcal{G}$ is a rooted subtree of $\mathcal{G}(\sigma(D))$, it follows that $\sigma(D) \sqsubseteq C$. On the other hand, by construction $\sigma(X) \sqsupseteq \sigma'(X)$, and thus, $C \equiv \sigma'(D) \sqsubseteq \sigma(D)$. It remains to construct $\mathcal{G}$ appropriately and to prove the properties claimed.

To do so, just as for $\mathcal{FLE}$, we employ the $\forall$-mapping φ on $\mathcal{G}(\sigma'(D))$. According to Proposition 6.3.5, there exists an injective homomorphism ψ from $\mathcal{G}(C)$ into the $\bot$-extension

$$\mathcal{H} := \varphi(\mathcal{G}(\sigma'(D)))_\bot$$

of $\varphi(\mathcal{G}(\sigma'(D)))$.

The first "approximation" of $\mathcal{G}$ is

$$\mathcal{G}' := \varphi^{-1}(\psi(\mathcal{G}(C))).$$

For $\mathcal{FLE}$, this would already yield the rooted subtree $\mathcal{G}$ of $\mathcal{G}(\sigma'(D))$ we are interested in. However, $\mathcal{G}'$ is not sufficient in the presence of unsatisfiable concepts. In order to see this point, assume that n is a node in $\mathcal{G}(C)$ labeled $\bot$. Then, $\mathcal{G}'$ contains all nodes $n' \in \varphi^{-1}(\psi(n))$. But the label of n' in $\mathcal{G}(\sigma'(D))$ need not necessarily contain $\bot$. Thus, $\mathcal{G}'(n')$ might not contain $\bot$, and hence, $\mathcal{G}' \sqsubseteq C$ does not hold in general. The inconsistency at the node $\psi(n)$ in $\mathcal{H}$ might rather be caused by an interaction of certain subtrees in $\varphi(\mathcal{G}(\sigma'(D)))$. One needs to extend $\mathcal{G}'$ by these subtrees. Before extending $\mathcal{G}'$ accordingly to $\mathcal{G}$, we will identify the subtrees in $\varphi(\mathcal{G}(\sigma'(D)))$ that contribute to the inconsistency in $\psi(n)$.

Let n be a node in $\mathcal{G}(C)$ labeled $\bot$. By definition of $\mathcal{H}$, the node $\psi(n)$ in $\mathcal{H}$ has $\bot$ in its label. Intuitively, a subtree of $\varphi(\mathcal{G}(\sigma'(D)))$ contributes to the inconsistency at $\psi(n)$, if the root, say m, of this subtree is connected to a predecessor of $\psi(n)$ via a $\forall$-path such that the label of this path corresponds to the label of the suffix of the path to $\psi(n)$, i.e., when propagating value restrictions onto existential restrictions, m would be propagated to $\psi(n)$. Formally, this set of nodes m is defined as follows: Let $N_{\psi(n)}$ be the set of all nodes m in $\varphi(\mathcal{G}(\sigma'(D)))$ with a (not necessarily direct) predecessor m' such that (i) m' has $\psi(n)$ as its (not necessarily direct) successor; and (ii) if the path from the root of $\varphi(\mathcal{G}(\sigma'(D)))$ to $\psi(n)$ is labeled $r_1 \cdots r_k$ and the path to m' is labeled $r_1 \cdots r_l$, $l \leq k$, then the path from m' to m is a $\forall$-*path* in $\varphi(\mathcal{G}(\sigma'(D)))$ labeled $r_{l+1} \cdots r_k$. Observe that, by definition, $\psi(n) \in N_{\psi(n)}$. Now, we define

$$C_{\psi(n)} := \bigsqcap_{m \in N_{\psi(n)}} C_{\varphi(\mathcal{G}(\sigma'(D)))m}$$

to be the conjunction of (at least) all those parts of $\varphi(\mathcal{G}(\sigma'(D)))$ that contribute to the inconsistency at the node $\psi(n)$.

Lemma 6.3.17. $C_{\psi(n)} \equiv \bot$.

As an immediate consequence of the definition of φ, we also obtain the following lemma.

Lemma 6.3.18. $C_{\psi(n)} \equiv \bigsqcap_{m \in \varphi^{-1}(N_{\psi(n)})} C_{\mathcal{G}(\sigma'(D))m}$.

Because of Lemma 6.3.18, one may be tempted to extend $\mathcal{G}'$ by $\mathcal{G}(\sigma'(D))_m$ for every $m \in \varphi^{-1}(N_{\psi(n)})$. However, the size of such an extension might not be polynomially bounded in the size of the matching problem $C \equiv^? D$. Therefore, we can only extend $\mathcal{G}'$ by certain parts of $C_{\psi(n)}$. Since $depth(\sigma'(X)) \leq depth(C)$, we know that $depth(C_{\psi(n)}) \leq depth(C) + depth(D)$. By Theorem 6.3.8, $C_{\psi(n)}$ contains an unsatisfiable subexpression $C'_{\psi(n)}$ of size polynomially bounded in $depth(C) + depth(D)$. According to Lemma 6.3.18, $\mathcal{G}(C'_{\psi(n)})$ is built from rooted subtrees $\mathcal{G}_{n,m}$ of $\mathcal{G}(\sigma'(D))_m$, $m \in \varphi^{-1}(N_{\psi(n)})$. Note that some of the trees $\mathcal{G}_{n,m}$ might correspond to $\top$. Clearly, these trees do not contribute to the inconsistency. Now, $\mathcal{G}'$ is extended to $\mathcal{G}$ by adding all $\mathcal{G}_{n,m} \not\equiv \top$ to $\mathcal{G}'$. Of course, all predecessors of m in $\mathcal{G}(\sigma'(D))$ must be added as well to obtain a (connected) tree.

Formally, $\mathcal{G}' = (N', E', n_0, \ell')$ is extended to $\mathcal{G} = (N, E, n_0, \ell)$ as follows: Let $M := \{n \in \mathcal{G}(C) \mid \bot \in \mathcal{G}(C)(n)\}$ and $M_n := \{m \mid m \in \varphi^{-1}(N_{\psi(n)}), \mathcal{G}_{n,m} \not\equiv \top\}$. For $n \in M$, $m \in M_n$, $\mathcal{G}_{n,m} = (N_{n,m}, E_{n,m}, m, \ell_{n,m})$, $N''' := \bigcup_{n \in M} \bigcup_{m \in M_n} N_{n,m}$, and $\mathcal{G}(\sigma'(D)) = (N'', E'', n_0, \ell'')$, let

- $N := N' \cup N''' \cup \{m \mid m$ is a predecessor in $\mathcal{G}(\sigma'(D))$ for some node in $N'''\}$;
- $E := E'' \cap N \times (N_R \cup \forall N_R) \times N$;
- $\ell(n') := \ell'(n') \cup \bigcup_{n \in M, m \in M_n} \ell_{n,m}(n')$ where $\ell'(n') := \emptyset$ in case $n' \notin N'$ and $\ell_{n,m}(n') := \emptyset$ in case $n' \notin N_{n,m}$.

With the tree $\mathcal{G}$ thus defined, we are able to show that $\mathcal{G}$ contains (at least) all those parts of $\mathcal{G}(\sigma'(D))$ necessary for $\mathcal{G}$ to be subsumed by C.

Lemma 6.3.19. $\mathcal{G} \sqsubseteq C$.

Proof. We show that ψ is a homomorphism from $\mathcal{G}(C)$ into the $\bot$-extension $\varphi(\mathcal{G})_\bot$ of $\varphi(\mathcal{G})$. Since $\varphi(\mathcal{G}) \equiv \mathcal{G}$ (cf. Lemma 6.3.11) and $\mathcal{G}(C) \equiv C$, Remark 4.3.1 completes the proof.

We first show that ψ is an homomorphism from $\mathcal{G}(C)$ into $\varphi(\mathcal{G})$ when the labels of the nodes are not taken into account, i.e., for the time being, we ignore the second condition in Definition 4.3.2. By definition of $\mathcal{H}$, ψ is an injective homomorphism from $\mathcal{G}(C)$ into $\mathcal{H}$, the $\bot$-extension of $\varphi(\mathcal{G}(\sigma'(D)))$. Thus, when ignoring the labels, ψ is a homomorphism from $\mathcal{G}(C)$ into $\varphi(\mathcal{G}(\sigma'(D)))$. But then, since $\mathcal{G}' = \varphi^{-1}(\psi(\mathcal{G}(C)))$ is a rooted subtree of $\mathcal{G}$, ψ is also a homomorphism from $\mathcal{G}(C)$ into $\varphi(\mathcal{G})$ still ignoring the labels.

It remains to take the labels of the nodes in $\mathcal{G}(C)$ into account. For every concept name P, negation $\neg P$, or $\bot$ in the label of a node $n \in \mathcal{G}(C)$, we need to show $P, \neg P, \bot \in \varphi(\mathcal{G})_\bot(\psi(n))$, respectively.

First, assume $P \in \mathcal{G}(C)(n)$. The case $\neg P \in \mathcal{G}(C)(n)$ can be dealt with analogously. We know that $\psi(\mathcal{G}(C))$ is a rooted subtree of $\mathcal{H}$. In particular, $\mathcal{H}$ coincides with $\varphi(\mathcal{G}(\sigma'(D)))$ except that some labels of nodes in $\mathcal{H}$ are extended by $\bot$. Consequently, there must exist a node n' in the set $\varphi^{-1}(\psi(n))$ with $P \in \mathcal{G}(\sigma'(D))(n')$. Then, by construction $P \in \mathcal{G}(n')$.

Now, assume that $\bot \in \mathcal{G}(C)(n)$. By construction of $\mathcal{G}$, we can add $\bot$ to the label of $\psi(n)$ in $\varphi(\mathcal{G})$ without changing the semantics of $\varphi(\mathcal{G})$.

This shows that ψ is a homomorphism from $\mathcal{G}(C)$ into the $\bot$-extension of $\varphi(\mathcal{G})$. □

The following lemma shows that $\mathcal{G}$ is indeed "small". Let $N_D(X)$ and $\mathcal{G}_{\sigma'(X),m}$ be defined as above Lemma 6.3.1.

Lemma 6.3.20. *The size of $\mathcal{G}$ is polynomially bounded in the size of the matching problem $C \equiv^? D$.*

Proof. We first investigate the size of $\mathcal{G}' = \varphi^{-1}(\psi(\mathcal{G}(C)))$. Since ψ is a homomorphism with domain $\mathcal{G}(C)$, we know $|\psi(\mathcal{G}(C))| \leq |\mathcal{G}(C)|$.

Let $n \in \psi(\mathcal{G}(C))$ and $m \in N_D(X)$ for a variable X in D. Then, because $\sigma'(X)$ is in $\forall$-normal form, we know by definition of φ that $\varphi^{-1}(n)$ shares at most one node with $\mathcal{G}_{\sigma'(X),m}$. Thus, the number of nodes in the intersection of the set of nodes of $\mathcal{G}_{\sigma'(X),m}$ and $\mathcal{G}'$ is linearly bounded in the size of $\psi(\mathcal{G}(C))$. Furthermore, the number of variables and nodes $m \in N_D(X)$ is linear in the size of D. Consequently, when taking all nodes in $\mathcal{G}_{\sigma'(X),m}$ for all variables X in D and all $m \in N_D(X)$, and intersecting this union of nodes with $\mathcal{G}'$, then the cardinality of the resulting set is polynomially bounded in the size of the matching problem. Finally, observe that $\mathcal{G}(\sigma'(D))$ is obtained by instantiating $\mathcal{G}(D)$ at m by $\mathcal{G}_{\sigma'(X),m}$ for all variables X in D and $m \in N_D(X)$. As a result, the number of nodes in $\mathcal{G}'$ is polynomially bounded in the size of the matching problem.

Now, let n' be a node in $\mathcal{G}'$. Then there exists a node n in $\psi(\mathcal{G}(C))$ such that $n' \in \varphi^{-1}(n)$. By definition, the label of n' in $\mathcal{G}'$ is a subset of the label of n in $\psi(\mathcal{G}(C))$.

This shows that the size of $\mathcal{G}'$ is polynomially bounded in the size of the matching problem.

By definition, $\mathcal{G}$ is obtained from $\mathcal{G}'$ by adding the trees $\mathcal{G}_{n,m}$ to $\mathcal{G}'$. The number and size of the trees $\mathcal{G}_{n,m}$ is polynomially bounded in the size of the given matching problem. Thus, $|\mathcal{G}| - |\mathcal{G}'|$ is polynomially bounded, and since $|\mathcal{G}| = |\mathcal{G}'| + |\mathcal{G}| - |\mathcal{G}'|$, so is $|\mathcal{G}|$. □

Intuitively, $\sigma(X)$ is now defined in such a way that $\mathcal{G}(\sigma(X))$ contains all those parts of $\mathcal{G}_{\sigma'(X),m}$ in $\mathcal{G}(\sigma'(D))$ that belong to the intersection of $\mathcal{G}(\sigma'(D))$ and $\mathcal{G}$.

Definition 6.3.6. *Let $\mathcal{G}_{\sigma'(X),m}$ and $\mathcal{G}$ be defined as specified above, and let $\mathcal{G}(\sigma'(X)) = (N', E', n_0', \ell')$. Define $\psi_{X,m}$ to be the isomorphism from $\mathcal{G}_{\sigma'(X),m}$ into $\mathcal{G}(\sigma'(X))$. Then, we define $\mathcal{G}(\sigma(X)) = (N, E, n_0, \ell)$ as rooted subtree of $\mathcal{G}(\sigma'(X))$ as follows:*

- $N := \{n \in N' \mid \text{ there exist } m, n' \text{ with } n = \psi_{X,m}(n'), \ n' \in \mathcal{G}_{\sigma'(X),m}, \text{ and } n' \in \mathcal{G}\}$;
- $E := E' \cap (N \times (N_R \cup \forall N_R) \times N)$;
- $n_0 := n_0'$;
- $\ell(n) := \bigcup_{\substack{n',m \\ n=\psi_{X,m}(n')}} \mathcal{G}_{\sigma'(X),m}(n') \cap \mathcal{G}(n')$.

Now, $\sigma(X)$ is defined to be the concept description corresponding to $\mathcal{G}(\sigma(X))$.

The following lemma says that σ is in fact the desired matcher.

Lemma 6.3.21. *The substitution σ specified in Definition 6.3.6 is a matcher for $C \equiv^? D$ of size polynomially bounded in the size of the matching problem, and $\sigma \preceq_d \sigma'$. In particular, σ only contains identifiers used in C.*

Proof. By Definition 6.3.6, for every variable X, $\mathcal{G}(\sigma(X))$ is a rooted subtree of $\mathcal{G}(\sigma'(X))$. Thus, $\sigma'(X) \sqsubseteq \sigma(X)$, which with Lemma 3.2.1 guarantees $\sigma'(D) \sqsubseteq \sigma(D)$. This shows that $\sigma(D) \equiv C$.

Since $\mathcal{G}(\sigma(X))$ is a subtree of $\mathcal{G}(\sigma'(X))$ it follows that $\mathcal{G}(\sigma(D))$ is (isomorphic to) a subtree of $\mathcal{G}(\sigma'(D))$. The tree $\mathcal{G}$ is a subtree of $\mathcal{G}(\sigma'(D))$ as well. Using Definition 6.3.6, it is easy to verify that $\mathcal{G}$ is even a subtree of $\mathcal{G}(\sigma(D))$. Thus, $\sigma(D) \sqsubseteq \mathcal{G}$. Lemma 6.3.19 implies $\sigma(D) \sqsubseteq C$.

The fact that $\mathcal{G}(\sigma(X))$ is a rooted subtree of $\mathcal{G}(\sigma'(X))$ also implies that $\sigma \preceq_d \sigma'$. By assumption, σ' only contains identifiers that occur in C. Thus, this holds for σ as well.

It remains to investigate the size of σ. By Lemma 6.3.20, the size of $\mathcal{G}$ is polynomially bounded in the size of the matching problem. Moreover, by construction $|\mathcal{G}(\sigma(X))| \leq |\mathcal{G}|$. Consequently, the size of σ is polynomial bounded in the size of the matching problem. □

Theorem 6.3.9 is an immediate consequence of Lemma 6.3.21. Together with the hardness result for deciding the solvability of $\mathcal{ALE}$-matching problems modulo equivalence, it proves the main complexity result of this subsection.

Corollary 6.3.15. *Deciding the solvability of $\mathcal{ALE}$-matching problems modulo equivalence is NP-complete.*

6.3.5 Computing i-Minimal Matchers in $\mathcal{ALE}$

The approach for computing minimal i-complete sets in $\mathcal{ALE}$ exactly corresponds to the one for $\mathcal{EL}$ (Section 6.3.1), i.e.,

1. Compute an s-complete set.
2. Extract a minimal i-complete set from the set computed in the first step.

The second step can be carried out in time polynomial in the size of the computed s-complete set using an oracle for deciding subsumption (Remark 3.2.1).

The main technical problem we are faced with is to come up with an algorithm for computing s-complete sets of matching problems modulo subsumption. Just as for $\mathcal{EL}$, the algorithm presented here solves the more general problem of computing s-complete sets for matching modulo *equivalence*. Again, this algorithm can easily be turned into a matching algorithm tailored to matching modulo subsumption.

The $\mathcal{ALE}$-Matching Algorithm for Computing s-Complete Sets. The main idea of the matching algorithm for $\mathcal{ALE}$ is the same as for $\mathcal{EL}$, i.e., based on homomorphisms from the description tree of the concept pattern D into the description tree of the concept description C, one defines candidate matchers and checks if these candidates really solve the matching problem.

Following Theorem 4.3.1, the $\mathcal{EL}$-matching algorithm (Figure 6.1) is modified as follows: (i) instead of the trees $\mathcal{G}(C)$ and $\mathcal{G}(D)$, we now consider $\mathcal{G}_C$ and $\mathcal{G}_D^\top$, where the $\top$-normal form of D is obtained by considering concept variables as concept names; (ii) homomorphisms are computed with respect to Definition 4.3.2, i.e., subtrees can be mapped onto a single incoherent node. Just as for $\mathcal{EL}$, the variables in $\mathcal{G}_D^\top$ are ignored when relating the labels of nodes (see (6.7) for the modified condition on labels).

This straightforward extension of the $\mathcal{EL}$-matching algorithm is sufficient to solve the $\mathcal{ALE}$-matching problem $C_{ex} \sqsubseteq^? D_{ex}$, where C_{ex} is the $\mathcal{ALE}$-concept description already introduced in Section 4.3:

$$C_{ex} := \forall r.(\exists s.Q \sqcap \forall s.\neg Q) \sqcap \exists s.(P \sqcap \exists r.\neg P),$$
$$D_{ex} := \forall r.(\forall r.X \sqcap \exists r.P) \sqcap \exists s.\exists r.X.$$

There exists exactly one homomorphism φ from $\mathcal{G}_{D_{ex}}^\top$ into $\mathcal{G}_{C_{ex}}$ (see Figure 6.6). Following the $\mathcal{EL}$-matching algorithm, φ gives rise to the matcher σ with $\sigma(X) := lcs\{\bot, \neg P\} \equiv \neg P$. The singleton set $\{\sigma\}$ is indeed an s-complete set.

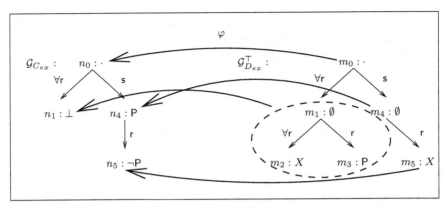

Fig. 6.6. Computing i-Minimal Matchers in $\mathcal{ALE}$.

However, as illustrated by the next example, this simple extension of the $\mathcal{EL}$-matching algorithm does not work in general.

Example 6.3.3. Consider the $\mathcal{ALE}$-matching problem $C'_{ex} \sqsubseteq^? D'_{ex}$, where

$$C'_{ex} := (\exists r.\forall r.Q) \sqcap (\exists r.\forall s.P),$$
$$D'_{ex} := \exists r.(\forall r.X \sqcap \forall s.Y).$$

The description trees corresponding to C'_{ex} and D'_{ex} are depicted in Figure 6.7. Obviously, $\sigma := \{X \mapsto Q, Y \mapsto \top\}$ and $\tau := \{X \mapsto \top, Y \mapsto P\}$ are solutions of the matching problem. However, there does not exist a homomorphism from $\mathcal{G}_{D'_{ex}}^\top$ into $\mathcal{G}_{C'_{ex}}$. Indeed, the node m_1 can be mapped either on n_1 or on n_2. In the former case, m_2 can be mapped on n_3, but then there is no way to map m_3. In the latter case, m_3 must be mapped on n_4, but then there is no node m_2 can be mapped on.

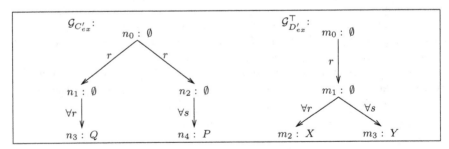

Fig. 6.7. The Description Trees for C'_{ex} and D'_{ex}.

The problem is that Theorem 4.3.1 requires the subsumer to be in $\top$-normal form. However, the $\top$-normal form of the instantiated concept pattern depends on the matcher, and thus cannot be computed in advance. For instance, in Example 6.3.3 the instances $\sigma(D'_{ex})$ and $\tau(D'_{ex})$ of D'_{ex} are not $\top$-normalized since they contain $\forall s.\top$ and $\forall r.\top$, respectively. The description tree for the $\top$-normalized concept description $\sigma(D'_{ex})$ does not include the node m_3 and the $\forall s$-edge leading to it. Analogously, for $\tau(D)$, m_2 would be deleted.

This illustrates that the instances of a pattern are not necessarily in $\top$-normal form and that the $\top$-normal form depends on the particular instance. However, only those matchers cause problems that replace variables by the top-concept. Therefore, instead of considering homomorphisms originating from $\mathcal{G}_D^\top$, the algorithm computes homomorphisms from the so-called $\top$-patterns of D.

Definition 6.3.7. *The concept pattern E is called $\top$-pattern of D iff E is obtained from D by replacing some of the variables in D by $\top$.*

In our example, we obtain the following $\top$-normalized $\top$-patterns for D'_{ex}: D'_{ex}, $\exists r.(\forall r.X)$, $\exists r.(\forall s.Y)$, and $\exists r.\top$. Matching these patterns against C'_{ex}, the extended matching algorithm described above computes the following sets of solutions: $\emptyset$, $\{\sigma\}$, $\{\tau\}$, and $\{\{X \mapsto \top, Y \mapsto \top\}\}$. The union of these sets provides us with an s-complete set of solutions of $C'_{ex} \sqsubseteq^? D'_{ex}$.

The matching algorithm for $\mathcal{ALE}$ obtained from these considerations is depicted in Figure 6.8. Here $\ell(n)$ denotes the label of n in $\mathcal{G}_{D'}^\top$. Just as for the $\mathcal{EL}$-matching algorithm (Figure 6.1), the homomorphism from $\mathcal{G}_{D'}^\top$ into $\mathcal{G}_C$ ignores variables in the label of nodes in $\mathcal{G}_{D'}^\top$ (see (6.7) for the modified condition on labels). As we will see later on, removing the test in the last line of the algorithm (i.e., adding σ to $\mathcal{C}$ without checking $C \sqsupseteq \sigma(D)$), provides us with an algorithm for matching modulo subsumption.

Input: $\mathcal{ALE}$-matching problem $C \equiv^? D$
Output: s-complete set $\mathcal{C}$ of matchers for $C \equiv^? D$

$\mathcal{C} := \emptyset$
For all $\top$-patterns D' of D do
    For all homomorphisms φ from $\mathcal{G}_{D'}^\top$ into $\mathcal{G}_C$
        Define σ by
            $\sigma(X) := lcs(C_{(\mathcal{G}_C)_{\varphi(m)}} \mid X \in \ell(m))$ for all variables X in D' and
            $\sigma(X) := \top$ for all variables X in D not contained in D'
        If $C \sqsupseteq \sigma(D)$ then $\mathcal{C} := \mathcal{C} \cup \{\sigma\}$

Fig. 6.8. The $\mathcal{ALE}$-Matching Algorithm.

Soundness of the $\mathcal{ALE}$-Matching Algorithm. We now prove that i) every element in the set $\mathcal{C}$ computed by the matching algorithm in Figure 6.8 is a matcher of the matching problem $C \equiv^? D$ and ii) the set $\mathcal{C}$ is s-complete.

Similar to $\mathcal{EL}$ (Section 6.3.1), the prove is based on two lemmas. The first lemma says that all substitutions σ computed by the matching algorithm satisfy $C \sqsubseteq \sigma(D)$.

Lemma 6.3.22. *Let D' be a $\top$-pattern of D, φ be a homomorphism from $\mathcal{G}_{D'}^{\top}$ into $\mathcal{G}_C$, and let σ be the corresponding substitution computed by the matching algorithm in Figure 6.8. Then, $C \sqsubseteq \sigma(D)$.*

Proof. We first show that $C \sqsubseteq \sigma(D')$. Let X be a variable in D'. Then, for every node m in D' with X in its label there exists a node n in $\mathcal{G}_C$ with $\varphi(m) = n$. By the definition of σ it follows that $C_{(\mathcal{G}_C)_n} \sqsubseteq \sigma(X)$. Thus, according to Theorem 4.3.1 there exists a homomorphism from $\mathcal{G}_{\sigma(X)}^{\top}$ into $(\mathcal{G}_C)_n$.

For this reason, one can extend φ to a homomorphism from $\mathcal{G}$ into $\mathcal{G}_C$ where $\mathcal{G}$ is obtained by instantiating $\mathcal{G}_{D'}^{\top}$ by (copies of) $\mathcal{G}_{\sigma(X)}^{\top}$ for all variables X in D'. It is easy to see that $\mathcal{G} \equiv \sigma(D')$, which by Theorem 4.3.1 implies $C \sqsubseteq \sigma(D')$.

Now, by the definition of $\top$-patterns and since $\sigma(Y) = \top$ for all variables in D that are not contained in D', we obtain $\sigma(D) \equiv \sigma(D')$. This shows $C \sqsubseteq \sigma(D)$.   □

As an immediate consequence of this lemma, we obtain that every substitution σ in $\mathcal{C}$ is a matcher of the problem $C \equiv^? D$: The lemma guarantees that C is subsumed by $\sigma(D)$ and the algorithm explicitly checks $\sigma(D) \sqsubseteq C$ before adding σ to $\mathcal{C}$. The following lemma shows that $\mathcal{C}$ is an s-complete set.

Lemma 6.3.23. *If σ' is a matcher for $C \equiv^? D$, then there exists a matcher σ in the set $\mathcal{C}$ computed by the matching algorithm depicted in Figure 6.8 with $\sigma \sqsubseteq_s \sigma'$.*

Proof. Let σ' be a matcher of $C \equiv^? D$. Then, $C \sqsubseteq \sigma'(D)$. Define $T := \{X \mid X$ is a variable in D and $\sigma'(X) \equiv \top\}$. Furthermore, let D' be the $\top$-pattern of D where the variables in T are substituted by $\top$. We can conclude $\sigma'(D) \equiv \sigma'(D')$. Thus, $C \sqsubseteq \sigma'(D')$. By Theorem 4.3.1 this means that there exists a homomorphism φ' from $\mathcal{G}_{\sigma'(D')}^{\top}$ into $\mathcal{G}_C$.

In what follows, we use φ' to construct a homomorphism φ from $\mathcal{G}_{D'}^{\top}$ into $\mathcal{G}_C$, i.e., a homomorphism computed by our matching algorithm. Then, we show $\sigma \sqsubseteq_s \sigma'$ for the substitution σ corresponding to φ.

In order to derive φ from φ', we need to show that $\mathcal{G}_{D'}^{\top}$ is (isomorphic to) a subtree of $\mathcal{G}_{\sigma'(D')}^{\top}$. To show this, let $\mathcal{G}$ be the description tree obtained by instantiating $\mathcal{G}_{D'}^{\top}$ by (copies of) $\mathcal{G}_{\sigma'(X)}^{\top}$ for all variables X in D'. We claim that $\mathcal{G}$ is isomorphic to $\mathcal{G}_{\sigma'(D')}^{\top}$:

In general, the description tree $\mathcal{G}_E^{\top}$ for some $\mathcal{ALE}$-concept pattern E can be obtained by iteratively removing those nodes of $\mathcal{G}(E)$ that i) are connected to their direct predecessor by a $\forall$-edge, ii) have an empty label, and iii) do not have outgoing edges.

Now, the description tree $\mathcal{G}(\sigma'(D'))$ is obtained by instantiating $\mathcal{G}(D')$ by (copies of) $\mathcal{G}(\sigma'(X))$ at every node in $\mathcal{G}(D')$ with X in its label and every variable X in D'. By definition, $\sigma'(X) \not\equiv \top$ for all variables X in D'. Thus, the nodes in the subtree $\mathcal{G}(D')$ of $\mathcal{G}(\sigma'(D'))$ containing variables are not removed when $\mathcal{G}(\sigma'(D'))$ is $\top$-normalized. For this reason, one can obtain $\mathcal{G}^\top_{\sigma'(D')}$ by first $\top$-normalizing $\mathcal{G}(D')$, which yields $\mathcal{G}^\top_{D'}$, and then instantiating $\mathcal{G}^\top_{D'}$ by $\mathcal{G}^\top_{\sigma'(X)}$. This implies that $\mathcal{G}$ is isomorphic to $\mathcal{G}^\top_{\sigma'(D')}$.

But then, $\mathcal{G}^\top_{D'}$ is a subtree of $\mathcal{G}^\top_{\sigma'(D')}$. Therefore, restricting φ' to $\mathcal{G}^\top_{D'}$, provides us with a homomorphism φ from $\mathcal{G}^\top_{D'}$ into $\mathcal{G}_C$.

Let σ be the substitution computed by the matching algorithm for D' and φ. It remains to show $\sigma \sqsubseteq_s \sigma'$:

If X is a variable in D but not in D', we know $\sigma'(X) \equiv \top$. Thus, $\sigma(X) = \top \sqsubseteq \sigma'(X)$.

Now, let X be a variable in D' and let m be a node in $\mathcal{G}^\top_{D'}$ with X in its label. Define $n := \varphi(m)$. When restricting φ' to $\left(\mathcal{G}^\top_{\sigma'(D')} \right)_m$, one obtains an homomorphism from $\left(\mathcal{G}^\top_{\sigma'(D')} \right)_m$ into $(\mathcal{G}_C)_n$. Now, recall that $\mathcal{G}$, as defined above, is isomorphic to $\mathcal{G}^\top_{\sigma'(D')}$. This implies that $\left(\mathcal{G}^\top_{\sigma'(D')} \right)_m$ contains a rooted subtree isomorphic to $\mathcal{G}^\top_{\sigma'(X)}$. Therefore, there exists a homomorphism from $\mathcal{G}^\top_{\sigma'(X)}$ into $(\mathcal{G}_C)_n$. Then, Theorem 4.3.1 ensures $C_{(\mathcal{G}_C)_n} \sqsubseteq \sigma'(X)$ (for all nodes $n = \varphi(m)$ with $m \in \ell(X)$). Hence, using that $\sigma(X)$ is defined to be the lcs of the concepts $C_{(\mathcal{G}_C)_n}$, it follows that $\sigma(X) \sqsubseteq \sigma'(X)$. $\qquad\square$

Together, Lemma 6.3.22 and Lemma 6.3.23 show:

Theorem 6.3.10. *For a matching problem modulo equivalence, the set C computed by the algorithm depicted in Figure 6.8 is s-complete.*

Similar to the $\mathcal{EL}$-matching algorithm (Figure 6.1), it is easy to see that replacing the last line of the $\mathcal{ALE}$-matching algorithm (Figure 6.8) by $C := C \cup \{\sigma\}$ provides us with a matching algorithm for matching modulo subsumption.

Theorem 6.3.11. *The algorithm depicted in Figure 6.8 is an algorithm for computing s-complete sets for matching modulo subsumption when replacing the last line by $C := C \cup \{\sigma\}$, i.e, omitting the test.*

Complexity of Computing s-Complete and i-Complete Sets. Example 6.3.1 and 6.3.2 immediately carry over to $\mathcal{FLE}$- and $\mathcal{ALE}$. As a result, Corollary 6.3.5 and 6.3.6 are valid for $\mathcal{FLE}$ and $\mathcal{ALE}$ as well.

Corollary 6.3.16.   *1. For $\mathcal{ALE}$-, $\mathcal{FLE}$-matching problems modulo equivalence*
   a) the cardinality of a (minimal) s-complete set of matchers may grow exponentially in the size of the matching problem;
   b) the size of s-minimal matchers may grow exponentially in the size of the matching problem.

2. *For* $\mathcal{ALE}$-, $\mathcal{FLE}$-*matching problems modulo subsumption*
   a) *the cardinality of (minimal) s-complete and i-complete sets of match-ers may grow exponentially in the size of the matching problem;*
   b) *the size of s-minimal and i-minimal matchers may grow exponentially in the size of the matching problem.*

As already mentioned in Section 6.3.1, a minimal i-complete set for matching modulo equivalence contains at most one element. Moreover, Theorem 6.3.7 and 6.3.9 imply that the size of matchers in i-complete sets for $\mathcal{FLE}$- and $\mathcal{ALE}$-matching problems modulo equivalence can polynomially be bounded in the size of the problem.

Again, similar to $\mathcal{EL}$ in Section 6.3.1, we use the matching algorithm (Figure 6.8) to prove exponential upper bounds for the cardinality and size of s- and i-complete sets.

According to [BKM99], the size of $\mathcal{G}_C$ can exponentially be bounded by the size of C. Since the size of $\mathcal{G}_{D'}^\top$ for some $\top$-pattern D' of D is linear in D this implies that the number of mappings from $\mathcal{G}_{D'}^\top$ into $\mathcal{G}_C$ is at most exponential in the size of the matching problem. Also, the number of $\top$-patterns of D is exponentially bounded by the size of D. As a result, the number of matchers in $\mathcal{C}$ computed by the matching algorithm is at most exponential in the size of the matching problem.

As shown in [BKM99], the size of $lcs(C_{(\mathcal{G}_C)_{\varphi(m)}} \mid X \in \ell(m))$ can be bounded by the product $\prod_{m, X \in \ell(m)} |(\mathcal{G}_C)_{\varphi(m)}|$. Due to the fact that the number of nodes m in $\mathcal{G}_{D'}^\top$ is linear in the size of the matching problem and the size of $(\mathcal{G}_C)_{\varphi(m)}$ is at most exponential in C, the size of the lcs can exponentially be bounded in the size of the matching problem. As an easy consequence of results in [BKM99], the lcs can even be computed in expo-nential time. Thus, the size of every substitution computed by the matching algorithm is at most exponential in the size of the given problem. To sum up, we can derive the following upper bounds from the matching algorithm depicted in Figure 6.8.

Corollary 6.3.17. *1. For* $\mathcal{ALE}$-, $\mathcal{FLE}$-*matching problems modulo equiva-lence*
   a) *the cardinality of a (minimal) s-complete set of matchers can expo-nentially be bounded in the size of the matching problem; and*
   b) *the size of s-minimal matchers can exponentially be bounded in the size of the matching problem.*
2. *For* $\mathcal{ALE}$-, $\mathcal{FLE}$-*matching problems modulo subsumption*
   a) *the cardinality of (minimal) s-complete and i-complete sets of match-ers can exponentially be bounded in the size of the matching problem; and*
   b) *the size of s-minimal and i-minimal matchers can exponentially be bounded in the size of the matching problem.*

We now turn to the computational complexity of the matching algorithm itself. As shown in [DHL$^+$92], subsumption of $\mathcal{ALE}$-concept descriptions is NP-complete. Since a substitution σ computed by the matching algorithm is of size at most exponential in the size of the matching problem $C \equiv^? D$, it follows that $C \sqsupseteq \sigma(D)$ can be decided in non-deterministic exponential time in the size of the matching problem. Thus, there exists a decision algorithm using only exponential space. Recalling that the number of $\top$-patterns D' of D and the number of mappings from $\mathcal{G}_{D'}^\top$ into $\mathcal{G}_C$ is at most exponential in the size of D and that the lcs specified in the matching algorithm can be computed in time exponential in the size of the matching problem, the matching algorithm in Figure 6.8 runs in space exponential in the size of the matching problem.

As mentioned above, for i-complete sets it is sufficient to compute only one matcher of size polynomially bounded in the size of the matching problem. Thus, i-complete sets can be computed by an exponential time algorithm by simply enumerating all substitutions up to the polynomially upper bound and testing which substitution solves the matching problem.

According to Theorem 6.3.11, for matching modulo subsumption we can dispense with the last subsumption test in the algorithm in Figure 6.8. Thus, for this problem we obtain an exponential time algorithm for computing s-complete (and therefore, i-complete) sets of matchers. We summarize these complexity results in the following corollary.

Corollary 6.3.18.   *1. For $\mathcal{ALE}$-, $\mathcal{FLE}$-matching problems modulo equivalence*
   a) s-complete sets can be computed by an algorithm using exponential space in the size of the matching problem; and
   b) i-complete sets can be computed by an exponential time algorithm.
   2. For $\mathcal{ALE}$-, $\mathcal{FLE}$-matching problems modulo subsumption both s- and i-complete sets can be computed by exponential time algorithms.

It is an open problem whether s-complete sets for matching modulo equivalence can also be computed by exponential *time* algorithms.

As usual, given s-complete (i-complete) sets, minimal sets can be derived by employing the subsumption algorithms for $\mathcal{FLE}$ and $\mathcal{ALE}$ (Remark 3.2.1). Note, however, that the size of the matchers in these sets might already be of exponential size in the size of the matching problem. Consequently, first computing complete sets and then deriving minimal complete sets only provides us with an exponential space algorithm for computing minimal complete sets. Up to now, it is not known whether there exist more efficient algorithms for this task which directly produce minimal complete set.

6.3.6 Computing d-Minimal Matchers in $\mathcal{ALE}$

As argued in Section 3.2.3, the second step for computing solutions of matching problems $C \sqsubseteq^? D$, is to compute minimal d-complete sets for matching problems $\sigma(D) \equiv^? D$ where σ is an i-minimal matcher of the problem $C \sqsubseteq^? D$. Recall that (minimal) d-complete sets contain all d-minimal (i.e., reduced) matchers in $\forall$-normal form up to s-equivalence.

In this subsection, we present a (naïve) algorithm for computing such sets for $\mathcal{ALE}$- and $\mathcal{FLE}$-matching problems modulo equivalence. The algorithm makes use of the following lemma.

Lemma 6.3.24. *For an $\mathcal{ALE}$-matching problem $C \equiv^? D$, the size of the d-minimal matchers in $\forall$-normal form can polynomially be bounded in the size of the matching problem.*

Proof. Let σ'' be some matcher of $C \equiv^? D$ in $\forall$-normal form. By Proposition 6.3.6, there exists a matcher σ', with $\sigma' \preceq_d \sigma''$ and $depth(\sigma'(X)) \leq depth(C)$ for all variables X in D. Clearly, because of $\sigma' \preceq_d \sigma''$, σ' is in $\forall$-normal form as well. Now, let σ be the matcher of $C \equiv^? D$ specified in Definition 6.3.6 using σ'. Lemma 6.3.21 implies that σ is of size polynomially bounded in the size of the matching problem and that $\sigma \preceq_d \sigma' \preceq_d \sigma''$.

If we now assume that σ'' is a d-minimal, then the above argument shows that there exists a matcher σ in $\forall$-normal form of size polynomially bounded in the size of the matching problem with $\sigma \preceq_d \sigma''$. Because σ'' is d-minimal it follows that $\sigma = \sigma''$, i.e., $\sigma(X) = \sigma''(X)$ for all variables X in D. Thus, σ'' is of size at most polynomial in the size of the matching problem. $\square$

Note that the construction of σ (Definition 6.3.6) also works for $\mathcal{FLE}$-matching problems. In fact, the proof is easier since one does not need to take unsatisfiable concepts into account. Thus, the lemma also holds for matching problems in $\mathcal{FLE}$.

A naïve algorithm for computing (minimal) d-complete sets can now be specified as follows: i) compute all substitutions (in $\forall$-normal form) up to the polynomial bound and filter out those that do not solve the matching problem, are not d-minimal, or are s-equivalent to previously computed matchers. It is easy to see that d-minimality can be tested by a polynomially time algorithm with an oracle for testing subsumption.

Corollary 6.3.19. *(Minimal) d-complete sets for $\mathcal{ALE}$- and $\mathcal{FLE}$-matching problems modulo equivalence can be compute by an exponential time algorithm.*

For $\mathcal{EL}$, we have developed a much more sophisticated algorithm, which is based on the fact that minimal d-complete sets consist of all s-maximal matchers (up to s-equivalence), where the images of the variables are reduced (cf. Theorem 6.3.5). For $\mathcal{FLE}$, we conjecture that Theorem 6.3.5 still holds. Thus, it might be possible to extend the algorithm for computing minimal d-complete sets in $\mathcal{EL}$ to $\mathcal{FLE}$.

Unfortunately, Theorem 6.3.5 does not hold for $\mathcal{ALE}$. Consider, for example, the $\mathcal{ALE}$-matching problem $\exists r.A \sqcap \forall r.\neg A \equiv^? X \sqcap Y$. The substitutions $\sigma_k := \{X \mapsto \exists r. \cdots . \exists r.A, Y \mapsto \forall r. \cdots . \forall r.\neg A\}$ for $\exists$- and $\forall$-chains of length

k are s-incomparable and s-maximal matchers of this problem with reduced images. However, these matchers are not d-minimal. In this example, the only d-minimal matcher is the one that maps X and Y to the bottom-concept.

Just as for $\mathcal{EL}$ (cf. Section 6.3.1), we can show that the cardinality of a d-complete set can grow exponentially in the size of the matching problem. On the other hand, Lemma 6.3.24 guarantees that the size of matchers in d-complete sets can be polynomially bounded in the size of the matching problem.

Corollary 6.3.20. *For $\mathcal{ALE}$- and $\mathcal{FLE}$-matching problems modulo equivalence*

- *the cardinality of d-complete sets may grow exponentially in the size of the matching problem;*
- *the size of matchers in d-complete sets can be polynomially bounded.*

As pointed out in Section 3.2.3, minimal d-complete sets are computed for matching problems of the form $\sigma(D) \equiv^? D$ where σ is an i-minimal matcher. The size of this problem may already be exponential in the size of the input matching problem $C \sqsubseteq^? D$. In particular, this means that matchers in minimal d-complete sets can be of size exponential in the size of the original matching problem modulo subsumption.

7. Conclusion

We have pointed out that, during the last fifteen years, DLs have been well-investigated with respect to their expressive power and the complexity of the standard inferences. Sound and complete inference algorithms are now available for a great variety of DLs. However, in some applications (e.g., the ones for the CLASSIC DL-system at AT&T) it has turned out that additional non-standard inferences, such as lcs, msc, and matching, are needed to support the construction and maintenance of DL knowledge bases. To this end, first ad hoc implementations of such non-standard inferences have been integrated into CLASSIC. However, the inference algorithms underlying these implementations were mostly incomplete and formal properties of the non-standard inferences, such as their computational complexity, had not been studied. This situation corresponds to the level of development for standard inferences in the first phase, where DL-systems have been developed without having complete algorithms at hand and without an exact understanding of the complexity of the underlying reasoning problems (see Section 2.1).

The goal of this book was therefore to take the research on non-standard inferences, as they have been proposed for CLASSIC applications, to a level that corresponds to (and partly exceeds) the one at the end of the second phase for standard inferences. That is, we aimed at providing (provably) sound and complete algorithms for the novel inferences together with an in-depth analysis of their complexity. With the investigations carried out here for the three inferences lcs, msc, and matching we have indeed reached this goal for the languages $\mathcal{ALNS}$, $\mathcal{ALN}^*$, and $\mathcal{ALE}$. The considered languages are expressive enough to be useful in CLASSIC applications and other technical applications like chemical process engineering. Moreover, the complexity results show that, in many cases, the devised algorithms are optimal from the worst-case complexity point of view.

Unlike standard inferences, non-standard inferences produce concept descriptions as output, which are presented to the user (e.g., the lcs of concept descriptions and solutions of matching problems). Therefore, besides the mere algorithmic complexity, additional formal properties of non-standard inferences have been explored, too. These properties include the existence and size of the lcs and msc as well as the size of (interesting) matchers and the cardinality of complete sets of (interesting) matchers.

R.Küsters: Non-Standard Inferences in Description Logics, LNAI 2100, pp. 229–234, 2001.
© Springer-Verlag Berlin Heidelberg 2001

In what follows, we will summarize the main results presented in this book in more detail and mention the problems that have been left open. Finally, we sketch the new techniques developed and conclude with some remarks on the future of non-standard inferences.

Least Common Subsumer and Most Specific Concept

It has turned out that, for the three languages $\mathcal{ALNS}$, $\mathcal{ALN}^*$, and $\mathcal{ALE}$, the size of the lcs of a sequence of concept descriptions may grow exponentially in the size of the sequence. On the one hand, this means that in applications it will be necessary to rewrite the lcs using concepts defined in a TBox to obtain smaller representations of the lcs. First theoretical and empirical results on rewriting the lcs show that, although the concept descriptions returned by an lcs algorithm may fill several pages of output, the rewritten descriptions only consist of a few symbols, which can easily be read and comprehended by the user [BKM00]. Thus, in combination with rewriting the exponential blow-up of the size of the lcs does not seem to be a problem in practice. On the other hand, this blow-up implies that every algorithm requires in the worst-case exponential time to compute the lcs. All algorithms presented here for the three DLs exactly meet this exponential lower bound. Although previous lcs algorithms were also optimal in this sense, they could only handle sublanguages of $\mathcal{ALNS}$. Moreover, they did not distinguish between partial and total attributes. However, as shown in the present book, for (sublanguages of) $\mathcal{ALNS}$, the existence and the size of the lcs vitally depends on the kind of interpretation used for attributes. Altogether, for the three DLs in question, we now have a good understanding regarding the existence and the computational complexity of the lcs.

The msc turned out to be much harder to handle, both conceptually and computationally. In order to guarantee the existence of the msc in $\mathcal{ALNS}$, it is necessary to allow for cyclic $\mathcal{ALNS}$-concept descriptions, i.e., those that are defined via a cyclic TBox interpreted by the greatest fixed-point semantics. However, since subsumption for cyclic $\mathcal{ALNS}$-concept descriptions is undecidable (as shown by Nebel [Neb90b]), in this book we have restricted ourselves to a decidable fragment of this language, cyclic $\mathcal{ALN}$-concept descriptions (which correspond to $\mathcal{ALN}^*$-concept descriptions). For this language, there exists a double exponential time algorithm for computing the msc. It remains an open problem whether there exists a more efficient msc algorithm. The only lower bound obtained so far is that the msc may grow exponentially in the size of the underlying ABox. Similarly to the case of $\mathcal{ALN}$ and $\mathcal{ALNS}$, we have shown that in $\mathcal{ALE}$ the msc does not exist in general. We conjecture that, to guarantee the existence of the msc in $\mathcal{ALE}$, one again needs to allow for cyclic $\mathcal{ALE}$-concept descriptions. However, proving this remains open. Summing up, the results on the msc reveal that in order to guarantee the existence of the msc, languages are required that allow for *cyclic* definitions of concepts interpreted with the greatest fixed-point semantics. In systems that do not support this capability one either needs to resort to approximations of the msc or extend the expressive power of the DL accordingly.

Matching of Concept Descriptions

The known results on matching in DLs have been extended in two directions. First, the intuitive notion of "interesting" matchers has been formalized, an issue not addressed until now. Second, matching algorithms have been designed for DLs that are more expressive than the ones treated so far. In the following, the main contributions are summarized.

Interesting Matchers. Although this notion might vary depending on the application in question, we have identified two general properties all matchers displayed to the user should obey. One property is that (in case of matching modulo subsumption) the matcher should bring the pattern as close to the concept description it is matched against as possible. Such matchers are called *i-minimal* and are formally defined via a precedence ordering. In fact, i-minimal matchers are the ones the first matching algorithms proposed in the literature tried to compute. These algorithms even produced least matchers, i.e., those that substitute every variable by an as specific concept description as possible. However, least matchers do not exist for any DL (e.g., $\mathcal{ALE}$). Moreover, they usually contain redundancies, which make them hard to read and to comprehend. This brings us to the second property matchers should obey, namely, they should be free of redundancies. Matchers satisfying this property are called *reduced*. While i-minimality is easy to formalize independently of the underlying DL, the notion of reduction heavily depends on the DL of choice and it is a non-trivial task to come up with an adequate definition. Only for $\mathcal{ALN}$ and $\mathcal{ALE}$ reduced matchers have been specified here. For $\mathcal{ALNS}$ and $\mathcal{ALN}^*$, we have discussed the problems one encounters when trying to capture the notion of reduction in a formal way.

Solving Matching Problems. Besides the formalization of "interesting" matchers, the main challenge was to actually solve matching problems in $\mathcal{ALNS}$, $\mathcal{ALN}^*$, and $\mathcal{ALE}$, thereby extending the known results for $\mathcal{FL}_0$ and $\mathcal{FL}_\neg$ substantially. More precisely, we have investigated both the problem of deciding whether a matching problem has a solution (decision problem) and the problem of computing matchers (computation problem).

Although in most cases the user is more interested in solutions of the computation problem, i.e., the actual matchers, the decision problem is important in that it gives first insight into the complexity of computing (interesting) matchers. It is easy to see that for all considered languages the decision problem for matching modulo subsumption has the same complexity as the (normal) subsumption problem because matching modulo subsumption can be tested by simply checking whether substituting all variables by the top-concept solves the problem. Thus, the decision problem for matching modulo subsumption is not of interest, for it does not give additional insight into the complexity of matching. For matching modulo equivalence things are quite different. Here, matching might add complexity compared to the (normal) equivalence test: Although in $\mathcal{ALNS}$ and $\mathcal{EL}$ testing for equivalence can be carried out in polynomial time, matching modulo equivalence in these languages is PSPACE-hard and NP-hard, respectively. This implies that there cannot exist polynomial time computation algorithms for matching modulo equivalence in these languages since otherwise there would exist polynomial time decision algorithms. The complexity lower bounds also show that same-as equalities and existential restrictions increase the complexity of matching since in $\mathcal{ALN}$ and its sublanguages the decision problem is still polynomial. This impact of the different constructors on the complexity of the decision problem is also confirmed by the complexity of the computation problem discussed next.

As mentioned above, previous matching algorithms were restricted to (sublanguages of) $\mathcal{FL_\neg}$, and they exclusively computed least matchers; thus matchers that satisfy the first property of "interesting" matchers, i.e., being i-minimal. In this book, algorithms have been designed to compute least matchers for the extensions $\mathcal{ALNS}$ and $\mathcal{ALN}^*$ of $\mathcal{FL_\neg}$. Interestingly, whereas in $\mathcal{FL_\neg}$ (and as it turns out, also in $\mathcal{ALN}$) the size of least matchers can polynomially be bounded in the size of the matching problem, in $\mathcal{ALNS}$ and $\mathcal{ALN}^*$ it may grow exponentially. Thus, every algorithm computing these matchers requires (at least) exponential time. The algorithm for $\mathcal{ALNS}$ proposed here exactly meets this complexity lower bound. For $\mathcal{ALN}^*$, however, we only have a double exponential time algorithm. Conceptually, for $\mathcal{ALE}$ things become even more involved since not every solvable $\mathcal{ALE}$-matching problem must have a least matcher. Therefore, *sets* of i-minimal matchers must be computed. As before, the size of i-minimal matchers may grow exponentially in the size of the given matching problem. But now, the cardinality of the set of i-minimal matchers may grow exponentially as well. Fortunately, there still exists an exponential time algorithm computing this set. In practice, one will need some heuristics to cut down the number of different matchers presented to the user, who otherwise would be overwhelmed by the possibly huge number of matchers. Moreover, even if only one matcher is displayed, its description might fill many pages of output. Thus, the size of a single matcher must also be cut down. One way of achieving this is to rewrite the concept descriptions assigned to every single variable using names defined in a TBox; an approach successfully applied for the lcs [BKM00]. However, rewriting matchers in this way reduces the size of the matchers only locally by separately looking at the substitution of every single variable. The readability of the matchers can be improved even further, if in a preprocessing step, "global" redundancies are eliminated from the matchers, taking into account the informations already represented in the concept patterns and the interaction of the variables occurring therein. We captured these global redundancies by the notion of reduced matchers.

In the present book, this notion has been formalized for $\mathcal{ALN}$- and $\mathcal{ALE}$-matching problems. Such matching problems have, in general, more than one reduced matcher. Their number may grow exponentially in the size of the given matching problem. Still, we have shown that the size of a single reduced matcher can be bounded polynomially. As a direct consequence, a naïve exponential time algorithm can enumerate all these matchers. Although from a theoretical point of view such an algorithm is worst-case optimal, it has only little use in practice. For $\mathcal{ALN}$, an improved algorithm has therefore been developed, which derives all reduced matchers from the least matcher computed in a preprocessing step. For the sublanguage $\mathcal{EL}$ of $\mathcal{ALE}$, we have also devised an improved algorithm, which, roughly speaking, is the dual algorithm of the one computing i-minimal matchers.

Overall, for matching in $\mathcal{ALNS}$, $\mathcal{ALN}^*$, and $\mathcal{ALE}$, the notion of interesting matchers as well as the decision and computation problem are well-investigated by now, although some open problems remain.

The Underlying Techniques

All results on non-standard inferences presented in this book are based on structural characterizations of subsumption, which are closely related to the structural subsumption algorithms employed in the first two phases for standard inferences. However, in order to handle cyclic concept descriptions and existential restrictions, these algorithms needed to be extended. One can distinguish between two different approaches, the language-based and the graph-based approach.

In the language-based approach, concept descriptions are represented by sets of regular languages, so-called value-restriction sets. This approach is particularly useful for cyclic concept descriptions, like $\mathcal{ALN}^*$-concept descriptions. Subsumption between such descriptions can be characterized in terms of inclusions of the corresponding value-restriction sets. We have shown that taking the intersection of these sets yields the lcs of the underlying $\mathcal{ALN}^*$-concept descriptions. For the msc, the main problem was to generalize the notion of value-restriction sets to individuals defined in an ABox. Finally, based on the language-based approach, matching in $\mathcal{ALN}^*$ was reduced to solving equation systems over regular languages.

In the graph-based approach, concept descriptions are turned into so-called description graphs, i.e., labeled directed graphs. This approach proves very useful for languages that contain constructors like same-as equalities (as they occur in $\mathcal{ALNS}$-concept descriptions) and existential restrictions (occurring in $\mathcal{ALE}$). Subsumption in these languages can be characterized in terms of homomorphisms between description graphs. We have shown that the lcs corresponds to the product of these graphs, and it turned out that matching problems can be solved by computing homomorphisms between description graphs. Remarkably, the lcs operation must be used as a subprocedure to actually compute (interesting) matchers. For certain matching problems and "admissible" DLs, it is even possible to come up with a generic matching algorithm, whose main component is a subprocedure computing the lcs. This algorithm has been employed to solve $\mathcal{ALNS}$-matching problems.

Rewriting of concept descriptions, as introduced and studied in [BKM00], as well as the difference operator [Tee94] show that the techniques developed in this book are also applicable to other non-standard inferences. Moreover, the hope is that the language- and the graph-based approach can be combined in such a way that, for instance, cyclic $\mathcal{ALE}$-concept descriptions can be handled. (As pointed out above, cyclic concept descriptions are necessary to guarantee the existence of the msc.) A combination of the two approaches will probably make use of finite tree-automata operating on infinite trees [Tho90].

The Future of Non-Standard Inferences

As pointed out, the results presented in this book take the research on non-standard inferences to a level that corresponds to (and partly exceeds) the one for standard inference at the end of the second phase (see Chapter 2). That is, for several DLs expressive enough for certain applications, non-standard inferences are now equipped with a formal basis in terms of precise definitions, provably sound and complete algorithms, and first complexity results.

The next challenge is to reach a level corresponding to what is known for standard inferences today. From a theoretical point of view, the main question is in how far tableau-algorithms or automata-theoretic techniques can be used to solve non-standard inferences in expressive DLs. Most likely, one will need to combine tableau- and automata-theoretic techniques with the structural approaches employed here. The hope is that the results accomplished until now can facilitate this certainly non-trivial task.

From a practical point of view, it is important to further evaluate the novel inferences in applications. The experiences may reveal that, in addition to the non-standard inferences investigated in this book, additional non-standard inferences are needed. As pointed out already, rewriting is one such novel inference, and certainly, there will be others as well. Again, the formal basis established in this book may help to formalize and study such inferences.

References

[AKVW93] A. Aiken, D. Kozen, M. Vardi, and E. Wimmers. The Complexity of Set Constraints. In E. Börger, Y. Gurevich, and K. Meinke, editors, *Proceedings 1993 Conf. Computer Science Logic (CSL'93)*, volume 832 of *Lecture Notes in Computer Science*, pages 1–17. European Association Computer Science Logic, Springer, September 1993.

[AvBN98] H. Andréka, J. van Benthem, and I. Németi. Modal languages and bounded fragments of predicate logic. *Journal of Philosophical Logic*, 27:217–274, 1998.

[Baa91] F. Baader. Augmenting Concept Languages by Transitive Closure of Rules: An Alternativ to Terminological Cycles. In J. Mylopoulos and R. Reiter, editors, *Proceedings of the 12th International Joint Conference on Artificial Intelligence (IJCAI'91)*, pages 446–451, Sydney, 1991. Morgan Kaufmann Publishers.

[Baa96] F. Baader. Using Automata Theory for Characterizing the Semantics of Terminological Cycles. *Annals of Mathematics and Artificial Intelligence*, 18(2–4):175–219, 1996.

[BBK01] F. Baader, S. Brandt, and R. Küsters. Matching under side conditions in description logics. In B. Nebel, editor, *Proceedings of the Seventeenth International Joint Conference on Artificial Intelligence, IJCAI'01*, 2001. To appear.

[BBM+92] R. J. Brachman, A. Borgida, D. L. McGuinness, P. F. Patel-Schneider, and L. A. Resnick. The CLASSIC Knowledge Representation System or, KL-ONE: The Next Generation. In ICOT Staff, editor, *Fifth Generation Computer Systems '92: Proceedings of the International Conference on Fifth Generation Computer Systems (FGCS'92)*, pages 1036–1043, Tokyo, Japan, 1992. IOS Press.

[BBM98] F. Baader, A. Borgida, and D.L. McGuinness. Matching in Description Logics: Preliminary Results. In M.-L. Mugnier and M. Chein, editors, *Proceedings of the Sixth International Conference on Conceptual Structures (ICCS-98)*, volume 1453 of *Lecture Notes in Computer Science*, pages 15–34, Montpelier (France), 1998. Springer–Verlag.

[BC86] J. Biskup and B. Convent. A Formal View Integration Method. In Carlo Zaniolo, editor, *Proceedings of the 1986 ACM SIGMOD International Conference on Management of Data*, pages 398–407, Washington, D.C., USA, 1986. ACM Press.

[BE89] A. Borgida and D.W. Etherington. Hierarchical Knowledge Bases and Efficient Disjunctive Reasoning. In R.J. Brachman and R. Reiter H.J. Levesque, editors, *Proceedings of the 1st International Conference on Principles of Knowledge Representation and Reasoning (KR'89)*, pages 33–43, Toronto, Canada, 1989. Morgan Kaufmann Publishers.

[BFH+94] F. Baader, E. Franconi, B. Hollunder, B. Nebel, and H.J. Profitlich. An Empirical Analysis of Optimization Techniques for Terminological Representation Systems or: Making KRIS get a move on. *Applied Artificial Intelligence. Special Issue on Knowledge Base Management*, 4:109–132, 1994.

[BFL83] R. J. Brachman, R. Fikes, and H. J. Levesque. Krypton: A Functional Approach to Knowledge Representation. *IEEE Computer*, 16(10):67–73, 1983.

[BFT95] P. Bresciani, E. Franconi, and S. Tessaris. Implementing and testing expressive description logics: a preliminary report. In *Proceedings of the International Symposium on Knowledge Retrieval, Use, and Storage for Efficiency, KRUSE'95.*, Santa Cruz, USA, 1995.

[BH91a] F. Baader and P. Hanschke. A Scheme for Integrating Concrete Domains into Concept Languages. In J. Mylopoulos and R. Reiter, editors, *Proceedings of the 12th International Joint Conference on Artificial Intelligence, IJCAI-91*, pages 452–457, Sydney (Australia), 1991. Morgan Kaufmann Publishers.

[BH91b] F. Baader and B. Hollunder. A Terminological Knowledge Representation System with Complete Inference Algorithms. In *Proceedings of the First International Workshop on Processing Declarative Knowledge*, volume 572 of *Lecture Notes in Computer Science*, pages 67–85, Kaiserslautern (Germany), 1991. Springer–Verlag.

[BH91c] F. Baader and B. Hollunder. KRIS: Knowledge Representation and Inference System, System Description. *ACM SIGART Bulletin*, 2:8–14, 1991.

[BK98] F. Baader and R. Küsters. Computing the Least Common Subsumer and the Most Specific Concept in the Presence of Cyclic $\mathcal{ALN}$-Concept Descriptions. In O. Herzog and A. Günter, editors, *Proceedings of the 22nd Annual German Conference on Artificial Intelligence, KI-98*, volume 1504 of *Lecture Notes in Computer Science*, pages 129–140, Bremen, Germany, 1998. Springer–Verlag.

[BK00a] F. Baader and R. Küsters. Matching in Description Logics with Existential Restrictions. In A.G. Cohn, F. Giunchiglia, and B. Selman, editors, *Proceedings of the Seventh International Conference on Knowledge Representation and Reasoning (KR2000)*, pages 261–272, Breckenridge, CO, 2000. Morgan Kaufmann Publishers.

[BK00b] A. Borgida and R. Küsters. What's not in a name: Some Properties of a Purely Structural Approach to Integrating Large DL Knowledge Bases. In F. Baader and U. Sattler, editors, *Proceedings of the 2000 International Workshop on Description Logics (DL2000)*, number 33 in CEUR-WS, Aachen, Germany, 2000. RWTH Aachen. Available via http://SunSITE.Informatik.RWTH-Aachen.DE/Publications/CEUR-WS/Vol-33/.

[BKBM99] F. Baader, R. Küsters, A. Borgida, and D. McGuinness. Matching in Description Logics. *Journal of Logic and Computation*, 9(3):411–447, 1999.

[BKM98a] F. Baader, R. Küsters, and R. Molitor. Computing Least Common Subsumers in Description Logics with Existential Restrictions. LTCS-Report 98-09, LuFG Theoretical Computer Science, RWTH Aachen, Germany, 1998. See http://www-lti.informatik.rwth-aachen.de/Forschung/Reports.html.

[BKM98b] F. Baader, R. Küsters, and R. Molitor. Structural Subsumption Considered From an Automata Theoretic Point of View. In *Proceedings of the 1998 International Workshop on Description Logics (DL'98)*, pages 30–34, Trento, Italy, 1998.

[BKM99] F. Baader, R. Küsters, and R. Molitor. Computing Least Common Subsumers in Description Logics with Existential Restrictions. In T. Dean, editor, *Proceedings of the 16th International Joint Conference on Artificial Intelligence (IJCAI'99)*, pages 96–101, Stockholm, Sweden, 1999. Morgan Kaufmann Publishers.

[BKM00] F. Baader, R. Küsters, and R. Molitor. Rewriting Concepts Using Terminologies. In A.G. Cohn, F. Giunchiglia, and B. Selman, editors, *Proceedings of the Seventh International Conference on Knowledge Representation and Reasoning (KR2000)*, pages 297–308, Breckenridge, CO, 2000. Morgan Kaufmann Publishers.

[BL84] R.J. Brachman and H.J. Levesque. The Tractability of Subsumption in Frame-based Description Languages. In *Proceedings of the 4th National Conference on Artificial Intelligence (AAAI'84)*, pages 34–37, Austin, Texas, 1984. AAAI Press.

[BLN86] C. Batini, M. Lenzerini, and S.B. Navathe. A Comparative Analysis of Methodologies for Database Schema Integration. *Computing Surveys*, 18(4):323–364, 1986.

[BLR97] C. Beeri, A.Y. Levy, and M.-C. Rousset. Rewriting queries using views in description logics. In L. Yuan, editor, *PODS '97. Proceedings of the Sixteenth ACM SIG-SIGMOD-SIGART Symposium on Principles of Database Systems, 1997, Tucson, Arizona*, pages 99–108, New York, NY 10036, USA, 1997. ACM Press.

[BM96] A. Borgida and D. L. McGuinness. Asking Queries about Frames. In L.C. Aiello, J. Doyle., and S.C. Shapiro, editors, *Proceedings of the Fifth International Conference on Principles of Knowledge Representation and Reasoning (KR'96)*, pages 340–349, Cambridge, Massachusetts, USA, 1996. Morgan Kaufmann Publishers.

[BM00] F. Baader and R. Molitor. Building and Structuring Description Logic Knowledge Bases Using Least Common Subsumers and Concept Analysis. In B. Ganter and G. Mineau, editors, *Proceedings of the 8th International Conference on Conceptual Structures (ICCS2000)*, volume 1867 of *Lecture Notes in Artificial Intelligence*, Darmstadt, Germany, 2000. Springer-Verlag.

[BMPS+91] R. J. Brachman, D. L. McGuinness, P. F. Patel-Schneider, L. A. Resnick, and A. Borgida. Living with CLASSIC: When and how to use a KL-ONE-like language. In J. Sowa, editor, *Principles of Semantic Networks*, pages 401–456. Morgan Kaufmann Publishers, San Mateo, Calif., 1991.

[BN98] F. Baader and P. Narendran. Unification of Concept Terms in Description Logics. In H. Prade, editor, *Proceedings of the 13th European Conference on Artificial Intelligence (ECAI-98)*, pages 331–335, Brighton, UK, 1998. John Wiley & Sons Ltd. An extended version has appeared in J. Symbolic Computation 31:277–305, 2001.

[Bor94] A. Borgida. On The Relationship Between Description Logic and Predicate Logic. In *Proceedings of the Third International Conference on Information and Knowledge Management (CIKM'94)*, pages 219–225, Gaithersburg, Maryland, 1994. ACM Press.

[BPS94] A. Borgida and P. Patel-Schneider. A Semantics and Complete Algorithm for Subsumption in the CLASSIC Description Logic. *Journal of Artificial Intelligence Research*, 1:277–308, 1994.

[Bra77] R. J. Brachman. What's in a concept: Structural foundations for semantic networks. *International Journal of Man-Machine Studies*, 9:127–152, 1977.

[Bra78] R.J. Brachman. Structured inheritance networks. In W.A. Woods and R.J. Brachman, editors, *Research in Natural Language Understanding*, Quarterly Progress Report No. 1, BBN Report No. 3742, pages 36–78. Bolt, Beranek and Newman Inc., Cambridge, Mass., 1978.

[BS85] R. J. Brachman and J. G. Schmolze. An overview of the KL-ONE knowledge representation system. *Cognitive Science*, 9(2):171–216, 1985.

[BS94]   F. Baader and J.H. Siekmann. Unification Theory. In D.M. Gabbay, C.J. Hogger, and J.A. Robinson, editors, *Handbook of Logic in Artificial Intelligence and Logic Programming*, pages 41–125. Oxford University Press, Oxford, UK, 1994.

[BS96a] F. Baader and U. Sattler. Description Logics with Symbolic Number Restrictions. In W. Wahlster, editor, *Proceedings of the Twelfth European Conference on Artificial Intelligence (ECAI-96)*, pages 283–287, Budapest, Hungary, 1996. John Wiley & Sons Ltd.

[BS96b] F. Baader and U. Sattler. Knowledge Representation in Process Engineering. In *Proceedings of the International Workshop on Description Logics*, Cambridge (Boston), MA, U.S.A., 1996. AAAI Press/The MIT Press.

[BS00]   F. Baader and U. Sattler. Tableaux Algorithms for Description Logics. In *Proceedings of the International Conference on Automated Reasoning with Analytic Tableaux and Related Methods (TABLEAUX 2000)*, volume 1847 of *Lecture Notes in Artifical Intelligence*, pages 1–18, University of St. Andrews, Scotland, 2000.

[BS01]   F. Baader and W. Snyder. Unification Theory. In J.A. Robinson and A. Voronkov, editors, *Handbook of Automated Reasoning*. Elsevier Science Publishers, 2001. To appear.

[Bür90] H.J. Bürckert. Solving Disequations in Equational Theories. In M.E. Stickel, editor, *Proceedings of the 9th International Conference on Automated Deduction*, Lecture Notes in Compute Science 310, pages 178–192, Kaiserslautern, Germany, 1990. Springer-Verlag.

[CA99]   S. Castano and V. De Antonellis. A Schema Analysis and Reconciliation Tool Environment for Heterogeneous Databases. In *1999 International Database Engineering and Applications Symposium (IDEAS 1999)*, pages 53–62, Montreal, Canada, 1999. IEEE Computer Society.

[Cal96] D. Calvanese. Reasoning with Inclusion Axioms in Description Logics: Algorithms and Complexity. In W. Wahlster, editor, *Proceedings of the 12th European Conference on Artificial Intelligence, ECAI-96*, pages 303–307, Budapest, Hungary, 1996. John Wiley & Sons.

[CBH92] W.W. Cohen, A. Borgida, and H. Hirsh. Computing Least Common Subsumers in Description Logics. In William Swartout, editor, *Proceedings of the 10th National Conference on Artificial Intelligence*, pages 754–760, San Jose, CA, July 1992. MIT Press.

[CDGR99] Diego Calvanese, Giuseppe De Giacomo, and Riccardo Rosati. Data integration and reconciliation in data warehousing: Conceptual modeling and reasoning support. *Network and Information Systems*, 2(4):413–432, 1999.

[CGL+98a] D. Calvanese, G. De Giacomo, M. Lenzerini, D. Nardi, and R. Rosati. Description Logic Framework for Information Integration. In A.G. Cohn, L.K. Schubert, and S.C. Shapiro, editors, *Proceedings of the 6th International Conference on the Principles of Knowledge Representation and Reasoning (KR-98)*, pages 2–13, Trento, Italy, 1998. Morgan Kaufmann Publishers.

[CGL+98b] D. Calvanese, G. De Giacomo, M. Lenzerini, D. Nardi, and R. Rosati. Information Integration: Conceptual Modeling and Reasoning Support. In *Proceedings of the 6th International Conference on Cooperative Information Systems (CoopIS-98)*, pages 280–291, New York City, New York, USA, 1998. IEEE-CS Press.

[CGL99] D. Calvanese, G. De Giacomo, and M. Lenzerini. Reasoning in Expressive Description Logics with Fixpoints based on Automata on Infinite Trees. In T. Dean, editor, *Proceedings of the 16th International Joint Conference on Artificial Intelligence (IJCAI'99)*, pages 84–89, Stockholm, Sweden, 1999. Morgan Kaufmann Publishers.

[CH94a] W. W. Cohen and H. Hirsh. Learnability of description logics with equality constraints. *Machine Learning*, 17(2/3):169–199, 1994.

[CH94b] W. W. Cohen and H. Hirsh. Learning the CLASSIC Description Logic: Theoretical and Experimental Results. In J. Doyle, E. Sandewall, and P. Torasso, editors, *Proceedings of the Fourth International Conference on Principles of Knowledge Representation and Reasoning (KR'94)*, pages 121–133, Bonn, Germany, 1994. Morgan Kaufmann Publishers.

[CL93] T. Catarci and M. Lenzerini. Representing and using interschema knowledge in cooperative information systems. *Journal of Intelligent and Cooperative Information Systems*, 2(4):375–398, 1993.

[CLN99] D. Calvanese, M. Lenzerini, and D. Nardi. Unifying Class-Based Representation Formalisms. *Journal of Artificial Intelligence Research*, 11:199–240, 1999.

[Com91] H. Comon. Disunification: a survey. In J.-L. Lassez and G. Plotkin, editors, *Computational Logic — Essays in Honor of Alan Robinson*, pages 322–359. MIT Press, 1991.

[DE92] F.M. Donini and A. Era. Most Specific Concepts Technique for Knowledge Bases with Incomplete Information. In T.W. Finin, C.K. Nicholas, and Y. Yesha, editors, *Proceedings of the International Conference on Information and Knowledge Management (CIKM'92)*, volume 752 of *Lecture Notes in Computer Science*, pages 545–551. Springer-Verlag, 1992.

[DHL+92] F.M. Donini, B. Hollunder, M. Lenzerini, A. Marchetti, D. Nardi, and W. Nutt. The complexity of existential quantification in concept languages. *Artificial Intelligence*, 53:309–327, 1992.

[DLN90] F.M. Donini, M. Lenzerini, and D. Nardi. An Efficient Method for Hybrid Deduction. In Luigia Carlucci Aiello, editor, *9th European Conference on Artificial Intelligence (ECAI'90)*, pages 246–252. Pitman, 1990.

[DLNN91a] F. Donini, M. Lenzerini, D. Nardi, and W. Nutt. The complexity of concept languages. In *Proceedings of the 2nd International Conference on Principles of Knowledge Representation and Reasoning (KR'91)*, pages 151–162, Cambridge, Mass., 1991.

[DLNN91b] F. Donini, M. Lenzerini, D. Nardi, and W. Nutt. Tractable concept languages. In J. Mylopoulos and R. Reiter, editors, *Proceedings of the 12th International Joint Conference on Artificial Intelligence (IJCAI'91)*, pages 458–463, Sydney, Australia, 1991.

[DLNN97] F.M. Donini, M. Lenzerini, D. Nardi, and W. Nutt. The Complexity of Concept Languages. *Information and Computation*, 134:1–58, 1997.

[DLNS94] F.M. Donini, M. Lenzerini, D. Nardi, and A. Schaerf. Deduction in Concept Languages: From Subsumption to Instance Checking. *Journal of Logic and Computation*, 4(4):423–452, 1994.

[Eil74] S. Eilenberg. *Automata, Languages and Machines*, volume A. Academic Press, New York/London, 1974.

[FL79] N.J. Fisher and R.E. Ladner. Propositional dynamic logic of regular programs. *Journal of Computer and System Sciences*, 18:194–211, 1979.

[FN00] E. Franconi and G. Ng. The i.com Tool for Intelligent Conceptual Modelling. In *7th Intl. Workshop on Knowledge Representation meets Databases (KRDB'00)*, Berlin, Germany, 2000.

[FP96] M. Frazier and L. Pitt. Classic Learning. *Machine Learning Journal*, 25:151–193, 1996.

[Gia95] G. De Giacomo. *Decidability of Class-Based Knowledge Representation Formalisms*. PhD thesis, Università degli Studi di Roma "La Sapienza", 1995.

[Gia96] G. De Giacomo. Eliminating "converse" from converse PDL. *Journal of Logic, Language, and Information*, 5:193–208, 1996.

[GJ79]   M.R. Garey and D.S. Johnson. *Computers and Intractability: A Guide to the Theory of NP-Completeness.* Freeman, San Francisco, 1979.

[GL94a] G. De Giacomo and M. Lenzerini. Boosting the correspondence between description logics and propositional dynamic logics. In *Proceedings of the Twelfth National Conference on Artificial Intelligence (AAAI-94),* pages 205–212, Seattle, WA, 1994. AAAI-Press/the MIT-Press.

[GL94b] G. De Giacomo and M. Lenzerini. Concept languages with number restrictions and fixpoints, and its relationship with mu-calculus. In A.G. Cohn, editor, *Proceedings of the Eleventh European Conference on Artificial Intelligence, ECAI-94,* pages 411–415, Amsterdam, The Netherlands, 1994. John Wiley and Sons.

[GL96]   G. De Giacomo and M. Lenzerini. TBox and ABox reasoning in expressive description logics. In L.C. Aiello, J. Doyle, and S.C. Shapiro, editors, *Proceedings of the 5th International Conference on Principles of Knowledge Representation and Reasoning (KR'96),* pages 316–327, Boston, USA, 1996. Morgan Kaufmann Publishers.

[GLN92] W. Gotthard, P.C. Lockemann, and A. Neufeld. System-Guided View Integration for Object-Oriented Databases. *IEEE Transactions on Knowledge and Data Engineering,* 4(1):1–22, 1992.

[GOR97] E. Grädel, M. Otto, and E. Rosen. Two-Variable Logic with Counting is Decidable. In *Proceedings of 12th IEEE Symposium on Logic in Computer Science (LICS '97),* pages 306–317, Warsaw, Poland, 1997. IEEE Computer Society Press.

[GOR99] E. Grädel, M. Otto, and E. Rosen. Undecidability Results on Two-Variable Logics. *Archive for Mathematical Logic,* 38:213–354, 1999.

[Grä73] G. Grätzer. *General Lattice Theory,* volume 52 of *Lehrbuecher und Monographien aus dem Gebiete der exakten Wissenschaften.* Birkhäuser Verlag, Basel, 1973.

[Grä99a] E. Grädel. Decision procedures for guarded logics. In *Automated Deduction - CADE16. Proceedings of 16th International Conference on Automated Deduction,* volume 1632 of *Lecture Notes in Computer Science,* Trento, Italy, 1999. Springer-Verlag.

[Grä99b] E. Grädel. Why are modal logics so robustly decidable? *Bulletin of the European Association for Theoretical Computer Science,* 68:90–103, 1999.

[GW99]   Erich Grädel and Igor Walukiewicz. Guarded Fixed Point Logic. In *LICS,* pages 45–54, Los Alamitos, California, July 1999. IEEE Computer Society Press.

[Hay77] P.J. Hayes. In defense of logic. In R. Reddy, editor, *Proceedings of the 5th International Joint Conference on Artificial Intelligence (IJCAI'77),* pages 559–565, Cambridge, Mass, 1977. William Kaufmann. A longer version appeared in *The Psychology of Computer Vision* (1975).

[Hay79] P.J. Hayes. The logic of frames. In D. Metzing, editor, *Frame Conceptions and Text Understanding,* pages 46–61. Walter de Gruyter and Co., 1979.

[HB91]   B. Hollunder and F. Baader. Qualifying Number Restrictions in Concept Languages. In J.F. Allen, R. Fikes, and E. Sandewall, editors, *Proceedings of the Second International Conference on Principles of Knowledge Representation and Reasoning, KR-91,* pages 335–346, Boston (USA), 1991. Morgan Kaufmann Publishers.

[HM00]   V. Haarslev and R. Möller. Expressive ABox Reasoning with Number Restrictions, Role Hierarchies, and Transitively Closed Roles. In A.G. Cohn, F. Giunchiglia, and B. Selman, editors, *Proceedings of the Seventh International Conference on Knowledge Representation and Reasoning (KR2000),* pages 273–284. Morgan Kaufmann Publishers, 2000.

[HNS90] B. Hollunder, W. Nutt, and M. Schmidt-Schauss. Subsumption Algorithms for Concept Description Languages. In *Proceedings of the 9th European Conference on Artificial Intelligence (ECAI'90)*, pages 348–353, Stockholm, Sweden, 1990.

[Hol90] B. Hollunder. Hybrid Inferences in KL-ONE-based Knowledge Representation Systems. In *Proceedings of GWAI'90*, volume 251 of *Informatik-Fachberichte*, pages 38–47. Springer-Verlag, 1990.

[Hor98a] I. Horrocks. The FaCT system. In *Proceedings of the International Conference on Automated Reasoning with Analytic Tableaux and Related Methods (Tableaux'98)*, volume 1397 of *Lecture Notes in Artificial Intelligence*, pages 307–312, Berlin, 1998. Springer-Verlag.

[Hor98b] I. Horrocks. Using an Expressive Description Logic: FaCT or Fiction? In A.G. Cohn, L. Schubert, and S.C. Shapiro, editors, *Proceedings of the Sixth International Conference on Principles of Knowledge Representation and Reasoning (KR'98)*, pages 636–647, Trento, Italy, 1998. Morgan Kaufmann Publishers.

[HP98] I. Horrocks and P.F. Patel-Schneider. FaCT and DLP. In Harrie de Swart, editor, *Proceedings of the International Conference on Automated Reasoning with Analytic Tableaux and Related Methods (TABLEAUX-98)*, volume 1397 of *Lecture Notes in Artificial Intelligence*, pages 27–30, Berlin, 1998. Springer-Verlag.

[HPS99] I. Horrocks and P.F. Patel-Schneider. Optimizing Description Logic Subsumption. *Journal of Logic and Computation*, 9(3):267–293, 1999.

[HS99] I. Horrocks and U. Sattler. A Description Logic with Transitive and Inverse Roles and Role Hierarchies. *Journal of Logic and Computation*, 9(3):385–410, 1999.

[HST99] I. Horrocks, U. Sattler, and S. Tobies. Practical Reasoning for Expressive Description Logics. In Harald Ganzinger, David McAllester, and Andrei Voronkov, editors, *Proceedings of the 6th International Conference on Logic for Programming and Automated Reasoning (LPAR'99)*, number 1705 in Lecture Notes in Artificial Intelligence, pages 161–180. Springer-Verlag, 1999.

[HST00] I. Horrocks, U. Sattler, and S. Tobies. Practical Reasoning for Very Expressive Description Logics. *Logic Journal of the IGPL*, 8(3):239–263, 2000.

[HT00] I. Horrocks and S. Tobies. Reasoning with Axioms: Theory and Practice. In A. G. Cohn, F. Giunchiglia, and B. Selman, editors, *Principles of Knowledge Representation and Reasoning: Proceedings of the Seventh International Conference (KR2000)*, pages 285–296, Breckenridge, CO, 2000. Morgan Kaufmann Publishers.

[HU79] J.E. Hopcroft and J.D. Ullman. *Introduction to Automata Theory*. Addison-Wesley Publ. Co., 1979.

[KB99] R. Küsters and A. Borgida. What's in an Attribute? Consequences for the Least Common Subsumer. Technical Report DCS-TR-404, Rutgers University, USA, 1999. Will appear in the Journal of Artificial Intelligence Research, 2001.

[KBR86] T. Kaczmarek, R. Bates, and G. Robins. Recent Developments in NIKL. In *Proceedings of the 5th National Conference on Artificial Intelligence (AAAI'86)*, volume 2, pages 978–985, Philadelphia, PA, 1986. Morgan Kaufmann Publishers.

[KL94] K. Knight and S.K. Luk. Building a Large-Scale Knowledge Base for Machine Translation. In *Proceedings of the 12th National Conference on Artificial Intelligence (AAAI)*, volume 1, pages 773–778, Seattle, WA, USA, 1994. AAAI Press.

[KLP97] D. Koller, A.Y. Levy, and A. Pfeffer. P-CLASSIC: A Tractable Probablistic Description Logic. In *Proceedings of the Fourteenth National Conference on Artificial Intelligence and Ninth Innovative Applications of Artificial Intelligence (AAAI/IAAI-97)*, pages 390–397, Providence, Rhode Island, 1997. AAAI Press/The MIT Press.

[KM01] R. Küsters and R. Molitor. Computing Least Common Subsumers in $\mathcal{ALEN}$. In B. Nebel, editor, *Proceedings of the 17th International Joint Conference on Artificial Intelligence (IJCAI 2001)*, Seattle, USA, 2001. Morgan Kaufmann Publishers. To appear.

[Kob91] A. Kobsa. First Experiences with the SB-ONE Knowledge Representation Workbench in Natural Language Applications. *SIGART Bulletin*, 2(3):70–76, 1991.

[Kor82] J. Korevaar. On Newman's Quick way to the Prime Number Theorem. *Mathematical Intelligencer*, 4:108–115, 1982.

[Koz77] D. Kozen. Lower Bounds for Natural Proof Systems. In *18th Annual Symposium on Foundations of Computer Science (FOCS18)*, pages 254–266, Providence, Rhode Island, 1977. IEEE.

[Koz83] Dexter Kozen. Results on the propositional mu-calculus. *Theoretical Computer Science*, 27:333–354, 1983.

[Küs98] R. Küsters. Characterizing the Semantics of Terminological Cycles in $\mathcal{ALN}$ using Finite Automata. In *Proceedings of the Sixth International Conference on Principles of Knowledge Representation and Reasoning (KR'98)*, pages 499–510, Trento, Italy, 1998. Morgan Kaufmann Publishers.

[Lad77] R.E. Ladner. The Computational Complexity of Provability in Systems of Modal Propositional Logic. *SIAM Journal of Computing*, 6(3):467–480, 1977.

[Lei95] E. Leiss. Implicit language equations: Existence and uniqueness of solutions. *Theoretical Computer Science A*, 145:71–93, 1995.

[Lei99] E. Leiss. *Language Equations*. Springer-Verlag, 1999.

[Lut99] C. Lutz. Complexity of terminological reasoning revisited. In *Proceedings of the 6th International Conference on Logic for Programming and Automated Reasoning (LPAR'99)*, volume 1705 of *Lecture Notes in Artificial Intelligence*, pages 181–200, Tbilisi, Georgia, 1999. Springer-Verlag.

[Mac91] R. MacGregor. Inside the LOOM classifier. *SIGART Bulletin*, 2(3):88–92, 1991.

[MB87] R. MacGregor and R. Bates. The LOOM knowledge representation language. Technical Report ISI/RS-87-188, University of Southern California, 1987.

[MB95] D.L. McGuinness and A. Borgida. Explaining Subsumption in Description Logics. In *Proceedings of the 14th International Joint Conference on Artificial Intelligence (IJCAI'95)*, pages 816–821, Montréal, Québec, Canada, 1995. Morgan Kaufmann Publishers.

[McG96] D.L. McGuinness. *Explaining Reasoning in Description Logics*. PhD thesis, Department of Computer Science, Rutgers University, October, 1996. Also available as a Rutgers Technical Report LCSR-TR-277.

[MDW91] E. Mays, R. Dionne, and R. Weida. K-Rep system overview. *SIGART Bulletin*, 3(2):93–97, 1991.

[MFRW00] D.L. McGuinness, R. Fikes, J. Rice, and S. Wilder. An Environment for Merging and Testing Large Ontologies. In A.G. Cohn, F. Giunchiglia, and B. Selman, editors, *Proceedings of the Seventh International Conference on Knowledge Representation and Reasoning (KR2000)*, pages 483–493, Breckenridge, CO, 2000. Morgan Kaufmann Publishers.

[MHN98] R. Möller, V. Haarslev, and B. Neumann. Semantics-Based Information Retrieval. In *Proceedings of the International Conference on Information Technology and Knowledge Systems (IT&KNOWS-98)*, pages 48–61, Vienna, Budapest, 1998.

[Min75] M. Minsky. A framework for representing knowledge. In P. Winston, editor, *The Psychology of Computer Vision*, McGraw-Hill, New York, 1975.

[MIP+98] D.L. McGuinness, C. Isbell, M. Parker, P.F. Patel-Schneider, L.A. Resnick, and C. Welty. A Description Logic-based configurator on the Web. *ACM Sigart Bulletin*, 9(2):20–22, 1998.

[MMK99] T. Mantay, R. Möller, and A. Kaplunova. Computing Probabilistic Least Common Subsumers in Description Logics. In W. Burgard, T. Christaller, and A.B. Cremers, editors, *Advances in Artificial Intelligence, 23rd Annual German Conference on Artificial Intelligence (KI-99)*, number 1701 in Lecture Notes in Computer Science, pages 89–100, Bonn, Germany, 1999. Springer–Verlag.

[Mol00] R. Molitor. *Unterstützung der Modellierung verfahrenstechnischer Prozesse durch Nicht-Standardinferenzen in Beschreibungslogiken*. PhD thesis, LuFG Theoretische Informatik, RWTH Aachen, Germany, 2000.

[Mor75] M. Mortimer. On languages with two variables. *Zeitschrift fuer mathematische Logik und Grundlagen der Mathematik*, 21:135–140, 1975.

[MPS98] D.L. McGuinness and P.F. Patel-Schneider. Usability Issues in Knowledge Representation Systems. In *Proceedings of the 15th National Conference on Artificial Intelligence (AAAI-98) and of the 10th Conference on Innovative Applications of Artificial Intelligence (IAAI-98)*, pages 608–614, Menlo Park, 1998. AAAI Press.

[MRI95] D.L. McGuinness, L. Alperin Resnick, and C. Isbell. Description Logic in practice: A CLASSIC application. In *Proceedings of the 14th International Joint Conference on Artificial Intelligence (IJCAI'95)*, pages 2045–2046. Morgan Kaufmann Publishers, 1995. Video Presentation.

[MW98a] D.L. McGuinness and J.R. Wright. An industrial strength Description Logic-based configurator platform. *IEEE Intelligent Systems*, 13(4):66–77, 1998.

[MW98b] D.L. McGuinness and J.R. Wright. Conceptual modeling for configuration: A description logic-based approach. *Artificial Intelligence for Engineering Design, Analysis, and Manufacturing Journal*, 12:333–334, 1998.

[Neb87] B. Nebel. On Terminological cycles. In *KIT Report 58*, Technische Universität Berlin, 1987.

[Neb90a] B. Nebel. Reasoning and Revision in Hybrid Representation Systems. In *Lecture Notes in Computer Science*, volume 422. Springer-Verlag, 1990.

[Neb90b] B. Nebel. Terminological reasoning is inherently intractable. *Artificial Intelligence*, 43:235–249, 1990.

[Neb91] B. Nebel. Terminological cycles: Semantics and computational properties. In J. Sowa, editor, *Formal Aspects of Semantic Networks*, pages 331–361. Morgan Kaufmann Publishers, San Mateo, 1991.

[NM99] F.N. Noy and M.A. Musen. SMART: Automated Support for Ontology Merging and Alignment. In *Proceedings of the Twelfth Workshop on Knowledge Acquisition (KAW'99)*, Banff, Canada, 1999.

[Pat89] P.F. Patel-Schneider. Undecidability of Subsumption in NIKL. *Artificial Intelligence*, 39(2):263–272, 1989.

[Pel91] C. Peltason. The BACK System - An Overview. *SIGART Bulletin*, 2(3):114–119, 1991.

[Qui68] M. Quillian. Semantic memory. In M. Minsky, editor, *Semantic Information Processing*, pages 216–270, Cambridge, Mass., 1968. MIT Press.

[Sat96] U. Sattler. A Concept Language Extended with Different Kinds of Transitive Roles. In G. Görz and S. Hölldobler, editors, *20. Deutsche Jahrestagung für Künstliche Intelligenz*, volume 1137 of *Lecture Notes in Artificial Intelligence*. Springer-Verlag, 1996.

[Sat98] U. Sattler. *Terminological knowledge representation systems in a process engineering application*. PhD thesis, LuFG Theoretical Computer Science, RWTH-Aachen, Germany, 1998.

[Sav70] W.J. Savitch. Relationship between nondeterministic and deterministic tape complexity. *Journal of Computer and System Science*, 4:177–192, 1970.

[Sch91] K. Schild. A correspondence theory for terminological logics: Preliminary report. In *Proceedings of the 12th International Joint Conference on Artificial Intelligence (IJCAI'1991)*, pages 466–471, Sydney, Australia, 1991. Morgan Kaufmann Publishers.

[Sch94] K. Schild. Terminological cycles and the propositional μ-calculus. In *Proceedings of the Fourth International Conference on Principles of Knowledge Representation and Reasoning, KR'94*, pages 509–520, Bonn, Germany, 1994. Morgan Kaufmann Publishers.

[SS89] M. Schmidt-Schauß. Subsumption in KL-ONE is undecidable. In R. J. Brachman, editor, *Proceedings of the 1st International Conference on Principles of Knowledge Representation and Reasoning (KR'89)*, pages 421–431, Toronto, Ont., 1989. Morgan Kaufmann Publishers.

[SS91] M. Schmidt-Schauss and G. Smolka. Attributive Concept Descriptions with Complements. *Artificial Intelligence*, 48(1):1–26, 1991.

[Tee94] G. Teege. Making the Difference: A Subtraction Operation for Description Logics. In J. Doyle, E. Sandewall, and P. Torasso, editors, *Proceedings of the Fourth International Conference on the Principles of Knowledge Representation and Reasoning (KR-94)*, pages 540–550, Bonn, Germany, 1994. Morgan Kaufmann Publishers.

[Tho90] W. Thomas. Automata on infinite objects. In J. van Leeuwen, editor, *Handbook of Theoretical Computer Science*, volume B, pages 133–191. Elsevier Science Publishers, Amsterdam, 1990.

[Val84] L. G. Valiant. A Theory of the Learnable. *Communications of the ACM*, 27(11):1134–1142, 1984.

[Var97] M. Vardi. Why is modal logic so robustly decidable? In N. Immerman and P. Kolaitis, editors, *Descriptive Complexity and Finite Models*, volume 31 of *DIMACS Series in Discrete Mathematics and Theoretical Computer Science, AMS*, pages 149–184, 1997.

[Woo75] W.A. Woods. What's in a link: Foundations for semantic networks. In D.G. Bobrow and A.M. Collins, editors, *Representation and Understanding: Studies in Cognitive Science*, pages 35–82. Academic Press, 1975.

[WS91] W.A. Woods and J.G. Schmolze. The KL-ONE family. *Computers and Mathematics with Applications, special issue on knowledge representation*, 23(2-5):133–177, 1991.

[WWV⁺93] J.R. Wright, E.S. Weixelbaum, G.T. Vesonder, K. Brown, S.R. Palmer, J.I. Berman, and H.H. Moore. A knowledge-based configurator that supports sales, engineering, and manufacturing at AT&T network systems. *AI Magazine*, 14(3):69–80, 1993.

[YZ91] S. Yu and Q. Zhuang. On the State Complexity of Intersection of Regular Languages. *ACM SIGACT News*, 22(3):52–54, 1991.

Index

Lecture Notes in Artificial Intelligence (LNAI)

Lecture Notes in Computer Science